Printed in the United States of America.

10 9 8 7 6 5 4 3 2 1

Permissions:
University of North Texas Press
1155 Union Circle #311336
Denton, TX 76203-5017

The paper used in this book meets the minimum requirements
of the American National Standard for Permanence
of Paper for Printed Library Materials, z39.48.1984.
Binding materials have been chosen for durability.

Library of Congress Cataloging-in-Publication Data

This corner of Canaan : essays on Texas in honor of Randolph B. Campbell / edited by Richard B. McCaslin, Donald E. Chipman, and Andrew J. Torget.
1st ed.
p. cm.
Includes bibliographical references and index.
ISBN 978-1-57441-503-2 (cloth : alk. paper)
ISBN 978-1-57441-517-9 (ebook)
1. Texas—History. 2. Texas—Historiography. I. McCaslin, Richard B. II. Chipman, Donald E. III. Torget, Andrew J., 1978- IV. Campbell, Randolph B., 1940-
F386.5.T53 2013
976.4—dc23

2012039590

This Corner of Canaan:

Essays on Texas in Honor of Randolph B. Campbell

Edited by
Richard B. McCaslin,
Donald E. Chipman,
and Andrew J. Torget

UNT PRESS

University of North Texas Press
Denton, Texas

"'Dont you see?' he cried. 'Dont you see?
This whole land, the whole South, is cursed,
and all of us who derive from it, whom it ever
suckled, white and black both, lie under the
curse? . . . What corner of Canaan is this?'"

—William Faulkner, "The Bear"

Contents

INTRODUCTION

Editors' Preface . . . . *ix*
Richard B. McCaslin, Donald E. Chipman, and Andrew J. Torget

Teacher, Mentor, Friend: A Reflection . . . . *xv*
Laura Lyons McLemore

PART I: *Texas Identity*

Chapter 1: *Texas Identity: Alternatives to the Terrible Triplets* 3
Walter L. Buenger

Chapter 2: *History, Memory, and Rebranding Texas as Western for the 1936 Centennial* 37
Light Townsend Cummins

PART II: *Texas Before the Civil War*

Chapter 3: *José Antonio Pichardo and the Limits of Spanish Texas, 1803–1821* 61
Donald E. Chipman

Chapter 4: *Sam Houston, Indian Agent* 83
Carol A. Lipscomb

Chapter 5: *Stephen F. Austin's Views on Slavery in Early Texas* 107
Andrew J. Torget

PART III: *Texas in Civil War and Reconstruction*

Chapter 6: *Landholding in Brazos County, Texas: Frontier, War, and Reconstruction* 131
Carl H. Moneyhon

Chapter 7: *Soldiering on the Texas Coast and the Problem of Confederate Nationalism* 157
Andrew F. Lang

Chapter 8: *North Texans and Civil War Amnesty: Helpless Instruments in the Hands of Rebellion?* 185
Bradley R. Clampitt

Chapter 9: *Texas Reconstruction in Popular Memory: What Really Happened in Hill County in 1871* 203
Richard B. McCaslin

PART IV: *Texas and the New South*

Chapter 10: *The Roots of Southern Progressivism: Texas Populists and the Rise of a Reform Coalition in Milam County* 229
Gregg Cantrell

Chapter 11: *African-American Housing and Health Patterns in Southwestern Cities, 1865–1900* 265
Alwyn Barr

Chapter 12: *Populism and the Poll Tax in Cooke County, Texas* 293
Mark Stanley

PART V: *Texas and the Twentieth Century*

Chapter 13: *Investing in Urban: The Woman's Monday Club and the Entrepreneurial Elite of Corpus Christi, Texas* 311
Jessica Brannon-Wranosky

Chapter 14: *Denton County, Texas, and the Draft During the First World War* 335
Gregory W. Ball

Chapter 15: *"Gente Decente": Tejanos Jovita González and Edmundo E. Mireles* 361
Harriett Denise Joseph, Alix Riviere, and Jordan Penner

Chapter 16: *National Ideal Meets Local Reality: The Grassroots War on Poverty in Houston.* 385
Wesley G. Phelps

Contributors' Biographies 403

Index 407

INTRODUCTION

Editors' Preface

This volume reflects a shared debt that many of us owe to the scholarly work of Randolph B. "Mike" Campbell. Among those whose work intersects with Texas, there are few whose legacy and influence loom as large as Campbell's. Over the course of almost fifty years, his books, essays, journal articles, and public lectures have painted a nuanced portrait of the Texas past that has become a model for the field. Perhaps just as important, Campbell's work as a teacher and mentor to both students and colleagues, and his leadership in shaping public memory throughout the Lone Star State, have embodied the ideal of what it means to be a professional historian. The essays presented here reflect the breadth and depth of his profound influence on the field, his colleagues, his students, and our modern understanding of the history of Texas.

Campbell's career can, perhaps, best be understood as a bridge between two edges of the American South: Virginia and Texas. As he often points out, Campbell was born in Nelson County, Virginia, where he grew up in the rural, segregated South. His father toiled at various odd jobs to support his family—"working for a living," as Campbell says—and he encouraged his son to get an education. When Campbell began taking classes at the nearby University of Virginia (UVA), his mother often sat with him in history courses, and she urged him to pursue graduate work in the field. After earning his doctoral degree in history from UVA in 1966, Campbell left Virginia for his first full-time job at North Texas State University in Denton (now the University of North Texas, or UNT). What proved remarkable about Texas, it seemed to Campbell, was how much it felt like Virginia to him. There was something profoundly southern about his new home, and the influential scholarship that Campbell published during the decades that followed would revolve around this deeply felt conviction about connections between places like Virginia and Texas.

If Texas as a southern place became an enduring theme of Campbell's work, a dedication to understanding that development through the eyes of those who lived it became his defining method. An indefatigable researcher, Campbell explored the lives of men and women, both obscure and famous, in the depths of county courthouses, where their lives and fortunes, trials and challenges could be understood in details that could be recovered nowhere else. His research focused on the history of Texas during the nineteenth century, when the arrival of many Anglos created the southern culture that Campbell found so familiar. An early adopter of new statistical and quantitative methods, his initial work mined census data and employed computer-aided analysis to answer long-standing questions about the economic and social structure of the antebellum South, using Texas materials. In August 1974, the *Journal of Southern History* published his article, "Planters and Plain Folk: Harrison County, Texas, as a Test Case, 1850–1860," which won the *Journal's* 1973–74 award for best article. Encouraged, Campbell formed a research partnership with his UNT colleague, Richard G. Lowe, to expand the use of Texas census records to provide new perspectives on the antebellum South. The result was the publication of *Wealth and Power in Antebellum Texas* by Texas A&M University Press in 1977. Ten years later, this same partnership published *Planters and Plain Folk: Agriculture in Antebellum Texas* with Southern Methodist University Press.

Campbell's first decade of work in Texas history strengthened his belief that the state was essentially southern in heritage, and that conviction led him to examine the role of slavery in the Lone Star State. He began this momentous task with research on Harrison County, which had the largest slave population of any county in Texas on the eve of the Civil War (and had already been a focus of several of his publications). The result was *A Southern Community in Crisis: Harrison County, Texas, 1850–1880*, published by the Texas State Historical Association (TSHA) in 1983. This pivotal work provided a nuanced portrait of the rise and fall of a slaveholding community during one of the most tumultuous periods in American history, and its methodology reflected the expansion of Campbell's research to include deep mining of county courthouse records. *A Southern Community in Crisis* demonstrates conclusively the analytical power of grass-roots research methods, and it continues to serve as a model for community-level studies.

The culmination of his work on slavery, however, came with the publication of *An Empire for Slavery: The Peculiar Institution in Texas, 1821–1865*, by Louisiana State University Press in 1989. The product of five years of dogged research in county courthouses across the state, *An Empire for Slavery* exposed the depth to which slavery penetrated the economic, social, and political life of antebellum Texas. This landmark volume challenged both historians and the public to come to terms with the profound influence that American slavery wielded on the development of Texas, and it garnered no fewer than five awards, including the TSHA's Coral H. Tullis Memorial Prize for the most important book on

Texas. It remains the only full-scale study of slavery in Texas, and it is frequently cited by scholars of Texas, the Southwest, American expansion, and the antebellum South.

Campbell's growing reputation brought him new opportunities. He served as the 1993–94 president of the TSHA, as well as an advisory editor (and author of numerous essays) for the acclaimed six-volume encyclopedia, *The New Handbook of Texas*, published in 1996 and later launched online by the TSHA. And he continued to produce influential works. In 1993 he published a biography, *Sam Houston and the American Southwest*, which proved so successful that its third edition appeared in 2007. His earlier work on the legacies of slavery—and thus the problems of race and citizenship—pushed Campbell to focus his attention on Reconstruction. In 1998 he published *Grass-Roots Reconstruction in Texas, 1865–1880,* with Louisiana State University Press, which told the story of how Texans experienced the aftermath of emancipation on the local level. With this work, Campbell again demonstrated the power of community records to challenge public memory and popular misconceptions of the state's past (focusing, in this case, on race relations, voting patterns, and economic development). In so doing, Campbell offered his readers what he often termed "a useable history."

The wider importance of Campbell's work was recognized beyond the borders of Texas. In 2000, Oxford University Press asked him to write a new and comprehensive history of Texas, incorporating and synthesizing several decades of new scholarship on the region, which Oxford hoped to offer to students, scholars, and the general public. *Gone to Texas: A History of the Lone Star State* appeared in 2003 and was named that year's best book on Texas by the Texas Philosophical Society. The book became generally accepted as the standard history of the state, and a second edition appeared in 2012. By then, Campbell had been elected to membership in the Texas Philosophical Society and the Texas Institute of Letters, and he had been named a Fellow of the TSHA. In 2008, the TSHA named Campbell its first Chief Historian, and in 2011 he became the first holder of the Lone Star Professorship at UNT.

Campbell's ground-breaking research on nineteenth-century Texas has shaped our modern understanding of that era. His work in long-overlooked data in the state and local records allowed him to tell the history of Texas in that period with accuracy few can match. Putting aside cherished popular conceptions of such pivotal issues as the place of slavery in the region, the effects of the Civil War, and the legacy of

Reconstruction, Campbell recovered a useable past that paved the way for future scholars to construct their own analytical narratives free from many outworn interpretations. And he continues to publish through his fifth decade at UNT, even as he directs the publication efforts of the TSHA.

The essays in this volume, quite naturally, reflect the influence of both Campbell and his scholarship on the field of Texas history. The first section addresses questions of Texas identity and the ongoing struggle of historians to define the southern and western heritage of the region. The second section focuses on defining influences and people—Spaniards, Mexicans, Indians, Anglo Americans, African Americans—who continually remade Texas throughout the early nineteenth century. The third section focuses on one of the defining moments in southern and Texas history, the Civil War and its legacies through the Reconstruction era. The fourth section addresses Texas in the late nineteenth century, as the region became a crucible of the economic, political, and social upheavals that overtook the United States during those years. The final section examines an urbanizing Texas that struggled to find a balance between the heritage of the nineteenth century and the challenges of the twentieth century. Throughout these sections, the contributions by both colleagues and former students expose how the two principal themes of Campbell's career—Texan identity and grassroots research—continually shaped and reshaped the history of this region.

The title of this volume reflects the intersections of those themes in Campbell's career. The book's epigraph comes from a short story by William Faulkner, the most famous and celebrated author of the South. Faulkner spent a lifetime grappling with the dark legacies of slavery, war, and race in Southern memory. For Faulkner, local context meant everything, and he sought to unravel the meaning of Southern history by writing about the lives of men and women, black and white, rich and poor, as they struggled beneath the weight of the past. Many of his stories and novels played out in an imagined Mississippi county, Yoknapatawpha, which Faulkner used as his stage for exploring what one small corner of the South could reveal about larger truths in the American past. Faulkner ended his career as a writer-in-residence at UVA at the same moment that Campbell began his on the same campus. And for Campbell, as much as for Faulkner, understanding the history of a southern place like Texas meant struggling to understand what life was like for those who lived along this far-flung edge of the South.

In "The Bear," Faulkner's Ike McCaslin rages at a black man about how the South remains haunted by its past. "What corner of Canaan is this?" he demands to know. What follows is our attempt to pay tribute to how Mike Campbell has shaped our understanding of this particular corner of Canaan.

Richard B. McCaslin, Donald E. Chipman, Andrew J. Torget
University of North Texas

Randolph B. "Mike" Campbell, Lone Star Professor, University of North Texas. Courtesy of the University of North Texas

Teacher, Mentor, Friend: A Reflection

Laura Lyons McLemore

I have had many good teachers; I recall them very well and even specific things I learned from each, but only a few were life-changing—my first grade teacher, my twelfth grade teacher, my thesis committee, and then there was the Virginian, Randolph B. Campbell. Dr. Campbell did not just want to teach a prescribed curriculum; he wanted to teach students; he wanted to change the world (at least his corner of it), and he wanted his students to help him do it.

On the first day of my first class in the Department of History at the University of North Texas, I sat in my desk unsure of my expectations, not knowing a lot about the "Age of Jefferson and Jackson." I opened my spiral notebook to the first page, took out a pencil, and waited. One by one the chairs in the classroom filled, and everyone began to settle down. As if on cue, in strode the professor, a thin wiry figure with salt and pepper hair cut close to his head, wire-rimmed glasses perched on the bridge of his nose, striding swiftly, long arms swinging palms down as if he were swimming, propelling himself forward not only with his legs, but by pushing the air resistance behind him. When he turned and faced the class, his hands came up, and they remained in the air for the rest of the class. At the first "aboot," I knew, without an introduction, that he was from Virginia, and by the end of the hour, I was certain this was the person I wanted to direct my dissertation. When class was over, I sat for a moment disappointed that I would have to wait until Wednesday for the next installment. So it was that I first learned it was possible to become so engrossed in a lecture that I did not want it to end, and I thought, "I want to be able to do that."

If this person was to be my model, then, my next step was to find out what his specialization was and adopt it. Fortunately, Randolph B. Campbell was interested in the early history of Texas, serendipitous since I was employed by an institution whose founding board read like a who's who of the Texas Republic. I had a field, I had a professor, and by the end of two semesters, I had a topic, and a goal.

In the six years that followed, I learned more and faster than I ever thought possible, and it amazes me, even now, how automatically and how frequently I call upon that knowledge. Having come from a background in language and literature, I had some practice in deriving meaning from texts. I was familiar with primary sources; my job was preserving them. From Dr. Campbell, I learned how to mine for information as though hunting for treasure. "Ah," he would say, "how little it takes to make a historian happy!" And he was right.

He was right about a lot of things—like what I should pursue for my dissertation. Knowing what I know now, I appreciate the challenge he faced far better than I did then—how to combine intellectual history with Texas history. Campbell found a way, and not only did his guidance lead to a dissertation, it will probably keep me thinking, questioning, and searching for answers for the rest of my life.

Along the way he provided glimpses of memorable insight himself. In my academic career, I had studied the subtleties of language, the meanings of poetry, the workings of myths and archetypes in cultures and society, but in Texas history I grappled anew with the definition of "hero." "We have so few heroes today," Campbell would say, "because we have had so little sacrifice." And he was right, again.

That is not to say, of course, that Americans or Texans were unfamiliar with sacrifice. However, as a student of Randolph Campbell, I came to understand that too often the sacrifices were self-inflicted and unnecessary, that failure or refusal of a people to understand their own role in their circumstances produced often insurmountable obstacles to improving those circumstances. Perhaps this was the most valuable lesson of all, life-changing even. Certainly, it caused me to take a longer view and a closer look at where the United States had run into trouble and why. As a citizen and a teacher, I never looked back from this turning point. This, I think, was the goal—to enable students and fellow Texans to view history honestly and clear-eyed, so that they could steer new courses and not keep bottoming out in the same ruts or sacrificing unnecessarily for the sake of a heroic "mystique," when there were new avenues of opportunity for Texas and the United States more worthy of sacrifice and more productive of true heroes.

Having inspired in me an appetite for research and a desire to share what I learned, Dr. Campbell told me I would probably have more time to engage in those pursuits as an archivist than as a teacher. He was wrong about that, but he was right about almost everything else. The mantle he encouraged us, his students, to assume—to seek the facts, to accept the truths they revealed, and to share the insights we gained—is not always light but it has always been rewarding. This semester, as we ended our second week of class, "Jacksonian America," I glanced down at my watch. "We have to go!" I exclaimed. "We're out of time!" A student in the first row started. "Has it been an hour already?" That is what I wanted to be able to do. How could I ask for a greater teacher, mentor, friend, who changes the world—one student at a time—and inspires those students to do the same?

PART I:
Texas Identity

Littlefield Fountain by Pompeo Coppini, The University of Texas at Austin. Photograph by Debbi Robertson, Fort Worth

Texas Identity: Alternatives to the Terrible Triplets

Walter L. Buenger

For more than a century Texas historians have nurtured three competing views on Texas identity. These terrible triplets, now well into a vital and vigorous old age, have a family resemblance and a similar effect on the study of the state. One stubbornly insists that Texas remains and always has been unique and exceptional. Another brusquely argues that Texas, at least since the early 19th century, has been southern and nothing except the 19th century matters much anyway. The third chimes in, often petulantly, that no, Texas has always been and remains western. A case can be made for all three positions, but not for all people and all times in the Texas past. All three share the family traits of obscuring as much as they reveal, of being excessively focused on the period 1820–1900, of being inspired by present realities, and of ignoring change over time. Most terrible of all, the cacophony the three raise has grown boring and shows little promise of leading to fresh insights about the Texas past.[1]

Instead, if given the space and oxygen to flourish, three interconnected alternative approaches promise a more relevant, compelling, and accurate history of Texas. Conceive of Texas as a border region with ties and influences stretching back and forth across multiple regional and national boundaries, as a place whose cultural identity has been constructed and reconstructed repeatedly through the conflict and cooperation of disparate groups originally from across those borders, and as a region that as a consequence of those borders and that constructed identity explained and influenced other parts of North America and beyond. Except perhaps for the period of roughly 1845 to 1890, Texas exemplified and often broke the trail for trends and patterns of change common to broad areas of North America and often perceived by Texans to be common to the civilized and progressive countries of the world. More often than not, Texas was American and universal instead of exclusively southern, western, or exceptional.[2]

Before exploring this alternative view, consider those terrible triplets more fully in the chronological order of the evidence often used to undergird them. Exceptionalism rests most commonly on the assumption that Texas alone experienced a revolution from Mexico and an extended period as an independent republic. The irony here, of course, is that Anglo Texans did not consider themselves unique at the time, but thought of themselves as exercising a basic American right of revolution. As the Matagorda Committee of Safety put it in October 1835, "We would be unworthy of the nation from which we sprung, of the name of Americans and of freemen, unworthy of the paradise we live in, were we to lie supinely still, and tamely suffer the bonds of servitude to be thrown around us." Texans argued in 1835 and into 1836 that they sought to work within the Mexican Constitution of 1824 and that they like other Mexican citizens sought freedom and liberty, but that Mexico was turning into a military despotism. In the tradition of George Washington they had no choice but armed rebellion. American symbols, American memories, and American values guided them. Yet they also saw themselves as exemplifying a struggle for liberty against despotism that stretched back to the Roman republic and included the recent efforts by the Greeks to free themselves from Turkish control. When M. W. Smith spoke to the citizens of Harrisburg in 1835, he recited a long list of those who had resisted dictatorship, including recent examples in Mexico, but he concluded with this telling point, "Santa Ana will I trust find in some son of Washington the corrector of his errors." Texans saw themselves as part of a longstanding worldwide movement, but when it came time to stir citizens to action the prime examples of correct behavior were all American. None argued Texans were exceptional or unique.[3]

Of course, other major currents propelled Texans to revolution, and one of them, the expansion and acceptance of slavery, ran counter to the trends in much of the United States and the western world. Historians have long debated and disputed slavery's role in the Texas Revolution, but most agree that to some extent it played a part in the increasing estrangement of Anglo Texans and elite Tejanos from the Mexican government. When listing the causes for going to war with that government, however, Texans seldom spoke of slavery. In this they followed a very American pattern for the 1830s in which citizens North and South sought to minimize the public discourse on slavery and southerners could still occasionally debate whether slavery conflicted with liberty. White southerners and northerners alike also remained committed to white supremacy. In that sense, Anglo Texans remained American in 1836 when they declared independence and, after failing to gain admission to the United States, organized a republic that guaranteed the right of whites to own blacks.[4]

While some have long argued that this republic made and continues to make Texas unique and exceptional, Anglo Texans, or Texians as some styled themselves, demonstrated no real desire to be an independent republic and joined the United States as soon as their mother country would let them. (Besides, other states passed through a brief phase as republics.) Ironically, given their support for secession in order to defend slavery barely fifteen years later, the need to ensure the security of slaves and slavery from Mexican invasion numbered high among the reasons influential Anglo Texans supported annexation to the United States in the 1840s. Whatever glories came with the Republic of Texas were fanciful at the time or tacked on long after the fact. As I often tell students, the Alamo had a flat roof in 1836 and that iconic profile was added on a decade later. That remains a basic metaphor for Texas, especially Texas during the Revolution and Republic period.[5]

Repeatedly, from the Republic to now, when Texans needed something more from their history and their memory of the past, something to calm their nervousness about modernity, something to ease their transition into a national and international economy, something to justify a political point of view, or something to shore up the power of their group, they trotted out the shibboleth of Texas exceptionalism. It remains a concept that has always had more to say about the present and those arguing about that present than the past. Assertions of exceptionalism, widely heard in many places and thus not all that exceptional, offered a comforting balm that eased the alienation and fears of the present, aided in the acquisition and maintenance of power, and justified current public policy. Insistence by the public and historians on exceptionalism is, ironically, as much an American characteristic as it is a Texas characteristic. Seen in this light, mindlessly hewing to Texas exceptionalism obscures our understanding of the past and of the place of Texas in the larger narrative of the history of North America.[6]

One of the things it most obscures was that antebellum white Texans owned slaves at the same rate as Virginians and that they seceded from the Union to defend their right to own black Texans. You still hear from Texas college students, politicians, and sympathizers with the Confederacy that economic causes or defense of the principle of states' rights caused secession. Texans at the time knew otherwise. As the leaders of the Texas Secession Convention of 1861 explained to those curious about the need for secession, at the time of annexation Texas "was received as a commonwealth holding, maintaining and protecting the institution known as negro slavery—the servitude of the African to the white race within her limits—a relation that had existed from the first settlement of her wilderness by the white race, and which her people intended should exist in all future time." Anglo Texans defended a specific right, the right to own slaves and to maintain white supremacy, not abstract concepts of states' rights or any other example of mistreatment by the North. Moreover the architects of secession went on to explain that the state's "institutions and geographical position established the strongest ties between her and other slave-holding States." When Anglo Texans from the South, the "whites" of secessionist rhetoric, came to the region in the 1820s, they began a process of linking Texas with the South. As slavery and white supremacy grew in importance, that linkage with the South grew apace.[7]

An increasingly rigid defense of slavery after 1845, secession to defend slavery, joining the Confederacy, losing the Civil War, Reconstruction, and the aftermath of Reconstruction all marked Texas as profoundly southern and distinct from the rest of the United States, both in reality and in the minds of most Anglo and African-American Texans at the time. Texans and southerners turned in a new direction after 1845. They changed in the same manner and at the same pace, and they became much more alike than ever before. The events of the late 1840s through the mid-1880s, especially the virulent and full-throated defense of slavery and a racial caste system and the wartime need to force conformity, uniformity, and Confederate nationalism on a diverse population, made the South more distinct from the rest of the United States than it had ever been. With time and defeat in the Civil War, the memories of sacrifice in the struggle against the rest of the United States added to this sense of distinctiveness. Over and over Texans were urged to remember their "illustrious dead," to—in the words of a speaker at an 1884 veterans reunion—"teach our children to rise up and call them blessed." Texans and other southerners reconstructed their identity, and to the extent that the South lay outside the American mainstream and the thrust of change in much of the world, the era from 1845 to 1890 proved the exception to the norm. Even though by the 1880s calls to remember the southern dead might be balanced by an increasing recognition of northern wartime sacrifice, Texans were first and foremost southern rather than American. That statement needs to be qualified by the assertion that there were many types of Texans and southerners. Likewise the traits that made the region distinct, especially white supremacy and racism, could be found nationwide to some degree. Still, until about 1890 Texans, especially the Anglo Texan majority, resided physically, intellectually, and culturally in the region that by the conclusion of the Civil War southerners and non-southerners alike regarded as the most distinct and the most outside the American norm of any part of the United States.[8]

This distinctiveness and all of its cultural markers lingered in Texas. Long after 1890, more Texans earned their living from growing cotton than raising cattle, and cotton still remains important to the economy. To this day religious characteristics and other markers of southern culture indicate the persistence of ties to the South in all parts of the state.[9]

Still, most Texans stopped thinking of themselves as exclusively southern between the 1890s and the 1920s, and some of them—European Texans, Mexican Texans, and Indian Texans—never did quite fit the southern model, although they certainly rubbed up against it. Even African-American Texans, who had their own brand of southerness, had already moved more easily into the American mainstream, in part through such distinct celebrations of freedom as Juneteenth. A steady shift from loud celebration of the South by the Anglo Texan majority to a clearer focus on Texas began as early as 1888 when a speaker at a reunion of Confederate and Union veterans declared that "Texas is almost a universe, broad in philanthropy and broad in patriotism." Texans passed the tipping point in this conversion in 1915 when the legislature, by concurrent resolution, for the first time mandated public celebration of March 2. The most interesting part of the resolution read "there is now no adequate recognition of March 2—Texas Independence Day." Until 1915, March 2 passed much as any other day. After 1915, Texans routinely paused on that date to remember the Texas Declaration of Independence signed in 1836.[10]

Soon celebrations of Texas blended subtly into celebrations of being American. Unlike others in the ex-Confederate states, Texans more easily, more quickly, and more completely moved back into the American mainstream both in their eyes and in the eyes of other Americans because the Alamo and other similar mythic moments marked them as distinct from the South of slavery and the Civil War and instead enthusiastically American. Nothing demonstrated the transformation to full-throated Americanism more clearly than the 1920s Ku Klux Klan. Populated exclusively by Anglo and Protestant Texans who were still the majority of the state's population, this organization railed against Catholics, Jews, German Texans, African-American Texans, and Mexican Texans and claimed to be "100% American." No Klan parade was complete without the ostentatious display of the flag of the United States. While the Klan's roots in the former Confederacy during Reconstruction received frequent mention in Texas, a rapidly growing Klan characterized much of the country in the early 1920s and everywhere stressed Americanism. Ironically, as we shall see, the Klan's opponents stressed its un-American characteristics. By the 1920s, however, all Texans spoke about being Americans. As one Texas Klansman wrote in 1922, "I believe in the United States of America and its leadership among the nations of the earth." If a sense of exceptionalism was at work, it was American exceptionalism, and the trappings of Americanism more than balanced all examples of southerness. Texans had clearly returned and been accepted into the American fold and while they still celebrated southern history, they celebrated even more the history of Texas and of the entire American experience.[11]

In the decades after the 1920s, the process of Texans setting themselves apart from the South accelerated. In our time, how can a state still be southern that does not claim to be southern, and where secession goes largely unremembered and uncelebrated 150 years later, except in the idle rhetoric of an ill-informed governor? It is hard to escape the conclusions that on some level Texas and Texans stopped being overwhelmingly southern a century ago and that some Texans, and more than an insignificant minority, were never southern.[12]

Some might say that instead Texas was part of the American West, at least as defined by New Western Historians. Ethnic diversity and a fast-growing urban presence characterized the state after 1850. Cattle, Indians, and the army all played a major role in events after 1865. The federal government, be it through Indian removal or the construction of the Houston Ship Channel, made the state into an economic powerhouse by the 1920s. In the 20th century defense spending powered the economy and population growth. Texans, at least after 1920, certainly often thought of themselves as western and they still identify with cowboys—of the Dallas variety or otherwise. Thanks in part to John Wayne, the movies, and novels, the outside world thinks of Texas and Texans as western. Texans gladly profit from this image, and some may even believe it. Again, as with the Texas image, being western made Texans fit more easily into an America where virulent racism reminded non-southerners on a routine basis that the South remained distinctive at least into the 1960s.[13]

This image, however, often did not fit circumstances. No western state had almost 400 lynchings of blacks by whites between the 1880s and the 1930s, as Texas did. Racial violence of the most horrific scale should remind us all that Texas was not a movie scene. It was not an imagined world. It was a place that trailed only Georgia and Mississippi in the number of recorded lynchings, and as in those states, participants in those events often numbered in the hundreds and occasionally in the thousands. The torture inflicted on Jesse Washington by the huge white mob at Waco in 1916 matched the brutality and sadism of anything that happened anywhere in the South. Segregation continued long after lynching stopped, and in 1969 the University of Texas was the last all-white college football team to win a national championship. Texas was not California; it was not even New Mexico.[14]

Yet in fascinating ways, Texas moved toward New Mexico after 1890 and in the process became first western and then American. No one better personified this shift than George W. Littlefield, an influential banker, cattleman, and Confederate veteran. Beginning in 1914, Major Littlefield, as he was known, endowed a fund at the University of Texas for the preservation of material needed to write what he hoped would be a more accurate history of the South. In announcing the creation of this fund, the editor of the Jefferson *Jimplecute* described Littlefield as "one of those southerners who believes that the south's side of the late unpleasantness has never been fairly presented." Littlefield owned and operated extensive ranches in Texas and New Mexico, and he decorated his new bank building in Austin with scenes of ranch life. He might have been a quintessential southerner, but he also became a westerner whose legacy celebrated the West as much as it celebrated the South.[15]

As Littlefield demonstrated, Texas did not precisely match New Mexico, but by the 1910s it was not Mississippi either. Even Texans far less entrepreneurial than Littlefield readily abandoned or modified images and folkways of the South and the Civil War that hindered their economic and social advancement. Instead of remaking the South or re-envisioning the southern past, they often turned to American, western, and Texan images and tropes. They thus pointed themselves to an American future. Throughout 1912, for example, the editor of the Omaha *Breeze*, looked around Texas, compared current conditions to twenty years before, and heralded the "limitless resources to be developed" and "limitless opportunities to be utilized" in his state. Week after week that small-town newspaper carried news and opinions about how to achieve economic growth and social progress. In a particularly revealing comment the editor declared: "Old ideas are rapidly passing out and giving place to improved conditions." Obsessive fealty to a combative and assertive separate South and a maudlin attachment to an idyllic Old South complete with a defense of slavery were among those ideas. In that sense, celebration of the West, like the new-found focus on the history of Texas, served as a way station to full integration into an American identity that better fit a people determined to make progress in the market place and in the life of their community. Texans and their fellow Americans forgot one Texas past and remembered others, thereby binding themselves more closely together. Instead of recalling the Waco Horror or other vestiges of the slave South, Texans and outsiders told tales of cowboys, cattle drives, and the martyrs of the Alamo.[16]

In their own form or fashion all of the ex-Confederacy traveled at least part way back into the American mainstream, but Texans' use of history and their reconstruction of their culture gave them a clear advantage. It was not surprising that they appear to have led other former Confederate states in this move back toward an American identity and concomitant economic and social change. On the Fourth of July, 1890, the United Confederate Veterans held their first convention in Chattanooga, Tennessee. In keeping with the spirit of conciliation between the North and South that filled many of the speeches given by participants, the front cover of the convention proceedings featured a United States flag, while the back cover featured a Confederate flag. Those who celebrated their Confederate military heritage did so on a very American holiday and with the symbols and words of sectional reconciliation. In this they trailed Texans by some six years and perhaps by an equal level of commitment. In 1884 veterans of the blue and the gray armies met together in Dallas, a practice they continued for the rest of the decade. As the keynote speaker put it at the 1888 reunion in San Antonio: "Here the blue and gray meet together to bond themselves more thoroughly into one union." Not only did the Texans, like the United Confederate Veterans, celebrate reconciliation with symbols and words, veterans of both sides shook hands, shared food and drink, and swapped stories.[17]

Some could argue that in using Texas history and the image of the West to help move away from southern separateness and toward an American identity, Texans were unique, even exceptional. They differed from citizens of other ex-Confederate states. The history of the Texas Revolution and Republic and western imagery made the passage back to the nation easier and less tension-fraught. Texans moved earlier and more completely into the national orbit on such issues as woman suffrage, and Texas women voted in the Democratic primary in 1918 well in advance of women voting in other ex-Confederate states. Still they shared with other ex-Confederates what one historian of the South called the "same push and pull between region and nation." Texans accommodated more easily, more quickly, and more thoroughly to this tension, but the buried layers of the past remained. From time to time those layers resurfaced, as they did with the 1969 all-white national championship football team. In 1966, however, with an all-black starting lineup, the Texas Western University basketball team defeated the all-white University of Kentucky team for the national championship. The first team with an all-black starting five to win the championship drew its players from around the nation and set a pattern for teams to come. Southern folkways retreated quickly, and by 1970, when the University of Texas again won the national championship, the football team included African Americans.[18]

Just as some might retreat to Texas exceptionalism to explain this move away from the South, others might highlight Texas regionalism. In a type of terrible triplets writ small, the eastern third of Texas, the argument goes, remained southern. The central third, the most culturally diverse and distinctive part of the state, had a unique mix of people and events that marked it as exceptional. Meanwhile the western third, including El Paso, the home of that 1966 national championship basketball team, became western. This regionalism argument drew heavily from the legacy of Frederick Jackson Turner and Walter Prescott Webb. From Turner came the concept that Texans moved into the western frontier reinvigorating their culture while civilizing the region. He emphasized process—moving west into new land created a frontier mindset and way of life. For Webb the land, especially the relative aridity of western Texas, shaped and formed a new people and a new way of life. They brought traits and ways of thinking and acting with them that were bent by the new environment in new directions. The place mattered. For both Turner and Webb and for those who combine place and process in looking at the creation of identity, frontier Texans always reached an end point, a point where a distinct region and culture emerged and remained.[19]

This regionalism argument ignored the migration patterns of Texans, who typically moved from the east, north, and south to western Texas, leaving behind close family connections and importing the cultural habits and institutions of the places they left behind. Texans, too, shared common experiences, the bonds of politics and government, and memories of the past. They engaged in the same rituals and shared the same image in the minds of those outside the state. The novelist William Humphrey recalled, for example, that in 1936 in his hometown of Clarksville, in Northeast Texas, the "Battle of the Alamo was refought weekly." Meanwhile, farmers near Plainview in West Texas plowed with mules and grew cotton, as in Clarksville. At about the same time farmers in Central Texas began integrating Mexican-American labor into the tenant-farming and cotton-growing agricultural system they shared with the area around Clarksville. Certainly in 1936 the eastern third of Texas shaded toward the South, the western third shaded to the West, and the central third fell a bit in between. Considerable diversity characterized counties within those broad sections, and as always that complicated any attempt to describe even East Texas, Central Texas, and West Texas as uniform. Still, in important ways citizens in Plainview and points east in Texas had more in common with citizens in Clarksville than they did with those in neighboring states.[20]

Texans always possessed a certain unity, but not constancy and uniformity. Especially as the 20th century dawned, political campaigns, state-oriented issues and reform movements, the influence of state law and governmental agencies, private associations such as the Texas State Historical Association or the Texas Federation of Women's Clubs, and associations dedicated to preserving memories of the past such as the Daughters of the Republic of Texas all touched every corner of the state. While pockets of the state tended to vote consistently for one faction or the other and while support for reform varied, every area of the state had at least a sizeable minority who shared much in common with those in other regions. The Texas public heard the same things, fought about the same issues, and grappled with the same problems. Take woman suffrage as an example. Support for the issue ebbed and flowed after the 1880s, but it never disappeared. Support tended to be strongest in the cities and larger towns of the state, places most influenced by the outside world. Better-off women and better-educated women led the movement. Mary Eleanor Brackenridge, for example, came from a family that grew wealthy in the cotton trade and banking, and she was one of the earliest women to serve on a bank board of directors. She also had an active public life as a pillar of the Presbyterian Church, a dedicated club woman, and a generous philanthropist in San Antonio, and for twenty years she served as a regent of what is now called Texas Woman's University. In 1913 she became the first president of the Texas Woman Suffrage Association, and she used her wealth and status to argue for equal rights for women in a variety of areas.[21]

But other towns far smaller than San Antonio scattered through the state had their own less prominent advocates of suffrage, and in the years leading up to World War I they shared in the public debate in Texas on this issue. Even in tiny Schulenberg to the east of San Antonio, the high school graduates of 1911 debated woman suffrage, and the local newspaper printed arguments in favor of suffrage. Adele A. Eilers, the author of the two-page article, argued that granting women the right to vote would be good for women, good for men, and good for society as a whole. As she put it: "This is the day of progress. A country must progress or it will fall behind and another take its place." If the United States, if Texas, and if Schulenburg hoped to make progress women must vote. It would transform them into better citizens and transform society as well. Perhaps the suffrage debate never penetrated to the most isolated rural areas, but Schulenburg's population numbered only a little more than a thousand in the 1910s. Connected by an increasingly sophisticated transportation and communication system to the outside world, Schulenburg and its equivalents across Texas shared in the emergence of a modern state where women voted by 1918.[22]

Woman suffrage and other such public issues linked all areas of Texas together. Certainly their level of acceptance and support varied, and such factors as the demographic makeup of the local population, economic interests, local memories of the past, and other characteristics that might be better classified as regional rather than statewide helped explain this variation. Still, after 1890 in particular, Texas became more one place than a series of poorly connected island communities isolated from each other by their past, their geography, their limited connections to the outside world, and their economic interests. Instead they were a place that shared in such very American and very Texan debates as whether to extend suffrage to women.

Thus even in their regional guise, the terrible triplets of Texas often obscured more than they uncovered. Characterizations of the state or its regions as exceptional, southern, or western, however, all revealed much about the time those arguments were put forward and in the process shed light on the influence of borders, the mutability of culture, and the American influences on all of Texas. Texans became less southern by 1920 because they wanted to leave behind defeat in the Civil War, the reality of slavery, and the stranglehold of the Lost Cause mentality on economic and social advancement. They wanted to become Americans to take better advantage of the opportunities opening up to them both inside and beyond their borders. Texans were more western in the 1950s, when they introduced the oversized replica of a cowboy to their state fairgrounds, because it fit their image of a rapidly advancing state and it fit the image others had of them at the time. It fit their image on the world stage. Texans conceived of themselves as exceptional in the 1960s and 1970s because they could not be homogenized into the whole since they had a history, manufactured and one-sided though it might have been. Thus these self characterizations tell us a great deal about Texans and what influenced them in the 1920s, the 1950s, and the 1970s, but little about previous and following decades.[23]

In fact these terrible triplets and their regional variations were all ahistorical in that none of them considered change over time. (Ironically enough, however, the relative acceptance or rejection of these concepts served as markers of how Texans changed over time.) Texans never reached an end point in the process of change. A permanent, indelible, and unchangeable imprinting of Texas by place, experience, or event never happened. What was true of Texas in 1800 was not true of Texas in 1950. Texas changed, and so did its basic identity and culture. In other words, those who rely solely on one of the terrible triplets are not only wrong, they are simplistic. Texas in 1865 was very much like the South as it then existed. The state was as southern as it would ever be, but it was not at all like the South in 1795. By 1920, when the burgeoning Ku Klux Klan paraded under the American, not Confederate, flag, Texans and Texas had evolved in a different direction from other ex-Confederate states. Unique circumstances may have faced Texans in 1836. They did not in 1963 when Texan Lyndon Johnson became a very American president. Texas was not western at all in 1861. It was more so in 1890. It is less so in the 21st century, even in El Paso where the connection of the region to an international economy and to Mexico mattered much more than westerness.[24]

These three faulty preconceptions of Texas also suffer from tunnel vision and a warping focus on the time period 1820–1890 and on Anglo Texans. Exceptionalists believe that the Texas character was molded and formed for the better by the epic events of those seventy years, and if you scratch beneath the surface you quickly see that this exceptionalism applies to whites only. Ironically, those who never forget the rebel yell typically stress the mirror image. Everything evil about Texas, most especially racism, violence, intolerance, bigotry, anti-intellectualism, and other alleged southern characteristics, grew from the 19th century, and they were all creations of whites only. Despite the efforts of New Western Historians, the white cowboy circa 1885 remains the dominant western trope applied to Texas. In fact, in all three cases you could go a step further and declare that the dominant actors remain white males from the period 1820 to 1890. Perhaps over simplifications, stereotypes, and ahistorical approaches imbue all characterizations of the past based on present perceptions, but the impact on Texas history remains especially pernicious.[25]

In essence then, the terrible triplets all obscure the varied people and events of the Texas past. What role for the 18th century or the 20th century is there in such discourses other than to trot through as quickly as possible? Where are Tejanos in this story or German Texans? African Americans were more than victims; they were creators of the Texas past. You cannot understand men in the past without women. Masculinity could not have existed without femininity. As late as 1845 Indians dominated much of Texas, and while that may be exceptional it is certainly not what the exceptionalists had in mind. Carried to extremes, the terrible triplets become simply silly, requiring that one group and one time be accepted as of overarching importance. That is an approach that has not been creditable among mainstream historians for almost fifty years. No wonder that Texas historians still get charged with being parochial.[26]

Moreover, focusing on the terrible triplets obscures what should be obvious to any well read contemporary historian. Cultural identity was constructed and reconstructed over time. It was the product of human action and interaction, not just impersonal forces and seismic events. Twentieth century Texans made themselves non-southern with a non-southern memory of the past. They stopped over at celebrating and remembering being Texan, exceptional, and western, but they eventually reached being American. What they made themselves should not be ignored in favor of what we think they should have really been or the past they should have really remembered. Obviously this does not change the reality of what Texans were in 1865, but to the extent that changes in public memories of the past changed behavior and culture in the 1910s and later, the new way of thinking of the past mattered.[27]

These mutable public memories that raised first one triplet and then another to preeminence and the many weaknesses of the terrible triplets in explaining Texas and its regions suggest that explanatory alternatives deserve much more widespread use. Historians and the public should recognize that Texas was always a border region (a place in between), that identity and culture have been constructed and reconstructed by diverse human actors, and that Texas fit more often than not within the framework of United States history and beyond. Essentially then the alternatives to the terrible triplets begin with understanding the implications of admitting that others besides Anglo males from the South mattered in the history of Texas, that the essence of Texaness was not formed for all time between 1820 and 1890, and that Texans shared in and sometimes pioneered the trends and characteristics of all Americans and others in the western world.[28]

Instead of one experience or one time creating an indelible mark on Texas or its regions, change occurred constantly with people from across different borders exerting greater influence at different times. As late as the 1790s, Indians, male and female, called the shots in most of what is now Texas. Comanches who had moved south into the Texas area from mid-America clearly dominated all those they came in contact with. Spanish-speaking settlements were profoundly shaped by both Indian Texans who had merged into the local population and Indian Texans like the Comanches who remained in their own tribal units. Recent scholarship insists that the Indian presence remained strong through the 1840s and later. You cannot understand Texas culture, identity, or politics without that realization. Indians crossed borders into Texas, and their contact with other Texans as much as anything else determined the course of events.[29]

By the 1840s, however, blacks and whites from the American South had begun arriving in Texas in large numbers—large enough numbers to quickly swamp any Old Texians and to challenge Indian dominance. A new culture, identity, and politics emerged that by 1861 allowed for secession with the Lower South. During the 1850s, however, Europeans began arriving in Texas in substantial numbers and by the 1880s German-speaking Texans significantly outnumbered Spanish-speaking Texans. These Europeans changed the culture, identity, and politics of the cities and counties where they clustered and of the entire state. Statewide prohibition lost in 1911 in Texas whereas it had been successful in most other southern states. The culture, identity, and politics built by the intersection of ethnic communities with the larger population proved the difference.[30]

By 1911 as well, Mexican immigration to Texas had trended up. The Tejano population began increasing noticeably as early as the 1890s, and then surged with the turmoil of the Mexican Revolution of 1910 and the increased labor needs in Texas during World War I and the early 1920s. After receding during the 1930s, Tejano numbers increased rapidly after 1941. Indeed the Civil Rights movement assumed a different character in the Texas of the 1950s and 1960s because the state had long since moved beyond a black-white binary typical of Mississippi.[31]

By the 1980s people from job-poor states like Michigan flocked to Texas cities and suburbs, again changing the culture, identity, and politics of the state, and perhaps making possible the rise to dominance in the 1990s of the Republican Party. The use of western images and western heroes by such politicians as Ronald Reagan aided this transformation, but they were not its only source and the influence of these images extended across the country. Viewed from this long sweep, Texas does not seem southern, western, or even particularly exceptional. Instead people, influences, and cultures from beyond the border lines of the state shaped and re-shaped what transpired within the state.[32]

More specifically, instead of being unique, southern or western, Texas was joined to the rest of the world. The Atlantic World, the Comanche Empire extending beyond Texas, the industrialization of textiles that drove the expansion of a southern cotton culture, the economic and political dislocations of Central Europe, the Mexican Revolution of 1910, United States immigration reform and economic change in the 1960s, and the seismic shifts in manufacturing patterns and the global economy after the 1960s all shaped Texas.[33]

Yes, Texas sprang from its particular location in a specific border region. It sprang from the combination of specific population groups and their interaction with each other. Out of this came some exceptional behavior. Take that previously mentioned successful drive to give women the vote in Texas in the 1910s—a most unsouthern thing by the way. Some might say it was western in this regard, taking after Colorado. Some might say that gender roles were unique in frontier Texas, and that the interactions between men and women that shaped attitudes towards what was proper for each sex varied from the norm. Yet the suffrage movement grew in cities and towns, usually cities and towns energized by increasing cultural and economic connections built by the world cotton trade and international banking, and it grew because of the influence of women deeply intertwined in those commercial networks like Mary Eleanor Brackenridge. Border influences brought the suffrage movement to Texas. Texas has never been able to escape the twists and turns of its border connections in the way that Mississippi has and does. So Molly Ivins' joke about Texas being "Mississippi with good roads" is funny, but wrong.[34]

Instead those border influences, people, and cultures met in Texas constructing and reconstructing culture and identity. Gender roles that more nearly matched those of Europe and the United States outside the South were one example of this construction and reconstruction process, a process requiring historians to adopt a new way of conceptualizing the Texas past. Before 1820, Texas was an Indian world with only a small European presence heavily influenced by its position on the Northern Frontier of New Spain. Between 1820 and 1845, Texas culture and identity transitioned from a place on the Northern Frontier to a place on the western frontier of the American South. United States influences and symbols and habits of mind grew increasingly strong only to take on a decidedly and preeminently southern texture by the end of the era. From 1845 to 1890 the southern nature of Texas grew more complete. Southerness faded from 1890 to 1920, another era of pronounced and relatively rapid change in culture and identity as the state moved toward celebration of a Texan past and a western image as way stations on the path back to full participation in American and western European culture and economic activity. From 1920 to about 1985, Texans shared about as fully as they ever did in the pattern of a broader America and of the industrialized western world. The years after 1985 appear even in short-sighted perspective to be another era of rapid transition with the influence of California-style conservatism, an increasingly global and interconnected economy, migration from the Rust Belt, and a surge in immigration from Mexico and Central America making for a difficult to read mix. Borders shaped Texas, and Texas culture and identity changed and evolved.

Yet from time to time, some shard from the past poked up in the present. While the Indian presence has virtually disappeared, secession still gets an occasional mention and white-on-black violence brings back memories of a southern past. The Texas Revolution and Republic remain potent symbols. The image of a large white cowboy still graces the Texas State Fair. Conceiving of Texas identity and culture as being constructed and reconstructed demands the acceptance of ambiguity and the realization that the Reconstruction process never totally erased the past.

Likewise conceiving of Texas as a place influenced by its location between other people, places, and cultures demands that we accept that some of those groups of people remained distinctive for decades. Culture and language and such specific experiences of Texas Germans as the struggle against Prohibition and the Ku Klux Klan kept them distinctive into at least the 1930s and by some measures into the 1950s. The experiences of African-American Texans in slavery, Reconstruction, segregation, and the Civil Rights Movement kept them distinctive at least into the 1980s, and the divide between black and white remains powerful to the present day. Tejanos, too, remain somewhat distinct from either African Americans or Anglos. Their struggle to be accepted and respected in Texas after 1836, the large scale movement from Mexico after 1910, and the continued vitality of the Spanish language set them apart. Historians inclined to look for complexity and nuance will find it in Texas history.[35]

Yet despite this ambiguity, complexity, and nuance, in fact on some level because of those characteristics, Texas and Texans have often either followed or led American patterns. Texas revolutionaries called up American symbols and myths. German and Czech movement to Texas fit within an American pattern of large-scale European immigration between 1840 and 1920. White racism and white-on-black violence were more intense in Texas and the South, but were part of a broader American pattern. Civil Rights was an American movement. Mexican Americans and immigrants from Central America now live scattered across the country and comprise significant minorities in numerous states.

Texans, too, often led in the transformation of American culture and life. Consider the changing gender roles that accompanied the movement of women into the public sphere in the early 20th century. Mary Eleanor Brackenridge and other Texas women voted in primaries at least, well ahead of women in most of the country. Thanks to the vote of the state legislature Texas became the ninth state overall and the first ex-Confederate state to ratify the amendment to the U.S. Constitution giving women the right to vote. Texans actually elected the first woman governor, even though the timing of her inauguration in 1925 made her the second woman governor to hold office in the United States. Tellingly, all of this occurred in one of those transition times when Texans were increasingly free from the mores of the Lost Cause and the Old South and moving toward full participation in the patterns of the rest of the United States and the industrialized world. Agitation for prohibition, calls for increased emphasis on public education and health, participation in a nationwide and worldwide suffrage movement, and a changing place for women in the economy and in public life all contributed to this transformation. Miriam A. Ferguson, the first woman governor of Texas, drove her own car to the governor's mansion on inauguration day. Her two daughters, both university graduates, bobbed their hair and helped with the campaign. Texans were Americans by 1925, not exceptional, southern, or western.[36]

Texans were Americans, but they were not "Super-Americans" as suggested by John Bainbridge in 1961 and they were not "a nation in every sense of the word" as suggested by John Steinbeck at about the same time. Calling Texans Super-Americans casts them as cartoon characters, reducing a complex, nuanced, and ambiguous past to the level of Yosemite Sam. Further it obscures the time when they were more southern than American. Calling Texas a nation simply reverses the coin, making Texans the equivalent of John Wayne playing Davy Crockett in the movies. Both images boil down to Anglo myths, useful in supporting the superiority and self image of white Texans above all others, but in reality all Texans never much wanted to go it alone and they followed as well as led other Americans. Just as Texans were not always southern and only tangentially western, by 1961 they were not Super-Americans and not a nation unto themselves.[37]

As always these images, myths, collective memories, and misconceptions reflected their time. Exceptionalism and classic western images in particular soothed the discontents of the present, providing a balm for the intrusion of modern suburbs or modern life styles. Some of the state's most celebrated writers have expressed a profound since of loss, not about the South and slavery of course, but about the West and the exceptional nature of Texas. Walter Prescott Webb, J. Frank Dobie, and even Larry McMurtry fell in this category. Meanwhile, those who wrote about the South and growing up on a cotton farm like William A. Owens remain largely forgotten. The West and Texas exceptionalism sell. What Randolph B. Campbell calls "the cold history of being southern" does not.[38]

All serious historians and others who want to explore the identity of Texas owe Campbell a debt. His work on slavery and many other writings underscore just how southern Texans really were in the 19th century. He has long sought to revise Texas history in the face of romanticism and traditionalism. While never making enough headway with the general public, in some ways he may have been too successful with historians. Some twenty years ago, Paul D. Lack wrote that all historians who seriously sought to understand the history of Texas from 1820 to 1845 worked in the shadow of Eugene C. Barker, an historian who in the first third of the 20th century produced much work of great merit but whose outsized stature made it difficult for later historians to move beyond his views of Texas history. Campbell's insistence on the essential southerness of Texas and the overriding importance of the mid-19th century experience has worked in a similar fashion. Still, Campbell has advised historians to "take fully into account the power of collective memories and make those memories themselves a means of understanding Texas' past." If they do that, they just may agree that Texas was shaped by the many people and influences that crossed its borders, that Texans made and remade their culture, and that Texans were often more American than southern. Campbell, unlike Barker, has offered his fellow historians a way forward beyond his core teachings. This requires accepting as evidence something more than counting the number of lynchings and documenting the similarities of the all white primary and other pillars of the Jim Crow system in Texas with those in Georgia. It requires accepting the importance, mutability, and translucent power of culture.[39]

Among Texans perhaps none demonstrated the importance, mutability, and power of collective memory and culture more than George Washington Littlefield, that Texas tycoon who personified the complexities of his state's identity. Born in Panola County, Mississippi, in 1842, Littlefield entered a world in which George Washington reigned as the premier symbol of what it meant to be an American. It was a time when construction began on the Washington Monument and when newspapers routinely filled their columns with accounts of the father of the country. Washington's grip on the American psyche held even in the South, and perhaps especially in the South. Casting him as a defender of liberty, southerners placed his image on the Confederate Seal.[40]

Washington's name and the complex imagery it conjured fit Littlefield well. He moved to Texas in 1850 with his family, elite plantation and slave owners, and he grew up in Gonzalez County. When war broke out in 1861, Littlefield enlisted in Terry's Texas Rangers and fought at Shiloh and Chickamauga, rising to the rank of major and company commander. Injured during the war, he returned home to Texas and engaged in a variety of business ventures, including driving cattle north to the railhead in Kansas soon after the war. He acquired substantial land holdings in Gonzales and Hays counties and eventually bought and sold large ranches in West Texas and New Mexico. In 1883 he moved to Austin where, in 1890, he organized American National Bank. His bank's name deserves note. At a time when banks routinely took the name of the city or region where they were located, his bank was American in scope. Moreover it was a national bank instead of the still common private banks that remained dominant in some parts of Texas in 1890. National banks, however, were almost always better equipped to deal with national corporations, especially railroads, and Littlefield had a keen eye for catching the wave of the future. His name and his bank's were American and national, not simply southern and local.[41]

Yet Littlefield's place in our own memories remains tied to his efforts to commemorate the South. As mentioned, in 1914 he funded the collection of documents that would tell a "balanced" history of the South and the Civil War. Late in that decade, having earlier helped in the building of two other Confederate monuments, he negotiated with the sculptor Pompeo Coppini to build a Confederate memorial on the campus of The

University of Texas. Coppini persuaded Littlefield, who served as a regent of the University, to commission a work that would honor "the boys of the University of Texas who died so that American democracy might spread all over the world, while honoring the leaders you most admire as America's great men." Littlefield agreed, and shortly before his death in 1920 he accepted Coppini's design. The monument as eventually installed included a fountain with a large winged Columbia and statues of Robert E. Lee, Jefferson Davis, James Stephen Hogg, Albert Sidney Johnston, Woodrow Wilson, and John H. Reagan. Littlefield deemed southern, American, and Texan icons worthy of remembrance, and at least one of those southerners, Lee, by the 1920s was rapidly becoming an American hero often linked to George Washington.[42]

Take in, then, Littlefield, whose life and works commemorated and enshrined collective memories. As much a gilded age entrepreneur as Andrew Carnegie, he preached sobriety and virtue to his relatives and cowhands. He proudly remembered the South and the Confederacy and wanted others to understand his Lost Cause from his point of view. Yet his bank was an American bank, a national bank, and one decorated with western images. His fountain and accompanying statues mixed American, southern, and Texan prototypes, but the overall drift of Littlefield's life and his legacy was clear. He made Texas American. He rode the leading edge of the economic currents of the nation and the industrialized world toward prosperity. He grew and changed over the course of his life with events like World War I making him even more American.[43]

Littlefield stood for Texas and its evolving identity. Texans celebrated American symbols in the 1840s and before. In the 1860s Anglo Texans in particular fought for the Confederacy and long after defensively and reflexively defended the Confederate cause and an idealized South. Along the way, a growing number of Texans grew increasingly entwined with western and Texan images and realities. By 1920 Texans were American and concerned with spreading American democracy to the world. Under that crust lay southern, Texan, and western images and realities that would surface intermittently for decades. Understanding this complexity, nuance, ambiguity, and mutability frees us to leave behind the terrible triplets that define Texas as exceptional, southern, or western. Texas identity was and is a product of its borders, constructed and reconstructed over time, and typically more American than anything else. Why else would Randall B. Woods give his study of that quintessential Texan, Lyndon Johnson, the title *LBJ: Architect of American Ambition?*[44]

The editor of the *Schulenburg Sticker,* the newspaper that helped publicize the issue of woman suffrage, and the voters of surrounding Fayette County, whose people crossed borders from Mexico, the American South, and Central Europe to build and rebuild their culture, deserve the last word. In August 1924 Texas voters faced a contentious choice in the Democratic run-off primary for governor between Miriam Ferguson and Felix D. Robertson, who was backed by the Ku Klux Klan. As the editor pointed out, voters confronted "an unprecedented situation." No woman had ever been elected governor of any state in the United States, and many in Texas opposed women holding office. But the editor insisted that electing a Klansman would sow racial and ethnic animosity, encourage strife between religious groups, and violate the American concept of religious freedom "embedded into the very marrow of our bones." Calling on all voters to go to the polls on August 23, 1924, the editor exhorted his fellow citizens, "forget that Miriam Ferguson is a woman, and remember that you are an American." Historians and all others interested in the topic of Texas identity should do likewise, for more often than not Texans remembered they were American. Some at least also often remembered that they had ties, intellectually and culturally, beyond the borders of the United States. Miriam Ferguson won decisively with a record turnout in Fayette County and across Texas and went on to become the state's first woman governor in part because that was so.[45]

Notes

1. For a good overview of the various approaches to Texas history and the impact of those approaches see Richard B. McCaslin, *At the Heart of Texas: One Hundred Years of the Texas State Historical Association, 1897–1997* (Austin: Texas State Historical Association, 2007). Also see Laura Lyons McLemore, *Inventing Texas: Early Historians of the Lone Star State* (College Station: Texas A&M University Press, 2004); Walter L. Buenger, "Three Truths in Texas," in Walter L. Buenger and Arnoldo DeLeón, eds., *Beyond Texas Through Time: Breaking Away from Past Interpretations* (College Station: Texas A&M University Press, 2011), 1–49.

2. On borders, the creation of identity, and the universalism of Texas see "Margins to Mainstream: The Brave New World of Borderlands History," *Journal of American History* 98 (Sept. 2011): 337–437. I have one important caveat with the arguments put forward in this special issue and that concerns the use of the term borderlands. This is often still seen as

the place between Mexico and the United States, and as such it is bound to an historiography that stretches back over a hundred years and does not reflect or easily make room for the influence of culture, memory, and other more modern concerns. It stresses one border, that between Mexico and the United States. Instead, Texas lay between the Atlantic World, the Mid West, the South, the Rocky Mountain West, and Mexico. Borders on all sides and people and cultures from across those borders influenced its past. For an exploration of this border status see Walter L. Buenger, "Texas and the History of American Foreign Policy," *Diplomatic History* 36 (June 2012): 495–98. Also see Leigh Clemons, *Branding Texas: Performing Culture in the Lone Star State* (Austin: University of Texas Press, 2008); Gregg Cantrell, "The Bones of Stephen F. Austin: History and Memory in Progressive-Era Texas," in Gregg Cantrell and Elizabeth Hayes Turner, eds., *Lone Star Pasts: Memory and History in Texas* (College Station: Texas A&M University Press, 2007): 39–68; Walter L. Buenger, *The Path to a Modern South: Northeast Texas Between Reconstruction and the Great Depression* (Austin: University of Texas Press, 2001). Also see various essays in Buenger and DeLeón, *Beyond Texas Through Time*, especially Pekka Hämäläinen, "Into the Mainstream: The Emergence of a New Texas Indian History," 50–84.

3. *Telegraph and Texas Register* (San Felipe de Austin), Oct. 17, 1835; *The Texas Republican* (Brazoria), Aug. 22, 1835. Also see *Telegraph and Texas Register*, Oct. 26, 31, Nov. 7, 14, 1835; *Texas Republican*, Oct. 17, 31, Nov. 14, 1835; Mar. 2, 1836. George Washington's symbolic role in all of the United States, including his appearance on the Confederate Seal, is discussed in this essay. See in particular note 40.

4. On slavery and the Texas Revolution see Paul D. Lack, *The Texas Revolutionary Experience: A Political and Social History, 1835–1836* (College Station: Texas A&M University Press, 1992); Randolph B. Campbell, *An Empire for Slavery: The Peculiar Institution in Texas, 1821–1865* (Baton Rouge: Louisiana State University Press, 1989); Gregg Cantrell, *Stephen F. Austin: Empresario of Texas* (New Haven: Yale University Press, 1999). For an introduction to the complicated role that slavery played in the politics of the 1830s and 1840s, see William W. Freehling, *The Road to Disunion: Secessionists at Bay, 1776–1854* (New York: Oxford University Press, 1990).

5. On the roof line of the Alamo see "The Alamo," by Mary G. Ramos, for the *Texas Almanac 1992–1993* [http://www.texasalmanac.com/topics/history/alamo (accessed Apr. 6, 2012)]. On the troubled life of the Republic, slavery, and annexation to the United States, see Freehling,

Secessionists at Bay, 353–439; Randolph B. Campbell, *Gone to Texas: A History of the Lone Star State,* 2nd ed. (New York: Oxford University Press, 2012), 157–84; Joel H. Silbey, *Storm Over Texas: The Annexation Controversy and the Road to Civil War* (New York: Oxford University Press, 2005).

6. On memory, Texas exceptionalism, the Texas Revolution, and the Republic see Holly Beachley Brear, *Inherit the Alamo: Myth and Ritual at an American Shrine* (Austin: University of Texas Press, 1995); Richard R. Flores, *Remembering the Alamo: Memory, Modernity, and Master Symbol* (Austin: University of Texas Press, 2002); Buenger, *Path to a Modern South*, 253–60. For an introduction to the literature on memory and exceptionalism, see Michel-Rolph Trouillot, *Silencing the Past: Power and the Production of History* (Boston: Beacon Press, 1995); W. Fitzhugh Brundage, ed., *Where These Memories Grow: History, Memory, and Southern Identity* (Chapel Hill: University of North Carolina Press, 2000); John Bodnar, *Remaking America: Public Memory, Commemoration, and Patriotism in the Twentieth Century* (Princeton: Princeton University Press, 1992); Michael Kammen, *Mystic Chords of Memory: The Transformation of Tradition in American Culture* (New York: Knopf, 1991); David W. Blight, *Race and Reunion: The Civil War in American Memory* (Cambridge: Harvard University Press, 2001); Kirk Savage, *Standing Soldiers, Kneeling Slaves: Race, War, and Monuments in Nineteenth-century America* (Princeton: Princeton University Press, 1997); W. Fitzhugh Brundage, *The Southern Past: A Clash of Race and Memory* (Cambridge: Harvard University Press, 2005); Kerwin Lee Klein, "On the Emergence of Memory in Historical Discourse," *Representations* 69 (Winter 2000): 127–50.

7. "A Declaration of the Causes which Impel the State of Texas to Secede from the Federal Union, February 2, 1861," in Ernest W. Winkler, ed., *Journal of the Secession Convention of Texas 1861* (Austin: Texas Library and Historical Commission, 1912), 61–65 [https://www.tsl.state.tx.us/ref/abouttx/secession/2feb1861.html (accessed Apr. 6, 2012)].

8. *Report of the Proceedings of the Various Associations of Ex-Confederates Held at Dallas, Dallas County, Texas, August 6th, 7th, 8th, and 9th, 1884* (Dallas: Dallas Herald Printing House, 1884), 5. On Civil War memories in Texas, see also Kelly McMichael, "'Memories are Short But Monuments Lengthen Remembrances:' The United Daughters of the Confederacy and the Power of Civil War Memory," in Cantrell and Turner, *Lone Star Pasts*, 95–118; Kelly McMichael, *The Civil War Monument Movement in Texas* (Denton: Texas State Historical Association

Press, 2009). On southern distinctiveness and its creation and elaboration in the Civil War era see Drew Gilpin Faust, *The Creation of Confederate Nationalism; Ideology and Identity in the Civil War South* (Baton Rouge: Louisiana State University Press, 1988); Anne Sarah Rubin, *A Shattered Nation: The Rise and Fall of the Confederacy, 1861–1868* (Chapel Hill: University of North Carolina Press, 2005); Gaines M. Foster, *Ghosts of the Confederacy; Defeat, the Lost Cause, and the Emergence of the New South, 1865–1913* (New York: Oxford University Press, 1987); Charles R. Wilson, *Baptized in Blood: The Religion of the Lost Cause, 1865–1920* (Athens: University of Georgia Press, 1980); Nina Silber, *The Romance of Reunion: Northerners and the South, 1865–1900* (Chapel Hill: University of North Carolina Press, 1993); David Goldfield, *Still Fighting the Civil War: The American South and Southern History* (Baton Rouge: Louisiana State University Press, 2002); Karen L. Cox, *Dixie's Daughters: The United Daughters of the Confederacy and the Preservation of Confederate Culture* (Gainesville: University Press of Florida, 2003); Blight, *Race and Reunion*; Brundage, *Southern Past*. For a compelling argument that the South has essentially always been a reflection of the larger United States that perhaps slights the importance of culture and memory in creating distinctiveness in the minds of those both in and outside the South, see Laura F. Edwards, "Southern History as U.S. History," *Journal of Southern History* 75 (Aug. 2009): 1–32, and "What Constitutes a Region?" *Diplomatic History* 36 (June 2012): 483–86. For an effective argument in support of the long-term importance of race and the distinctiveness and continuity of southern politics, see Michael Perman, *Pursuit of Unity: A Political History of the American South* (Chapel Hill: University of North Carolina Press, 2009), and *The Southern Political Tradition* (Baton Rouge: Louisiana State University Press, 2012). For the view that this focus on unity and constancy misses key parts of the southern population, see Jacquelyn Dowd Hall, "The Long Civil Rights Movement and the Political Uses of the Past," *Journal of American History* 91 (Mar. 2005): 1,233–63.

9. For a fuller discussion of the persistence of many southern characteristics and their pervasiveness in Texas, see Walter L. Buenger, "Texas and the South," *Southwestern Historical Quarterly* 103 (Jan. 2000): 309–26.

10. *Proceedings of the Annual Meeting of the Blues and the Grays Ex-Confederate and U.S. Soldiers Held at San Antonio, Tex., September 16th, 17th and 18th, 1888* (San Antonio: Johnson Bros., 1888), 13; *Proceedings of the Daughters of the Republic of Texas, Twenty-Fourth Annual*

Meeting, Austin, Texas, April 20–21, 1915 (Austin: Von Boeckman-Jones, 1915), 8. On those who remained outside the southern mainstream in Texas even during the Civil War and Reconstruction, see James Marten, *Texas Divided: Loyalty and Dissent in the Lone Star State, 1856–1874* (Lexington: University of Kentucky Press, 1990); David Pickering and Judy Falls, *Brush Men and Vigilantes: Civil War Dissent in Texas* (College Station: Texas A&M University Press, 2000); Richard B. McCaslin, *Tainted Breeze: The Great Hanging at Gainesville, Texas, 1862* (Baton Rouge: Louisiana State University Press, 1994). Also see Elizabeth Hayes Turner, "Juneteenth: Emancipation and Memory," in Cantrell and Turner, *Lone Star Pasts*, 143–75.

11. *The Texas 100 Percent American*, April 21, 1922. Also see Walter L. Buenger, "Memory and the 1920s Ku Klux Klan in Texas," in Cantrell and Turner, *Lone Star Pasts*, 119–42; Walter D. Kamphoefner, "The Handwriting on the Wall: The Klan, Language Issues, and Prohibition in the German Settlements of Eastern Texas," *Southwestern Historical Quarterly* 112 (July 2008): 52–66; Charles C. Alexander, *Crusade for Conformity: The Ku Klux Klan in Texas, 1920–1930* (Houston: Texas Gulf Coast Historical Association, 1962); Nancy MacLean, *Behind the Mask of Chivalry: The Making of the Second Ku Klux Klan* (New York: Oxford University Press, 1994). For a more general description of the transformation of Texas from a place that emphasized its ties to the South to a place that remembered Texas and gradually to a place that celebrated its American roots see Cantrell, "Bones of Stephen F. Austin"; Buenger, *Path to a Modern South*.

12. On Governor Rick Perry and talk of secession see *Politico*, Aug. 10, 2011 at http://www.politico.com/news/stories/0811/61030.html (accessed Apr. 6, 2012); *Statesman*, Apr. 17, 2009 at http://www.statesman.com/news/content/region/legislature/stories/04/17/0417gop. html (accessed Apr. 6, 2012).

13. For a good snapshot of the diversity of the late 19th century Texas population see L. L. Foster, *Forgotten Texas Census: First Annual Report of the Agricultural Bureau of the Department of Agriculture, Insurance, Statistics, and History, 1887–88* (Austin: Texas State Historical Association, 2001). For a probing look at how Texas fits into western history, see Ty Cashion, "What's the Matter with Texas? The Great Enigma of the Lone Star State in the American West," *Montana: The Magazine of Western History* 55 (Winter 2005): 2–15. Also see Glen Sample Ely, *Where the West Begins: Debating Texas Identity* (Lubbock: Texas Tech University Press, 2011); Ty Cashion, *The New Frontier: A Contemporary*

History of Fort Worth and Tarrant County (San Antonio: Historical Publishing Network, 2006); Patricia Nelson Limerick, *The Legacy of Conquest: The Unbroken Past of the American West* (New York: W. W. Norton, 1987); Richard White, *It's Your Misfortune and None of My Own; A New History of the American West* (Norman: University of Oklahoma Press, 1991); Donald Worster, *Under Western Skies: Nature and History in the American West* (New York: Oxford University Press, 1992); Patricia Nelson Limerick, Clyde A. Milner II, and Charles E. Rankin, eds., *Trails Toward a New Western History* (Lawrence: University of Kansas Press, 1991); David M. Wrobel and Michael C. Steiner (eds.), *Many Wests: Place, Culture, and Regional Identity* (Lawrence: University of Kansas Press, 1997). For a fascinating examination of how the Texas West fit other trends within industrializing America, see Jacqueline M. Moore, *Cowboys and Cattlemen: Class and Masculinities on the Texas Frontier, 1865–1900* (New York: New York University Press, 2010). On the influence of the movie industry, see Don Graham, *Cowboys and Cadillacs: How Hollywood Looks at Texas* (Austin: Texas Monthly Press, 1983); Don Graham, *State of Mind: Texas Culture and Its Discontents* (Austin: University of Texas Press, 2011).

14. On lynching in Texas, see Patricia Bernstein, *The First Waco Horror: The Lynching of Jesse Washington and the Rise of the NAACP* (College Station: Texas A&M University Press, 2005); William D. Carrigan, *The Making of a Lynching Culture: Violence and Vigilantism in Central Texas, 1836–1916* (Urbana: University of Illinois Press, 2004); Cynthia Skove Nevels, *Lynching to Belong: Claiming Whiteness through Racial Violence* (College Station: Texas A&M University Press, 2007); Buenger, *Path to a Modern South*, 19–26. On integration, see Amilicar Shabazz, *Advancing Democracy: African Americans and the Struggle for Access and Equity in Higher Education in Texas* (Chapel Hill: The University of North Carolina Press, 2004); Charles H. Martin, *Benching Jim Crow: the Rise and Fall of the Color Line in Southern College Sports, 1890–1980* (Urbana: University of Illinois Press, 2010); Ricky F. Dobbs, *Yellow Dogs and Republicans: Allan Shivers and Texas Two-party Politics* (College Station: Texas A&M University Press, 2005).

15. Jefferson *Jimplecute*, July 9, 1914. Also see David B. Gracy II, "Littlefield, George Washington," Handbook of Texas Online (http://www.tshaonline.org/handbook/online/ articles/fli18) , accessed Feb. 13, 2012, Published by the Texas State Historical Association; Dallas *Morning News*, Apr. 30, 1914.

16. Omaha *Breeze*, Apr. 17, May 8, 1912. My point here is not that the South did not change or that Texas or Texans completely and immediately ceased being southern, but that Texas and Texans followed a different and more accelerated path because their border influences facilitated the construction and re-construction of a different culture. Especially after the 1920s they more easily (but never completely) put behind them a virulent defense of segregation and a closed racial system. Concerning changes in the South and the importance of race and memory in determining those changes, see Foster, *Ghosts of the Confederacy*; Brundage, *Southern Past*; Brundage, *Where These Memories Grow*. On how opponents of lynching used the media to create an image of the savage South, see Bernstein, *First Waco Horror;* Buenger, *Path to a Modern South*, 104–31.

17. *Annual Meeting of the Blues and the Grays*, 11. Also see *First Annual Convention of the United Confederate Veterans, July 3rd, 4th, 5th, 1890 in Chattanooga, Tenn.* (n.p., n.d.); *Report of the Proceedings of the Various Associations of Ex-Confederates Held at Dallas, Dallas County, Texas, August 6th, 7th, 8th, and 9th, 1884* (Dallas: Dallas Herald Printing House, 1884).

18. Edward L. Ayers, *The Promise of the New South: Life After Reconstruction* (New York; Oxford University Press, 1992), 437. Also see William A. Link, *The Paradox of Southern Progressivism, 1880–1930* (Chapel Hill: University of North Carolina Press, 1992). On woman suffrage, see A. Elizabeth Taylor, "Woman Suffrage," Handbook of Texas Online (http://www.tshaonline.org/handbook/online/articles/viw01), accessed Feb. 16, 2012, Published by the Texas State Historical Association. On the integration of college sports in Texas, see Martin, *Benching Jim Crow*; Frank Fitzpatrick, *And the Walls Came Tumbling Down: the Basketball Game that Changed American Sports* (Lincoln; University of Nebraska Press, 2000).

19. On Texas regionalism, see Cashion, "What's the Matter with Texas;" Ely, *Where the West Begins*. Ely in particular stresses the importance of the environment and the emergence of West Texas as a fixed region. For the classic expression of the relevance of place and process and the shift from "flux to fixity" see William Cronon, George Miles, and Jay Gitlin, "Becoming West," in William Cronon, George Miles and Jay Gitlin, eds., *Under An Open Sky: Rethinking America's Western Past* (New York: W. W. Norton, 1992), 23. Also see Robert V. Vine and John Mack Faragher, *The American West: A New Interpretive History* (New

Haven: Yale University Press, 2000); Patricia Nelson Limerick, *Something in the Soil: Legacies and Reckonings in the New West* (New York; W. W. Norton, 2000).

20. William Humphrey, *No Resting Place* (New York: Delacort Press, 1989), 9. Also see Buenger, "Texas and the South;" Neil Foley, *The White Scourge: Mexicans, Blacks, and Poor Whites in Texas Cotton Culture* (Berkeley: University of California Press, 1997). For the argument that 1936 marked a decisive moment in the Americanization of Texas, see Kenneth B. Ragsdale, *The Year America Discovered Texas: Centennial '36* (College Station: Texas A&M University Press, 1987).

21. A. Elizabeth Taylor, "Brackenridge, Mary Eleanor," Handbook of Texas Online (http://www.tshaonline.org/handbook/online/articles/fbr04), accessed Apr. 6, 2012, Published by the Texas State Historical Association; A. Elizabeth Taylor, "The Woman Suffrage Movement in Texas," *Journal of Southern History* 17 (May 1951): 194–215.

22. *Schulenburg Sticker*, June 23, 1911.

23. On changes in how Texans thought about themselves, see Buenger, *Path to a Modern South*, 223–260; Cantrell, "Bones of Stephen F. Austin;" Michael Phillips, "Why is Big Tex Still a White Cowboy? Race, Gender, and the 'Other Texans,'" Buenger and DeLeón, *Beyond Texas Through Time*, 125–78. For a popular history from the 1960s that depicted Texas as exceptional, see T. R. Fehrenbach, *Lone Star: A History of Texas and Texans* (New York: Macmillan, 1968). For further perspective on the evolution of Texaness, see Graham, *State of Minds,* and *Giant Country: Essays on Texas* (Fort Worth: TCU Press, 1998).

24. For a good narrative history of Texas that despite presenting evidence to the contrary maintains that Texas has remained essentially southern, see Campbell, *Gone to Texas*. Again, the South and southerners also changed. They entered again into a fuller participation in the life of the United States, but not in the same way or at the same speed as Texas and Texans. Because of the South's or at least the southern elite's determined defense first of slavery and then of segregation, lynching, and other aspects of the often violent enforcement of racial differences, the South long remained the most distinctive and set-apart region of the United States. See Perman, *Pursuit of Unity*, but balance that with Edwards, "Southern History as U.S. History." For a useful reminder that there were many Souths with many memories, just as there were many aspects to Texas and Texans, see W. Fitzhugh Brundage, "Contentious and Collected: Memory's Future in Southern History," *Journal of Southern History* 75 (Aug. 2009): 751–66.

25. For more detail on the back and forth struggle between traditionalists who often view Texas as either exceptional or western and revisionists who view Texas as southern see Buenger, "Three Truths in Texas," 1–49.

26. On how the study of Texas history has changed and why see the various essays in Buenger and De León, *Beyond Texas Through Time*.

27. On memory and culture, see Victoria E. Bonnell and Lynn Hunt, eds., *Beyond the Cultural Turn: New Directions in the Study of Society and Culture* (Berkeley: University of California Press, 1999); Brundage, "Contentious and Collected;" Gregg Cantrell and Elizabeth Hayes Turner, "A Study of History, Memory, and Collective Memory in Texas," in Cantrell and Turner, *Lone Star Pasts*, 1–14.

28. For reflections on how the South fits in the broader national history that might also be applied to Texas see Edwards, "Southern History as U.S. History," 533–64. Also see Walter L. Buenger and Arnoldo DeLeón, "Editor's Introduction," in Buenger and DeLeón, *Beyond Texas Through Time*, xi–xx; Buenger, "Three Truths in Texas." For a good recent example of the connection of Texas to the nation and the world, see William R. Childs, *The Texas Railroad Commission: Understanding Regulation in America to the Mid-Twentieth Century* (College Station: Texas A&M University Press, 2005).

29. For a sampling of the recent literature on Texas Indians, see Juliana Barr, *Peace Came in the Form of a Woman: Indians and Spaniards in the Texas Borderland* (Chapel Hill: University of North Carolina Press, 2007); Pekka Hämäläinen, *The Comanche Empire* (New Haven: Yale University Press, 2008); F. Todd Smith, *From Dominance to Disappearance: the Indians of Texas and the Near Southwest, 1786–1859* (Lincoln: University of Nebraska Press, 2005); Brian DeLay, *War of a Thousand Deserts: Indian Raids and the U.S.-Mexican War* (Yale, 2008). Also see Hämäläinen, "The Emergence of a New Texas Indian History," in Buenger and DeLeón, *Beyond Texas Through Time*, 50–84. On Spanish Texas see Donald E. Chipman and Harriett Denise Joseph, *Spanish Texas, 1519–1821*, rev. ed. (Austin: University of Texas Press, 2010).

30. For an overview of demographic change, see Terry G. Jordan, "A Century and a Half of Ethnic Change in Texas, 1836–1986," *Southwestern Historical Quarterly* 89 (Apr. 1986): 385–422. On the 1911 Prohibition elections see Lewis L. Gould, *Progressives and Prohibitionists: Texas Democrats in the Wilson Era* (Austin, University of Texas Press, 1973), 28–57.

31. For an introduction to the complex demographic history of Tejanos, see Jordan, "Ethnic Change in Texas," 385–422; Buenger, *Path to a Modern South*, 141–73; Lawrence A. Cardoso, *Mexican Emigration to the United States, 1897–1931* (Tucson: University of Arizona Press, 1980). For a sampling of the growing literature on the Mexican-American Civil Rights movement, see Anthony Quiroz, *Claiming Citizenship: Mexican Americans in Victoria, Texas* (College Station: Texas A&M University Press, 2005); Cynthia Orozco, *No Mexicans, Women, or Dogs Allowed: The Rise of the Mexican American Civil Rights Movement* (Austin: University of Texas Press, 2009); Emilio Zamora, *Claiming Rights and Righting Wrongs in Texas: Mexican Workers and the Politics of Job Opportunity, 1939–1947* (College Station: Texas A&M University Press, 2008); Ignacio M. García, *White But Not Equal: Mexican Americans, Jury Discrimination and the Supreme Court* (Tucson: University of Arizona Press, 2008); Guadalupe San Miguel Jr., *Brown, not White: School Integration and the Chicano Movement in Houston* (College Station: Texas A&M University Press, 2001). For useful insight and comparison between the African-American and the Mexican-American Civil Rights Movement, see Carlos Blanton, "Deconstructing Texas: the Diversity of People, Place, and Historical Imagination in Recent Texas History," in Buenger and DeLeón, *Beyond Texas Through Time*, 179–220; Carlos Blanton, "George I. Sánchez, Ideology, and Whiteness in the Making of the Mexican American Civil Rights Movement, 1930–1960," *Journal of Southern History* 72 (Aug. 2006): 569–604; Brian D. Behnken, *Fighting Their Own Battles: Mexican Americans, African Americans, and the Struggle for Civil Rights in Texas* (Chapel Hill: University of North Carolina Press, 2011).

32. Sean P. Cunningham, *Cowboy Conservatism: Texas and the Rise of the Modern Right* (Lexington: University Press of Kentucky, 2010); Robert A. Goldberg, "The Western Hero in Politics: Barry Goldwater, Ronald Reagan, and the Rise of the American Conservative Movement," in Jeff Roche, ed., *The Political Culture of the New West* (Lawrence: University Press of Kansas, 2008), 13–50; M. Ray Perryman, *Survive and Conquer, Texas in the '80s: Power—Money—Tragedy . . . Hope!* (Dallas: Taylor Publishing Company, 1990); Steven H. Murdoch, *The New Texas Challenge: Population Change and the Future of Texas* (College Station: Texas A&M University Press, 1997).

33. On borders and borderlands, see the special section in *Journal of American History* 98 (Sept, 2011): 337–454. On the continual movement of new groups into Texas, see Campbell, *Gone to Texas*.

34. Molly Ivins, April 3 [1997] [http://www.creators.com/opinion/molly-ivins/molly-ivins-april-3-1997-04-03.html (accessed July 6, 2012)]. For an example of a suffrage leader with links to the broader world, see Judith N. McArthur and Harold L. Smith, *Minnie Fisher Cunningham: A Suffragist's Life in Politics* (New York: Oxford University Press, 2005).

35. For a starting point in understanding the persistence of language, ethnicity, and diversity in Texas, see Blanton, "Deconstructing Texas," 179–220. Also see Walter D. Kamphoefner, "German Texans: In the Mainstream or Backwaters of Lone Star Society?" *Yearbook of German-American Studies* 38 (2003): 119–38; Emilio Zamora, Cynthia Orozco, and Rodolfo Rocha, eds., *Mexican Americans in Texas History: Selected Essays* (Austin: Texas State Historical Association Press, 2010); Shabazz, *Advancing Democracy*; Carlos Blanton, *The Strange Career of Bilingual Education in Texas, 1836–1981* (College Station: Texas A&M University Press, 2004).

36. *Fort Worth Press,* Aug. 1, 1924; M. M. Crane to M. S. Duffie, Aug. 18, 1924, Martin McNulty Crane Papers, 1834–1974 (Dolph Briscoe Center for American History, University of Texas); Norman D. Brown, *Hood, Bonnet, and Little Brown Jug: Texas Politics, 1921–1928* (College Station: Texas A&M University Press, 1984), 211–96; Shelley Sallee, "'The Woman of It': Governor Miriam Ferguson's 1924 Election," *Southwestern Historical Quarterly* 100 (July 1996): 1–16.

37. John Steinbeck, *Travels with Charley: In Search of America* (New York: Curtis Publishing, 1961), 173. Also see John Bainbridge, *The Super-Americans; A Picture of Life in the United States, as Brought into Focus, Bigger than Life, in the Land of the Millionaires—Texas* (Garden City, NY: Doubleday, 1961); James E. Crisp, *Sleuthing the Alamo: Davy Crockett's Last Stand and Other Mysteries of the Texas Revolution* (New York: Oxford University Press, 2005); Graham, *State of Minds*, 125–33; Brear, *Inherit the Alamo*; Flores, *Remembering the Alamo*; Raúl A. Ramos, *Beyond the Alamo: Forging Mexican Ethnicity in San Antonio, 1821–1861* (Chapel Hill: University of North Carolina Press, 2008).

38. Randolph B. Campbell, "History and Collective Memory in Texas; the Entangled Stories of the Lone Star State," in Cantrell and Turner, *Lone Star Pasts*, 279. Also see Graham, *State of Minds*, 26–34.

39. Campbell, "History and Collective Memory in Texas," 280. Also see Paul D. Lack, "In the Long Shadow of Eugene C. Barker: The Revolution and the Republic," in Walter L. Buenger and Robert A. Calvert, eds., *Texas Through Time: Evolving Interpretations* (College Station:

Texas A&M University Press, 1991), 134–64. Ely also comments on the long shadow of Campbell and others who advocate for a statewide and persistent southern identity in Texas. See Ely, *Where the West Begins*, 6–7. For expressions of the essential southerness of Texas, see Randolph B. Campbell, "Statehood, Civil War, and Reconstruction, 1846–1876," in Buenger and Calvert, *Texas Through Time*, 165–96; Campbell, *Empire for Slavery*; Randolph B. Campbell, *Grass-roots Reconstruction in Texas, 1865–1880* (Baton Rouge: Louisiana State University Press, 1997). Campbell's emphasis on Texas' enduring ties to the South was more muted in *Gone to Texas*, but see 468–71.

40. For the basic details of Littlefield's life, see Gracy, "Littlefield, George Washington." Also see J. Evetts Haley, *George W. Littlefield, Texan* (Norman: University of Oklahoma Press, 1943). For an introduction to the symbolic use of Washington, see Barry Schwartz, *George Washington: The Making of an American Symbol* (New York: Free Press, 1987); Kammen, *Mystic Chords of Memory*. On the Confederate Seal see "Great Seal of the Confederacy," http://americanhistory.si.edu/military-history/collection/object.asp?ID=677 (accessed Apr. 6, 2012).

41. From the creation of the national banking system during the Civil War until the 1980s, banking in Texas operated on several levels, with private banks that often predated the war remaining important through 1907 and state-chartered banks adding to the mix. Private banks were largely unregulated, while state and national banks had capital requirements and other regulations that influenced their formation. From their appearance in Texas shortly after the Civil War, however, national banks, whose creation usually required substantial capitalization, typically captured the business of corporations operating across state lines. For background information on late 19th and early 20th century banking in Texas, see Walter L. Buenger and Joseph A. Pratt, *But Also Good Business: Texas Commerce Banks and the Financing of Houston and Texas, 1886–1986* (College Station: Texas A&M University Press, 1986), 12–63; Avery L. Carlson, *A Monetary and Banking History of Texas* (Fort Worth: Fort Worth National Bank, 1930).

42. Quoted in McMichael, *Sacred Memories*, 61. Also see Carol Morris Little, *A Comprehensive Guide to Outdoor Sculpture in Texas* (Austin: University of Texas Press, 1996), 62–65. For an introduction to the connections between Washington and Robert E. Lee and Lee's changing place in the American imagination, see Richard B. McCaslin, *Lee in the Shadow of Washington* (Baton Rouge: Louisiana State University Press, 2001); Thomas L. Connelly, *The Marble Man: Robert*

E. Lee and His Image in American Society (New York: Knopf, 1977); Brian Holden Reid, *Robert E. Lee: Icon for a Nation* (Amherst, N.Y.: Prometheus Books, 2007).

43. To place Littlefield in the context of other American industrial leaders see Moore, *Cowboys and Cattlemen*. For commentary on Littlefield as champion of the history of the South, supporter of the war effort in World War I, western rancher, leading banker, and friend of higher education see Fort Worth *Star-Telegram*, Nov. 10, 1920.

44. Randall B. Woods, *LBJ: Architect of American Ambition* (New York: Free Press, 2006). Also see the revealing essay showing how Johnson was Texan and American, Larry L. King, "The Alamo Mindset: Lyndon B. Johnson and Vietnam," *Of Outlaws, Con Men, Whores, Politicians and Other Artists* (New York: Viking Press, 1980), 253–74.

45. *Schulenburg Sticker*, Aug. 22, 1924, p. 1. E. A. Bosl published the *Sticker*, but it is not entirely clear if he was also the editor. See *Schulenburg Sticker*, Aug. 29, 1924, p. 4. Also see Brown, *Hood, Bonnet, and Little Brown Jug*, 211–96; Sallee, "'The Woman of It,'" 1–16. For voting returns see *Schulenburg Sticker*, Aug. 29, 1924, p. 1; Mike Kingston, Sam Attlesey and Mary Crawford, *The Texas Almanac's Political History of Texas* (Austin: Eakin Press, 1992), 204–7. Also see Daphne Dalton Garrett, "Fayette County," Handbook of Texas Online (http://www.tshaonline.org/handbook/online/articles/hcf03), accessed July 02, 2012, Published by the Texas State Historical Association. Texas voting laws in the 1920s were in an almost constant state of flux and still varied to some degree from county to county, especially in the party primaries. In general, African-American Texans could not vote in the Democratic primary, but Tejanos and European immigrants could. For a quick snap shot, consult *Dallas Morning News*, Aug. 28, 29, 30, 1920; Aug. 22, 23, 24, 25, 1924. Also see Charles L. Zelden, *The Battle for the Black Ballot: Smith v. Allwright and the Defeat of the Texas All-White Primary* (Lawrence: University Press of Kansas, 2004); Darlene Clark Hine, *Black Victory: The Rise and Fall of the White Primary in Texas*, New Ed. (Columbia: University of Missouri Press, 2003).

Texas celebrated its western heritage and bright future at the State Fair in 1936. Courtesy of Dallas Historical Society

History, Memory, and Rebranding Texas as Western for the 1936 Centennial

Light Townsend Cummins

Whether Texas is southern or western in its basic historical character has long been debated by historians of the Lone Star State and the Southwest. Numerous articles, essays, and books have explicitly touched on this subject over the decades. Several scholars have played significant roles in this debate. Notably, Frank Vandiver wrote a timely book in 1975 titled *The Southwest: South or West?* Vandiver inconclusively found vestiges of both influences that shaped the region historically. An important contribution to this debate occurred twenty-eight years after Vandiver's book when Randolph B. Campbell published his monumental survey text, *Gone to Texas: A History of the Lone Star State*. Campbell came down solidly on the side of southern heritage as the primary historical underpinning of the Texas experience. This landmark volume, in addition to serving as a solid and eminently accessible textbook of the state's history, persuasively argued that Anglo-American Texas had its roots indisputably in the Old South. Campbell substantiated this conclusion by undertaking a close analysis of the Texas past to show that the state has consistently manifested southern characteristics in its historical attributes and continues to do so in the current era. One of the most recent entries in this lively debate is the work of historian Glen Sample Ely, who contends that Texas is predominantly western in its twentieth-century culture, especially those parts of the state that lie west of Interstate 35.[1]

The complex notions of Texas being seen as western, southern, or a combination of both are rooted in the subtle relationship between history and memory. There are differences between the study of history as an academic exercise and the existence of historical memory in any given society. Campbell's contention that the Lone Star State is essentially southern can be classified as history. His analysis is historiographical and based on documents gleaned from archival research in a wide variety of sources, the formulation of historical models that interpret past events, and the application of such constructs in creating a sustainable historiographical opinion. Memory is different from such history. It constitutes popular, publicly held views of the past that generally inform people about their historical origins, whether or not these are supported by the archival record.[2]

Not every Texan, therefore, would agree with Campbell's contention about the southern influences on the Texas ethos. Instead, for those who view the state through the prism of public memory, Texas is more appealingly rooted in the western frontier than southern heritage in terms of its modern imagery and the perceptions of current popular culture. The two sides have an explicit disagreement on this point. "The memory of Texas as western," Campbell has written, "has some basis in fact . . . Texas, however, is far more southern than western and has been so for nearly two hundred years."[3] He can make such a bold observation because, as chief historian of the Texas State Historical Association, he is absolutely and solely about the business of creating scholarly history, sustained by academic research and forging historiographical interpretation from those efforts. As a professional historian, Campbell uses research in order to comment on how the past created the world in which we live.[4]

On the other hand, many Texans have a marked tendency to view their state's past within the parameters of public memory instead of the thorough conclusions offered by scholarly history. That is because memory is a primary component of group identity, something that speaks to the very essence of why and how one defines being Texan, especially the Anglo-American aspects of myth, mystique, and memory. "For individuals and groups alike," W. Fitzhugh Brundage has remarked, "memory forms an essential component of their social identity."[5] Only a small part of group memory is produced by academic scholarship dealing with the past. As Gregg Cantrell and Elizabeth Hayes Turner observe, "today, document-based historical research of the sort found in scholarly history books sometimes contributes to shaping collective memory, but a larger role is probably played by the history lessons taught in schools, visits to museums, monuments, historical sites, or public celebrations; and the viewing of historically themed art, television, and movies—to name a few."[6] This means that scholarly historians must sometimes grapple with the very real potential of disagreeing in their conclusions with the content of public memory.[7] Sometimes these disagreements can be profound, extending to questions about what actually happened as an historical event and what did not. There is, therefore, often tension between scholarly history and public memory, with each serving different purposes when considering what people choose to remember, forget, emphasize, and honor about the past. The power of collective memory cannot be overlooked in considering the basic nature of Texas history. "The seemingly simplistic observation of a photograph, a gravesite, or even a high school yearbook," Yvonne Davis Frear argues, "invokes an historical memory that is often different from what is printed in history textbooks and scholarly monographs."[8]

Given the potential differences between scholarly history and public memory as ways to conceptualize the past, this essay does not imply that Randolph B. Campbell is off the mark when he says that Texas has strong predominant southern attributes that are manifested well into our own time. I agree with him. It is my opinion that, by scholarly standards as held by historians, Texas remains southern and does so without historical debate. At the same time, however, there exists a significant western, frontier theme in Texas public memory that cannot be sustained in the same way as historical viewpoints about southernisms.[9] In fact, this western-based public memory predominates in many quarters over and above any recognition of the state's relationship to southern history. Campbell, for one, certainly realizes this inherent dichotomy in considering the Texas past and its public memory. "When modern Texans in cities such as Houston," he has noted, "put on their boots and Stetsons and head for the rodeo or hearken back to the days of movie westerns that portrayed their state as cowboys, rustlers, and gunfighters, they are drawing on a collective memory that, although it has a basis in fact, is not the essence of Texas."[10]

Urban Houstonians can attend the rodeo dressed in their western finery because there has been a marked and overriding disconnect between the scholarly history of the state and its public memory since the 1930s. Southern attributes had ceased to be the state's primary and overriding historical image by the end of that decade. By then, Texans had come to consider themselves as westerners within the parameters of public memory. In so doing, they chose to ignore their southern historical origins as an explanation of their modern existence. Popular culture during the 1930s increasingly presented Texas to the nation and the world as a western place. Cattle and cowboys became the new overriding historical metaphors for Texas iconography. Campbell indeed has noticed this disconnection and conceded one reason for it when he wrote that "the cold history of being southern is not as pleasing as the warm memory of being western."[11] Historian Michael Phillips put it even more bluntly when he noted: "Texans embraced the western cowboy identity embodied by Big Tex [at the State Fair] and imitated by Bush in part because it sells well to tourists and because it cleanses the Anglo public memory of the state's Southern past."[12]

The mechanisms and methods whereby the public memory of Texas changed from southern to western during the 1930s form the basis for this essay. Although some historians, including Campbell along with Walter L. Buenger and Gregg Cantrell, have called attention to the deemphasizing of the southern image in Texans' collective remembering during the early twentieth century, as early as the Progressive Era, no scholar has yet studied the process whereby the basic underpinnings of public memory actually moved to a western frontier orientation. I contend that this change was rooted in the concept today called "branding," a term that was unknown in the years of change that this essay will consider. Nonetheless, during the Great Depression decade of the 1930s especially, there was an explicit effort to remake the popular image of Texas within a western context. The South had come to be viewed as a benighted region that existed outside the mainstream of American progress. For example, President Franklin D. Roosevelt unabashedly called the South the nation's number one economic problem.

For many Americans, things that were southern embodied in basic historical orientation various retrograde notions that looked to an increasingly irrelevant past. As Cantrell has reminded us about the shift from southern to western in the arena of public memory: "By the second decade of the twentieth century . . . the sentimentality of the Lost Cause with its reminders of slavery, defeat, military occupation, and poverty, held little appeal for the forward-looking leaders who wanted to build a progressive future for Texas." The result, he notes, was that Texas emerged "as a quintessentially western and American state" where "the dominant public memories . . . of Texas history continue to be western symbols," something that some historians have occasionally overlooked. Leigh Clemons has also pointed out that this branding of Texas was essentially male-oriented and racially biased. These efforts to present a new image of Texas had an "historical emphasis on white, male Texans and the importance of whiteness in the construction of Texan Cultural identity." Hispanic Texas scholars have seconded this viewpoint. John Morán González observes that these activities of rebranding "fundamentally reshaped the general representational contours of modern Texas, articulating what had been a commonly assumed yet loosely coordinated narrative of Anglo-Texan Progress."[13]

Starting in the decade after World War I, things "western" were seen by many people across the country as positive, progressive, and vitiating forces in a new emerging national life. When California became the destination for Dust Bowl migrants, it also a emerged as a national metaphor for renewing the American spirit, a viewpoint that in one fashion or another eventually dominated the entire western United States during the 1930s. Texans thus adopted the west and western imagery during the Depression decade in a broad based historical rebranding of the state. This was a grassroots, *sui generis* intellectual movement across Texas, especially in literature, historiography, and the arts. On the other hand, this rebranding also occurred as a consciously and carefully calculated effort that took place in the world of advertising, popular culture, and business. The deliberate aspect of this rebranding can be seen, for example, in the activities for the Texas Centennial Celebration of 1936. As part of those celebratory activities, the primary objective of which was to present Texas to the nation in a positive fashion, a number of advertising executives, event organizers, and participants in the Centennial made concerted efforts to characterize the state as being western instead of southern. "For the first time in the state's history," one student of the Texas Centennial has written, "its agents developed a national publicity campaign, funded by legislative appropriation and based on its colorful history, romantic myths, and cultural symbols."[14] That campaign helped to make Texas "western."

This branding involved a conscious effort to recast the public memory of Texas, especially as manifested in popular culture, from southern norms to western. "Collective or historical Memory is not simply the articulation of some shared subconscious but rather the product of intentional creation," historian W. Fitzhugh Brundage has noted. He added, "Collective remembering forges identity, justifies privilege, and sustains cultural norms."[15] That is exactly what happened during the Texas Centennial as organizers of the celebration provided white elites with a revamped public memory rooted in the western frontier tradition as a justification for their elite status in the state. What follows in this essay will examine this rebranding of Texas during the 1930s within the dual context of the intellectual movement of the decade and also by considering the actual events of the Centennial Celebration. In reality, these two historically distinct aspects of the rebranding were mutually complementary and can be seen as different aspects of the same broad based movement. "Those strategies were developed in the years leading up to the Texas Centennial Celebration of 1936," as Clemons notes, and "which grew out of an economic crisis that fueled an identity shift in Texas cultural memory."[16]

In the area of intellectual expression, the years after World War I witnessed the predominance of regionalism as an important interpretive vehicle for viewing United States history and culture. Scholars such as John Dewey, Lewis Mumford, and others argued that the nation was a combination of distinct regional cultures. The practitioners of regionalism undertook "a search for what might be called the indigenous or the primal basic America, a desire for a stable community identity, and a reverence for the past—especially the memories that could bring a sense of order and certainty."[17] The sociologist Howard Odom became a champion of this interpretive viewpoint when he wrote several important volumes during the 1930s that defined the South as a distinct regional culture, a contention seconded by southern agrarians and their literary movement. "Regionalists," as one student of the Texas Centennial era has observed, "advocated a reverence for the past, the values of tradition, and a sense of place amid the homogenizing aspects of modernization." For many Texas intellectuals, this meant the frontier, the west, and the images of the cowboy who, "in all his mythic grandeur, served as a symbol of a simpler, more rugged frontier age." [18] Hence, in Texas during the early years of the twentieth century, Texas regionalists looked more and more to the West as the basis of their regionalism. In some cases, regionalists were quite explicit regarding a preference for western themes in defining the region. Such was the case for the *Southwest Review*, a scholarly journal that proved to be an eloquent voice for Texas regionalism during the 1920s and 1930s. Founded at The University of Texas in 1915, it moved to Southern Methodist University in 1924. That year its editor, Jay Hubbell, proclaimed that the *Review*'s "pages will be open to all who write well; but it will especially encourage those who write on western themes, for it is a magazine for the Southwest."[19]

A shift in scholarly history paralleled the change in public memory. At the start of the twentieth century, most important Texas historians viewed the state historically as part of the South. Charles W. Ramsdell of The University of Texas had successfully established the southern heritage of the state in his teaching, his publications, and in his professional activities.[20] By the late 1920s, the historiographical orientation of that history department (which in those years had an overwhelming influence on Texas historiography) began to become increasingly western. Eugene C. Barker, for example, cast Stephen F. Austin within the context of the westward movement instead of southern expansionism. Walter P. Webb greatly accelerated this reorientation with his seminal book *The Great Plains*, which offered environmental determinism rather than southern heritage as an important cause of Texas regionalism. As a University of Texas history professor, Webb had already become concerned that the western heritage of the state had not been as fully appreciated as it should be. In the mid-1920s, for example, he helped organize a protest by historians and writers of the West to decry a lack of full acceptance by eastern book reviewers.[21] Webb's monumental book *Texas Rangers*, published the year prior to the centennial celebration, went to great lengths to present Texas as western. In its pages, Webb adopted a western viewpoint when he interpreted Texas history as a contest of three civilizations: Native American, Spanish, and Anglo-American pioneer folk, not southerners.[22] The 1936 motion picture *The Texas Rangers*, starring Fred McMurray and Jack Oakie, was based on Webb's book, thus bringing his western-based ideas to the nation as part of the popular culture of the movies. This motion picture attracted a great deal of attention in the Lone Star State when Paramount Pictures sponsored its world premiere at Dallas's Majestic Theatre on August 21, 1936.[23]

The 1930s also witnessed the emergence of a professionally manifested folklore that presented Texas as western. For example, J. Frank Dobie became known as "Mr. Texas" during that decade after having emerged as a tireless proponent of the western, ranching heritage of Texas. As his biographer later described his University of Texas office: "Once entering his lair, students couldn't be blamed for feeling as though they had stepped into a ranch headquarters. Western art filled the walls, and coyote and deerskin rugs blanketed the floor. . . . Above everything, dominating the entire room, was an impressively huge skull from a Texas longhorn."[24] Dobie also served in a crossover capacity between the southern to western intellectual changes of the decade and the Texas Centennial when he served on the Board of Historians of the celebration, in which capacity he labored mightily to advance the image of the state as part of the West.

These same intellectual changes can be seen in the worlds of Texas art, music, and architecture. Building on the earlier work of artist Frank Reaugh, Texas painters and sculptors participated in a reorientation of art starting in the 1920s that brought them into conformity with the regional movement that was sweeping the nation. The creation of the Public Works of Art Project in late 1933 provided jobs for many Texas artists to execute public commissions. Most of these projects revolved about western themes.[25] This helped forge in the artistic community a significant underpinning for their interpretation of the Texas regional experience. It should be noted, in that regard, that art can have an impact on culture and memory. "When such images become part of the popular culture," historian James E. Crisp has noted, "they can have a powerful and lasting effect on a community's collective memory."[26] Painters such as Jerry Bywaters, Otis Dozier, Alexandre Hogue, Everette Spruce, Tom Lea, and a host of others turned to western themes as an important attribute that characterized their work. Bywaters and Dozier, for example, took regular sketching trips to the Big Bend region of Texas, and Hogue became known for western landscapes. Tom Lea almost single-handedly legitimized the Trans-Pecos west as part of the Texas artistic heritage.

As well, artistic communities were established in the western part of the state that further motivated this rebranding. The San Cristoval arts community near San Angelo and the summer arts encampment at Sul Ross State College in Alpine further underscored the western influences on Texas artistic expression.[27] Sculptors including Allie Victoria Tennant, Pompeo Coppini, and Waldine Tauch also turned to western themes during the decade. As part of the construction of the centennial exposition at Dallas, for example, Tennant sculptured the famous *Tejas Warrior* (a statue of a Native American) that today still graces the main entrance to the Hall of State at Fair Park. Coppini chose to present the heroes of the Alamo as western frontiersmen in appearance, instead of southerners, when he crafted his famous Cenotaph that commemorates that signal event in Texas history.[28] The adopting of this "new regional" style of expression became in Texas art circles the most important criteria by which an artist was defined as a member of this movement. Those who did not embrace this style were not only criticized, but sometimes ostracized as well, by younger Texas artists who saw themselves as new regionalists.[29]

Texas music underwent a similar reorientation during the 1930s. The rise in popularity of country and western music, most often then styled as hillbilly music or western swing, became a notable occurrence of the decade. Bob Wills, Milton Brown and the Brownies, and a host of other such bands filled the radio airwaves and record stores of Texas with a popular, new, and indigenous brand of music that was unmistakably western in its orientation.[30] Western themes also emerged in the more classical compositions of David Guion, which were rooted in things western. Guion mirrored on the Texas scene the same sorts of western influences seen in the nationally oriented compositions of individuals such as Aaron Copland. No greater embodiment of these musical changes can be seen than in the career of Texan Gene Autry. He successfully popularized western music in ways that helped propel it to new heights of popularity across various venues in the nation's mass culture. Autry's vision of Texas in this musical style could be readily seen by the mid-1930s in the diverse media of radio, musical records, and motion pictures. A highpoint in these efforts occurred in 1936 when Autry made a motion picture at the Central Centennial Celebration held at Dallas entitled *The Big Show*, one of the first Hollywood movies filmed on location. His film crew used Fair Park and the celebration as the backdrop for a western that featured cowboy themes interspersed with a large measure of country and western music.[31]

Texas architecture also shifted in the period after World War I from southern norms to a new, western-oriented vernacular that was predominating by the late 1930s. Prior to the late 1920s, architects such as John Staub manifested a strong reliance on antebellum southern styles of decoration, embellishment, and residential planning. His design for Bayou Bend, the Hogg family home in the subdivision of River Oaks, can be seen as the zenith of this architectural orientation. Indeed, all of River Oaks (a residential area planned by Will C. Hogg and his family in the mid-1920s) consisted of grand homes that exhibited a strong reliance on the southern plantation style as one of its basic inspirations.[32] New forms of residential architecture, however, had become popular by the early 1930s, especially in the case of work undertaken by O'Neil Ford, David R. Williams, and Atlee B. Ayers. These architects turned to non-southern themes as motivations for architectural plans, especially in designing elite, upper-class residences across the state. Ayers became the master of the mission style, as seen predominantly in the dozens of homes he designed in the Olmos Park, Alamo Heights, and Monte Vista districts of San Antonio. Travelling to Mexico for his inspiration, Ayres made popular a mission style of design that tied Texas architecturally to California and other parts of the west during the 1930s.

The Drane home at Corsicana, jointly designed in 1926 by Ford and Williams, became the prototype for what eventually became known as the "ranch house," a new style of residence that quickly spread across Texas and the entire nation. Ford and Williams worked together to create a new regional architecture for Texas based on non-southern, pioneer norms. They travelled the Texas hill country to view German houses, and also looked at historical dwellings in San Antonio. Williams later wrote: "These little houses . . . are natural, native Texas art, suited to our climate and indigenous to our soil. We should use them as sources from which to draw a beautiful architecture which we could call our own."[33] If

River Oaks in Houston was the last great bastion of southern residential architecture in the 1920s, many of the homes of Highland Park in Dallas became the first significant manifestation in the 1930s of a Texas vernacular style rooted in western sensibilities, largely through new architectural assumptions advanced by Ford and Williams.

The official activities of the Texas Centennial Celebration of 1936 codified, legitimized, and sanctioned the broad based intellectual changes in Texas viewpoints that were already redefining the state as western instead of southern. The most obvious and best-known aspect of the westernization of the centennial celebration was found at Fort Worth's Frontier Exposition, largely promoted by the expansive Amon G. Carter with the assistance of the New York City showman Billy Rose.[34] With Rose as producer, Carter mounted a grand show in his city that featured Broadway performers, musical comedy stars, and other entertainment figures, all of whom presented Texas as being western in character. Carter even enlisted well-known fan dancer Sally Rand, who operated an all-female musical attraction of scantily clad chorus girls called "Sally Rand's Nude Ranch," thereby imparting a western flavor to burlesque itself although the performers—with some measure of prudence—wore body stockings as part of their western-themed costumes. Carter and his exposition attracted national attention in newspapers, on the radio, and in newsreels. The western character of the Fort Worth celebration relentlessly advanced the notion that it was located in the city "where the west began." Carter kept the Fort Worth exposition solidly before the state and nation with a constant emphasis on the western character of Texas. Celebrating the Texas Centennial as a part of the West, however, was a phenomenon not limited to Carter at Fort Worth. The idea of the celebration originated in the 1920s among the business leaders and advertising executives of the state, who viewed the centennial as an opportunity to highlight Texas progress to the rest of the nation and thus advance the state's commercial prospects. A number of centennial offices and agencies thus consciously adopted the viewpoint that Texas should be characterized in terms of its western heritage, doing so instead of presenting its southern background.

This was most certainly the case regarding the Centennial Board of Control, the state entity created by the legislature to oversee the celebration and dispense the public funds that would underwrite some of its events. The publicity office of the Board of Control instructed its employees to highlight things western in the various stories and news items it issued about the centennial. As Centennial historian Kenneth Ragsdale has noted: "The state's cultural icons therefore became part and parcel of their promotional baggage. Combined, they merged into an eclectic logo that symbolized Texas—ten-gallon hats, six shooters, high-heeled boots, Texas Rangers, bluebonnets, and sex," the latter involving the highlighting of feminine beauty in much of the publicity they generated.[35] The Dallas advertising firm of Tracy-Locke-Dawson received a contract to implement a barrage of publicity for the statewide celebration that highlighted the western nature of the state. Dale Miller, working in the publicity office, became a master of presenting the state in this fashion. In particular, much of what he did in advertising the Centennial would today be classified as branding a public image for Texas. He was relentless, later recalling of his work in this regard: "We took it on as a crusade."[36] A distinctive ten-gallon cowboy hat became the official headgear of the celebration. Miller visited Hollywood, where he met with radio and motion picture producers to arrange for plugs and publicity on behalf of the Centennial. He enlisted the assistance of Texans including Ginger Rogers and John Boles from the film community to advance a western view of Texas. He stressed western themes in all activities. Beyond the publicity office itself, much of the business and commercial advertising that emanated from Houston, Dallas, and San Antonio public relation firms during 1935 and 1936 explicitly contained western images and themes.

The publicity office seldom missed an opportunity to link Texas with the West. Starting in late 1935 the Centennial Board of Control published a tabloid newspaper entitled *The Centennial News*. One of its first issues proudly proclaimed a somewhat tenuous link with California, "The destinies of Texas and California have been inexorably linked since the birth of both," citing as its reason that both states were once a part of Mexico. Indeed, the start of the centennial year found Governor James V. Allred and a host of Texans visiting California where, among other activities, they attended the Rose Bowl football game that included Southern Methodist University. "Governor James V. Allred," the *Centennial News* proclaimed early in January, "who recently returned to Texas after an extensive visit to California, carried the Texas Centennial message to the Pacific coast, and if his reception is any indication of that section's interest in the Centennial, California will be well represented in the Lone Star State in 1936." That same issue of the *Centennial News* featured a photograph of a cattle drive taken on the Smith Brothers Ranch near Marfa, the caption of which proved particularly revealing regarding the western viewpoint of the paper. "Scenes such as this one," in issues to come, the editor promised his readers, "will present a true-to-life story of the traditional West to the many visitors who will flock to Texas this year for the Texas Centennial Celebrations. To many, Texas holds the romance of early trail-blazing adventures and delightful stories of cowboy days." Such images became a regular feature of the publication.[37]

One of the most elaborate publicity events of the Centennial involved a nationwide, ten-day tour by train during April and May of 1936, organized by Dale Miller. Comprising a group of Texans that included Governor Allred, the trip also included R. L. Thornton, the Dallas banker who was in charge of the celebration there, The University of Texas Longhorn Band, and Captain Leonard Pack of the Texas Rangers. Pack brought along his show horse, named Texas, who had been trained to perform a series of tricks. The publicity train traveled through Arkansas, Tennessee, Ohio, and Pennsylvania before arriving in Washington, D.C., where a bevy of politicians greeted the entourage. A visit with President Roosevelt at the White House proved a highlight of the trip, during which time the president promised to visit the Centennial Exposition at Dallas later in the year. After leaving the nation's capital, the tour headed to New York City, where Gotham welcomed them with gusto. The New York City reception drove home the western heritage of Texas. "Sights and sounds of the frontier," the *New York Times* told its readers, "filled a good part of the Pennsylvania station a few minutes before 8 o'clock last night when the Texas Centennial Special with a delegation of 100, headed by the Governor of the State, pulled in as cowboy yells were sent up by about 500 native sons and city officials." A western-themed parade led by the Longhorn band escorted the Texans, many of them dressed in western garb, to the New Yorker Hotel. "At the New Yorker," the *Times* reported, ". . . Captain Pack, undaunted, rode his mount right through the doorway and into the crowded foyer."[38]

As one study of the centennial has noted, "Texas Centennial officials also capitalized on the cowboy's popularity, often with little regard for historical authenticity." No less a figure than Tom Connally, United States Senator from Texas, embodied this view. Connally chaired the United States Centennial Commission, the federal agency created by Congress to provide funds to underwrite events in Texas related to the celebration. Statues, dramatic productions, buildings, markers, and events of the fairs at Fort Worth and Dallas all received significant funding from Connally's commission, which played a significant role in setting the discourse of the Centennial. "The cowboy image looms large in the history and development of Texas," the senator wrote in the summer of 1936. "That romantic figure," he continued, "has given a touch of color to Texas since the days of the Alamo and San Jacinto. Texas this year celebrates its centennial of independence and the cowboy is entitled to a large place in that celebration."[39] Images of the cowboy abounded in Centennial publicity materials, especially as images for the covers of travel brochures and tourist flyers. Celebrities visiting the celebrations in Dallas and Fort Worth often posed for photographers while wearing cowboy garb and ten-gallon hats. Juvenile actress Shirley Temple obliged promoters when Centennial officials made her an honorary Rangerette. She posed for the cover of the *Centennial News* exuberantly waving a ten-gallon hat while dressed in cowboy clothes that included boots with longhorn designs on her chaps. Even FBI Director J. Edgar Hoover posed for a publicity photo in a ten-gallon hat while being lassoed by Centennial Rangerettes.[40]

This western, frontier viewpoint also permeated the version of Texas history as adopted by the Board of Historians, a group of three individuals selected by the Board of Control to oversee the historical content of the hundreds of monuments, statues, historical markers, and commemorative plaques that would be placed around the state as part of the official celebration of the Centennial. Historian Kelly McMichael has observed that "monuments and the process of choosing, fundraising, building, and unveiling provide a select group with the opportunity to shape society's memory of an event." Creating monuments, she further notes, involves "creating memory—controlling memory" and this "constitutes real societal power."[41] In the case of the Centennial, it was the State of Texas that officially exercised this power through the Board of Historians. Louis Wiltz Kemp served as its chair, while Reverend Paul Foik and J. Frank Dobie were its two other members. The Board spent a good deal of time disagreeing about which personages and events from Texas history would be commemorated. In the end, Dobie clashed vehemently with Kemp over many of the decisions made by the Board. However, all three of the members steadfastly supported the presentation of Texas as being historically more part of the western frontier historical experience than southern regarding the various monuments and markers it recommended. This proved significant for changing public memory in Texas, because history written in stone by its nature is more durable than history written in ink.

"Monuments attempt to mold a landscape of collective memory," one present-day historian has written, "to conserve what is worth remembering and discard the rest."[42] That is most certainly what Kemp thought regarding the monument program he directed, which quickly came to represent his views about Texas history. Kemp was a Houston oil executive who lived from 1881 until 1956. An engineering graduate of The University of Texas, he joined the Texas Company in 1908 and remained with Texaco for the rest of his professional career. He was, in that capacity, a person who played a significant role in the development of the infant Texas oil industry. Throughout his life, Kemp was also an avid historian and collector of Texana. He played a key role in the improvement and development of the Texas State Cemetery in Austin. He was a member of the Texas State Library Board and served as president of the Texas State Historical Association from 1942 to 1946. He was considered one of the best informed people on Texas history.[43]

Like others of his generation, Kemp had a particular view of Texas history; namely, it was the story of Anglo-American frontier folk as part of the nineteenth century westward movement of the United States. In holding his viewpoint, he rejected an overt presentation of the Texas heritage as southern. Instead, he emphasized the period of the Texas Revolution as a chapter in growth of the western frontier. The Alamo became a metaphor for westward expansion. For him, the story to be told during the Centennial rested on the exploits of pioneers and frontier heroes who brought the best of Anglo-American civilization from the United States to Texas.[44] In total, he supervised the writing of more than a thousand inscriptions, plaques, and historical markers on statues, centennial buildings, and other physical constructions marking the centennial. Only two of these make explicit reference to the South as a source of heritage for Texas. The statue of David Ellis erected at Waxahachie characterized him as "nurtured in the culture of the Old South," while the historical marker placed at Elisabet Ney's Liendo Plantation noted that it was the "location of lavish southern hospitality." On the other hand, almost one hundred markers styled various Texas historical figures as "pioneers" and never once used the term "southerner." More than two dozen inscriptions cast antebellum Texas as part of the "frontier" and, not surprisingly, more than one hundred forts or sites of former forts received Centennial historical markers.[45]

A pro-western orientation can also be seen in assessing the more than two dozen bronze statues of Texas founders funded by state monies provided by Kemp's board. It should be noted that most of the subjects were presented as frontiersmen instead of southerners. In that regard, a minor controversy involved the statue of James Butler Bonham that was erected in the city named for him. The people of Bonham did not like the first model presented to them by sculptor Allie V. Tennant. She dressed her subject in frontier buckskin. The civic leaders of Bonham complained that their town was named for a southerner who may well never have worn such an outfit. They instead wanted their statue to be dressed in a frock coat and four-in-hand tie, which would have been the southern custom of his era. Tennant relented and altered the statue's dress accordingly, although at the last minute she added a powder horn hung over the shoulder of Bonham's suit jacket.[46]

Western images and themes also permeated the central exposition at Dallas's Fair Park. Most of the architects involved in planning the construction of Centennial markers, memorials, and buildings rejected norms of expression that had been popular in the southern United States. Such was the case for George Dahl. As the chief architect of the Centennial celebration at Dallas's Fair Park, Dahl embraced the internationalist style of modernism that had since been called "Art Deco." He worked closely with Dallas civil leader R. L. Thornton in bringing a distinctive look to the celebration in that city.[47] Like Dahl, architect Donald Nelson also left an enduring mark on the Centennial, especially in meeting the goal of presenting Texas as a modern place. A native of Chicago, Nelson attended the Atelier Parsons of the Architectural Sketch Club before studying at M.I.T., from which he received an architectural degree. He helped design many of the buildings at the Century of Progress Exhibition in Chicago before coming to Dallas to do the same for the Texas Centennial.[48] Along with George Dahl, Nelson brought a decidedly international style of modernism to much of the construction at Dallas's Fair Park. In addition, he designed many of the marble bases and stone pediments for a number of the statues and markers placed around the state. This very modern style further removed the architecture of the Centennial from vernaculars popular in the South, which in many cases still harked back to the more embellished style of the City Beautiful movement, which relied on beaux-arts and neo-classicist aesthetics.[49]

Many of the artistic embellishments of the distinctive buildings constructed at Fair Park for the Centennial reinforced western traditions. For example, in the State of Texas Building, which was the state's official edifice (now known as the Hall of State), Dorothy Austin's cowboy statue, Tom Lea's murals, cowboy tiles fashioned by Ethel Wilson Harris, the *Tejas Warrior*, and the wood carvings of Lynn Ford all evoked the West. Importantly, in the Hall of Heroes section of the building, the six monumental statues sculpted by Coppini of Sam Houston, Stephen F. Austin, James Fannin, and others present these Texas figures as westerners rather than southerners in their styles of dress and imagery. As well, during the run of the celebration from June to November 1935, western heritage was manifested by the publicity department finding a way to invoke the Texas Rangers. Centennial officials freely dispensed honorary commissions in the Rangers to an ever-increasing number of dignitaries, including national and state political leaders, movie stars, and opera singers. Bill Langley, a member of the Dallas Celebration public relations office, created the Centennial Rangerettes, who served as hostesses and publicity subjects for the event. They worked hard to present a western image. "They emerged as an unlikely composite guaranteed to attract national attention," one historian of the Centennial has recalled, as "beautiful girls clad in western regalia—ten-gallon hats, colorful bandanas, plaid shirts, riding breeches (and sometimes cowboy chaps,) Justin boots and spurs."[50] Other events at Dallas, including the musical pageant "The Cavalcade of Texas," also highlighted the state's western orientation.

As a result of the intellectual changes and the official sanctions provided by the Centennial Celebration, the public image of Texas had been rebranded as western by the late 1930s. Newspaper articles and journalistic analyses of the state tended to refer to it as western rather than southern. Texans increasingly viewed themselves as westerners. In some measure, these changes in imagery and regional identification came partially in response to the reality that Texas was certainly far less southern in the mid 1930s than it had been at the start of the twentieth century. The arrival of a petroleum-based economy, the growth of industry, the urbanization of the state's major cities, and a transportation revolution that included both an increasing reliance on air travel and the construction of a state highway system all worked to remove Texas from the southern orbit in which it had been operating in previous decades. In sum, it can be stated accurately that many people throughout the world today perceive Texas as western rather than southern. Such would not have been the case without the cultural shifts of the 1930s that were legitimized by the Texas Centennial. Public memory can sometimes be more compelling to those who look to the past for their identity than reading and understanding the documentary-based research that produces scholarly history.

Notes

1. Randolph B. Campbell notes that the arrival of Anglo immigrants in the 1820s "began making Texas southern" and this continued thereafter. "Texas was essentially a part of the Old South." This orientation, he contends, continues into modern economic and political practices. See *Gone to Texas: A History of the Lone Star State* (New York: Oxford University Press, 2003), 297, 242–44, 287–89, 325–26, 419–29, 457–63, 469–70. See also Frank E. Vandiver, *The Southwest: South or West?* (College Station: Texas A&M University Press, 1975), and Glen Sample Ely, *Where the West Begins: Debating Texas Identity* (Lubbock: Texas Tech University Press, 2011).

2. David Glassburg, "History and Memory," in *A Companion to American Cultural History*, ed. Karen Halttunen (Oxford, England: Blackwell Publishing, 2008), 371–80.

3. Randolph B. Campbell, "History and Collective Memory in Texas: The Entangled Stories of the Lone Star State," in Gregg Cantrell and Elizabeth Hayes Turner, eds., *Lone Star Pasts: Memory and History in Texas* (College Station: Texas A&M University Press, 2007), 279.

4. An extensive literature on the relationship between history and memory has emerged over the last quarter century. As early as the 1920s, the French scholar Maurice Halbwachs articulated the concept of memory in his *Les cadres sociaux de la mémoire* (Paris: Presses Universitaires de France, 1925). See also Halbwachs, *On Collective Memory* (Chicago: University of Chicago Press, 1992). Pierre Nora, a modern academic, further defined the nature of memory in his *Realms of Memory: Rethinking the French Revolution*, 3 vols. (New York: Columbia University Press, 1996–98.) Analyzing the ways in which history relates to memory has in recent years become so important for scholars that the journal *History and Memory* was established in the late 1970s. This journal, as its mission, "explores the manifold ways in which the past shapes the present and is shaped by present perceptions. The journal focuses on a wide range of questions relating to the formation of historical consciousness and collective memory." [http://muse.jhu.edu/journals/ham/ (accessed June 4, 2011)]. See also John Bodnar, *Remaking America: Public Memory, Commemoration, and Patriotism in the Twentieth Century* (Princeton, N.J.: Princeton University Press, 1991.)

5. W. Fitzhugh Brundage, "No Deed But Memory," *Where These Memories Grow: History, Memory, and Southern Identity* (Chapel Hill: University of North Carolina Press, 2000), 4.

6. Cantrell and Turner, *Lone Star Pasts,* 2.

7. For a good example of how an historical museum can present interpretations of the past based on public memory that runs counter to scholarly history, see Walter L. Buenger, "The Story of Texas? The Texas State History Museum and Forgetting and Remembering the Past," *Southwestern Historical Quarterly* 105 (Jan. 2002): 481–93.

8. Yvonne Davis Frear, "Generation Versus Generation: African Americans in Texas Remember the Civil Rights Movement," in Cantrell and Turner, *Lone Star Pasts*, 204.

9. This is an essential point made by Ely in *Where the West Begins: Debating Texas Identity*.

10. Campbell, "History and Collective Memory in Texas," Cantrell and Turner, *Lone Star Pasts,* 279.

11. Ibid., 279.

12. Michael Phillips, "Why is Big Tex Still a White Cowboy?" in *Beyond Texas Through Time*, Walter L. Buenger and Arnoldo de León, eds. (College Station: Texas A&M University Press, 2011), 162.

13. Gregg Cantrell, "The Bones of Stephen F. Austin: History and Memory in Progressive Texas," in Cantrell and Turner, *Lone Star Pasts*, 66–67; Leigh Clemons, *Branding Texas: Performing Culture in the Lone Star State* (Austin: University of Texas Press, 2008), 10; John Morán González, *Border Renaissance: The Texas Centennial and the Emergence of Mexican American Literature* (Austin: University of Texas Press, 2009), 32.

14. Kenneth Ragsdale, *Centennial '36: The Year America Discovered Texas* (College Station: Texas A&M University Press, 1987), 142–43.

15. W. Fitzhugh Brundage, "Introduction," in Cantrell and Turner, *Lone Star Pasts,* xiv.

16. Clemons, *Branding Texas*, 104.

17. Michael C. Steiner, "Regionalism in the Great Depression," *Geographical Review* 73 (Oct. 1983): 432.

18. Kevin Edward Mooney, "Texas Centennial Music and Identity," Ph.D. Diss., University of Texas at Austin, 1998, pp. 14–15.

19. Thomas S. Gossett, "A History of the Southwest Review, 1915–1942," M.A.Thesis, Southern Methodist University, 1948, p. 20.

20. Charles W. Ramsdell proved so successful as an historical advocate and apologist for the South, along with novelist Thomas Dixon, that one modern historian has expressed the opinion that the intellectual rationalizations provided by these two writers helped, at least for many white Texans, to justify a resurgence of the Ku Klux Klan after World War I. See Walter L. Buenger, "Memory and the 1920s Ku Klux Klan," in Cantrell and Turner, *Lone Star Pasts,* 121.

21. Robert L. Dorman, *Revolt of the Provinces: The Regionalist Movement in America, 1920–1946* (Chapel Hill: University of North Carolina Press, 1993), 93.

22. Walter Prescott Webb, *The Texas Rangers: A Century of Frontier Defense* (2nd ed.; Austin: University of Texas Press, 2003), 1–17.

23. As older southern views of memory in Texas faded into a new one, it should be noted that the premiere of this picture in Dallas was broadcast over radio by means of the Dr. Pepper Show to the nineteen stations of the Dixie Radio Network. The *Pepper-Upper Show*, as it was then known, billed itself as "The South's Premier Radio Program." See Program Flyer, Centennial Collection, Dallas Public Library, and Don

Graham, *State Fare: An Irreverent Guide to Texas Movies* (Fort Worth: TCU Press, 2008).

24. Steven L. Davis, *J. Frank Dobie: A Liberated Mind* (Austin: University of Texas Press, 2009), 75.

25. For example, many urban artists adopted western themes for the commissions under this program. See "PWAP Give and and Take a 'Thing' or Two," undated newspaper clipping, Dallas Art Association Scrapbook, 1933–1935, Dallas Museum of Art, Dallas, Texas.

26. James E. Crisp, "Memory, Truth, and Pain: Myth and Censorship in the Celebration of Texas History," in Cantrell and Turner, *Lone Star Past*, 75–94.

27. Rick Stewart, *Lone Star Regionalism: The Dallas Nine and Their Circle* (Austin: Texas Monthly Press, 1985), xii; Francine Carraro, *Jerry Bywaters: A Life in Art* (Austin: University of Texas Press, 1994), 101–2; Jerry Bywaters, "Otis Dozier: Growth and Maturity of a Texas Artist," *Southwest Review* 42 (Winter 1957), *passim;* Interview with Otis and Velma Dozier, June 10, 1965, Dallas, Texas, conducted by Sylvia Loomis, Archives of American Art, Smithsonian Institution.

28. Pompeo Coppini, *From Dawn to Sunset* (San Antonio: Naylor, 1949), 352–53; "Texas Centennial Hall of State," University of Texas Student's Clipping Bureau, Jan. 18, 1936, Commission of Control Scrapbook, 1935–1936, Box 4-20/567-2, Box 4-0/573-1, Commission of Control Records, State of Texas Archives, Austin, Texas; Frank Carter Adams, ed., *The State of Texas Building: Central Exhibition, Texas Centennial Celebrations* (Austin: Steck, 1937), n.p.; "Texas State Building Shrine of Art," Dallas *Daily Times Herald*, Nov. 1936, Allie V. Tennant Vertical File, Dallas Public Library; "Oral History Interview of Dorothy Austin Webberley by Dealey Campbell and Kevin Vogel," Jan. 12, 2010, Dallas Historical Society, Dallas, Texas.

29. Victoria H. Cummins, "Art in Your Own Backyard," unpublished paper presented to the East Texas Historical Association, Nacogdoches, Texas, Sept. 24, 2009.

30. Charles Townsend, *San Antonio Rose: The Life and Work of Bob Wills* (Champaign: University of Illinois Press, 1986); Gary Ginell, *Milton Brown and the Founding of Western Swing* (Champaign: University of Illinois Press, 1994); Bill C. Malone, *Country Music USA* (Austin: University of Texas Press, 1969).

31. Graham, *State Fare*, 21–22.

32. The River Oaks Corporation, and John Staub, came to prefer a tradition-oriented style that combined Latin colonial elements with

Georgia styles, along with influences from French Louisiana. It clearly rejected a Texan or western vernacular in favor of styles seen across the Gulf South. See Stephen Fox, *The Country Houses of John Staub* (College Station: Texas A&M University Press, 2007), 77–79.

33. Quoted in Mary Carolyn Hollers George, *O'Neil Ford, Architect* (College Station: Texas A&M Press, 1992), 22. David Williams further noted of his house designs: "These houses were designed in the Texas manner using the early Texas work as a source of inspiration." This quote appears in David Dillon, *The Architecture of O'Neil Ford: Celebrating Place* (Austin: University of Texas Press, 1999), 21. Williams was a *bon vivant* who greatly influenced the crafting of a modern Texas image. As his biographer, Muriel Quest McCarthy, has noted: "Williams was equally at ease telling Wild West tales and singing cowboy songs to an audience of youngsters, hosting a dinner party for Frank Lloyd Wright in the bohemian surroundings of his apartment-studio, or dining with the Roosevelts at the White House." See McCarthy, *David R. Williams: Pioneer Architect* (Dallas: Southern Methodist University Press, 1984), 4.

34. For a colorful portrait of Amon Carter, see Jerry Flemmons, *Amon: The Life of Amon Carter, Sr., of Texas* (Austin: Jenkins Publishing Company, 1978). The Fort Worth Frontier Exposition is the subject of Jan Jones, *Billy Rose Presents Casa Manana* (Fort Worth: Texas Christian University Press, 1999).

35. Ragsdale, *Centennial '36*, 142.

36. Ibid., 28. For the role that selling female beauty played, see Light Townsend Cummins, "From the Midway to the Hall of State at Fair Park: Two Competing Views of Women at the Dallas Celebration of 1936," *Southwestern Historical Quarterly* 114 (Jan. 2011): 225–51.

37. "Editorial: Texas, California, and Louisiana," *Centennial News*, Jan. 1, 1936, p. 2; "The West Welcomes Texas," *Centennial News,* n.d., p. 2. Copies consulted in the Cushing Memorial Library, Texas A&M University, College Station, Texas.

38. Ragsdale, *Centennial '36,* 150–54; "100 Dashing Texans Capture the City," *New York Times*, May 1, 1936.

39. Mooney, "Texas Centennial Music and Identity," 102.

40. "Texas Centennial—Pamphlets and Printed Materials" Box 4/16-117, Texas Commission of Control for Texas Centennial Celebrations, Texas State Archives and Library, Austin, Texas; *Centennial News*, Apr. 2, 1936; Centennial Scrapbooks, June 1936, Texas Commission of Control for Texas Centennial Celebrations, Texas State Archives and Library, Austin.

41. Kelly McMichael, "'Memories are Short but Monuments Lengthen Remembrances': The United Daughters of the Confederacy and the Power of Civil War Memory," in Cantrell and Turner, *Lone Star Pasts*, 96; "Train Trippers Give Invitations: To Leave April 26 for 17 Key Cities," *Centennial News*, Apr. 2, 1936.

42. Kirk Savage, *Standing Soldiers, Kneeling Slaves: Race, War, and Monument in Nineteenth-Century America* (Princeton, N.J.: Princeton University Press, 1997), 4.

43. Louis W. Kemp kept a file of sorts about his activities in support of Texas history which reveals both his frenetic support for all things historical in the Lone Star State and also his Anglo-centric frame of reference about the past. See Awards and Certificate Scrapbook: 1931–1955, Box 4M118, Louis Wiltz Kemp Papers, Dolph Briscoe Center for American History, The University of Texas at Austin. Biographical information about Kemp is contained in Box 2R215 of this same collection.

44. Kemp seldom, if ever, made any statements that cast Texas within a southern heritage. Instead, he constantly evoked Texas within a frontier, western, and pioneer history that stressed patriotism and Americanism. He summed up his work by saying: "We are concerned only in making or improving historical places and in honoring the memory of pioneer men and women who have rendered outstanding service to Texas." Quoted in Ragsdale, *Centennial '36*, 105.

45. These figures come from a tabulation of the data contained in Harold Schoen, *Monument Erected by the State of Texas to Commemorate the Centenary of Texas Independence* (Austin: Commission of Control for the Texas Centennial Commission, 1938).

46. "Bonham Model Completed by Allie Tennant," Dallas *Morning News*, Apr. 6, 1928; James Bonham Statue Vertical File, Bonham Public Library, Bonham, Texas.

47. "Dahl Calls '36 Exposition his Great Achievement," Clipping file, George Dahl Papers, Alexander Architectural Archive, The University of Texas at Austin.

48. "History of the Firm," Box 2, Folder 52, Donald S. Nelson: Architectural Records, Drawings, and Photographs, 1910–1975, Alexander Architectural Archive.

49. For a discussion of the City Beautiful style, see William Wilson, *The City Beautiful Movement* (Baltimore: Johns Hopkins University Press, 1989). This study notes that this style was particularly popular across the South in the 1920s (see 291–92).

50. Ragsdale, *Centennial '36*, 144–45.

PART II:

Texas Before the Civil War

"Carta Esférica" by Juan de Lángara, *Pichardo's Treatise*, 1: between 350 and 351

José Antonio Pichardo and the Limits of Spanish Texas, 1803–1821

Donald E. Chipman

From the Louisiana Purchase in 1803 to July 21, 1821, when the flag of Castile and León was lowered for the last time at San Antonio, Spanish Texas experienced its most turbulent and bloody years. The province faced an aggressive United States with its expansion-minded President Thomas Jefferson, and in 1813 Texas suffered the bloodiest war in its history, followed by an agonizing aftermath. To help retain its hold on Texas, Spain turned to a Mexican savant, man of letters, and cleric in the Oratory of San Felipe de Neri in Mexico City named José Antonio Pichardo. Appointed to record the legal claims of Spain to her exposed northern frontier after decades of ineffective administration reorganizations, Pichardo created a massive legal treatise that exhaustively recounted Spain's efforts to take and hold Texas against all challengers. Unfortunately for him, and Spain, he could not anticipate that events soon after his death would swiftly bring an end to Spanish control over the northern frontier.

Few other than those who study Texas history are familiar with Pichardo's name. He merits an entry in the fifth volume of the *New Handbook of Texas* and its on-line version, but his three-thousand-page report, accompanied by twenty maps, compiled at the request of the Spanish government during the reign of Charles IV (1788–1808), is less known. This massive treatise was translated and published in its entirety by historian Charles Wilson Hackett, with the assistance of Charmion Clair Shelby and Mary Ruth Splawn, in the early decades of the twentieth century.[1]

Pichardo began his work with an account of Christopher Columbus's first voyage, followed by a discussion of the Papal Line of Demarcation (1493) and the Treaty of Tordesillas (1494), as well as a summary of Spain in America amid its English and French competitors. It was the year 1762, however, that riveted his attention and fueled his prolix compilations, which began in 1808. His work would increase henceforth almost exponentially until his death in 1812. Pichardo made clear his overall intentions with these words: "Thus far we have proved by most weighty arguments that Spain was the one legitimate and absolute owner of all land in which the French founded La Louisiana . . . and that, consequently, the French acted with much injustice and iniquity in settling it . . . ."[2]

Prior to the Treaty of Paris, which ended the French and Indian War (1754–1763), the great struggle for empire in North America was lost by France to the benefit of Spain, who had been an ally of the French. Toward the end of the conflict in late 1762, France transferred the Louisiana territory it had first settled in 1699 to Spain. To Pichardo, the ceding of Louisiana "froze" its boundaries from that time forward, and it made no difference to the Cuernavaca-born cleric that the limits of Texas and Louisiana were left unsettled, because both were indisputably Spanish.[3]

To the Spanish Crown, acquiring Louisiana made a big difference. The Viceroyalty of New Spain was too large to function efficiently as a single administrative unit. It stretched south to north from the northern border of Panama to the Spanish Southwest, and, incredibly, east to west from the Caribbean Islands to the Philippines. To add the huge Louisiana territory to an already overburdened viceregal government in Mexico made no sense to Charles III, the reform-minded Bourbon monarch of Spain (1759–1788). So the king, with the approval of his advisory councils, placed Louisiana under the Captaincy General of Cuba, headquartered in Havana.[4] At that point, defining the limits of Texas and Louisiana became very important, and so a series of actions was taken that would lead directly to the appointment of Pichardo. The boundaries he studied would remain of great concern until the Adams-Onís Treaty was signed in 1819 and ratified by the United States Senate and Spanish Cortes in 1821.

Louis XV of France had urged Spain to take immediate control of Louisiana, but that did not happen for several years. French settlers in New Orleans opposed the transfer, expelled the first Spanish governor, and delayed Spanish control of Louisiana until 1769. By then, plans were well underway for reorganizing the entire northern frontier of New Spain, which would have significant consequences for Spanish Texas.[5] Always attentive to the political realities of North America, Charles III was an ardent proponent of the experimentation, innovation, and rationality that always characterized the Spanish component to the Age of Enlightenment. In 1763 the king commissioned José de Gálvez as inspector general for public finance in New Spain. He would spend the next six years in that capacity. In the year following Gálvez's appointment, Charles III selected the Marqués de Rubí as "inspector of presidios on the northern frontier of New Spain."[6]

Rubí arrived at Los Adaes, the colonial capital of Texas, in mid-September 1767. He found appalling conditions there. The garrison contained sixty-one men, but just twenty-five horses were fit for service, and the presidials had only two functional muskets. None of the soldiers had uniforms. All were dressed in rags, some without hats, shirts, or shoes. Since Texas was no longer a frontier province after Spain's acquisition of Louisiana, Rubí saw no reason to continue any Spanish presence in East Texas or western Louisiana, whether military, civilian, or religious. This decision and its consequences would later complicate Pichardo's task of defining clear boundaries.[7]

Despite protests, especially from ranchers and clerics in East Texas, a royal order known as the New Regulations for Presidios was issued in September 1772. Among other provisions, it designated San Antonio as the capital of Texas. By royal decree, the population of East Texas, which numbered perhaps five hundred in all save for a few who fled into the piney woods to avoid eviction, was removed to San Antonio. Later, after a successful appeal to the viceroy in Mexico City, some of the displaced settlers were allowed to return to their homes and ranches. However, without authorization, these pioneers in a region Spain had chosen to depopulate founded Nacogdoches in 1779.[8]

This struggling frontier outpost depended on manufactured items from Louisiana, such as clothing and furniture, but Spain's outdated mercantile restrictions strictly prohibited trade between Texas and Louisiana, despite both being Crown provinces. Not surprisingly, smuggling was so commonplace that even one of Nacogdoches's leading citizens, Antonio Gil Ibarbo, who ironically served as judge of illegal trade seizures, was arrested as a contrabandist in late 1791 and jailed in San Antonio. Acquitted of all charges four years later, Gil Ibarbo did more than anyone, including the Spanish government, to ensure that Nacogdoches—important in defining the limits of East Texas—was one of colonial Texas's four important towns, as later noted by Pichardo in his voluminous report.[9]

Shortly prior to the founding of Nacogdoches, the Spanish government on the recommendation of José de Gálvez, who had returned to Spain to assume the post of minister of the Indies, again chose to reduce the administrative sphere of New Spain. In May 1776 officials in Madrid created the Commandancy General of the Interior Provinces, itself an enormous territorial unit that included Texas, Coahuila, Nueva Vizcaya, New Mexico, Sinaloa, and Sonora as well as Upper and Lower California. The Interior Provinces, so named because one had to go inland from Mexico City to reach them, became in effect an autonomous government under the control of a commandant general. The first to serve with that title was Teodoro de Croix.[10] Despite an almost bewildering number of reorganizations, divisions, and cohesions, Texas would remain under the control of a commandant general until 1821.[11]

It was the responsibility of the commandant general of the Interior Provinces as well as the viceroy of New Spain to protect the northern frontier from Anglo-American encroachment. In 1783 Juan Gassiot, a senior staff member of the commandant general, recognized that challenge and sent a prescient warning to Felipe de Neve, the first to succeed Croix. Gassiot warned that Great Britain's former North American colonies, by then the United States, contained "active, industrious, and aggressive people." These same people, continued Gassiot, then freed from the burden of war with their founding nation "will constantly menace the dominion of Spain in America and it would be an unpardonable error not to take all necessary steps to check their territorial advance. . . ."[12] Gassiot's warning was echoed by Vicente Manuel de Zéspedes, the first governor of Florida after it retroceded to Spain from Great Britain in 1783. He characterized Anglo-American frontiersmen as "nomadic like Arabs and . . . distinguished from savages only in color, language, and the superiority of their depraved cunning and untrustworthiness."[13]

The concerns of Gassiot and Zéspedes were borne out almost immediately after the 1783 Treaty of Paris ending the American Revolutionary War. At the end of the first year that followed the treaty, an estimated fifty thousand Anglo-American settlers crossed the Appalachian Mountains and moved westward. By fall 1785 they needed a way to get their crops of wheat and tobacco to market, because transporting bulky goods to the east across the mountains was impractical, if not impossible.[14] The right of Anglo Americans to transport their crops via the Mississippi River and deposit them at New Orleans depended entirely on the concurrence of Spain, which controlled both banks of the Great River and the port. This circumstance gave the Spanish government and Captaincy General officials in Havana a powerful bargaining chip. In the mid-1780s, extended negotiations between John Jay, secretary of foreign affairs for the United States, and Diego de Gardoqui, Spanish minister to the American states, failed to produce any settlement of lasting consequence. For example, the two diplomats by 1786 signed a preliminary agreement whereby Spain would practice "forbearance" regarding the use of the Mississippi by Americans in exchange for a commercial treaty favorable to her. The accord, however, failed to win the necessary approval of nine states in the Articles of Confederation Congress.

By the early 1790s, Spanish officials in Mexico and Texas—in a move that foreshadowed nineteenth-century Argentine President Domingo Faustino Sarmiento's comment that to "govern is to populate"—welcomed American immigrants from any quarter in Texas, almost regardless of their intentions. They recognized that Texas was severely under populated as evidenced by twelve general and local censuses taken between 1777 and 1793. Over the course of the years from 1777 to 1790, the population had risen from 3,103 to only 3,168.[15]

In the 1790s, the Interior Provinces averaged six inhabitants per square league (approximately seven square miles). But both Texas and Coahuila had slightly fewer than two residents per square league, barely more than the desert region of Baja California with one person per square league. Despite these numbers, the commandant general, Nemesio Salcedo y Salcedo (1802–1810), was not one who would welcome Anglo Americans of any stripe. Indeed, as he commented from his headquarters in Chihuahua, all foreigners were untrustworthy and he underscored that view with these words: "They are not and will not be anything but crows to pick out our eyes."[16]

Salcedo's view of non-Spaniards hardened in part because of Irish-born Philip Nolan's interests in Texas. By 1789 Nolan, having emigrated to the United States, wound up in New Orleans. There he learned of the opportunities of rounding up mustangs in Texas for sale in Louisiana. Operating with passports provided by Louisiana governors, Nolan made three forays into Texas in the 1790s, capturing increasing numbers of wild horses on each occasion. By 1799 he aroused the suspicions of Commandant General Pedro de Nava. Based upon little or no evidence, Nava believed the mustanger was likely an agent of Anglo-American designs on Texas. He ordered the governor of Texas to arrest him if he again entered Texas, which Nolan did in October 1800. On this occasion, the Irish immigrant led a party of eighteen armed men to a site in present-day McLennan or Hill County, where they began capturing and corralling wild horses. Some five months after entering Texas, the Nolan party on March 22, 1801, woke to find themselves surrounded by Spanish troops, who immediately opened fire. Within minutes, Nolan died when struck in the head by a musket ball. Later that same day, the remaining members of Nolan's party surrendered. They were eventually marched off to varying fates in Mexico.[17]

In the meantime, Spanish concerns about the intentions of Anglo Americans in Texas were exacerbated by events taking place in Europe. The well-known pressures brought by Napoleon Bonaparte on Spain that forced the retrocession of Louisiana by the Treaty of San Ildefonso on October 1, 1800, and the subsequent purchase of the Louisiana Territory from France by the United States, which was formalized on April 30, 1803, need not be recounted.[18] That they greatly affected Texas, however, is another matter. In both instances, Texas moved from being an interior to frontier province, but the latter agreement brought Anglo Americans as unwelcome neighbors in Louisiana who would almost immediately contest Spanish claims to Texas and beyond.

As historian David J. Weber has observed, neither Spain nor France had formalized the borders of their North American possessions with precision, and given that the Louisiana territory had twice changed hands in just three years, "Spain, then, had much to negotiate with the new owners of Louisiana, but the American expansionist president, Thomas Jefferson, seemed to prefer coercion to negotiation." To be sure, Jefferson had "numbers" on his side when he assumed the presidency of the United States in 1801 and began to press his advantage at the expense of Spain. At that time, Texas had a non-Indian population of just greater than 3,000, while Kentucky alone, which became a state in 1792, had experienced an astonishing jump in population to 221,000.[19] Whatever the justification for Jefferson's actions during most of his two terms in office, it is clear that one of the most intelligent of all presidents favored bold action over scholarly disputation.

The vagueness regarding the limits of the Louisiana territory, as mentioned by Weber, was nicely summed up in comments made by the French minister of finance, François Barbé-Marbois, in 1803. In congratulating the American ministers, Robert R. Livingston and James Monroe, on the treaty of cession, Barbé-Marbois remarked on the ill-defined limits of Louisiana and said "that if an obscurity did not already exist, it would be good policy to put one there."[20] Jefferson would seize upon that very obscurity to assert nothing less than preposterous claims for the borders of Louisiana. The American president insisted that Louisiana extended to the Rocky Mountains, in effect claiming for the United States all lands drained by the Mississippi and Missouri rivers and their watersheds. Jefferson also insisted that the territory included New Mexico, northern Nuevo Santander between the Río Grande and the Río Nueces, and all of Texas. Manuel Godoy, in effect the real ruler of Spain from 1800 to 1808 rather than the feckless Charles IV, of course disputed Jefferson's claims. Godoy, however, narrowly defined Louisiana as "encompassing little more than present-day Louisiana, eastern Arkansas, and eastern Missouri."[21]

But it was Jefferson who would aggressively move on his assertions. Spain would respond, at first militarily and diplomatically, and then by way of reasoned arguments and historical evidence to support its claims to empire in North America. And José Antonio Pichardo would do just that—the very approach eschewed by Jefferson. The American president, seldom a fan of a powerful national government unless it suited his purposes, believed lands claimed by the United States belonged to its citizens. He therefore believed his soon-launched explorations ought to be underwritten at government expense. This gave him and the United States a decided advantage over Spain. It had fewer resources and would soon be further weakened by the designs of Napoleon.

Aside from the Meriwether Lewis and William Clark expedition from St. Louis to the mouth of the Columbia River in 1804–1806, Jefferson sponsored lesser known expeditions that brought Anglo Americans in close proximity to Spanish settlements in Texas. For example, Thomas Freeman and Peter Custis led a group up the Red River in 1806, and in the same year a closely related enterprise sent Zebulon Pike to explore the headwaters of the Arkansas and Red rivers and spy on Santa Fe. Pike and his men while camped on the upper Río Grande were captured by Spanish soldiers, interrogated in Santa Fe, and sent by way of El Paso del Norte, Chihuahua, and Monclova to San Antonio. Freed but ordered to leave Texas, Pike and his followers returned to the United States in July 1807.[22]

By then the well-known claims of Jefferson on the limits of Louisiana, coupled with explorations by Anglo Americans along and into lands claimed by Spain for more than two centuries, had already prompted a strong military response by Spain. Nemesio Salcedo, the no-nonsense commandant general of the Interior Provinces, had begun stationing troops east of the Sabine River at the abandoned site of Los Adaes. At the end of 1805, Spanish troops in Texas numbered 700, with 141 of them stationed at Nacogdoches. Spain also reassigned Lt. Col. Simón de Herrera, one of its most capable military commanders, to Texas. War between Spain and the United States seemed imminent. But by fall 1806, cooler heads had begun to silence the saber rattling.[23]

Salcedo ordered Herrera "not to begin the action or attack the Americans without an entire and absolute certainty of evicting them from the disputed territory." From Spain, Charles IV also commanded that every effort be made to end differences peaceably with the Americans, but the king authorized no concession on the contested territory. At the same time, the United States softened its stance. General James Wilkinson, commander of United States forces in Louisiana, offered a compromise.

American troops would withdraw east of Arroyo Hondo if Spanish forces would pull back to the right bank of the Sabine River. The resulting Neutral Ground Agreement preserved peace between the two countries, and provided an opportunity for Pichardo to take a more peaceful approach to the dispute.[24]

The Spanish acted on a directive issued by Charles IV, dated May 20, 1805, that called for the compilation of data and maps pertinent to determining the true boundary between Texas and Louisiana. The commission was nonetheless not formalized until nearly two years later with the selection of fray Melchor de Talamantes at its director, who was appointed by Viceroy José de Iturrigaray in New Spain. The Peruvian-born intellectual, intending to travel to Spain by way of Mexico, decided instead to stay in Mexico City. There Talamantes began his work in 1807 and continued with diligence for a year. In 1808, when news of Napoleon's invasion of Spain and the placement there of his brother Joseph as king reached Mexico, Talamantes quit the work of the commission and associated himself with liberal-minded *criollos,* who thought they should have a voice in ruling Mexico as members of a junta in the name of their true king. For his involvement with those elements in Mexico, Talamantes was arrested in September 1808, tried by the Mexican Inquisition, and sentenced to death. The judges in a rare act of clemency lifted the death sentence on Talamantes and instead sent him under guard to Spain. While awaiting passage in Veracruz, Talamates fell ill—a not uncommon occurrence in the mosquito-infested port city—and died there in May 1809. By then he had been replaced by fray José Antonio Pichardo, who would take up the task of completing the exhaustive treatise that bears his name.[25]

Although the Neutral Ground Agreement had brought about a compromise on the borders of Spanish East Texas and American western Louisiana that avoided armed conflict, Jefferson still insisted that the Louisiana territory extended to the Río Grande. So the commission given to Pichardo in 1808 had much importance. His appointment in October came from aged Viceroy Pedro de Garibay, the interim successor of Iturrigaray. The language used in choosing Pichardo to head the commission speaks volumes about the state of affairs in Mexico at this time and the respect accorded the appointee. Garibay wrote, "Since Father Fray Melchor Talamantes, the Merced religious is embarrassed, for reasons which are notorious, in continuing on the commission on the boundaries of our possessions with those of the united province [United States], to which he had been named by your Excellency's predecessor, it becomes necessary that there be appointed another well-informed individual, one of sufficient ability for the fulfillment of this important commission . . . ." The praise accorded Pichardo also emphasized his "knowledge . . . of those regions, and because of his well-known ability and critical judgment."[26]

Pichardo, in accepting the commission, acknowledged his fears of inadequacy: "A cold sweat broke out all over my body on finding myself appointed to such a large undertaking. I felt my shoulders too weak for a burden so heavy. My knowledge of those regions between which the division line had to be run, [*sic*] was limited . . . . My geography was not sufficient to give me as much information as was needed to locate the boundaries in question. . . . But obedience to the commands of my superiors, love of country, and the desire to serve God and the king confronted me . . . . Consequently, I bowed my shoulders and accepted the burden."[27]

It was indeed a burden. What Pichardo set out to do can be stated succinctly: he had to determine the territorial extent of what France had ceded to Spain in 1762 and whether that which Spain receded to France in 1800 was exactly the same. If so, it logically followed that what the United States acquired by purchase in 1803 was again precisely the same lands. He thought he had the answer in the text of a letter written by don Carlos Martínez de Yrujo, Spanish minister to the United States during the administrations of John Adams and Thomas Jefferson. The minister's letter, sent to all foreign ministers then accredited to the United States, was published in the *Gaceta de México*, Mexico's first periodical. Its pertinent lines read: "Louisiana was ceded to France on the same terms as France had ceded to Spain; [and] . . . Spain re-ceded to France that which the latter had ceded to Spain." Although the syntax is tortuous, the meaning is clear.[28]

The approach taken by Pichardo in determining the true borders between Louisiana and Spanish-claimed domains in North America was argumentative and far from chronological in order, thus making his treatise difficult to follow. Nevertheless, he studied existing maps and drew some of his own; he searched government archives in Mexico and commissioned reports from knowledgeable people in the field; and he studied journals and reports of French and Spanish explorers. Of particular interest to the Mexican cleric were the mentions of native peoples.[29] Also of interest to Pichardo were rivers and smaller streams mentioned in the accounts of Spanish officials who responded to the French challenge in what historian Robert S. Weddle has called the Spanish Sea, meaning lands touching waters of the Gulf of Mexico from Florida to Yucatán.[30] If Pichardo could locate these waterways on maps, it did much to validate Spanish claims to lands through which they flowed.

Again, it is well to remember the Mexican friar's strong conviction that all of Louisiana belonged to Spain, and that all French entries into that territory were illegal. It therefore comes as no surprise that Pichardo focused on the coming in 1685 of René Robert Cavelier, sieur de la Salle, to the Texas Gulf Coast and Spain's most important overland response to this intrusion in the person of Alonso de León. Pichardo next cited a letter from fray Damián Massanet to his friend don Carlos Sigüenza y Góngora. Massanet accompanied De León on his 1690 expedition, which occurred in response to the French intrusion, and founded Mission San Francisco de los Tejas in eastern Texas. In his missive, Massanet mentioned the very things that most interested Pichardo—the Ríos Bravo and Magdalena, as well as the names of small Indian groups, some never again identified by name.[31]

Typical of Pichardo's un-chronological approach, he soon directed his attention to don Diego de Peñalosa. The former governor of New Mexico from 1661 to 1664 claimed to have visited the province of Gran Quivira to the east of Santa Fe. After leaving New Mexico under a cloud, don Diego ran afoul of the Mexico Inquisition for his misdeeds and conduct as governor, and he was banished for life from New Spain and the Caribbean islands by the Holy Tribunal in Mexico City in early February 1668. He nonetheless landed on his feet in France at the very time La Salle sought a license at the court of Louis XIV to found a colony in lands near northern New Spain. At Versailles, Peñalosa spun out tales of the riches of Gran Quivira, which in truth he had never visited. Pichardo wisely chose not to use Peñalosa's claims to validate his case for defining Spanish-explored lands in North America. More concerned about Peñalosa's shameful banishment than the veracity of his self-serving statements made at the French court, Pichardo labeled him a "perfidious Spaniard" and a "wicked man, enemy of God, of his king, and of his native country . . . ."[32]

Although it should not have been necessary for Pichardo to document Spanish claims to lands north of Mexico explored by Francisco Vázquez de Coronado, he nonetheless believed he could not afford to be less than thorough in his treatise. The Mexican savant asserted that Coronado had explored Cíbola, Tiguex, and Quivira provinces in the early 1540s. That these lands were not again visited by Spaniards for forty years did not invalidate their being possessions of the Crown, because Coronado "took possession of the said plains, of all the land which he saw, and of that which extended as far as the possessions which previously Juan Ponce de León . . . and others had taken in the east in Florida and on the eastern bank of the Mississippi." Again, in defiance of chronology, Pichardo also documented Álvar Núñez Cabeza de Vaca's exploration of coastal Texas during the late 1520s and early 1530s, thereby initiating Spain's claim to Texas. And of course, argued Pichardo, Coronado and Hernando de Soto had further strengthened Spain's rights in those lands "which the French unjustly possessed . . . under the false pretext that they were the first ones who discovered them."[33]

Pichardo, after examining Spanish land expeditions into realms long claimed by Spain, next turned his attention to where rivers rising in Texas entered the Gulf. He minced no words when claiming that his approach if done properly would have to operate on the assumption "that Monsieur d'Anville, like everyone else, whether Spaniard or foreigner, was entirely ignorant with regard to the coasts of the Mexican Gulf." The Mexican cleric cited the wise counsel given to Commandant General Croix in a letter from Athanase de Mézières in 1779: "All the southern part of Texas is a coast. Who will give an account of it? Who will give an account of the [region] where the rivers disembogue, the ports, bays, islands, and peninsulas, the number and fixed dwelling place of the execrable Carancaguaces?" As it turned out, the person who had been chosen to carry out that task was José Antonio de Evia, an experienced pilot.[34]

However, because of Spain's involvement in the American Revolution, nothing could be done until the war ended. At that point, Spain once again came into possession of the entire Gulf Coast. From 1783 to 1786, Evia carried out a systematic survey from the Florida Keys to Tampico. He also mapped the coast and its bays. His work "formed the basis for the Spanish Hydrographic Services's *Carta Esférica que comprende las costas del Seno Mexicana* (1799)." To document Spain's coastal exploration and mapping, Pichardo included the western portion of a later map (1799–1805) by Juan de Lángara of the Gulf Coast from the Mississippi River to the Río Grande.[35]

After the United States purchased Louisiana, Spain of course no longer controlled the entire upper Gulf Coast. Pichardo used Evia's survey and map as well as the Lángara map to assert that the United States had no right to claim lands within the Neutral Ground Agreement. Moreover, he argued that the proper boundary between Texas and Louisiana on the coast lay well east of where the Río Calcasieu, which defined the eastern boundary of the Neutral Ground, emptied into the Gulf. Instead, Pichardo maintained that the correct coastal boundary was where the Río Atchafalaya entered "La Bahía de Ascension," the present-day Atchafalaya Basin. He drew his own map of the coast to underscore that contention.[36]

Pichardo buttressed his contention that rivers themselves, not the full extent of the lands they drained, were the best means of determining "the boundaries of kingdoms, provinces, and properties" by citing the Bible (Genesis 15:18) and quoting the Greek geographer Strabo: "For in former times, and especially in the present, rivers conclude the entire argument by being the natural boundaries of the size and conformation of territories." He lamented that the French had chosen to go against "the decrees of God or other men" by refusing to accept that rivers marked the limits of territories. Instead, they wrongly contended that rivers should be the center of lands they occupied "and that whatever rivers, arroyos, marshes, canals, etc., may enter this river, or issue from it, together with all the territories and land that they bathe, mark the extent of their possessions on this river."[37] Having made his case, Pichardo unrelentingly asserted that the United States should accept the Río Atchafalaya as the appropriate boundary between Texas and Louisiana on the Gulf Coast.

In all, José Antonio de Pichardo's enormous compilation of the materials pertinent to determining the boundary between Texas and Louisiana, as translated by Hackett and colleagues, fills four big volumes with an aggregate pagination of 2,385. If, as historians such as Randolph B. Campbell contend, the history of a people starts with local sources, the Mexican friar paid far more than passing homage to that dictum. He sifted through voluminous materials in government archives, scoured private collections, commissioned reports from the field, and reproduced nearly two dozen maps drawn by others and himself.

Pichardo so committed himself to serve God and country with his scholarly pursuits that he literally worked himself to death. When he died, given that his commission came from a Crown directive, it is likely that his manuscript treatise passed into the hands of Luis de Onís, the Spanish minister accredited to the administrations of James Madison and James Monroe. That would have given the Spanish diplomat an important bargaining tool when negotiating a treaty in 1819 with the United States that bears his name and that of John Quincy Adams, Secretary of State in the Monroe cabinet.[38] But much more than Pichardo's great treatise came into play in determining the final boundaries between Texas and Louisiana.

Around the time of Pichardo's death in 1812, it was virtually impossible to separate the history of Spanish Texas from events taking place in Mexico, Europe, Louisiana, and the United States. For instance, fray Miguel de Hidalgo's struggle for independence in Mexico spilled over into Texas. This led to the abortive revolt of Juan Bautista de Las Casas against royalists in San Antonio and the temporary imprisonment of Texas Governor Manuel Salcedo, the freeing of Salcedo and the execution of Las Casas, and the restoration of Crown authority in Texas by the fall of 1811.[39]

A more serious threat to Texas remaining under the Spanish flag came from a partisan of fray Hidalgo, José Bernardo Gutiérrez de Lara. Gutiérrez, a rancher and merchant from Revilla in Nuevo Santander Province, sought aid from the United States in making Texas independent of Spain. He crossed royalist-controlled Texas without incident but ran into trouble in traversing the Neutral Ground. There the Mexican patriot lost his official papers while fleeing from a Spanish ambush. Upon reaching safety in Natchitoches, Gutiérrez traveled to Washington, where in December 1811 he received a cordial reception from United States officials, including Secretary of State Monroe and President Madison. However, despite his pleas for assistance, Gutiérrez failed to reach "any precise diplomatic understanding" with the Americans. The best he could accomplish in Washington was the promise of transportation by sea to New Orleans as well as a letter of introduction to William C. C. Claiborne, governor of the Louisiana Territory.[40]

From New Orleans, Gutiérrez traveled to Natchitoches, where he began preparations for an invasion of Texas. Among those joining him was Augustus William Magee, a West Point graduate and former lieutenant in the United States Army. The two men recruited about 130 Anglo Americans interested in "land, loot, and adventure." What many of those men failed to understand, however, was Gutiérrez's determination to free Texas from Spanish control to the benefit of an independent Mexico. Later, it would become clear that the Mexican insurgent never intended for Texas to become an independent republic.[41]

The self-styled Republican Army of the North crossed the Sabine River on August 8, 1812, but it never received official sanction from the United States. Rather, Secretary of State Monroe sent a diplomat to Chihuahua to express Washington's disapproval of any violations of Spanish-claimed territories by its citizens. Maintaining good relations with Spain at that time far outweighed any perceived advantage of supporting rebels in Texas. The Republican Army occupied Nacogdoches without incident because not a single citizen answered Spanish officer Bernardino Montero's appeal for volunteers to help defend the town. Worse, all but ten of Montero's command defected to the insurgents, forcing the captain and his few stalwarts to withdraw to San Antonio. At Nacogdoches, the invading army swelled its ranks to nearly three hundred.[42]

Gutiérrez and Magee marched inland to La Bahía and again captured it without a fight. They and their followers occupied the stone fort there and took possession of two or three cannons. Three days later, a superior force under the command of Governor Manuel Salcedo and Lt. Col. Simón de Herrera arrived and began a fruitless four-month siege that ended with the withdrawal of all Spanish troops to Béxar.[43] In early February 1813, during the final days of the siege, Magee died of undetermined causes, whereupon Gutiérrez assumed sole command of the rebel army and led it toward San Antonio. Salcedo and Herrera rallied royalist supporters and made a determined stand at Salado Creek, about eight miles southeast of Béxar. The resulting battle turned into a devastating rout of their forces. Later, Salcedo and Hererra surrendered in San Antonio. They were tried by a revolutionary junta, found guilty of treason against the Hidalgo movement, and sentenced to death. On the insistence of Anglo Americans, their sentences were reduced to imprisonment away from Béxar. The two men and their aides were marched out of San Antonio by a rebel captain at the head of sixty armed men. At the Salado Creek battle site, Salcedo, Herrera, and more than a dozen junior officers and non-commissioned men were dismounted and murdered with knives and sabers.[44]

The Spanish government in Mexico responded by sending a huge army into Texas under Joaquín de Arredondo, commandant general of the Eastern Interior Provinces, to avenge the death of its officials and officers. By this time, the Republican Army had changed leadership from Gutiérrez to José Álvarez de Toledo. On August 18, 1813, the decisive battle of Medina River lasted approximately three and a half hours. Some 1,300 of the 1,400 men commanded by Toledo were either killed in the fighting or executed by Arredondo after the battle. Serving in Arredondo's army was a young lieutenant, Antonio López de Santa Anna. Cited for bravery during the battle by Arredondo, Santa Anna came away from the carnage with a mistaken impression that Anglo Americans were totally inept combatants without discipline. And he would soon witness an example of "ethnic cleansing" carried out by Arredondo as he descended on defenseless San Antonio. En route, Arredondo captured 215 men suspected of being rebels and ordered the execution of "those deserving death." He remained in San Antonio for several months. There he ordered the execution of an additional forty men suspected of either insurgent activities or sympathies. The mothers, wives, and children of these unfortunates were confined in such crowded and stifling quarters that eight died of suffocation.[45]

The non-Indian population of Spanish Texas never recovered from the vengeance meted out by Arredondo. The province passed under the control of the independent Mexican nation with scarcely a protest from those living there in 1821. Royalists had repelled all incursions, whether that of Philip Nolan or the Republican Army of the North, but Texas's defenders had also become its predators. In the words of historian David J. Weber: "By 1821 it must have been difficult to tell whether royalists or rebels had done the most harm." In the words of Antonio Martínez, the last Spanish governor of Texas, the king's soldiers had "drained the resources of the country and laid their hands on everything that could sustain human life." For those still alive, San Antonio offered little beyond a beggarly existence, but things were even worse in Nacogdoches, which had "nearly expired." It seems certain that Texas in 1821 had a non-Indian population of fewer than 3,000—less than the 3,103 reported in the first census of 1777.[46] Such facts probably would have depressed Pichardo, who had worked so hard for a better outcome.

The baleful conditions in Texas obviously had no role in keeping the province under the Spanish flag long enough for it to pass under the control of the new Mexican nation. But it was nonetheless Spanish—far from being a possession of the United States, as asserted by Jefferson at the time of the Louisiana Purchase. During both the Madison and Monroe administrations, attention was focused far more on Florida than Texas. In terms of global power politics, many Americans no doubt saw Florida as someday becoming a possession of the United States. This discussion of the cession of Florida brought the resolution to the Texas question that Pichardo had tried hard to avoid.

Florida, as mentioned, had again become a Spanish province after the 1783 Treaty of Paris. But Spanish presence there, aside from St. Augustine on the east coast and Pensacola on the Gulf of Mexico, was more theory than actuality. Spain's tenuous hold became increasingly apparent to men in the Monroe cabinet, especially Secretary of State John Quincy Adams and Secretary of War John C. Calhoun. To them, Florida had become unacceptably troublesome as a haven for escaped slaves and a refuge for Creek Indians who raided into the United States and retreated to safety across the northern border of Florida. The Creek raiders, better known as Seminoles, or "runaways," were troublesome enough that Calhoun authorized General Andrew Jackson to pursue such Indians into Florida. Jackson's dislike of Spaniards and troublesome Indians and his loose regard for technicalities during his Florida campaign are too well known to dwell on. But his actions convinced the Spanish Crown that it could not long keep possession of Florida, which it had claimed since the sixteenth century and continuously settled at St. Augustine since 1565.

The king of Spain during the Jackson campaign was Ferdinand VII. In the words of historian Stanley G. Payne, the young monarch "proved in many ways the basest king in Spanish history. Cowardly, selfish, grasping, suspicious, and vengeful, D. Fernando seemed almost incapable of any perception of the commonweal." During Ferdinand's absence from Spain while a prisoner of the French from 1807 to 1814, Spain had adopted a liberal constitution in 1812 and summoned into session an elected parliament, or *cortes*. On his return to the Spanish throne, one of the first decisions of the king was to dismiss the *cortes*, throw out the constitution, and declare himself absolute in authority. Ferdinand's actions rankled young officers in the Spanish army who had remarkably liberal ideas; and during the first half dozen years of Ferdinand's reign, he survived a series of plots and uprisings led by them. Then in 1820 the king was captured after a much larger revolt led by Major Rafael del Riego at Cádiz that soon spread throughout much of Spain. As a condition for keeping his throne, Ferdinand had to reinstate the Constitution of 1812 and summon into session the Spanish parliament.[47] It was at this time that the 1819 treaty signed by Luis de Onís and Adams was sent to Spain, where it had to be ratified by the new *cortes*, operating within a constitutional monarchy.

Luis de Onís primarily used the United States's desire to acquire Florida as leverage in his negotiations with Adams. But he may also have drawn on the great treatise compiled by Pichardo to wrest concessions from the United States. The resulting treaty in 1819 almost certainly would not have been endorsed in its entirety by Pichardo, but he would have approved of the Sabine and Red Rivers serving as part of the boundaries that preserved Spanish lands in Texas and the Spanish Southwest. The Mexican cleric and scholar would likewise have been pleased by his insistence that Spanish lands on the upper Texas coast extended to the mouth of the Atchafalaya River. His assertion, supported by a map drawn by him, gave Luis de Onís bargaining power when he compromised on the Sabine River being part of the eastern boundary of Texas. On the other hand, Pichardo almost certainly would not have agreed to the cession of Spanish lands in Quivira, which he had so painstakingly documented as Spanish-explored and Spanish-claimed territories, dating from the expedition of Francisco Vázquez de Coronado in the early 1540s. Despite the hard labor of the Mexican friar, the world had changed, and Spain had lost its hold on much of the northern frontier it struggled to control for almost three centuries.

Notes

1. See Charles W. Hackett, *Pichardo's Treatise on the Limits of Louisiana and Texas* (4 vols.; Austin: University of Texas Press, 1931). I am grateful to the Abilene Christian University Library for lending me reprints (Freeport, N.Y.: Books for Libraries Press, 1971) of these four volumes. All citations are to the reprinted volumes.

2. Hackett, *Pichardo's Treatise*, 1: vi–vii.

3. The reader is reminded that Florida, also part of New Spain, passed to Great Britain under terms of the Treaty of Paris in 1763.

4. A captaincy-general functioned as a smaller viceroyalty in all respects except name. When the Captaincy General of Cuba was created after the Treaty of Paris in 1763, it became independent of the Viceroyalty of New Spain.

5. Donald E. Chipman and Harriett Denise Joseph, *Spanish Texas, 1519–1821* (Rev. ed.; Austin: University of Texas Press, 2010), 175.

6. Luis Navarro García, *Don José de Gálvez y la Comandancia General de las Provincias Internas de Nueva España* (Seville: Escuela de Estudios Hispano-Americanos de Sevilla, 1964), 158.

7. Declarations of Soldiers at Presidio Nuestra Señora del Pilar (1767), Archivo General de Indias, Guadalajara 274.

8. Herbert E. Bolton, "The Spanish Abandonment and Re-Occupation of East Texas, 1773–1779," *Quarterly of the Texas State Historical Association* 9 (Oct. 1905): 67–137.

9. Chipman and Joseph, *Spanish Texas,* 190–91. The other important municipalities in colonial Texas at this time were San Antonio, La Bahía (later Goliad), and Laredo.

10. David J. Weber, *The Spanish Frontier in North America* (New Haven: Yale University Press, 1992), 224–25. Technically, the Interior Provinces remained a part of the Viceroyalty of New Spain, because all supplies and correspondence bound for it had to enter Mexico through the port of Veracruz.

11. Chipman and Joseph, *Spanish Texas*, 279–80.

12. Carlos E. Castañeda, *Our Catholic Heritage in Texas* (7 vols.; Austin: Von Boeckmann-Jones, 1936–1958), 5: 10–11, as quoted.

13. Weber, *Spanish Frontier*, 272, as quoted. The formal transfer of Florida from Great Britain to Spain came on July 12, 1784.

14. Robert H. Ferrell, *American Diplomacy, A History* (Rev. ed.; New York: Norton, 1969), 59–60.

15. Alicia V. Tjarks, "Comparative Demographic Analysis of Texas, 1777–1793," *Southwestern Historical Quarterly* 77 (Jan. 1974): 296–303.

16. Ibid.; Weber, *Spanish Frontier*, 296, as quoted.

17. Chipman and Joseph, *Spanish Texas,* 226–28. For more detailed information on Nolan, see Maurine T. Wilson and Jack Jackson, *Philip Nolan and Texas Expeditions to the Unknown Land* (Waco: Texian Press, 1987).

18. See Robert S. Weddle, *Changing Tides: Twilight and Dawn in the Spanish Sea, 1763–1803* (College Station: Texas A&M University Press, 1995), 255.

19. Weber, *Spanish Frontier*, 274, 291.

20. Richard Sternberg, "The Western Boundary of Louisiana, 1762–1803," *Southwestern Historical Quarterly* 35 (Oct. 1931): 104, as quoted. See also William M. Maloy, comp., *Treaties, Conventions, International Acts, Protocols, and Agreements between the United States of America and Other Powers, 1776–1909* (2 vols.; Washington, D.C.: U.S. Government Printing Office, 1910), 1: 506.

21. Stanley G. Payne, *A History of Spain and Portugal* (2 vols.; Madison: University of Wisconsin Press, 1973), 2: 419; Weber, *Spanish Frontier*, 292, quotation.

22. Ibid., 292; Chipman and Joseph, *Spanish Texas*, 237–40.

23. Ibid., 238.

24. Odie Faulk, *The Last Years of Spanish Texas, 1778–1821* (The Hague: Mouton, 1964), 124; Chipman and Joseph, *Spanish Texas*, 238–39 (see map on 239).

25. Carlos E. Castañeda, "Melchor de Talamantes," in Ron Tyler, et al., eds., *The New Handbook of Texas* (6 vols.; Austin: The Texas State Historical Association, 1996), 6: 195 (hereafter cited as Tyler, *NHOT).*

26. Hackett, *Pichardo's Treatise*, 1: xvii, 21.

27. Ibid., 22.

28. Ibid., 41, as quoted.

29. About half of the second volume of *Pichardo's Treatise* is devoted to Indian nations encountered by Spanish expeditions.

30. See especially the first and second volumes in Weddle's trilogy, *Spanish Sea: The Gulf of Mexico in North American Discovery, 1500–1685* (College Station: Texas A&M University Press, 1985, and *The French Thorn: Rival Explorers in the Spanish Sea, 1682–1762* (College Station: Texas A&M University Press, 1991). The author's third volume is cited in n.18 above.

31. Hackett, *Pichardo's Treatise*, 1: 141–48. See p. 143 for a listing of eight Indian nations as well as two others on p. 144.

32. See ibid., 33 n.7 and 155, quotations. Hackett, more than a century later than the judgment of Peñalosa by Pichardo, completely dispelled Peñalosa's claims to having visited Gran Quivira. See his "New Light on don Diego de Peñalosa: Proof That He Never Made an Expedition from Santa Fe to Quivira and the Mississippi River in 1662," *Mississippi Valley Historical Review* 6 (Dec. 1919): 313–35.

33. Hackett, *Pichardo's Treatise*, 1: 69, 81 (first quotation), 95 (second quotation), 120, 407. De Soto never set foot in Texas, but Luis de Moscoso and the remnants of De Soto's army assuredly did in the early 1540s.

34. Hackett, *Pichardo's Treatise*, 1: 349. "Monsieur d'Anville" refers to the French geographer Jean Baptiste Bourguigon D'Anvile. Carancaguaces are more commonly known as Karankawas.

35. Robert S. Weddle, "Spanish Mapping of Texas," in Tyler, *NHOT*, 6: 9 (quotation); see Hackett, *Pichardo's Treatise*, "Lángara map," between l: 350 and 351.

36. See "Section of Pichardo's map of New Mexico and adjacent regions" (1811) in Hackett, *Pichardo's Treatise*, between 1: 474 and 475.

37. Hackett, *Pichardo's Treatise*, 3: 111–12.

38. For provisions of the Adams-Onís Treaty (now often called the Transcontinental Treaty), see Randolph B. Campbell, *Gone to Texas: A History of the Lone Star State* (New York: Oxford University Press, 2003), 94–95, map on 95.

39. Chipman and Joseph, *Spanish Texas*, 246–47.

40. David E. Narrett, "José Bernardo Gutiérrez de Lara: *Caudillo* of the Mexican Republic in Texas," *Southwestern Historical Quarterly* 106 (Oct. 2006): 198.

41. Richard W. Gronet, "The United States and the Invasion of Texas," *Americas* 25 (Jan. 1969): 293–94.

42. Ibid.; Harry W. Henderson, "The Magee-Gutiérrez Expedition," *Southwestern Historical Quarterly* 55 (July 1951): 46.

43. Ibid., 48–50; Narrett, "Gutiérrez de Lara," 195.

44. Félix D. Almaráz Jr., *Tragic Cavalier: Governor Manuel Salcedo of Texas, 1808–1813* (Austin: University of Texas Press, 1989), 168–71; Narrett, "Gutiérrez de Lara," 216–17.

45. Donald E. Chipman and Harriett Denise Joseph, *Notable Men and Women of Spanish Texas* (Austin: University of Texas Press, 1999), 226–27, 244–54. See also Ted Schwarz, *Forgotten Battlefield of the First*

Texas Revolution: The Battle of the Medina (Austin: Eakin Press, 1985), 82, 89, 102.

46. David J. Weber, *The Mexican Frontier, 1821–1846: The American Southwest under Mexico* (Albuquerque: University of New Mexico Press, 1982), 4, 10 (quotations); see also Joseph C. McElhannon, "Imperial Mexico and Texas," *Southwestern Historical Quarterly* 53 (Oct. 1949): 120. Weber estimated the non-Indian population of Texas in 1821 at 2,500.

47. Payne, *History of Spain and Portugal*, 2: 428 (quotation)– 30.

Sam Houston in Cherokee Dress, Artist Unknown, ca. 1830. Courtesy of Library of Congress [Original in San Jacinto Museum]

Sam Houston, Indian Agent

Carol A. Lipscomb

> A familiar knowledge of the Indians, their manners, and habits, and their intercourse with the Government of the United State from my boyhood through life placed within my possession facts and implanted in me a principle enduring as life itself. That principle was to protect the Indian against wrong and oppression, and to vindicate him in the enjoyment of rights which have been solemnly guaranteed to him by this Government.
>
> Sam Houston[1]

Sam Houston is revered as a Texas hero. At least twelve major biographies along with countless other works have chronicled the adventures of this larger-than-life American. But even before he entered the pages of Texas history, he had carved out a wide-ranging and remarkable career. Houston was an accomplished frontiersman, schoolmaster, soldier, lawyer, and politician who became governor of Tennessee—all before he ever set foot in Texas. That impressive variety of occupations also included a brief stint as United States subagent to the Cherokee Indians. Houston held that position for just short of six months, but that brief experience provided him with a cause he would champion for the rest of his life. Throughout his career, Houston urged a peaceful and conciliatory policy toward Indians that was remarkably out-of-step with the attitudes of his fellow white Texans. Houston's refusal to wage war on Indians as president of the Republic of Texas cost him political support and helped ensure the election of Mirabeau B. Lamar—who promised to wage war against Native Americans—as the Republic's next president. During his thirteen years in the United States Senate, Houston agitated Texas voters by arguing for fair treatment of Indians. Houston's attitudes proved remarkably consistent and unyielding to the popular attitudes of the day, indicating the deep impact his early experiences had on this otherwise consistently practical politician. Houston's support for the Indians rivals his commitment to the Union, his better-known character trait that also led to conflicts with his contemporaries in Texas.[2]

In January 1817, Second Lieutenant Houston had just been assigned to the Southern Division Adjutant General's office in Nashville, Tennessee. The young officer had spent the last thirty-four months recuperating from wounds he received in the Creek Indian War, where his daring at the Battle of Horseshoe Bend had brought him to the attention of Maj. Gen. Andrew Jackson. Houston's new assignment brought him once again into direct contact with General Jackson, who commanded the Southern Division. The two men, who would develop a lasting friendship, often talked about the Indian situation in Tennessee, and Jackson became aware of Houston's extensive knowledge of the Cherokees. The General learned that as a teenager Houston had lived among those Indians in eastern Tennessee. He spoke their language and had even been adopted into the tribe. Jackson was looking for someone to fill a vacant post of subagent to the eastern Cherokee, and Houston, promoted to first lieutenant soon after his arrival in Nashville, seemed ideal. Jackson recommended the young soldier for the position, and in September President James Monroe approved the appointment. Houston received orders from the War Department to report to his new post in October. As a subagent, he would be paid $1,000 per annum and receive four rations a day, a considerable increase over a first lieutenant's pay of thirty dollars a month plus allowances.[3]

Because Jackson was facing the possibility of war with Seminoles who were causing trouble along the border between Georgia and Spanish Florida, he needed to avoid a conflict with Cherokees in Tennessee, where unrest was brewing over objections to a new treaty. Jackson counted on Houston, who understood Indian character and customs, to overcome the reluctance of many members of the tribe to abide by the provisions of the Cherokee Treaty of 1817. That agreement, which Jackson had helped to negotiate, was unpopular with many of the tribe, who asserted that the Cherokees who signed it did not represent all factions of the tribe and therefore had no authority to relinquish their lands. The treaty was designed to relocate the eastern Cherokee to the Arkansas Territory.[4]

The United States government's policy of Indian removal involved negotiating the exchange of Indian land for tracts farther west, where the tribes would be relocated. The idea of removal was first suggested by President Thomas Jefferson in 1803. When he negotiated the Louisiana Purchase, Jefferson considered the possibility that the eastern Indians might exchange their homeland for comparable land west of the Mississippi. He suggested the idea to Cherokees and Choctaws, but never formally adopted the notion as part of his Indian policy. After the War of 1812, the idea gained more favor as a growing Anglo population demanded more and more land. Prevailing logic dictated that removing the Indians would take them out of harm's way of the advancing Anglo frontier and give them time to adopt the white man's way. The fact that the Cherokees, who had already reached a high degree of assimilation, were not exempt from the removal process is evidence that land acquisition was a primary motive behind the government's removal policy. Government officials worked to convince tribal leaders to agree to be moved, and the exchange of land was legalized by the treaty process. The Cherokee Treaty of 1817 was an indication of the growing support within the federal government for removal.[5]

To help implement government policy, agents were appointed to reside among the Indians and act as "go-betweens." Their duties included solving problems with frontier whites, promoting civilizing endeavors such as agriculture and domestic arts, and overseeing trade between the tribe and government licensed traders. The success of an agent depended on his character, his ability to gain the respect of the tribe he served, and his perceived authority among neighboring whites. The job of Indian agent was highly desirable, primarily because the pay was good. Houston later wrote that "the salary is equal to any office in the gift of the state." As with any position, the job attracted men of varying ability and character, but the federal government had many capable men who distinguished themselves as Indian agents. One of those was Colonel Return J. Meigs, a Revolutionary War veteran who served as an agent to the Cherokees from 1801 until his death in 1823. Meigs supervised the Hiwassee Agency near the mouth of the Hiwassee River in southeastern Tennessee, where Houston was appointed as his subagent.[6]

Meigs himself was a proponent of removal. He observed the increasing white intrusion onto Cherokee land and as early as 1808 had suggested that a solution might be found by encouraging the Indians to exchange their homelands for land in the west. The issue divided the tribe, but in early 1810 about eight hundred Cherokees migrated to the Arkansas River valley in present-day Arkansas. Others, including the Hiwassee band that had adopted young Houston, chose to remain on their homelands. Under the provisions of the 1817 treaty, they, too, would have to give up their land.[7]

When Lieutenant Houston arrived at the Hiwassee Agency, Meigs was not there. The agent had escorted a delegation of Indians to Washington, D.C. It was common practice for such delegations to travel to the country's capital to meet with the president, receive gifts, and discuss grievances. Meigs had appointed William Smith, a local merchant, as acting agent during his absence, but Smith was also away from the post. He had gone to Georgia to buy supplies and left his brother-in-law in charge of the agency. Smith had been away for more than three weeks, and Houston found the state of affairs at the agency to be less than ideal. Meigs had instructed Houston that funds totaling $2,000 would be available when the subagent arrived, but Smith's brother-in-law could produce only $884. Houston drew $200 to begin his work among the Hiwassee Cherokees, but "a want of instructions" necessitated a quick trip to Knoxville to confer with Gov. Joseph McMinn, who also served as Superintendent of Indian Affairs for the state of Tennessee. The governor told Houston that he would have to wait for Meigs's return to receive further instructions.[8]

Houston returned to the agency, where he encountered another impropriety relating to the source of supplies for the Indians. The Cherokees acquired most of their provisions from a store located at the army garrison. That business was operated by Smith, the acting agent. Houston questioned the ethics of that arrangement, but he was even more concerned with a specific problem created by the store's location. Smith was selling liquor to the Indians, and because the business was outside the boundary of the Cherokee Nation, Houston had no authority to stop the illegal sales. The newly arrived subagent wrote to Jackson about the problem, adding "you know how difficult it is to keep Indians sober and also how impossible it is to transact business with them when intoxicated." On Houston's suggestion, and with Secretary of War John C. Calhoun's approval, the store was moved to the Hiwassee Agency, where the subagent had some control over the commodities sold there.[9]

After addressing the immediate problems, Houston set about his main task. His instructions were to encourage the Cherokees to vacate the land they had ceded by treaty and join their tribesmen in the west. He was also responsible for making the necessary preparations for the tribe's relocation. The Indians were led by Oo-loo-teka, the chief also known by the Anglo name John Jolly, who had adopted Houston years earlier. Houston had no difficulty convincing Oo-loo-teka that the move west was in the best interest of the tribe, for the peace-loving chief had become reconciled to the necessity of relocation. And the subagent was determined to do all in his power to ease the hardships of removal for his adopted tribe.[10]

Houston learned that the Indians did not have enough blankets for the winter journey. According to provisions of the treaty, only heads of households were entitled to receive blankets. In a letter to Jackson, Houston expressed his grave concern for the "squaws" who could not make the trip "without the aid of a blanket." At Houston's request, Governor

McMinn authorized the issue of additional blankets. The allocation was approved by the War Department with the justification that blankets were a small price to pay for lands the Cherokees were vacating. Houston also worked to acquire tools and other goods to facilitate the emigration, and in late December he reported that he had five hundred Cherokees ready to leave, including Oo-loo-teka and his Hiwassee band.[11]

While Houston was making final preparations for the removal of the eastern Cherokees, he was confronted with another problem. The Cherokees already settled in Arkansas Territory had serious grievances and wished to send a delegation to Washington to discuss their concerns. Those western Cherokees, led by Tahlontuskee, wanted the federal government to guarantee the boundaries of their Arkansas land, which overlapped territory belonging to native western tribes, particularly the Osages and Pawnees. They also complained that they were not getting a fair share of the annual government annuity, most of which went to their eastern brothers. In order to alleviate that problem, they wished to obtain recognition as an independent tribe.[12]

The delegation of western Cherokees arrived in Knoxville in December. Houston was instructed by Governor McMinn to accompany them to Washington, but poor health delayed his joining them until mid-January 1818, when the group finally departed for the nation's capital. The delegation, comprised of seven Cherokee chiefs and headmen, an interpreter, and Houston as guide, arrived in Washington in February and there lodged at Brown's Indian Queen Hotel, the usual accommodation for the many Indian deputations that visited the capital.[13]

Each of the visiting chiefs received gifts of clothing and a blanket while they awaited a meeting with the president. Members of the delegation were also given sizable monetary "presents." Tahlontuskee received $1,000, and each of the other chiefs received $500. In a letter to McMinn, Secretary of War Calhoun confidently noted that the money gifts would "no doubt have important effects in aiding the operations now going on." However, government generosity was certainly not the motivation for bestowing money. In May 1818, Calhoun instructed Meigs that the expenses incurred by the delegation to Washington would be deducted from the Cherokee annuity.[14]

The Cherokee delegation met with Calhoun to discuss its problems before being treated to a formal reception with President James Monroe. The president assured the delegates that the boundaries of their western land would be "laid off" as soon as a treaty was concluded with the other native tribes. Monroe reiterated that "it is better for you and for us that all of the Cherokees should go to the Arkansaw," and he promised to supply the emigrants with "as much corn as you may want." He skirted the tender issue of a separate Western Cherokee nation, but he implied that independent status would not be necessary if the tribe united in Arkansas Territory. The Cherokees were generally pleased with the results of their trip, but Houston was not so fortunate.[15]

Dressed in Cherokee style, Houston had accompanied the delegation to its scheduled meeting with the Secretary of War. When the meeting ended, Calhoun detained Houston and demanded an explanation for the agent's outlandish costume. Houston's response that the attire improved his effectiveness as an Indian agent was not accepted by Calhoun, who severely reprimanded the young lieutenant for being out of uniform. The subagent's humiliation did not end there. Some ten days later, Houston was summoned to Calhoun's office and told that he had been accused of smuggling slaves out of Florida. He was also charged with preventing a Cherokee force from marching to the relief of army units fighting Seminoles. Houston was shocked by the allegations because he had, in fact, made every effort to stop illegal slave trafficking. The accusation that he had refused to allow the Indians under command of Col. Gideon Morgan, a Cherokee, to join Maj. Gen. Edmund P. Gaines in Florida was true, but Houston claimed valid reasons for making that decision.[16]

In order to refute the charges, Houston presented written evidence, in the form of letters, to Calhoun. On the basis of that evidence, Calhoun conducted an investigation that vindicated Houston. The Secretary of War became satisfied that Houston had done nothing improper, but no action was taken against Houston's accusers, members of Congress who were attempting to protect the real perpetrators of the illegal slave trade. Houston requested a written statement clearing his name, but Calhoun replied that was not necessary since no written charges had been filed. The young subagent felt slighted by Washington officials who failed to confront his accusers or offer any apology or regrets for the false accusation or any appreciation for his work with the Cherokees. On March 1, 1818, Houston wrote to General David Parker at the War Department: "Sir, you will please accept this as my resignation, to take effect from this date."[17]

Houston resigned his first lieutenancy in the army, but he continued to hold the civilian job of subagent to the Cherokee as he felt obligated to carry out those duties, and he was committed to helping the Indians. On March 16, Houston left Washington with his delegation and accompanied them as far as the Hiwassee Agency in Tennessee. When he arrived there, he was ordered by Governor McMinn to travel to the various villages to communicate President Monroe's message to the Cherokee people. Houston learned to his pleasure that in early February Chief Oo-loo-teka and 331 members of his band had departed for their new land in the west. Much to Houston's credit, the travelers were well supplied with blankets, tools, and seventy days of food rations per person.[18]

Houston might have continued to serve as Cherokee subagent had it not been for notification of salary reductions for the entire agency. In April 1818, a letter from the War Department advised him that his annual pay would be cut by more than half, from $1,296 to $500 per annum. Houston resigned his position rather than accept the decrease in pay. He had served as subagent for only six months but had learned much about the workings of the Indian agency. Despite the presence of some honest and dedicated people, there was still considerable graft and corruption. In a few short months he had uncovered missing funds, illegal alcohol sales, and unethical practices with regard to supplying food and other commodities to the Indians. Whether on a small scale or a large one the improprieties resulted in injustices perpetrated on the Indian people, which Houston could not abide. His job as subagent had given him new insight into the Indian situation and the inherent problems of the Indian agents.[19]

Although only twenty-five, Houston had already acquired a wide-ranging knowledge of Indians. He had observed their circumstances through a variety of experiences that began when he lived with the Cherokees as an adopted member of their tribe as a teenager. As a young soldier during the War of 1812, he had fought and killed Indians and suffered grievous wounds, so he knew the devastation war brought to both sides. His service in an Indian agency had given him new insight into the plight of Indians who were being forced from their land by the expanding white population. There were probably very few of Houston's contemporaries who could claim such wide-ranging experience with Indians. More important, as a result of his experiences, Houston had developed a great sympathy for the native people.

After leaving the agency, young Houston went to Nashville to study law, a course he completed in six months. Within a short time he received an appointment as Adjutant General for the state of Tennessee. In the fall of 1819, Jackson again recommended Houston for a post in an Indian agency, this time as agent to the western Cherokee in Arkansas Territory. In a letter to Secretary of War Calhoun, Jackson expressed his opinion that Houston's influence could draw the remaining eastern Cherokees from Georgia and Tennessee to Arkansas and unite the tribe, thereby saving the United States half the present expense. Jackson added, "I have no hesitation in saying that Col. Sam[ue]l Houston is better qualified for this station than any man of his age I am acquainted with . . . ." Houston, however, declined the position. His career as an attorney was going well, and he probably still resented the perceived slights he received from Calhoun the year before.[20]

Houston's law practice grew along with his notoriety, and in 1823 he was elected to the United States House of Representatives from the Ninth Tennessee District. He served two terms in Congress before staging a successful run for governor in 1826. But the failure of his short marriage to Eliza Allen and the resulting scandal "with its ten thousand imputed slanders" led Houston to resign as governor, his only explanation being that he was "overwhelmed by sudden calamities." He fled the state of Tennessee, leaving behind astounded friends and constituents, and returned to his Cherokee family, now residing on the Arkansas River in eastern Indian Territory. In the spring of 1829, Houston again took up the ways of the Cherokee, residing with Chief Oo-la-teka and dressing as one of the tribe. The chief welcomed Houston and at the same time invoked his help. He told his adopted son, "We are in trouble, and the Great Spirit has sent you to give us council [*sic*], and take trouble away from us . . . You will tell our sorrows to the great father, General Jackson." Houston was about to be involved in Indian affairs again.[21]

From his Cherokee friends, Houston learned of the many difficulties they had encountered since their move west. The tribe had first settled on land in northeastern Arkansas, the historic hunting ground of the Osages. Hostilities with that tribe coupled with increasing encroachment of whites forced the Cherokees to move a second time. This move, sanctioned by another treaty, took them to what is today eastern Oklahoma. Within a few days of his arrival in Cherokee country, Houston learned that his Indian friends were being victimized by their agent, Maj. Edward W. du Val, who had systematically defrauded his wards.[22]

Word of Houston's arrival in Indian Territory spread fast. He was a well-known public figure with influence in the highest office in the land, because Houston's friend and mentor Jackson now occupied the White House. Other tribes sought his help. At the behest of long-time trader August Pierre Chouteau, Houston visited Osage country, some one hundred miles to the northeast, where he learned of similar corruption at that agency. Chouteau, who had traded with the Osages for thirty years, complained that agent John Hamtramck cheated the Indians and asked Houston to report this to President Jackson. The respected trader even suggested that Houston become an agent and use his influence in Washington to help stop the corruption. After leaving Chouteau's trading post and the nearby

Osage agency at Three Forks, Houston visited the Creeks to hear about problems with their agent, David Brearley, and the agent of the Eastern Creeks, John Crowell. Houston later visited the Choctaws at their agency near Fort Smith for the same purpose. Their agent, Captain William McClellan, was honest, but Washington had ignored his pleas for help in controlling unscrupulous whites who were defrauding the Choctaws.[23]

The widespread corruption that Houston uncovered in the Indian agencies took a variety of forms, all injurious to the Indian people. They were being defrauded of their annuities by several corrupt practices. Agents sometimes dispensed funds inequitably, used them to bribe Indians, or refused to dispense them at all. Using the funds for their own speculation, some agents became rich at their wards' expense. When the Indians were paid, it was often with paper certificates of indebtedness rather than the gold payments promised by treaty. Many Indians did not understand paper money and were cheated out of their specie certificates for less than face value. There was also widespread graft in the purchase of food rations, which were often poor quality and not supplied on a timely basis. And there was the same problem that Houston had worked to correct at the Hiwassee Agency, where the agents themselves or their cohorts were selling liquor to the Indians.[24]

In October 1829, Houston witnessed firsthand the payment of annuities to the Cherokees and the resultant abuses that robbed his friends of the money due them under provisions of the Treaty of 1828. The Cherokees were owed a $50,000 lump indemnity, a $2,000 annuity, and various other payments from previous treaties, all due in gold. Agent du Val announced that there would be no gold, but rather certificates of indebtedness would be used to satisfy the government's debt. Houston described what happened: "Merchants who had connections with the agents, purchased up these certificates in a fraudulent manner for a mere song . . . Agent du Val himself opened up a store to facilitate trade in certificates. The agent's brother opened a whisky running station, and in six weeks he had sold two hundred and fifty barrels of liquor." When du Val later learned that Houston intended to travel to Washington to prefer charges against the various agents, he asked that Houston put the charges against him in writing, to which Houston gladly complied, keeping a copy for himself.[25]

Houston then began his campaign to correct the evils of the agency system. He wrote a number of letters to officials in Washington, including President Jackson and the Secretary of War, John Eaton. In June he forwarded a memorial from the Creeks listing their grievances, and he attached a personal note to Jackson saying that the complaints deserved investigation. In the fall of 1829 he wrote again to Jackson, volunteering his help with the Indian situation even though he held no official position in an Arkansas Indian agency. He told the president that since he had come to know the Indians, it had been his principal objectives "to meliorate the condition of the Indians, to suggest improvements to their growing institutions, to prevent fraud, and peculation, on the part of the Governments Agents among them, and to direct the feelings of the Indians in kindness to the Government . . . ." A few months later, Houston again wrote to Jackson offering ideas for making peace with the tribes in Arkansas Territory. If the government would survey the boundaries of each tribe's land, he wrote, give them annuities of from $5,000 to $10,000, and "follow the spirit of the treaties," peace was certainly possible. As Chouteau suggested, Houston added that unless Osage agent Hamtramck was removed, the Indians would "never prosper." He accused the agent of wrongdoings in the treatment of the tribe but gave no specifics.[26]

In January 1830, Houston traveled to Washington as a member of a Cherokee delegation to complain about corruption in the Indian agencies. He carried memorials from the various tribes along with other material supporting his charges. With the evidence he presented, Houston was successful in obtaining the dismissal of five Indian agents, including Hamtramck and du Val.[27]

While in the city, Houston saw another opportunity to help the Indians while earning some much-needed revenue for himself. He learned that the government was taking bids for a contract to supply rations for some 60,000 southern Indians who under the removal policy were to exchange their land for tracts west of the Mississippi. During the emigration, the government proposed to feed the Indians. With the backing of New York investor John Van Fossen, Houston entered a bid for the contract. He made his intentions clear to Van Fossen when he wrote, "to do ample justice to the Indians in giving to them full ration, and of good quality should we get the contract must be regarded as a 'sine qua non' with us." But that opportunity vanished when a subsequent bidding war became so controversial that Secretary of War Eaton withdrew the contract on the grounds that no Indian removal measure had as yet been passed by Congress. With no further prospects in Washington, Houston headed for his home in Cherokee country. As he traveled west he must have been pleased that he had some success in exposing the corruption that plagued the Indian agencies, and through his efforts at least five corrupt agents would no longer cheat the Indians.[28]

As he was leaving Washington, Houston heard a rumor that the sutler at Fort Gibson was about to be removed, and he applied to Secretary of

War Eaton for the job. In anticipation of this new opportunity, Houston loaded a keel boat with supplies from New York and Nashville to stock the Fort Gibson store. When he arrived in Cherokee country, he learned that the rumor was unfounded. There was no vacancy for the post he hoped to occupy, so with the goods he had shipped west, he opened a small store at his home, which he called Wigwam Neosho, located about three miles from Fort Gibson. Within a month, Houston found new reasons to resume his campaign to correct injustices in the Indian agencies. This time he used a newspaper to rally public opinion to his cause.

Houston had certainly made enemies, both in Indian Territory and in Washington, in his crusade against corruption. Those in the capital accused Houston of attempting to use his influence with President Jackson to obtain the rations contract. His accusers were the very men who had attempted to rig the bidding process in their favor. In a letter to Secretary of War Eaton in the summer of 1830, Houston defended his actions and added that he would publish a series of articles in the *Arkansas Gazette* "showing in what manner the agencies, have been, and are now managed in this quarter. The innocent will not suffer, the guilty ought not to escape." He added that he would sign the articles with the name Talohntusky.[29]

The five articles, written in Houston's flamboyant style, detailed the abuses in the Indian Agency that he had campaigned to correct. They provided a vivid account of the graft and corruption that Houston saw as well as the effect of questionable practices on the Indians. The first article signed Talohntusky appeared in the *Gazette* on June 22, 1830; it was followed by two more installments signed Talohntusky, one signed Standing Bear, and the final article on December 8, 1830, titled "Indian Matters" but not signed. Taken together, the articles are a scathing indictment of the agency system. Houston documented false promises made to Indian leaders, bribery in the War Department, schemes to take Indian land, the ration contract scandal, the theft of specie certificates, misappropriation of annuities, and the sale of liquor to Indians by their agents. He did not hesitate to name names, and his articles quickly drew indignant responses from the accused. Those replies, also printed in the *Gazette*, generally took the form of slanders against Houston rather than refutations of his charges. One of the replies was so vicious that the editor of the *Gazette* refused to print it in the body of the paper, relegating it instead to a supplement used for dueling challenges. One rebuttal, signed Tekatoka, was addressed "To Standing Bear alias Samuel Houston." It seems that despite the use of pseudonyms, the author's true identity was no secret.[30]

Houston's choice to write under an Indian pseudonym probably was not intended to hide his identity. He had certainly shown on more than one occasion that he was not afraid to speak his mind. It seems more likely that Houston chose not to use his own name because he wanted to focus attention on his subject rather than himself. In effect, he was giving a voice to the Indian. And signing with an Indian name gave a dramatic flair that helped draw attention to his articles. Publishing them in the *Arkansas Gazette* also assured a wide readership. The *Gazette* was the most influential newspaper in the Southwest, with a circulation of five hundred subscribers in 1829, but more important, it served as a reliable source of news in the west for papers in the east. Newspapers like *Niles' Weekly Register* in Baltimore often reprinted entire stories directly from the *Gazette.* Houston knew that his articles would likely be picked up by some influential eastern papers, greatly increasing their political impact. In the midst of publishing his articles, he wrote to Van Fossen in New York, "You will perhaps see in some of the northern papers, "chapters" signed "Tah-lou-tusky," and every fact contained you may rely upon as true! The author you may guess at."[31]

It is impossible to determine the exact effects of Houston's newspaper campaign to reform the Indian agencies. In his July 7, 1830, article signed Tah-Lohn-Tus-Ky, Houston hotly denounced the head of the Indian Bureau, Thomas L. McKenney, whom he called "the complaisant sycophant of those in power," and "a constant apologist of every delinquent Agent in the Indian Department." His stinging indictment of McKenney may have contributed to the superintendent's removal from office by President Jackson on August 16, 1830, although being a political enemy of Jackson was also a factor. McKenney's replacement, Samuel S. Hamilton, recognized the problems confronting the Bureau and proposed constructive changes to improve annuity disbursals and modify the trade and intercourse laws, but Congress generally ignored his proposals. Four years later, Congress finally passed the Indian Service Reorganization Act and a new Trade and Intercourse Act aimed at correcting some of the agency problems that Houston so vehemently denounced.[32]

In his efforts to help the Indians, Houston fought an uphill battle. It was a time when the white population east of the Mississippi expanded rapidly, and it was not popular to champion the cause of Indians, especially those who held desirable land. The majority of white public opinion did not favor Indians, and Houston knew that. In a letter to Jackson he wrote, "I am aware that this is not the most popular position for me to occupy in relation to the Indians, but justice and a regard to their real interests requires of me both risque [*sic*] and sacrifice if necessary."

Houston continued to use his influence to improve the lot of the Indians whenever he had an opportunity, even if it meant expending his political capital to do so. His articles, with their outspoken indictment of the agency system and descriptions of the effects of agency abuses, provided a reliable account of what was happening to Indians. Writing in the names of Talohntusky and Standing Bear, Houston seems to have found his political voice once again. The articles marked the beginning of the end of his self-imposed exile as he began to look for opportunities to reenter public life. He would find those in Texas.[33]

Houston's interest in Texas had been brewing for a decade. As early as 1822 he joined a group applying for grants of land in the Mexican state. Although those grants never came to fruition, a number of Houston's friends, including William H. Wharton, migrated to Texas in the 1820s and early 1830s and frequently encouraged him to join them there. It was widely known that Houston believed Texas should be independent of Mexico, and rumors abounded that he planned to foment some sort of revolution with the help of Indian allies. If he had such plans, they never materialized. His well-publicized caning of William Stanbery, an Ohio Congressman who had the audacity to accuse Houston himself of fraud in his dealings with Indians in the summer of 1832 may have prompted Houston to consider Texas even more strongly. He set out for Texas in the winter of 1832 intending to practice law and speculate in land, as well as to avoid paying a judgment for beating Stanbery, but he also was charged with what he later described as "a confidential mission."[34]

Houston had lobbied for this mission. On his last trip to Washington, he had informed the new Secretary of War, Lewis Cass, that he was traveling west, and he offered to gather information on the Plains tribes. The reasons for his offer were twofold. Obviously, he thought his Indian skills could be of value to the government, but the mission would also earn him some much needed income. The government was eager to establish peace with the western Indians, and a July 1832 letter from the War Department offered Houston the position of "special agent" for the purpose of holding talks with Plains Indians, particularly Pawnees and Comanches. The letter also stated that Houston would be allowed reasonable compensation for his services. He was given an official passport and further instructions to "do no act that could furnish even a plausible pretext of complaint on the part of Mexico."[35]

To fulfill this obligation, Houston traveled as far as San Antonio where, in the company of Mexican officials, he met with some Comanche leaders. He found them "well disposed" to make a treaty with the United States. The Indians promised to visit Fort Gibson in the spring to negotiate peace. Believing that his mission had been a success, Houston reported the results of his meeting to Secretary of War Cass and the Indian Commissioners at Fort Gibson. He also filed an expense account in the amount of $3,552. The Secretary replied that the amount was excessive for the information obtained. It seems the Department had received another informative letter in the spring of 1833 from Albert Pike, who had traveled extensively among the Indians. Pike offered the following comment on Houston's mission: "Governor Houston of Tennessee will effect nothing with the Comanches. He goes to treat with the southern portion of them who are already friendly—he will never meet one of the northern portion from whom is our only danger, and should he do so he would be immediately scalped." Houston's Comanches did not show up for the promised meeting at Fort Gibson, and Houston received only $1,200 for his efforts—it was a disappointing outcome for all concerned. Houston put his Indian cause aside as he turned his attention to the growing insurrection in Texas.[36]

Houston's leadership during the Texas Revolution led to his election as president of the newly independent Republic of Texas in 1836. The new government faced a number of pressing issues, and not the least among them was the question of how to deal with Texas's Indians. The Republic consisted of scattered frontier settlements that advanced north and west as the population grew. In 1836 the Anglo population approached 35,000, and that number continued to increase rapidly. Lieutenant James W. Abert, a United States soldier traveling the Santa Fe Trail, remarked that, "the way from Fort Gibson was literally lined with the wagons of emigrants to Texas." Most of them wanted land. Houston would have to deal with the same problem he had witnessed in the eastern United States—how to keep peace between Indians and the growing number of Anglos who wanted their land.[37]

Indian affairs became one of Houston's major concerns, and he tackled the issue with a plan that he believed would serve the best interests of Indians and whites. Texas had both native tribes and immigrant Indians who had fled from Anglo expansion in the eastern United States. Among those immigrants was a large contingent of Houston's adopted tribe, the Cherokees. Pursuing a plan that he believed would result in the best outcome for all concerned, Houston developed a policy of peace, friendship, and commerce. He negotiated treaties with the various tribes, advocated boundaries between Indian and Anglo land, and passed legislation to build forts and trading houses along those boundary lines to maintain peace. He favored organized protection of the frontier, but he opposed offensive expeditions against the Indians.[38]

Once again popular opinion was not in Houston's favor. The majority of Texans, as well as a majority in the Texas Congress, did not agree with their president's Indian policy, particularly with regard to giving Indians title to their land. For example, an 1836 treaty that guaranteed the Cherokees possession of their land was never ratified by the Texas Senate. During his first term as president, Houston did his best to assure that Indians got fair treatment, but his policy was largely unsuccessful due primarily to an uncooperative Congress, an impoverished treasury, and unsympathetic settlers who continued to encroach on Indian land. Houston's term as president was limited to two years, and in December 1838 Texans elected a leader who would handle the Indian situation in a radically different manner.[39]

Mirabeau B. Lamar had none of Houston's understanding and sympathy for Indians. Like the majority of Texans, he viewed them as impediments to the progress of civilized society, and he saw no possibility of peacefully resolving the problems between settlers and Indians. Lamar, instead, waged war on Texas's tribes, a war of extermination that in his two years as president left Texas with far fewer Indians. Many immigrant Indians residing in East Texas were killed, and the remainder were forced north into the Indian Territory. The Plains Indians were pushed west away from advancing settlers. Lamar's wars were costly in terms of lives lost and property destroyed, and they left the new republic with a staggering debt. This fiscal irresponsibility paved the way for Houston's reelection to the Republic's highest office in 1841.[40]

During Lamar's term, Houston did not sit idly by. In 1839 he was elected to the House of Representatives by the citizens of San Augustine. Houston noted that he did not seek the office but willingly accepted it, and he then used the position to continue to put forth his vision for the Republic, including the treatment of Indians. In a number of speeches before Congress, Houston argued for the land claims of the Cherokees, and he condemned the government's failure to recognize Indian treaty rights and protect Indian lands from continuing encroachment But he delivered his most fervent attack on Lamar's policy on January 8, 1840, after Hugh McLeod, a supporter of Lamar's war on the Indians, presented Houston with the hat of his friend, Cherokee Chief Bowl, who had been killed by Lamar's forces at the Battle of the Neches. That defeat forced the surviving Cherokees to flee to Indian Territory, opening up their land to white settlers. From his minority position, Houston had no option but to watch as the Cherokees were once again forced from their land. He must have been both angry and sad to learn the fate of his Cherokee friends, but he was powerless to effect a policy change.[41]

Houston officially entered the Republic's presidential race in the fall of 1840, and in September 1841 he won a decisive victory over Lamar's hand-picked successor, David G. Burnet. In his inaugural message to Congress, Houston announced that the government would return to the pacific Indian policy that he had always advocated. Since most of the immigrant Indians had been forced into the Indian Territory, the new policy was directed primarily toward tribes on the western frontier. Trading posts encouraged commerce, ranger companies patrolled the frontier for defensive purposes, peace talks were initiated with various tribes, and in 1843 a new law created the Bureau of Indian Affairs, headed by a superintendent and staffed by up to four agents and four interpreters. The same law imposed a boundary between Indians and whites along the line of trading posts. This policy, which Houston described as "satisfactorily tested," remained in effect for the duration of the Texas Republic, and with some success.[42]

During the ten-year life of the Republic, Houston continually advocated a policy that he believed served the best interests of both whites and Indians. His peace policy was not popular with the majority of Texans, especially those closest to the frontier, but most agreed it was less costly in terms of lives lost and dollars spent than a war of extermination. As the Anglo population continued to push the boundaries of Indian land, the Indians fought to keep them out, and depredations committed by both sides increased. Frontier protection became a major issue in the call for annexation. The people of Texas were confident that annexation would bring an end to their Indian problems. The burden of frontier defense would be assumed by the United States government, and Texans welcomed that prospect. An editorial in the *Telegraph and Texas Register* enthusiastically proclaimed that "the giant arms of the United States will soon sweep the few bands of hostile Indians from our borders." When annexation became official in late 1845, Houston did not give up his Indian cause. He continued to fight for the rights of Indians for the remainder of his public life.[43]

In February 1846 the people of Texas elected Houston to represent them in the United States Senate. When he assumed his Senate seat, the Indian question was still an important national issue, but government policy had changed in the fourteen years since Houston left Arkansas Territory for Texas. The removal of the eastern tribes was nearly complete, and as they settled into their new homes in Indian Territory, the government made concerted efforts to "civilize" and Christianize the displaced people. But new problems arose in the 1840s as the country grew. In the short span of three years the acquisition of Texas, Oregon, and California, along with the rest of the Mexican Cession, expanded the borders of the United States and brought the government into conflict with new groups of Indians. A new policy grew out of the idea of locating the tribes on reserves of land where they would be protected by trade and intercourse laws. The treaty process legalized the acquisition of Indian land, much as it had done since the country's founding. With the reservation system, administered primarily by the Bureau of Indian Affairs, Houston found many of the same problems he had fought to correct years earlier.[44]

During his thirteen-year tenure in the Senate, Houston continued to champion the cause of fair treatment for Indians, both in his home state of Texas and on the national level. His benevolent stance continued to run counter to majority opinion, but he held fast to his convictions, despite caustic criticism. Augustus C. Dodge, Senator from Iowa, accused the senator from Texas of "sickly sentimentality" with regard to the Indians. Houston replied that "it is a sickly sentimentality that was implanted in me when I was young, and it has grown up with me." He went on to say, "I am a friend of the Indian, upon the principle that I am a friend to justice." Houston condemned the injustice of concluding treaties with the Indians and then failing to uphold those compacts, telling his fellow Senators, "We are not bound to make them promises: but if a promise be made to an Indian, it ought to be regarded as sacredly as if it were made to a white man."[45]

This same injustice that Houston had worked to correct as a young Indian agent in 1818 was still a problem more than thirty years later. The Indians were not receiving the compensation that the government had promised them. Houston told his fellow Senators, "We rob them, first of their native dignity and character; we rob them next of what the Government appropriates for them." Of the $100 million appropriated by the government since its founding to benefit the Indians, Houston calculated that they had received less than $15 million as the bulk of the funds fell into the hands of corrupt agents, speculators, and traders. From the Senate floor Houston argued that the Indians "are too remote from the seat of government for their real condition to be understood here; and if the Government intends liberality or justice toward them, it is often diverted from the intended object and consumed by speculators."[46]

The Senator from Texas suggested that the Indians should be given a government of their own and allowed to send representatives to the House and the Senate. It was extremely unlikely that the Senate would adopt such a radical suggestion, and Houston knew that, but perhaps he reasoned that by advocating the extreme, he could win some lesser compensation for the Indians. In a speech delivered at Nacogdoches in May 1855, he once more suggested enfranchising the Indians, telling his audience that, "The Indians have few friends and he knew the reason why. They cannot vote. If they could vote these men [politicians] would soon make use of them and have them up the top of the pole." Opinions opposing Houston were just as radical. Senator John Pettit of Indiana argued that "the Indians were an inferior race" and "God Almighty had already condemned them" and "there is no use in doing anything for them." Houston countered this argument by recounting the accomplishments of the Cherokees, noting that, "Whenever they have had an opportunity, they have shown that they are not inferior to white men, either in sense or capability."[47]

Houston refused to abandon the Indian cause. On one occasion, he came to the Senate floor with all the books detailing Indian policy since the founding of the government. Telling his fellow Senators not to be alarmed, that he would "occupy but a short time," he proceeded to give a brief history of government dealings with Indians, noting the "solemn pledges" that had been broken and "the faithless conduct on the part of the government or its agents." He argued for protecting the Indians' land and adopting a system "to civilize and Christianize them."[48] Houston spoke on other occasions against sending mounted troops to wage war against the Indians. He was convinced that warfare was the most costly option that the government could adopt, and violence only begat more violence. If even a portion of the money used to fund the military solution was used to provide presents and supplies for the Indians and to send qualified agents to promote civilization, education, and Christianization, he had no doubt that peace could be attained. Houston asked his Senate colleagues, "Would it not be wiser to send a few wagons with presents than to send an army?" He argued this position again and again during his public life.[49]

Throughout his career, Houston held fast to his fight for fair treatment of Indians. He knew his stance was not popular. In addressing the Senate in 1854, he said, "I am aware, Mr. President, that in presenting myself as the advocate of the Indians and their rights, I shall claim but little sympathy from the community at large, and that I shall stand very much alone, pursuing the course which I feel it my imperative duty to adhere to." And adhere he did, despite vehement opposition. His resultant victories were small, but it can be argued that he made a difference. He was instrumental in the removal of corrupt agents in the early 1830s. At the same time, his exposure of corruption in the Indian agencies probably helped to bring on a wholesale revamping by Congress in 1834. During the time Houston served the Texas Republic, both as president and in the legislature, then later as governor of the state of Texas, he worked to establish peace between Texans and Indians, with some short-term successes. While serving in the United States Senate, Houston remained committed to the fight for fair treatment for Indians, despite the general unpopularity of his cause. The longevity of his commitment in the face of continual opposition is a true measure of Houston's political integrity and character. As it was, Indian culture barely survived—had there been no Sam Houston or others of like mind before and after him who advocated fair treatment for the Indians, the outcome might have been even more tragic.

Notes

1. Sam Houston, "Opposing the Kansas-Nebraska Bill," Feb. 14–15, 1854, in Amelia W. Williams and Eugene C. Barker, eds., *The Writings of Sam Houston, 1813–1863* (6 vols.; Austin: University of Texas Press, 1940; repr., Austin: Jenkins Publishing Company, 1970), 5: 469.

2. Among the biographies of Houston, the most extensive recent publication is James L. Haley, *Sam Houston* (Norman: University of Oklahoma Press, 2002). While Haley provides detailed information on Houston's early work with Indians, and links that experience to his policies as president of the Republic of Texas, he does not discuss many of his later efforts in their defense.

3. Extract from Division Orders, Nashville, Oct. 28, 1817 in Williams and Barker, *Writings of Sam Houston*, 1: 8; George Graham to Sam Houston, Sept. 29, 1817, in Letters Sent by the Secretary of War Relating to Indian Affairs, 1800–1824, Records of the Bureau of Indian Affairs, Record Group 75, National Archives, Washington, D.C. (Microfilm M15, Reel 4). George Graham served as Pres. James Monroe's acting secretary of war until Dec. 8, 1817, when the position was assumed by John C. Calhoun.

4. Randolph B. Campbell, *Sam Houston and the American Southwest* (New York: Harper Collins College Publishers, 1993), 8–9.

5. Francis Paul Prucha, *The Great Father: The United States Government and the American Indians* (Abridged ed., Lincoln: University of Nebraska Press, 1986), 64–77.

6. Houston to Joseph McMinn, Mar. 30, 1823 in Williams and Barker, *Writings of Sam Houston*, 1: 18; Prucha, *Great Father*, 57–59. For additional information on Return J. Meigs, see James S. McKeown,

"Return J. Meigs: United States Agent in the Cherokee Nation, 1801–1823" (Ph.D. Diss., Pennsylvania State University, 1984).

7. Theda Perdue and Michael D. Green, eds., *The Cherokee Removal: A Brief History with Documents* (Boston: Bedford Books of St. Martin's Press, 1995), 14–17.

8. Sam Houston, *Life of General Sam Houston: A Short Autobiography* (Austin: Pemberton Press, 1964), 3; Houston to Andrew Jackson, Dec. 18, 1818, Andrew Jackson Houston Collection, Texas State Library and Archives, Austin (hereafter cited as AJHC); Houston, "Indian Matters," *Arkansas Gazette*, Dec. 8, 1830, in Williams and Barker, *Writings of Sam Houston*, 1: 181. Joseph McMinn served three terms as governor of Tennessee, 1815–1823. During his lengthy administration, he worked in the best interests of both Indians and whites. Houston respected McMinn and the two men remained friends long after Houston left Tennessee. For a biographical sketch of McMinn, see Charles W. Crawford, ed., *Governors of Tennessee, I: 1790–1833* (Memphis: Memphis State University Press, 1979), 97–118.

9. Houston to Jackson, Dec. 18, 1818, AJHC; John C. Calhoun to Houston, Jan. 15, 1818, in Edwin Hemphill and Robert L. Meriwether, eds. *The Papers of John C. Calhoun* (16 vols.; Columbia: University of South Carolina Press, 1959), 2: 75; Graham to Joseph McMinn, Nov. 29, 1817, Lets. Sent by Sec. of War Relating to Indian Affairs, 1800–24 (M15, Reel 4).

10. Marshall De Bruhl, *Sword of San Jacinto: A Life of Sam Houston* (New York: Random House, 1993), 58–59; Jack Gregory and Rennard Strickland, *Sam Houston with the Cherokees, 1829–1833* (Austin: University of Texas Press, 1967), 17–18.

11. Houston to Jackson, Dec. 18, 1818, AJHC; Houston to Calhoun, Dec. 14, 1817; Calhoun to Houston, Jan. 3, 1818, in Hemphill and Meriwether, *Papers of Calhoun*, 2: 15, 55; Houston to William Smith, Dec. 11, 1817, Records of the Cherokee Indian Agency in Tennessee, 1801–1835, Records of the Bureau of Indian Affairs, RG75, NA (Microfilm M208, Reel 7); De Bruhl, *Sword of San Jacinto*, 58–59.

12. Cherokee Chiefs to Jackson, Apr. 18, 1817, in Harold Moser et al., eds., *Papers of Andrew Jackson* (8 vols. to date; Knoxville: University of Tennessee Press, 1991–), 4: 109–10; *Daily National Intelligencer* (Washington, D.C.), Feb. 3, 1818.

13. McMinn to Calhoun, Jan. 16, 1818, in Hemphill and Meriwether, *Papers of Calhoun,* 2: 76–77; McMinn to Return J. Meigs, Jan. 18, 1818, Recs. of Cherokee Agency in Tennessee, 1801–1835 (M208, Reel 7).

14. Calhoun to Thomas L. McKenney, Dec. 12, 1817, in Hemphill and Meriwether, *Papers of Calhoun,* 2: 32; Calhoun to McMinn, Mar. 16, 1818, Calhoun to Meigs, May 11, 1818, Lets. Sent by Sec. of War Relating to Indian Affairs, 1800–24 (M15, Reel 4).

15. Calhoun to McMinn, Mar. 16, 1818, ibid.; James Monroe, "Talk to the Cherokee Deputation of the Arkansas," Mar. 7, 1818, in Hemphill and Meriwether, *Papers of Calhoun*, 2: 180–81.

16. Donald Braider, *Solitary Star: A Biography of Sam Houston* (New York: G. P. Putnam's Sons, 1974), 44–46; Campbell, *Sam Houston and the American Southwest*, 9–10; Houston, *Life of General Sam Houston*, 3; Houston to Jackson, Dec. 6, 1818, AJHC.

17. Ibid.; Houston, *Life of General Sam Houston,* 3; Braider, *Solitary Star,* 45–46; Houston to Daniel Parker, Mar. 1, 1818, in Williams and Barker, *Writings of Sam Houston,* 1: 8. Houston was later paid $645.60 for the six months he served as subagent. He requested reimbursement for additional expenses totaling $170.09, but as late as 1822 he had not been paid. In a letter to Calhoun on July 6, 1822, Houston inferred that this was a result of Calhoun's "prejudice" against him. Referring to the events of 1818, Houston wrote, "I had hoped that all these matters would have rested, inasmuch, as the end intended was not realized; I know it well; it was to oblige a Senator—secure his interest, and crush a Sub-Agent." No record has been found of Houston getting this money. Calhoun to William H. Crawford, Mar. 4, 1818, in Hemphill and Meriwether, *Papers of Calhoun,* 2: 174; Houston to Calhoun, July 6, 1822, in Williams and Barker, *Writings of Sam Houston*, 1: 12.

18. Calhoun to McMinn, Mar. 16, 1818, in Hemphill and Meriwether, *Papers of Calhoun,* 2: 194; McMinn to Calhoun, Feb. 19, 1818, Recs. of Cherokee Agency in Tennessee, 1801–1835 (M208, Reel 7).

19. Houston, "Indian Matters," *Arkansas Gazette*, Dec. 8, 1830, in Williams and Barker, *Writings of Sam Houston*, 1: 182.

20. Jackson to Calhoun, Sept. 30, 1819, Jan. 17, 1820, Hemphill and Meriwether, *Papers of Calhoun,* 4: 581.

21. Houston, "Resignation as Governor of Tennessee," Apr. 16, 1829, Houston to Jackson, May 11, 1829, in Williams and Barker, *Writings of Sam Houston,* 1: 131–34; M. K. Wisehart, *Sam Houston: American Giant* (Washington: Robert B. Luce, 1962), 53.

22. Houston, "In Defense of the Indians," *Arkansas Gazette,* Aug. 14, 1830, in Williams and Barker, *Writings of Sam Houston,* 1: 164–70.

23. Wisehart, *Sam Houston: American Giant,* 53–55; Llerena Friend, *Sam Houston: The Great Designer* (Austin: University of Texas Press,

1954), 24–26; Marquis James, *The Raven: A Biography of Sam Houston* (1929; repr., New York: Macmillan Publishing Company, 1990), 106–16.

24. Houston, "Tah-Lohn-Tus-Ky on the Indians," *Arkansas Gazette*, June 22, 1830, in Williams and Barker, *Writings of Sam Houston*, 1:155–63; James, *The Raven,* 95–102.

25. Houston, "In Defense of the Indians," *Arkansas Gazette*, Aug. 14, 1830, in Williams and Barker, *Writings of Sam Houston,* 1: 164–70.

26. Houston to Jackson, Sept. 19, 1829, Houston to Jackson, n.d. [*ca.* 1830], in Williams and Barker, *Writings of Sam Houston*, 1: 140–43, 146–47; James, *The Raven,* 113.

27. Ibid., 135–36.

28. Houston to John Van Fossen, Apr. 4, 1830, in Williams and Barker, *Writings of Sam Houston,* 1: 147–48; James, *The Raven,* 135.

29. Houston to John Eaton, June 13, 1830, in Williams and Barker, *Writings of Sam Houston,* 1: 152–53.

30. The five articles written by Houston for the *Arkansas Gazette* were printed on June 22, July 7, Aug. 14, Sept. 8, and Dec. 8, 1830. All are reproduced in Williams and Barker, *Writings of Sam Houston,* 1:155–85; James, *The Raven,* 149.

31. Houston to Van Fossen, Aug. 22, 1830, in Williams and Barker, *Writings of Sam Houston,* 1: 187; Fred W. Allsopp, *History of the Arkansas Press for a Hundred Years and More* (Little Rock: Parke-Harper Publishing Company, 1922), 41–49.

32. Houston, "The Creek Indians," *Arkansas Gazette*, July 7, 1830, in Williams and Barker, *Writings of Sam Houston,* 1: 161–62; Robert M. Kvasnicka and Herman J. Viola, eds., *The Commissioners of Indian Affairs, 1824–1977* (Lincoln: University of Nebraska Press, 1979), 1–15.

33. Houston to Jackson, n.d. [*ca.* 1830], in Williams and Barker, *Writings of Sam Houston,* 1: 146.

34. For a discussion of Houston's suspected plans to lead an insurrection in Texas, see Gregory and Strickland, *Sam Houston with the Cherokees,* 137–54; Charles Edwards Lester, *The Life of Sam Houston: The Only Authentic Memoir of Him Ever Published* (New York: J. C. Derby, 1855), 65. On the fight with William Stanbery, see Haley, *Sam Houston*, 81–87.

35. Grant Foreman, *Pioneer Days in the Early Southwest* (1926; repr., Lincoln: University of Nebraska Press, 1994), 200–2; Houston to Lewis Cass, July 30, 1833, in Williams and Barker, *Writings of Sam Houston,* 2: 15–17.

36. Foreman, *Pioneer Days,* 200–3; Houston to Indian Commissioners at Fort Gibson, Feb. 13, 1833, Houston to Jackson, Feb. 13, 1833, Houston to Cass, July 31, 1833, in Williams and Barker, *Writings of Sam Houston,* 1: 272, 274, 276.

37. John Galvin, ed., *Through the Country of the Comanche Indians in the Fall of the Year 1845: The Journal of a U. S. Army Expedition Led by Lieutenant James W. Abert of the Topographical Engineers* (San Francisco: John Howell Books, 1970), 68.

38. For a concise account of the Republic of Texas' Indian policy, see Randolph B. Campbell, *Gone to Texas: A History of the Lone Star State* (2nd ed.; New York and Oxford: Oxford University Press, 2012), 157–84.

39. For a detailed analysis of Texas's Indian policy, see Anna Muckleroy, "The Indian Policy of the Republic of Texas, Parts 1, 2, 3, 4," *Southwestern Historical Quarterly* 25, 26 (Apr./July/ Oct. 1922, Jan. 1923).

40. Muckleroy, "Indian Policy of the Republic, Part 3," *Southwestern Historical Quarterly* 26 (Oct. 1922): 148.

41. Friend, *Sam Houston: Great Designer,* 95–96.

42. Houston, "To the Texas Congress," Dec. 14, 1844, in Williams and Barker, *Writings of Sam Houston,* 4: 392–98.

43. *Telegraph and Texas Register* (Houston), Dec. 10, 1845.

44. Prucha, *Great Father,* 94–111.

45. Houston, "Opposing the Nebraska-Kansas Bill," Mar. 3, 1854, in Williams and Barker, *Writings of Sam Houston,* 5: 504–22.

46. Ibid. 5: 520.

47. Ibid. 5: 518–20; Houston, "A Synopsis of a Speech at Nacogdoches," May 11, 1855, in Williams and Barker, *Writings of Sam Houston,* 6: 180–84.

48. Houston, "Opposing the Kansas-Nebraska Bill," Feb. 14, 1854, in Williams and Barker, *Writings of Sam Houston,* 5: 469–502.

49. Houston, "On an Increase of the Army, and the Indian Policy of the Government," Jan. 29, 31, 1855, in Williams and Barker, *Writings of Sam Houston,* 6: 111–56. For a list of the numerous occasions that Houston argued against waging war on Indians, see Williams and Barker, *Writings of Sam Houston,* 5: 155, note 2.

Stephen F. Austin, Portrait by William Howard, 1833. Courtesy of Dolph Briscoe Center for American History, The University of Texas at Austin

Stephen F. Austin's Views on Slavery in Early Texas

Andrew J. Torget

In 1830, Stephen F. Austin made a bold declaration to a group of potential settlers from Alabama who were interested in moving to Texas. "I am of the opinion," he informed them, "that Texas will never become a Slave state or country." Such sentiments might have struck his Alabama audience as strange, since Austin had spent the majority of the previous decade doing everything in his power to ensure the passage of proslavery laws in Mexico. Yet Austin now insisted that slavery would never take firm root within Texas, and that was for the best. Who, he asked, could "seriously wish that slavery should be entailed upon this country?" Before long, however, Austin reversed himself, and he began advocating once again for the long-term preservation of slavery in Texas. In 1833 Austin proclaimed that "Texas *must be* a slave country. Circumstances and unavoidable necessity compels it. It is the wish of the people there, and it is my duty to do all I can, prudently, in favor of it. I will do so."[1]

Who was the real Stephen F. Austin, the would-be antislavery advocate or the fierce defender of the rights of slaveholders? Historians have long struggled to reconcile the different voices of Austin on the matter. In his monumental 1925 biography of Austin, Eugene C. Barker carefully explored Austin's handling of the slavery issue throughout the 1820s and 1830s, as well as nearly every other aspect of Austin's public life. For Barker, Austin's perspective on slavery shifted in response to changing political circumstances in Mexico, as the *empresario* regularly recalibrated his approach to slavery in order to ensure the survival and success of his Texas colonies. The Austin that appeared in Barker's book was a shrewdly calculating man, and so Barker portrayed Austin's perspective on slavery as something that would shift whenever necessary. Gregg Cantrell, in contrast, delved far deeper into the private side of Austin in his excellent 1999 biography, arguing that Austin remained conflicted about the institution throughout his life. Austin, according to Cantrell, "knew that slavery was wrong" and so Austin's occasional pronouncements against slavery revealed the *empresario's* personal antipathy toward the institution. Austin's more frequent endorsements of slavery, Cantrell argued, reflected instead the *empresario's* practical capitulation to the era's "nearly irresistible social, economic, and political pressures to preserve and defend the institution." Randolph B. Campbell, in his ground-breaking study of slavery in Texas, argues that Austin was likely more committed to the institution than Barker claimed and less conflicted about it than Cantrell argues. In Campbell's telling, Austin emerges as a man who backed away from slavery only when it threatened his colonization project, and who ultimately "did more than any other individual to establish slavery in Mexican Texas."[2]

Despite their debates about Austin's personal convictions, most historians tend to agree with Campbell's judgment that Austin—more than anyone—played the central role in ensuring that slaveholders and enslaved people came to Texas during the 1820s and early 1830s. And the truth is that we will likely never have more than the most vague understanding of what Austin thought to himself during quiet moments about such complex matters as slavery and the enslaved. We can, however, build a detailed and nuanced portrait of how and why Austin conducted his public battles over the institution in the ways that he did. Reading through Austin's correspondence from the era reveals that there was almost no other issue that so consumed his discussions with Mexican officials as slavery. There was almost nothing that potential American colonists pestered him about in more detail than questions of the institution's future in Mexico. If we want to understand the development of the early Anglo colonies in Texas, then, we need to understand Austin's role at the center of discussions between Mexicans and Americans over slavery's future in North America. And the key to understanding Austin's views on slavery, it turns out, is to step back and look at them within the larger context of the world in which Austin lived, and the *empresario's* enduring conviction that, in the words of Gregg Cantrell, "the economic development of Texas depended on commercial agriculture, primarily cotton."[3]

Austin came to Texas during a period of momentous change in North America, when the rise of a new global cotton economy was reshaping both the continent and the larger Atlantic World. The seeds of this far-reaching change had been sown during the 1770s, when English manufacturers began experimenting with cotton as a cheaper, more durable, more comfortable alternative to wool. They soon discovered that cotton cloth could sell remarkably well in both domestic and European markets. Yet, for several decades, nothing happened because separating the seed from the fiber by hand was so labor-intensive as to make it unprofitable, and British industrialists thus found themselves unable to find a reliable supplier of raw cotton. Then, during the 1790s, the invention of various machines to remove seeds from cotton mechanically—to "gin" them—changed everything. Cotton suddenly became highly profitable, and American farmers rushed to produce the crop for the English market. Almost overnight new plantations sprang up across South Carolina, Georgia, and the Mississippi River Valley. From 1794 to 1800 virtually every tobacco planter in the territory around Natchez, Mississippi, converted his farm to cotton, and in only six years the Natchez District increased its cotton production from 36,000 pounds annually to more than 1.2 million.[4]

Nothing compared, however, to the explosive transformation that cotton wrought on the northern coast of the Gulf of Mexico during the 1810s, when a series of favorable circumstances converged to set off a frenzied land rush. With the defeat of the Creek Indians during the War of 1812, the United States federal government opened up fourteen million acres of prime Gulf Coast cotton lands (an area equal to half of modern-day Alabama) for public purchase at rock-bottom prices. Because several new strands of hybrid cotton seeds—which produced bigger bolls that were easier to pick—had also recently become available, each of those acres promised farmers more profit than ever. The tipping point came, however, when the market price for cotton doubled to nearly thirty cents per pound during the mid-1810s, making the crop more valuable than almost any other commodity in the Atlantic World. The result was one of the largest migrations in North American history, as hundreds of thousands of Americans hurdled themselves into the Gulf Coast territories to establish cotton farms and plantations. By the late 1810s, the combined populations of Louisiana, Mississippi, and Alabama bulged past 370,000, while the production of cotton in the region exploded. The number of cotton bales exported by the United States increased tenfold during the 1810s, and by 1820 the southern United States surpassed India as the world's leading cotton producer. The result was nothing less than the transformation of the Gulf Coast of North America into the epicenter of the international cotton economy, turning the southern United States into one of the most profitable places in the world.[5]

This was the world in which Austin lived when he began his Texas venture, and Austin saw his colonies as a natural extension of the expanding cotton frontier. Because Texas shared the same long growing season, rich soils, and ready access to Gulf Coast shipping ports that made Mississippi acreage so appealing (a point made repeatedly by

United States newspapers during the late 1810s) Austin believed that farmers who found themselves priced out of the American land market would take a chance on cotton lands in Texas. He was betting his entire colonial enterprise, in fact, on the idea that he could entice hundreds—perhaps thousands—of American farmers to abandon the United States for Mexico if he could offer them far more cotton land at far better prices than they could get in Mississippi or Alabama. The spectacular rise of cotton prices had transformed Gulf Coast acreage into a highly valuable commodity, and by the late 1810s the best cotton lands in the United States sold at auction for $50 an acre.[6] When the Panic of 1819 put most of those acres beyond the financial reach of small-time American farmers, Austin recognized a remarkable opportunity. And because he would be granted his own large tracts of lands—which he could then resell to new migrants—Austin hoped that by redirecting the American cotton frontier into northern Mexico he could make himself a wealthy man.

For Austin, then, the success of his colonies depended upon creating the right conditions for cotton planters to succeed in the region. This required the establishment of the necessary infrastructure to support the industry, and Austin petitioned repeatedly to both the Coahuila-Texas legislature and the governor of the state for the authority to establish a seaport near the colonies for exporting cotton. The *empresario* worked to build connections with businessmen in New York and New Orleans, hoping to use the promise of Texas cotton as collateral with merchants to obtain equipment and ships needed to connect his settlements to the markets. He advertised in newspapers across the American South about the agricultural promise of Texas soil, courted wealthy planters with promises of vast acreage, and encouraged his early settlers to import the machinery necessary to prepare their crops for shipment to New Orleans, New York, and Liverpool. Austin's brother and cousin even set up a partnership to erect a cotton gin along the banks of the Brazos River to process colonists' crops into processed bales. Yet Austin believed—and said, repeatedly, to anyone who would listen—that nothing would be more central to establishing a cotton empire in Texas than the institution of slavery. "The primary product that will elevate us from poverty is Cotton," Austin explained to a Tejano friend, "and we cannot do this without the help of slaves."[7]

For the overwhelming majority of white Americans of the era, like Austin, slavery was considered the indispensable engine for running a successful cotton economy. When cotton fever prompted American farmers to begin pouring into the Mississippi River Valley during the

1810s, they brought with them tens of thousands of enslaved people to work their new plantations. As demand for cotton boomed, so did the enslaved populations of Alabama, Mississippi, and Louisiana. By 1820, the combined slave populations of those states approached 150,000—every third person in Alabama was enslaved, while nearly half of Louisianans were.[8] Although cotton could be grown profitably without slaves (and often was on small family farms throughout the southern United States), most white Americans believed that only slave labor could enable plantations to achieve the scale that would make a man wealthy. And so white men of all classes—whether they already owned slaves or not—hoped to buy enslaved people for their farms, creating voracious new markets for slaves along the Gulf Coast. Even for those who objected to the morality of the institution—and Austin said, several times, that he did—slavery was considered by many white Americans to be an economic necessity in the world that cotton had made.

Knowing that slavery was, for his potential colonists, inseparable from the cotton economy, Austin wove the institution into every aspect of his colonial enterprise. Austin, for example, put incentives aimed directly at slaveholders into his land distribution policy and advertised them widely across the southern United States. The head of each family settling in his colony would receive a large tract of land—the specific number of acres would change several times, but eventually most farmers were eligible for 4,428—and would also receive additional acreage for every dependent they brought with them. A man could get an additional 200 acres for bringing his wife, 100 for every child, and 50 for every enslaved person he transported into Texas. The idea was to encourage Americans to bring their entire families into Mexico, and to provide a premium to slaveholders willing to make the journey. Austin sent these terms to his partner in New Orleans, Joseph Hawkins, so they could be published in the New Orleans newspapers. Once news of cheap cotton lands in Mexico began appearing in the Louisiana papers, Austin anticipated that word would soon spread across the American South. "I hope the newspapers in Mississippi, Tennessee, Kentucky and Missouri, will republish," he wrote to Hawkins. Within weeks, Austin's advertisements found their way into newspapers across the southern United States. In one reprinted letter, Austin laid out a hypothetical scenario to illustrate the vast land grants he would make to colonists. "A married man with two children and ten slaves would receive 1360 acres of land" for farming, he bragged, "and 2840 acres for a vachery, making together 4200 acres of land besides a town lot." Austin's letters offered American farmers, particularly those with slaves, far more land in Mexico than they could ever hope to own in the United States.[9]

The idea was to attract well-heeled planters from places like Mississippi and Alabama, people like Jared Groce, one of Austin's earliest settlers and the largest slaveholder in the colony. A Virginian by birth, Groce had meandered through South Carolina and Georgia, accumulating a large stock of enslaved men and women along the way, before ending up in Alabama in 1818 during the cotton rush to the Gulf Coast. Like many Americans, Groce had been impressed with newspaper reports of Austin's glowing descriptions of the agricultural promise of Mexican Texas. Determined to claim his share of Mexico's cotton lands, Groce drove his ninety slaves westward in a convoy of fifty wagons toward Mexico. After a stopover in New Orleans to purchase farming supplies, the caravan rolled through Nacogdoches along the San Antonio Road before arriving at the Brazos River in January 1822. Christening the tract of land he claimed "Bernardo," Groce ordered his ninety slaves to build cabins for their master and themselves, and to begin planting a cotton crop with seed they brought from Alabama.[10]

No other colonist brought as many slaves as Groce, although most came from the same portion of the United States. From 1825 to 1831, Austin recorded the names of each state his colonists abandoned on their way into northeastern Mexico. Nearly 90 percent came from the slaveholding regions of the United States, with Louisiana, Alabama, and Arkansas accounting for more than half of the settlers. Austin's advertisements, as he expected, had clearly resonated among white southerners in ways they simply did not among white northerners. Although most of these people—like most white families along the American cotton frontier—owned no slaves, the vast majority listed themselves as farmers and hoped to raise cotton. And a significant proportion of the colonists did bring enslaved people into Mexico territory. Those who imported slaves usually could afford only a few, such as William Rabb and Thomas Bell who each brought one enslaved person into the colony. Others had more means, such as Alexander Jackson (who had four slaves), James Ross (six slaves), and Benjamin Beeson (seven slaves). By 1825, only three years after American settlers began arriving in Texas, a census of Austin's colony revealed that a full quarter of the population was enslaved. Large slaveholders, such as Groce, accounted for a significant portion of those slaves, with eleven elite families in the colony holding an average of twenty-five slaves each. The majority of slaveholders had far fewer, with most families owning about three slaves.[11]

More families in Austin's colony depended on enslaved labor than the raw population numbers alone would suggest. Colonists with an abundance of slaves, such as Groce, profited on their human property by leasing slaves to settlers without the means to purchase their own. This practice expanded the ranks of those with access to enslaved labor, as well as the investment of non-slaveholders in the institution's preservation. A settler named Churchill Fulshear, for example, approached Groce in 1824 in hopes of leasing one of his slaves. Fulshear needed a slave to cut and split fence rails, most likely to fence in crop fields, and he offered Groce $20 to cover the "Two or three months" he imagined the job would require. Although Austin was fond of telling Mexican officials that he owned no slaves himself (in fact, he did from time to time), the *empresario* regularly relied on enslaved labor that he contracted from other slaveholders. In 1823, Austin leased from Groce the rights to Sally, Jack, and Kelly for $38 a month, and the following year he leased Lucy, Patsy, Elsy, and Henry from Thomas Westhall for $180. In a letter to his sister, Austin succinctly described how people in the colony without slaves—such as he and his brother, James "Brown" Austin—dealt with ongoing labor needs. "Neither of us own any negroes and have to depend on hiring," he explained. The practice of leasing slaves, personified in the colony's *empresario*, enabled many of his non-slaveholding colonists to take advantage of enslaved labor, thus extending the reach of the institution well beyond the ranks of those wealthy enough to purchase their own slaves.[12]

With the institution playing such a central role in the economic life of the colony, Austin did everything he could throughout the 1820s to ensure that slavery would remain legal in northern Mexico. The *empresario* promulgated a legal code for his colony in January 1824 that demonstrated the extent to which slavery made up a significant portion of the settlement's business. Intending his code as a means for providing stability to the colony, Austin addressed issues he felt most likely to cause problems: murder, theft, robbery, assault, slander, drunkenness, immorality, gambling, horse racing, and counterfeiting. The legal issues concerning slavery merited special consideration—only Indian relations occupied as much of the code—and Austin sought to establish security in enslaved property by instituting harsh deterrents. Anyone who harbored a runaway slave could be fined $500 and sentenced to hard labor; anyone who stole slaves or helped them escape risked a $1,000 fine and hard labor. Slaves who stole would receive as many as a hundred lashes of the whip. Any enslaved person found off their plantation without a pass was to be tied up, whipped, and returned to their master. And no one could trade with a slave without the permission of their master, lest such commerce encourage slaves to steal. The code itself was a clever mix of Spanish and English legal traditions, although its articles concerning slavery were thoroughly American. While the provisions for punishing slaves codified practices common in the southern United States, they violated Spanish precedents and Mexican laws, which dictated that slaves receive the same punishment as free men.[13]

Austin sought to provide a sound legal foundation for slavery in his colony because he received a steady stream of letters from potential colonists in the southern United States asking about the status of slavery in Mexico. His entire enterprise depended upon the steady movement of Americans into the region, and many migrants made clear that the absence of a full-throated endorsement of slavery by the Mexican government would prevent numerous farmers from abandoning the securities of the United States. "Three months ago I received more than one hundred letters from individuals in that country, well-known men of character, asking for reports about whether the Government would allow the free entry of Emigrants, and especially if they can bring in their Slaves," Austin reported in late 1824. In one of those letters, an Alabama planter named Charles Douglas warned Austin that "our most valuable inhabitants here own negroes" and "our planters are not willing to remove without they can first be assured of their being secured to them by the laws of your Govt." James Phelps sent a similar report to Austin from his home in western Mississippi. "Nothing appears at present, to prevent a portion of our wealthy planters from emigrating immediately to the province of Texas," Phelps wrote, "but the uncertainty now prevailing with regard to the subject of slavery." Even settlers already within the colony sent Austin similar pleas, telling the *empresario* that their compatriots in the United States would not join them without assurances that their slaveholdings would be secure in Mexico. If Austin wished for his colony to fill up with Americans, advised Randall Jones, a settler already in the colony, "nothing would facilitate that more than the admission of Slavery in this state."[14]

Most of that uncertainty was due to persistent antislavery rhetoric emanating from various parts of Mexico during the 1820s. As Mexicans began to build their nation from the rubble of New Spain, there was a widely held desire during the early years following independence to abolish slavery. For some, antislavery convictions grew out of the fervor of the revolution itself, as calls for freedom and independence pushed many to advocate for a more equal and equitable society. For others, there were numerous practical reasons for Mexico to outlaw slavery.

While slavery had been an important part of the Mexican economy during the sixteenth century, by the early 1800s Indian labor (often in the form of debt-peonage) provided most of the country's labor needs. Abolishing slavery, therefore, would require no meaningful sacrifice on the part of Mexico's industry, agriculture, or trade. Such a ban could, however, pay important dividends on the international political stage. England—which, at the time, was both the dominant global power and the biggest foreign investor in Mexico's economy—was actively working to disrupt the international slave trade, and Mexico would do well to avoid conflicts with the English over an institution that appeared to have little salience for the national economy. Most Mexicans, as a result, would have agreed with Juan Francisco Azcárate's declaration from the floor of the new Mexican congress that "there is not a better moment than this to prohibit slavery in the Mexican Empire."[15]

During the first years of his colony, Austin spent more time lobbying in favor of slavery than anything else in his efforts to secure support from Mexico City for his colonial enterprise. When Mexico's national congress took up the question of sanctioning Anglo colonization, most legislators recognized the strategic importance of populating Texas quickly and thus approved—if reluctantly—Austin's efforts to bring American farmers into Mexican territory. Many legislators, however, wanted his colonists to build their new farms without enslaved labor, forcing Austin to meet with congressmen personally to explain the interlaced connections between cotton farming and slavery. "I talked to each individual member of the junta of the necessity which existed in Texas, Santander, and all the other unpopulated provinces for the new colonists to bring slaves," Austin reported from Mexico City. Although Austin's frenzied efforts helped ensure that slavery would not be outlawed when the national colonization laws passed, the matter arose once more when Mexicans began writing their new constitution in 1823. As numerous Mexican statesmen spoke out against slavery, Austin again went on the offensive, arguing forcefully in numerous petitions that preserving slavery in Texas was indispensable to the successful development of the region. Erasmo Seguin, the Texas representative at the constitutional debates, received notes from Austin begging him to use "all your protection and influence" to ensure that Americans "could bring and keep their slaves" in northeastern Mexico. "They cannot emigrate without bringing them," Austin informed his Tejano ally.[16]

In his efforts to preserve slavery, Austin relied heavily on the Tejano leadership in San Antonio, who largely shared his ideas about the institution's necessity in a cotton economy. In the eyes of most Tejanos, the greatest challenge facing northeastern Mexico was the absence of any sizeable non-Indian population. The Comanches, along with numerous other tribes, had long controlled the region, frequently battering the weak outposts of San Antonio and La Bahía with violent and bloody raids. Without more people there could be no security in the region, no growth of Tejano commerce or trade, and no means for developing places like San Antonio into prosperous towns. The promise of attaining that population and security through the colonization of expatriate Americans thus had a strong appeal, and seemed to offer Tejanos their only realistic option for transforming Texas into a flourishing part of the Mexican nation. That these Americans would come from the southern United States and would therefore bring slaves with them proved a far lesser concern for Tejano leaders than the dire necessity of finding a way to stabilize the region and grow its economy. As one Tejano later explained to Austin, "I cannot help seeing the advantages which, to my way of thinking, would result if we admitted hard-working people, regardless of what country they come from . . . even hell itself." The Tejano leadership in San Antonio thus embraced Austin's perspective about the role that slavery needed to play in developing the region and became ardent supporters of allowing the institution to continue in Mexico.[17]

Austin needed all the political support he could muster. When Mexico's national constitution was published in 1824, it delegated difficult issues of colonization and slavery to the individual states to decide for themselves. Because the Mexican congress had also grafted Texas onto its more populous neighbor Coahuila—creating the state of Coahuila y Texas—the future of slavery in the region would now be determined in the Coahuilan capital of Saltillo, where the new state legislature gathered in 1826 to write a new state constitution. Word soon reached Austin that an antislavery bloc of Coahuila legislators planned to introduce a provision known as Article 13, which sought the unequivocal end to slavery in the region: "The state prohibits absolutely and for all time slavery in all its territory, and slaves that already reside in the state will be free from the day of the publication of the constitution in this capital." Austin, in concert with the Tejano leadership in San Antonio, moved quickly to pressure legislators in Saltillo to back away from abolition as a grave threat to continued Anglo migration into Texas, dispatching his brother, Brown Austin, to take their case personally to the state congress.[18]

The debates over slavery in Saltillo, which raged during the fall of 1826 and spring of 1827, forced the *empresario* to articulate his ideas about slavery and Texas in revealing ways. While Austin offered every defense he could conceive of to dissuade legislators from abolishing the institution, his central argument was that any attack on slavery would undermine American migration into Texas. "I made efforts to persuade rich men who owned slaves to emigrate because with them the country would make swift progress," he protested. "I told them that the Government would never take away slaves brought by them for their own use." "What would the world say," asked the *empresario*, "if in direct violation of that law and that guarantee, the Government were to take away that property from those colonists against their will?" Such an act would, he asserted, drastically undermine the new government's credibility and "the mistrust which is certain to follow will destroy all hope of further emigration."[19] The crux of the matter, for Austin, was that a ban on slavery would end American migration into his Mexican colony. Without guarantees that their slaveholdings would be respected by Mexican authorities, Austin believed that American farmers would choose to remain in the United States where they were assured of their property rights in slaves. Virtually free land in Mexico, Austin feared, would simply have no appeal to cotton planters in the United States if slavery did not remain legal in the region.

After months of persistent lobbying by both Austin and the Tejanos, the Saltillo congress finally passed a constitution that preserved the institution in the short-term while also providing for its ultimate demise. The revised version of Article 13 stipulated that slaves already in Texas would remain enslaved for life, and colonists would be permitted to bring new slaves into the region for another six months. At the close of the six-month window, however, migrants could bring no new slaves into Texas, and the children of those already enslaved would be considered free citizens of Mexico upon their birth. Although they had succeeded in avoiding immediate emancipation, Article 13 promised to end all further immigration of planters like Jared Groce to the Anglo colonies. Searching desperately for a way around the ban, Austin came up with a scheme to ask the Saltillo legislature for a new law guaranteeing that labor contracts signed in foreign countries would also be honored in Mexico. Although the proposal sounded innocent (which was necessary in order to pass the legislature), its underlying intent was more sinister: to create a legal loophole that would enable American slaveholders to force their slaves into ninety-nine-year labor contracts, thereby allowing slavery to continue in Texas under the name of indentured servitude. Austin sent his proposal to the Tejano leaders in San Antonio, and José Antonio Navarro and José Miguel de Arciniega, the Tejano representatives in Saltillo, brought it before the legislature. When the law passed as Decree 56 on May 5, 1828, Austin hoped it would reopen the gates of Texas to cotton farmers in the United States.[20]

Austin's words and deeds during both the national and state debates over slavery's future in Mexico demonstrate the remarkable depth of the *empresario's* commitment to slavery as a necessary means for supporting his colony. Preserving the institution was, for him, absolutely indispensable to ensuring the continued migration that served as the foundation for his entire colonial enterprise. He almost never defended slavery as inherently good for the enslaved people themselves, as some of his counterparts in the southern United States were beginning to do. The preservation of slavery was, instead, a necessary precondition for him to ensure that his cotton lands in Mexico could compete on the open market with similar lands in Mississippi and Alabama. So many of Austin's concerns about antislavery debates and legislation in Mexico therefore tended not to be about how such measures would affect the plantations already in operation in his colony. Rather, the *empresario* focused instead on how such matters would be covered and *perceived* in U. S. newspapers, where they could discourage further migration. In Austin's eyes, threats against slavery in Texas were primarily threats against American migration into Mexico. And if he needed to thwart the will of the state congress by passing a deceitful labor law in order to preserve slavery—and thus migration—into his colony, Austin was more than willing to do it.

The intricate connection between cotton and migration that lay at the base of Austin's attitude toward slavery can perhaps be seen most clearly in how he reacted to a challenge to the American cotton industry shortly after the Saltillo slavery debates. In May 1828, the United States Congress enacted a tariff aimed at protecting manufacturing and industry in their northeastern states from competition with British-made goods. Furious cotton farmers in the southern United States immediately protested the measure, dubbing it the "Tariff of Abominations," largely out of fear that the British would respond by cutting back on imports of American cotton. Reading about these debates in the newspapers, Austin became convinced that trade disputes between England and the United States could open the door for Texas farmers to displace U. S. planters as the primary cotton supplier to British textile mills. In lengthy proposals to the president of Mexico, his senator in the national congress, the minister of foreign relations, the commandant of the eastern interior provinces, and the governor of Coahuila-Texas, Austin proclaimed that "Mexican cotton can fill the void in the English market caused by the exclusion of the United States" and suggested that "the arrival of a single ship in Liverpool loaded with good-quality Mexican cotton would have a huge influence." Now was the time, Austin urged, for the government to put policies into place to foster a highly profitable cotton industry that would benefit all of Mexico. "It seems to me that the Mexican nation can take great advantage of this fight between those two nations," the *empresario* advised, "if it can encourage the Mexican people to dedicate themselves to growing cotton."[21]

For Austin, that meant Texas had an unprecedented opportunity to become a more appealing place to grow cotton than the southern United States and therefore open the floodgates to a new rush of American farmers eager for Mexican land. In a letter to the governor of Coahuila-Texas, Austin outlined various measures he believed necessary for Mexico to adopt in order to overtake the United States in supplying the British textile market: promote the rapid populating of Anglo colonies in Texas, allow for duty-free importation of cotton gins and baling equipment, and establish a trade agreement with England "favorable to the interests of the cotton farmers." The linchpin of Austin's plan, of course, was lifting the existing restrictions on slavery in the region. "Only article 13 of our constitution is preventing many wealthy and powerful people from moving to Texas," Austin informed the governor, insisting that "the only thing needed to promote the new Texas settlements is a Government act to repeal law 18 regarding slaves and suspend article 13 from the constitution for 10 years." If the government were to implement such policies, thus opening northeastern Mexico to an exodus of disgruntled American farmers looking for a new place to grow cotton for export to England, Austin promised that "in a very few years the State of Coahuila and Texas will have more wealth and trade than any other state in the entire Mexican federation."[22]

Rather than moving to endorse cotton and American migration, however, the national government of Mexico began challenging both slavery and colonization in alarming new legislation. In September 1829, President Vicente Guerrero suddenly declared an end to slavery throughout all of Mexico, promising to "free those who until today had been considered slaves." The result was a political firestorm in northern Mexico, as officials in both Saltillo and San Antonio refused to publish or enforce the decree. Protesting that Guerrero's proclamation was an egregious violation of the property rights of Texas slaveholders, Tejanos warned officials at the state and national level that any attempt to enforce it would lead to armed revolt among the Anglos. Bending under such pressure, Guerrero eventually rescinded his order for Texas.[23]

A more far-reaching challenge came, however, when Mexico City issued an outright ban on all future American immigration into Mexico with the law of April 6, 1830. In response to alarming reports that the Anglo presence in eastern Texas was growing beyond the ability of Mexico to control it, the national congress moved forcefully to strengthen Mexico City's control over Texas. While it granted Mexico's president the authority to establish new military posts in the region (as well as take various other measures "for the security of the Republic"), the most controversial portions of the new law sought to end all immigration from the United States into Mexico. "It is prohibited that emigrants from nations bordering on this Republic shall settle in the states or territory adjacent to their own nation," read the law's eleventh article, which also suspended all ongoing *empresario* contracts "not already completed." Because the illegal importation of enslaved people as indentured servants supported American migration into Texas, the law also mandated that "the government of each state shall most strictly enforce the colonization laws and prevent the further introduction of slaves." The law of April 6, 1830, was a sweeping reassertion of national control over colonization in Texas by cutting off the Anglo settlements from their connections to the United States.[24]

News of the law sent Austin into the depths of depression. He had lost his brother and closest confidant to yellow fever only months before. The *empresario* himself was then struck down by malaria, which confined him to bed on the edge of death for nearly a month. When word of the April 6 law arrived, Austin found himself struggling along the edge of mental and physical exhaustion during one of the lowest periods of his life. Anastacio Bustamante, Mexico's president, tried to reassure Austin in a letter of his continued goodwill toward the colonies despite the new restrictions. Austin was cordial in reply, but minced no words in protesting that the purpose of the law of April 6 "seems to be to destroy in one blow the happiness and prosperity of this colony which Your Excellency has always protected." Austin sent similar missives to officials in northeastern Mexico, perhaps hoping for another stand by state officials against Mexico City, but received little back in terms of hope or encouragement. "I do not know what to tell you," Ramón Músquiz told the *empresario*, "except to agree with your opinion and have the displeasure of informing you that it is now impossible to do anything to counteract the proposed law, which is bound to retard the growth of Texas."[25]

The national government's renewed efforts to halt the immigration of Americans and their slaves into Mexico—particularly in the wake of Guerrero's emancipation decree—prompted an exhausted Austin to temporarily abandon hope of securing from Mexico City sanctions for slavery in Texas. And so Austin began experimenting with the idea of perhaps ending enslavement in Texas as a means of saving his colonial enterprise. "I have always been opposed from principle to slavery," he announced in a letter he drafted to the Mexican secretary of state, Lucas Alamán, with obvious disregard for his previous endorsements of the institution. "As far as my influence extends I shall forever oppose slavery in Texas." Austin ultimately decided against sending the letter (perhaps he was not yet ready to make such definitive statements to Alamán), but the *empresario* began testing the idea of a slave-free Texas in correspondence with friends. Slavery had been a necessary evil during the beginning of his settlement, he now argued, but the future prosperity of the region now necessitated "the perpetual exclusion of slavery from this country."[26]

It is important to note that Austin made clear that his new-found opposition to the institution did not come from any moral concern for the rights of people of African descent. His sudden reservations about slavery, he insisted, sprang instead from fears that the black population in Texas might one day outnumber and overtake the white population. The massive slave revolt that had overthrown French power on the Caribbean island of Saint-Domingue (modern-day Haiti) provided a terrifying example to white Americans like Austin of the dangers that came with a rapidly expanding black population. To illustrate, he asked some planters in Alabama to calculate the likely increase of both black and white populations in slave states by 1910. "Compare the two sums," he advised, "and then suppose that you will be alive at the period above mentioned, that you have a long-cherished and beloved wife, a number of daughters, grand daughters, and great grand daughters." Although it would surely be in the economic interest of white Texans to preserve slavery, Austin warned that those same slaves might one day rise up against whites in a violent race war: "Satan entered the sacred garden in the shape of a serpent—if he is allowed to enter Texas in the shape of negros it will share the fate of Eden."[27]

Austin's flirtation with the idea of a slave-free Texas proved short-lived because he utterly failed to convince his fellow colonists. S. Rhoads Fisher, a recent emigrant from Pennsylvania, rejected the proposition as hopeless and unattainable fantasy. "Do you believe that cane and cotton can be grown to advantage by a sparce white population?" Fisher asked incredulously, "It is impossible!" The majority of settlers in Austin's colony, Fisher reminded him, "are from Slaveholding States—they have enrolled themselves in your register under the firm conviction that slavery would be tolerated, and they would be secure in the ownership of those brought by them." Although himself a non-slaveholder from the northern United States, Fisher could not imagine the cultivation of cotton or sugar cane without enslaved labor. "There is no country in the world where these articles are grown unless by the assistance of Slaves," he pointed out. And without slave-based agriculture driving a thriving economy in Texas, there would be no migration from the United States to sustain the colonies. "Therefore we must either abandon the finest portion of Texas to its original uselessness," concluded Fisher, "or submit to the acknowledged, but lesser evil of Slavery."[28]

Austin found that he could not escape the logic of cotton that was so deeply imbued on his colonists, and so he quickly disabused himself of notions that Americans would consider growing cotton in Texas without slaves. The settlers, he found, remained singularly fixated on acquiring "negros to make cotton to *buy more* negros," and nothing Austin said seemed capable of persuading them otherwise. "It is in vain to tell a North American that the white population will be destroyed some fifty or eighty years hence by the negroes, and that his daughters will be violated and Butchered by them," Austin lamented to a friend. "To say any thing to them as to the justice of slavery, or its demoralizing effects on society, is only to draw down ridicule upon the person who attempts it." Within months, Austin returned to lobbying for reopening Texas to slave importations and he petitioned the Saltillo legislature to rescind its restrictions on such traffic. "The wishes of my colonists have hurried me into this thing," he conceded in a letter from Saltillo, "but I am now in for the cuestion and there is no retreat." Austin had run head-long into a problem he helped create. By building his settlement on the lure of cotton profits, he found that by the early 1830s he simply could not pull his colonists back from the labor system they believed indispensable for such work. If Austin could not abandon cotton in building his colony, his settlers would not abandon using slaves to grow it. "Nothing is wanted but money," Austin concluded of his colonists, "and negros are necessary to make it."[29]

In 1833, Austin declared that "Texas *must be* a slave country. Circumstances and unavoidable necessity compels it." Austin's crucial phrase was "circumstances and unavoidable necessity," by which he meant the logic of cotton that demanded enslaved labor, and the fact that Americans would not continue to come into his colony to claim farm lands without assurances that slavery would be legal in Texas. "It is the wish of the people there," he acknowledged, "and it is my duty to do all I can, prudently, in favor of it. I will do so."[30] For Austin, the question of slavery had always been secondary to his larger vision for the development of Texas into a thriving extension of the American cotton frontier. Yet precisely because cotton served as the foundation of that vision, slavery became the primary means for accomplishing what Austin hoped to build in his settlement. Whatever his personal convictions about enslavement, Austin recognized that white Americans hoping to make their fortune in cotton along the Mexican borderlands considered slavery to be the indispensable institution. And so he committed himself to creating a slave country in Texas.

Notes

This essay's title is my homage to the pioneering work of Lester Bugbee, who published the first scholarly examination of Stephen F. Austin's perspective on slavery with his essay "Stephen F. Austin's Views on Slavery in Early Texas," which appeared in *The Texas Magazine*'s May 1897 issue. Bugbee was among the first scholars to examine the Austin papers, and his essay argued that Austin had himself been opposed to slavery during the 1820s, but chose to tolerate the institution because he believed that it could quicken the pace of American settlement of Mexico. "Temporarily, then," wrote Bugbee, "he declared himself in favor of a system which, under other circumstances, he should have opposed, and which no doubt he hoped would be limited to the introduction of those slaves who came with the first colonists." Tolerating slavery, according to Bugbee, was less a necessity to Austin than a convenient means of shoring up the early colonization efforts in Texas until the Anglo settlements could become well-established. Following Bugbee's death in 1902, his student Eugene C. Barker incorporated that interpretive framework into his own work, making Bugbee's writings on the subject one of the more enduring interpretive strands of scholarship on the Anglo colonization of Texas. This essay owes a debt to Bugbee's early work, even if my interpretations differ a great deal from his. I would also like to thank Thomas L. Torget, Alexandra A. Torget, Rick McCaslin, Don Chipman, Gregg Cantrell, and Eric Walther for insightful commentary on earlier drafts of this essay.

1. Stephen F. Austin to Richard Ellis, et. al., June 16, 1830, and Austin to Thomas F. Leaming, June 14, 1830, both in Eugene Barker, ed., *Annual Report of the American Historical Association for the Year 1919: The Austin Papers*, 3 vols. (Washington, D. C.: Government Printing Office, 1924, 1928; Austin: University of Texas Press, 1927), 2: 417–19, 2:

421–23 (first quotations); Austin to Wiley Martin, May 30, 1833, *Austin Papers*, 2:981 (second quotation; emphasis in original). The *Austin Papers* will hereafter be cited as *AP*, Stephen F. Austin as SFA.

2. Eugene C. Barker, *The Life of Stephen F. Austin, Founder of Texas, 1793–1836: A Chapter in the Westward Movement of the Anglo-American People* (1926; repr., Austin: University of Texas Press, 1969), particularly 201–2. Barker surmised his perspective thus: "Measured by any standard but that of the success of his colonies and the welfare of his colonists, Austin's attitude [toward slavery] appears unstable" (224); Gregg Cantrell, *Stephen F. Austin, Empresario of Texas* (New Haven: Yale University Press, 1999), particularly 189–90, 344 (quotes on 189); Randolph B. Campbell, *An Empire for Slavery: The Peculiar Institution in Texas, 1821–1865* (Baton Rouge: Louisiana State University Press, 1989), 32.

3. Cantrell, *Stephen F. Austin*, 190.

4. John Hebron Moore, *The Emergence of the Cotton Kingdom in the Old Southwest: Mississippi, 1770–1860* (Baton Rouge: Louisiana State University Press, 1988), 5; Robert V. Haynes, *The Mississippi Territory and the Southwest Frontier, 1795–1817* (Lexington: University Press of Kentucky, 2010), 12–13.

5. Daniel H. Unser, Jr., "American Indians and the Cotton Frontier: Changing Economic Relations with Citizens and Slaves in the Mississippi Territory," *Journal of American History* 72 (Sept. 1985): 315–16; Moore, *The Emergence of the Cotton Kingdom*, 8, 11–14; on cotton prices, see Stuart Bruchey, *Cotton and the Growth of the American Economy: 1790–1860* (New York: Harcourt, Brace & World, 1967), particularly the tables on 29–30; on population, see "Historical Census Browser," Geospatial Center, University of Virginia [http://fisher.lib.virginia.edu/ collections/stats/histcensus/ (accessed July 9, 2012)]; Adam Rothman, *Slave Country: American Expansion and the Origins of the Deep South* (Cambridge: Harvard University Press, 2005), 182–83; Haynes, *The Mississippi Territory*, 133; Daniel Walker Howe, *What Hath God Wrought: The Transformation of America, 1815–1848* (Oxford: Oxford University Press, 2007), 128–31.

6. Howe, *What Hath God Wrought*, 127.

7. SFA to Governor of Coahuila y Texas, Dec. 20, 1824, *AP*, 1:994–95; SFA to Congress of Coahuila y Texas, Feb. 4, 1825, *AP*, 2:1,036–37; Archibald Austin to SFA, Jan. 30, 1825, *AP*, 2:1,027–28; Nathaniel Cox to SFA, July 20, 1825, *AP*, 2:1,154; Articles of Partnership between James E. B. Austin and John Austin, Nov. 22, 1825, *AP*, 2:1,234; SFA to Emily Perry, Dec. 12, 1825, *AP*, 2:1,238; SFA to Gaspar Flores, [answering letter of Dec. 6, 1824], *AP*, 1: 984–85 (quotation).

8. In 1820, the populations were: Alabama (47,449 slaves out of 144,317 total people), Mississippi (32,814 out of 75,448), Louisiana (69,064 out of 153,407). All census numbers taken from the "Historical Census Browser."

9. SFA to Antonio Martinez, Aug. 18, 1821, *AP*, 1:407; SFA to Joseph H. Hawkins, July 20, 1821, *AP*, 1: 402–4 (first quotation); for reprints of Austin's advertisements, see *Washington Gazette* (Washington, D.C.), Aug. 15, 1821, quoting *Argus* (Frankfort, KY); *Arkansas Gazette* (Arkansas Post, AR), Sept. 29, 1821; *Edwardsville Spectator* (Edwardsville, IL), Oct. 2, 1821; *St. Louis Enquirer* (St. Louis, MO), Sept. 22, 1821; *Richmond Enquirer* (Richmond, VA), Nov. 20, 1821; *Richmond Enquirer*, Nov. 20, 1821; Washington *Gazette*, Nov. 15, 1821 (second quotation).

10. Sarah Groce Birlet, "Life of Jared Ellison Groce One of the Old Three Hundred and this oldest son, Leonard Wallace Groce," manuscript dated 1936, MSS #179, Woodson Research Center, Fondren Library, Rice University; Rosa Groce Berthlet, "Jared Ellison Groce," *Southwestern Historical Quarterly* 20 (Apr. 1917): 358–61.

11. Slaveholding, migration, and population statistics for 1825 come from Eugene C. Barker, "Notes on the Colonization of Texas," *Mississippi Valley Historical Review* 10 (Sept. 1923): 149–51; Barker, *Life of Austin*, 98. Names of specific slaveholders come from "Census of the District of Colorado for the Year 1825," *AP*, 2:1,244. According to Barker, the 1825 census listed 443 slaves among the 1,800 inhabitants of Austin's colony. Sixty-nine families held those slaves, with eleven families holding 271 slaves (61 percent of the slave population) and fifty-eight families holding 172 slaves (39 percent of the slave population). Of the migrants to Austin's colonies recorded from 1825 to 1831 (out of 902 applications, 864 noted places of origin with 806 from the United States), the states listed by Barker as providing the largest number of settlers were: Louisiana, 201; Alabama, 111; Arkansas, 90; Tennessee, 89; Missouri, 72; Mississippi, 56; New York, 39; Kentucky, 37; Ohio, 28; Georgia, 14; Pennsylvania, 14; Virginia, 13; New England, 20. As Barker points out, the points of departure for these colonists were usually western states (meaning that most of them had previously migrated from seaboard states), and therefore the list is not an indicator of the original birth state of the colonists.

12. Churchill Fulshear to SFA, Nov. 22, 1824, *AP*, 1:976 (first quotation); SFA to Jared Groce, Oct. 19, 1823, *AP*, 1:701; Contract for Hire of Slaves, Aug. 1, 1824, *AP*, 1:869–70; SFA to Perry, Dec. 12, 1825, *AP*, 2:1,238 (second quotation).

13. Stephen F. Austin, "Criminal Regulations," in David B. Gracy, II, ed., *Establishing Austin's Colony: The First Book Printed in Texas, with the Laws, Orders and Contracts of Colonization* (Austin: The Pemberton Press and Jenkins Publishing Company, 1970), 84–89; Eugene Barker, "The Government of Austin's Colony, 1821–1831," *Southwestern Historical Quarterly* 21 (Jan. 1918): 228–30; Joseph McKnight, "Stephen F. Austin's Legalistic Concerns," *Southwestern Historical Quarterly* 89 (Jan. 1986): 247–56.

14. SFA to Flores, [answering letter of Dec. 6, 1824], *AP*, 1:984 (first quotation); Charles Douglas to SFA, Feb. 25, 1825, *AP*, 2:1,047 (second quotation); James Phelps to SFA, Jan. 16, 1825, *AP*, 2:1,020 (third quotation); Randall Jones to SFA, June 4, 1824, *AP*, 1:809 (fourth quotation).

15. For an example of antislavery rhetoric that referenced the ideals of the Mexican War for Independence, see the congressional debate of Nov. 26, 1822, in *Actas Constitucionales Mexicanas* (1821–1824), (México: Instituto de Investigaciones Jurídicas. Universidad Nacional autónoma de México, 1980), Tomo VII, 64; on the British navy's efforts to curtail the international slave trade, see Robert Fogel, *Without Consent or Contract: The Rise and Fall of American Slavery* (New York: W. W. Norton, 1989), 216–18; on the financial influence of the British on early Mexico, particularly in regard to making loans to keep Mexico's treasury solvent and concerning investments in Mexican mining operations, see Stanley Green, *The Mexican Republic: The First Decade, 1823–1832* (Pittsburgh: University of Pittsburgh Press, 1987), 151–52 (on loans) and 129–33 (on mining); Session of October 18, 1821, *Diario de las Sesiones de la Soberana Junta Provisional Gubernativa del Imperio Mexicano, Instalada según Previene el Plan de Iguala y los Tratados de la Villa de Córdova*, in *Actas Constitucionales Mexicanas*, Tomo I, 124 (quotation).

16. For examples of antislavery perspectives among Mexican legislators during the debates over colonization during 1822, see Debates of Nov. 23 and 26, 1822, in *Diario de la Junta Nacional Instituyente del Imperio Mexicano*, reprinted in *Actas Constitucionales Mexicanas*, Tomo VII, 63–66; Juan Antonio Mateos, *Historia Parlamentaria de los Congresos Mexicanos*, (México: J. V. Villada, 1877), Tomo II, 25–29; SFA to José Felix Trespalacios, Jan. 8, 1823, *AP*, 1:567 (first quotation); SFA to Erasmo Seguin, ca. Jan. 1, 1824, *AP*, 1:718–19 (second quotation).

17. Juan Antonio Padilla to the Governor of Texas, Dec. 27, 1819, in Mattie Austin Hatcher, trans., "Texas in 1820," *Southwestern Historical Quarterly* 23 (July 1919): 61–62; Pekka Hämäläinen, *The Comanche*

Empire (New Haven: Yale University Press, 2008), 182–90; Andrew J. Torget, "Cotton Empire: Slavery and the Texas Borderlands, 1820–1837" (Ph.D. dissertation, University of Virginia, 2009), 111–12; Francisco Ruíz to SFA, Nov. 26, 1830, quoted in David J. Weber, *The Mexican Frontier, 1821–1846* (Albuquerque: University of New Mexico Press, 1982), 176.

18. Coahuila y Texas Congressional Session of Nov. 30, 1826, Congreso Constituyente, 1824–1827, Actas de Primera Sesión Ordinaria, Agosto 15, 1824 a Marzo 22, 1827, Archivo del Congreso del Estado de Coahuila, Saltillo, Mexico. The initial draft of Article 13 can also be found in SFA to the Coahuila y Texas State Legislature, Aug. 11, 1826, *AP*, 2:1,407; J.E.B. Austin to SFA, Aug. 22, 1826, *AP*, 2:1,430–34; J. E. B. Austin to SFA, Sept. 23, 1826, *AP*, 2:1,461–62.

19. SFA to Coahuila y Texas State Legislature, Aug. 11, 1826, *AP*, 1: 1,406–9 (quotes); SFA to Coahuila y Texas State Legislature, Nov. 20, 1826, *AP*, 2: 1,507–10.

20. Session of Mar. 11, 1827, Actas de Primera Sesión Ordinaria; Ramón Músquiz to SFA, Apr. 17, 1828, *AP*, 3:31; José Antonio Navarro to SFA, May 17, 1828, *AP*, 3:41; Músquiz to SFA, May 15, 1828, *AP*, 3:38. For the full text of the law, see "Decree No. 56," May 5, 1828, reprinted in H. P. H. Gammel, *The Laws of Texas, 1822–1897*, 12 vols. (Austin: Gammel Book Co., 1898), 1:213.

21. SFA to Manuel Ceballos, Sept. 20, 1828, *AP*, 3:110–15 (second quotation); SFA to Manuel de Mier y Terán, Sept. 20, 1828, *AP*, 3:116–18; SFA to Minister of Relations, Oct. 7, 1828, *AP*, 3:122–28 (first quotation); SFA to José María Viesca, Feb. 16, 1829, *AP*, 3:168–72. For an excellent treatment of the tariff controversy in the United States, and the perceptions of southerners that they could lose their position as the dominant source of cotton for the Atlantic economy, see Brian Schoen, *The Fragile Fabric of Union: Cotton, Federal Politics, and the Global Origins of the Civil War* (Baltimore: The Johns Hopkins University Press, 2009).

22. SFA to José Maria Viesca, Feb. 16, 1829, *AP*, 3:168–72.

23. Número 703, "Decreto del gobierno en uso de facultades extradinarias—Abolicion de la esclavitud en al República," Sept. 15, 1829, in Manuel Dublán y José María Lozano, *Legisación Mexicana o Colección Completa de Disposiciones Legislativas Expedidas desde la Independencia de la República* (Mexico: Imprenta del Comercio, 1876), Tomo II, 163 (quotation). On protests of Tejanos and Coahuilans see, for example, Ramón Músquiz to the Governor of Coahuila-Texas, Oct. 25,

1829, *AP*, 3:273–75; Navarro to SFA, Oct. 29, 1829, *AP*, 3:277–78; Juan Antonio Padilla to SFA, Nov. 26, 1829, *AP*, 3:291; José Maria Viesca to Agustín Viesca, Nov. 14, 1829, *AP*, 3:286–88.

24. Law of April 6, 1830, translated in Alleine Howren, "Causes and Origins of the Decree of April 6, 1830," *Southwestern Historical Quarterly* 16 (Apr. 1913): 415–17. The original Spanish can be found in Dublán y Lozano, *Legisación Mexicana*, Tomo II, 238–40.

25. Anastascio Bustamante to SFA, Mar. 20, 1830, translated in Howren, "Causes and Origins of the Decree of April 6, 1830," 419–20; SFA to Bustamante, May 17, 1830, quoted in Cantrell, *Stephen F. Austin*, 221; on Austin's depression, see Cantrell, *Stephen F. Austin*, 214–17 (first quotation); Músquiz to SFA, Apr. 29, 1830, Thomas W. Streeter Collection of Texas Manuscripts (WA MSS S-498-500), Beinecke Library, Yale University (second quotation).

26. On SFA's approach to the April 6, 1830, law, see Cantrell, *Stephen F. Austin*, 222–27; SFA to Lucas Alamán, May 18, 1830, *AP*, 3:384 (first quotation; SFA noted on the manuscript: "Copy of letter not sent"); SFA to Henry Austin, [June 1830?], *AP*, 3:405 (second quotation).

27. SFA to Ellis, et. al., June 16, 1830, *AP*, 3: 422; SFA to S. Rhoads Fisher, June 17, 1830, *AP*, 3:427.

28. Fisher to SFA, Aug. 23, 1830, *AP*, 3: 469–70.

29. SFA to Edward Livingston, June 24, 1832, *AP*, 3: 795 (first quotation; emphasis in original); SFA to Leaming, June 14, 1830, *AP*, 3:415 (second quotation); SFA to Samuel Williams, April 16, 1831, *AP*, 3:645 (third quotation); SFA to Livingston, June 24, 1832, *AP*, 3:795 (fourth quotation).

30. SFA to Martin, May 30, 1833, *AP*, 2:981 (emphasis in original).

PART III:

Texas in Civil War and Reconstruction

Harvesting Cotton in Texas. Courtesy of Library of Congress

Landholding in Brazos County, Texas: Frontier, War, and Reconstruction

Carl H. Moneyhon

One of the most persistent historical questions concerning the American Civil War and Reconstruction is what impact the war and the end of slavery had on local elites in the South. The answer to that question has varied. Some historians have seen relatively little change, while others have perceived a more radical transformation.[1] As historian James Roark points out, however, resolving these interpretations is difficult because of the narrow geographic focus of most of these studies.[2] Further, most of these studies have concentrated particularly on older plantation communities. The following study seeks to expand our knowledge of the war's impact by examining a different type of community, a frontier county of the Confederacy—Brazos County, Texas. It does so by exploring what happened to the local elite between 1850 and 1874. This investigation assesses their position every five years during this period, looking also at their persistence as members of the local elite from point to point.

Discovering how the events of the period under consideration affected the local elite necessarily begins with a definition of that group. Scholars have extensively debated how to apply a quantitative measure to status in the antebellum South with no widely held agreement. Even the definition of a "large planter" is in dispute, although recent studies have used ownership of twenty slaves as a line of demarcation between large planters and others.[3] In the case of Brazos County, however, this definition is hardly workable, since slaves had only begun to move into the area in 1850. The census that year counted only 142 slaves within the county, county tax rolls just 132.[4] Further, only one slave owner, John Millican, had the requisite number of slaves to be considered a large planter at that time. What, then, constitutes the local elite in such a county? Ultimately all definitions are arbitrary, but in other states at least 600 acres were considered necessary to justify a workforce of twenty slaves. Because the relatively low cost of land in Texas made larger acquisitions more possible, this study will consider individuals with a thousand or more acres as being part of the county's elite. Of course, such landowners also acquired slaves to raise cotton, and that aspect of their economic activity, which potentially exposed them to ruin after the war, will be considered as well.

Tax rolls provide the best source for such an investigation, since they provide a record of who actually owned land. Tax rolls also were made annually, allowing a close view of changes that might be connected to historical events with the potential of altering a community. In addition, assessments of personal property provide considerable insight into a landowner's possible economic activities. Although these records are not always completely reliable (assessors often under-assessed property, and personal property could be left off the books easily), they provide a better measure of what was going on at the local level than the decennial national census. Tax rolls, supplemented with census material, local histories, and newspaper accounts, serve as the basis for the analysis of large landowners that follows. It should be noted that this information offers only a picture of patterns and cannot always illuminate what happened to individuals, a task beyond the scope of this paper. They do, however, provide a useful perspective on the broader context of individual lives.

Anglo-American immigrants began settling what would become Brazos County in the 1820s. Originally part of Stephen F. Austin's second colony, the area was included in Washington County during the years of the early Republic. In 1841 the Texas Congress created Navasota County out of this area, then renamed it Brazos County in 1842.[5] These landowners settled in an area initially covered with woodlands, including oak, hickory, and pine. The land possessed considerable potential for farming and plantation agriculture, however, as it lay at the juncture of the Brazos and Navasota Rivers. A later assessment by the Bureau of the Census estimated that lands in the county could produce between 1,000 to 1,600 pounds of seed-cotton per acre on the average. The best lands lay in the Brazos River bottoms running along the western boundary of the county, where the production of as much as 2,000 pounds of seed-cotton per acre was possible. Away from the rivers, settlers found less productive prairie lands, but they still could produce up to 800 pounds of seed-cotton per acre.[6] Brazos County thus possessed considerable potential for farming, even if through its early years the lack of adequate transportation to markets at Houston or Galveston impeded that development.

This study begins with a look at the county tax rolls for 1850. The figures gathered by the assessor indicated that the county remained relatively undeveloped at this time. That's year's assessment showed only

102 taxpayers in the county. Of these only fifty-eight owned land other than town property, a number equal to 56 percent of the taxed residents. This rural property totaled 73,982 acres, about 19 percent of the approximately 376,320 total acres in the county. The average taxpayer at this time owned 1,276 acres. In addition to the small number of taxpayers and the small proportion of land that had been claimed, the low value of this property further reflected the lack of development in the county. The total assessed value was $63,335, an average of only eighty-five cents per acre (See Table 1).

Table 1: Land Ownership in Brazos County, 1850–1874

Year	*Land Owners*	*Acres Owned*	*Average Acreage*	*Landed Elite*	*Acres Owned by Landed Elite*	*Average Acreage for Landed Elite*
1850	58	73,982	1,276	22	58,447	2,476
1855	106	114,192	1,077	30	87,828	2,928
1860	199	135,336	680	34	76,360	2,246
1865	238	177,538	746	53	111,102	2,096
1870	476	237,509	499	59	138,191	2,342
1874	555	184,997	333	41	76,535	1,867

*Note. These and subsequent figures are derived from the manuscript tax rolls for Brazos County in the Texas State Archives and Library. Since they are transcribed from the original manuscript, figures may not always match the published reports for this time.

Brazos County may have been in the early stages of development, but a local elite already existed, exercising considerable control over the productive assets of the county. Twenty-one individuals and one estate, each of which possessed a thousand or more acres of land, constituted this elite. Overall, they claimed 58,447 acres of the total assessed. Their relatively strong economic position can be perceived from the fact that while they constituted 38 percent of landowners and 21 percent of all taxpayers, they owned 79 percent of the land. Clearly, at this early period this group held a disproportionate share of the land, potentially dominating other aspects of the local economy. That much of their land had not yet been developed, however, was reflected by its average valuation, which was essentially the same eighty-six cents per acre as all lands taxed within the county (See Table 2).

Table 2: Value of Lands in Brazos County, 1850–1874

Year	*Total Acreage*	*Total Value of Lands*	*Average Value per acre*	*Acreage of Landed Elite*	*Total Value of Lands of Landed Elite*	*Average Value of Lands of Landed Elite*
1850	73,982	$ 63,335	$ .86	59,447	$ 51,251	$ .86
1855	114,192	$205,216	$1.79	87,828	$151,744	$1.72
1860	133,336	$632,985	$4.68	76,360	$407,594	$5.47
1865	177,583	$452,420	$2.55	111,102	$279,141	$2.52
1870	237,509	$796,695	$3.35	138,191	$307,573	$2.23
1874	184,997	$641,390	$3.47	76,535	$180,850	$2.36

Already by 1850 the local elite consisted of individuals from a wide variety of backgrounds. Many were old settlers who had been there since the 1820s while others were relative newcomers. Inevitably some of the older residents were among the elite as land grant policy within the Austin Colony had made possible the acquisition of sizeable holdings. Among such individuals in 1850 were Elliott M. Millican, John Millican, and other heirs of Robert Hemphill Millican. They had divided two and a half sitios of land, over eleven thousand acres, which their father had received in 1824. Richard Carter was also a part of this elite group, arriving in the area in 1831 and receiving a league of land, 4,428 acres, from Austin. A later arrival was Thomas Bowman, who had received a land grant of 4,605 acres as a headright given to heads of household at the time of the Texas Declaration of Independence. Others appear to have arrived in the county some time after statehood. This includes the third largest landowner in the county, thirty-three-year-old Martha Jones of Virginia, who had more than five thousand acres.[7]

The value of the lands of the elite suggested the county remained at an early stage of economic development, and personal property assessments also appear to confirm that conclusion. At this time herding and ranching was a major part of the local economy. Tax rolls showed large herds of cattle within the county. Overall, taxpayers owned 6,548 head of cattle, and the landed elite played a major role in this enterprise. The 2,928 head of cattle that they claimed represented a disproportionate share of the county's cattle, 44 percent of all cattle compared with their representation of only 21 percent of the total population. Almost all of the elite had cattle. The largest herds were owned by the Millican family, with Elliott, John and others running over a thousand head. Still, others than the landed elite were engaged in the cattle business. How they managed to range their cattle is unclear. Wiatt Coleman, for example, had 250 cows but only 200 acres of land. Thomas Cress presented an even greater problem as he owned 319 head of cattle but no land at all. How he managed this cannot be discerned, although he may have rented land or simply grazed his herds on the unclaimed prairie lands that were part of the county at this time (See Table 3).[8]

Table 3: Cattle Ownership in Brazos County, 1850–1860

Year	*All Cattle*	*Elite Cattle*	*Elite Acreage*	*Elite Cattle per Acre*
1850	6,548	2,928	58,447	20
1855	10,940	4,057	87,828	21
1860	23,940	7,753	76,360	10

Cattle ranching was a major part of the local economy in the 1850s, but some indications point to the emergence of cotton cultivation as an important component in the overall picture. In this development the landed elites do not appear to have played an integral part. The 1850 census showed the small scale of cotton farming at that time, reporting that the county's farmers produced only 142 bales that year. That same year farmers to the south in Washington County grew 4,008 bales.[9] The 1850 manuscript agricultural census in the county does not include the page that reported which farmers grew this cotton, but slave ownership gives a partial clue to their identity as slaves were an integral part of cotton cultivation at this time. Only twenty-two taxpayers possessed slaves in 1850, and of these only five owned ten or more slaves, a number usually associated with at least the potential for being a smaller planter.

The five included John Millican with twenty-four and four others—S. A. Sparks, Alex McGahey, Mary Collins, and Jackson D. Williams—who owned between ten and nineteen slaves.[10] Of these five, only Millican was a member of the landed elite. Sparks had 920 acres; McGahey, an old settler who operated a ferry, had 350 acres; and Collins and Williams had none. Conversely, only eight of the twenty-two members of the elite owned any slaves at all, although Millican's slaves accounted for 18 percent of all the slaves in the county.

That the ownership of slaves by a landowner marks a shift in land usage from grazing to the cultivation of crops is supported by the higher assessed value of the land holdings of slave owners as compared to that of the taxpayers in general. While the landed elite were not yet turning from livestock to commercial farming, many farmers were. A look at the impact of the presence of slaves on the value of land in 1850 provides a useful measure to assess future change among the elite. Simply put, the property value of the twenty-one residents of Brazos County who had slaves outstripped that of their neighbors' lands. Combined, slave owners possessed 30,789 acres of land valued at $33,236. While representing only 20 percent of all taxpayers, they owned 42 percent of the assessed acreage and the value of their land constituted 79 percent of the overall land value in the county. With slaves on the land, the average value of property was $1.08 per acre as opposed to the county average of eighty-six cents. Slave ownership can thus be used to measure changes in the economic activities of the county's taxpayers (see Tables 4, 5, 6).

Table 4: Value of Land Belonging to Slave Owners, Brazos County, 1850–1860

Year	*Total Acreage*	*Total Value of Lands*	*Average Value per acre*	*SlaveOwners Acreage*	*Total Value of Land*	*Average Value of Land*
1850	73,982	$63,335	$ .86	30,789	$ 33,236	$1.08
1855	114,192	$205,216	$1.79	64,978	$119,391	$1.84
1860	135,336	$632,985	$4.68	82,874	$462,654	$5.58

Table 5: Slave Ownership, Brazos County, 1850–1860

Year	*Total Owners*	*Total Slaves-*	*Owners With Ten or More Slaves*	*Percent of Slave Owners*	*Slaves on Units of Ten or More*	*Percent of Slaves*
1850	22	132	5	22	75	57
1855	44	147	12	27	377	84
1860	99	733	18	18	500	68

Table 6: Slave Ownership by Landed Elites, Brazos County, 1850–1860

Year	*Landed Elite*	*Slave Owners in Class*	*Percentage of Landed Elite Owning Slaves*	*Slaves Owned by Landed Elite*	*Percentage of All Slaves in County*
1850	22	8	36	42	31
1855	30	17	57	338	76
1860	34	24	71	431	59

Although relatively undeveloped in 1850, Brazos County over the next five years would see considerable economic growth, and tax rolls clearly show these changes. What drove this growth is not clear. The fact that only one-fifth of the county's lands in 1850 had been taken possession of by local residents may have been an attraction. In addition, the promise of greater accessibility to markets may have been a factor. That potential was offered with the formation of the Galveston & Red River Railroad in 1853. Railroad promoters hoped to have their road open from Houston to the Brazos bottoms within a year in what proved to be an overly optimistic projection. Nonetheless, they did move forward with construction and at least created the hope among those engaged in farming that they could more easily get their crops to market.[11]

While the cause that brought each individual to Brazos County between 1850 and 1855 cannot be readily discerned, the tax rolls presented a clear pattern of development. The local population grew steadily, with the number of taxpayers reaching 174, an increase of 72 individuals and a growth rate of nearly 70 percent. In addition, this expanding population was acquiring land. Of the taxpayers in 1855, 106 were assessed as having land, and the proportion of landowners had increased from 56 to 60 percent of the total population. The 1855 assessment indicated that residents had nearly doubled the amount of land held in 1850, to 114,192 acres of the county's 376,320 acres.

Using the measure of development applied in 1850, it is clear that change within the county was not just quantitative but also qualitative. More people moved into Brazos County, but its residents also began to use the land more productively. In part, this is suggested by the decrease in the average size of holdings. In this period the average fell from 1,276 to 1,077 acres. This reduction intimates that less land may have been held for potential speculation and more was being developed into actual productive farm and ranch operations. This conclusion is further supported by the rise in the total value of assessed non-town property. Land valuations swelled at an even greater rate than population, rising from $63,355 to $205,216. The average assessed value of all land increased significantly from eighty-five cents to $1.79 per acre, indicating its existing worth and potential for greater productivity.

In this changing milieu the local elite increased as well, although not at the same rate as the general population. In 1850 there had been twenty-two large landholding units; in 1855 there were thirty, a 36 percent rate of growth. Their share of the total assessed lands in the county remained relatively unchanged, although they still held a disproportionate portion with 87,828 acres, an amount that constituted 77 percent of all the land assessed by the county's residents. The per-acre assessed value of the land of the elite suggests that as a group much of their land continued to be undeveloped. In fact, the average value of their land in 1855, although higher than in 1850, at $1.72 per acre was actually less than that for all land in the county. As shall be seen, this did not mean that individuals among the elite were not beginning to improve their land.

The tax assessment of 1855 provides an opportunity to measure another vital component of the character of the county's landed elite: its ability to survive over time and retain its status. This is measured by determining the percentage of taxpayers from 1850 who remained in the county and among its landed elite in 1855. This number will be referred to as persistence rate. A high rate of persistence suggests that the class found adequate economic opportunities over time to remain in place, and so the landed elite of Brazos County appear to have remained relatively stable. Of those who possessed more than one thousand acres in 1850, fourteen or 64 percent of the total remained landowners in the county in 1855 and retained their status.[12] While remaining in the elite, eleven of the fourteen did begin to dispose of some of their land. As examples, Elliott Millican, who had been the largest landowner in the county in 1850 with 8,522 acres, assessed only 7,082 in 1855, and John Millican reduced his holdings from 6,411 to 5,375 acres. On the other hand, three got more land. James and Thomas Bowman were the most acquisitive, adding 5,100 acres to the 2,900 they held earlier. Of the non-survivors, A. McMahan stayed in the county but lost enough land that he no longer could be considered part of the landed elite. Another, the estate of J. H. Millican, no longer existed. The fate of the remaining is unknown.

The fourteen survivors from among the 1850 landed elite were joined by seventeen newcomers in 1855. Emphasizing the opportunities that existed in the county is the fact that eight members of this group had been residents of the county in 1850 and had managed to acquire a thousand or more acres of land. In some cases the addition of property had been substantial. Wilson Reed, a forty-eight-year-old settler and farmer from Tennessee, achieved the greatest expansion when he increased his acreage from 420 to 2,214 acres. Others who moved up showed less spectacular growth. Charles Clayton, a stock raiser, reflected this more modest pattern, adding 462 acres to the 915 he held in 1850. Acquiring large amounts of lands was more pronounced among some newcomers. Samuel Holleday, for example, displaced the Millicans as the county's largest landowner, reporting 12,246 acres by 1855. William C. Wilson, an immigrant from Ohio, also moved into the elite, becoming one of the top four land owners with his 6,628 acres.

The economic lives of the landed elite appear to have been changing somewhat by 1855, although some aspects remained the same as in 1850. Raising cattle continued to be a significant activity for all landowners in Brazos County, and the landed elite remained active in this area. By 1855 cattle herds in the county had expanded from 6,548 head to 10,940 head, an increase of 67 percent. The herds of the large landowners reached 4,057 head of cattle at this time, adding to the numbers they owned in 1850. At the same time, their cattle represented a smaller proportion of those in the county, decreasing from 44 percent to 37 percent of all cows. At the same time, however, they were adding to the number of cows they were running per acre, from twenty cows in 1850 to twenty-one in 1855.

Cattle remained important, but many of the landed elite also appear to have been growing crops as well. This is suggested by the increasing number of slaves, the expansion of the number of slaves who were part of holdings of ten or more individuals, and the steady acquisition of slaves by the landed elite. Between 1850 and 1855 the number of slaves swelled from 132 to 447. At the same time, the number of slave owners who owned ten or more slaves increased from five to twelve. Of this twelve, six individuals owned twenty or more slaves, a number that easily gave them the capacity to engage in plantation agriculture. Three of this six had slaves in numbers that would have made them large planters in the more established areas of the South. John S. Wilson, the largest slave owner in the county, owned eighty-nine slaves. Thomas C. Wilson, the second largest, reported owning eighty slaves. John Millican, the third, had fifty.

Many of the landed elites still did not own enough slaves to be engaged in plantation agriculture, but a shift from their position in 1850 was clearly underway. The landed elite in Brazos County was becoming a slave owning elite. Seventeen of the thirty members of the landed elite owned slaves in 1855, or 57 percent of the class as opposed to 36 percent in 1850. The landed elite also now controlled a greater share of the slave labor force, with their 338 slaves comprising 76 percent of all the slaves in the county. While only one of the individuals with ten or more slaves possessed a thousand acres in 1850, seven of fifteen with this amount of slave property had more than a thousand acres in 1855. Five of the six individuals with twenty or more slaves owned more than a thousand acres of land. The figures clearly indicate that at this point the landed elites were coming to control not only land but also labor.

This increase in slave ownership among the landed elite to a considerable degree resulted from the arrival of newcomers with slaves. Of the twelve slave owners with ten or more slaves in 1855, only three had been in the county five years before. John Millican, who had been the county's largest slave owner in 1850, expanded his holdings from twenty-four slaves to fifty. The other two older residents included Richard Carter, who increased the number of slaves he owned from five to ten, and Elliott Millican, who acquired six slaves to add to the five he owned in 1850. All the other slave owners with ten or more slaves had arrived in Brazos County sometime after 1850.

Tax rolls in 1855, as in 1850, strongly suggest that with control over labor, slave owners were improving their lands and probably turning more to farming. Their property thus increased in value. At this time, the value of land owned by slave owners with ten or more slaves climbed to

$2.30 per acre, significantly higher than the $1.79 per acre value for the county as a whole. For the members of the landed elite who also owned slaves, the differentiation in value was even more striking. The 6,628 acres of Thomas Wilson, for example, was assessed at $3.85 per acre, nearly twice the average value. John Wilson's land had a similarly higher evaluation at $2.50 per acre. John Millican's property had the highest assessments in the county at $4.72 per acre. With slaves, the lands of at least some of the landed elite had radically climbed in value.

If the period 1850 to 1855 had been a time of economic promise, the next five years appeared even more encouraging. The hope created by the Galveston & Red River was not realized prior to 1855 as that road struggled with financing in its efforts at moving inland. The picture became more encouraging, however, when the Houston & Texas Central took over the G & RR in 1856 and the new company actually pushed into the interior. By January 1858 it reached Hempstead, within about thirty miles of Brazos County. Construction stalled there, however, as the company was forced to bridge the Navasota River and secure further financing itself. Nonetheless, farmers had easier access to markets with a railroad that promised to move goods from Hempstead to Houston in two hours. In 1860 the H&TC finally pushed into the county, establishing a terminus at Millican that at least for the next decade made the community a major center through which cotton in the county and the upper Navasota and Brazos rivers would move. As would be expected, the latter half of the 1850s witnessed a boom not only in the economy of that town but also in that of the county as a whole.[13]

The boom was marked at least in part by the steady increase in Brazos County's population. By 1860 the number of taxpayers in the county increased to 312 individuals. Landownership also continued to increase, with 198 taxpayers now owning land, an increase of 100 percent. In addition, the proportion of taxpayers who actually owned land also increased, reaching 63 percent. In addition to the growing number of landowners, changes in the size of land holdings suggested a further breakup of speculative holdings and the development of more intensive agriculture. The average acreage held by property owners dropped from 1,077 to 683 acres per owner. Land values also pointed to the possibility of more intensive development of the land, with the total assessment that year of $631,518 averaging out to $4.66 per acre, a 260 percent increase in the evaluation.[14]

The years 1855 to 1860 saw change not only for land owners overall but also for the local elite. The number of individuals with a thousand or more acres of land increased from thirty to thirty-four, but the average size of their holdings decreased to some extent. With individual acreage averaging 2,246, the size of the average holding among the elite had dropped 682 acres. In addition, the share of all assessed property owned by the landed elite dropped from 76 to 56 percent. That the larger landowners were further developing their land was reflected in the continued rise of the value of their land in comparison with that of their smaller neighbors. By 1860 the average value per acre for this landed elite reached an all-time high at $5.47 per acre.

As in the past, economic growth was marked by the continued expansion of the livestock component of the economy, but there was an important shift. Over the five-year period leading up to 1860, the number of cattle in the county more than doubled, reaching 23,940 head. The large landowners continued to run cattle, with the total in their herds reaching 7,753 head, but the importance of cattle for the landed elite appears to have been diminishing. Their herds increased overall, but their share of the total number in the county dropped from 37 to 32 percent. Further, the number of head that they ran per acre dropped from twenty-one to ten, possibly reflecting their continued shift to farming.

For the landed elite, cotton cultivation appears to have become an increasingly important part of their economic activities. Overall, the census of 1860 clearly showed the increasing importance of cotton in the county. Enumerators counted some 2,209 bales of cotton produced locally. The development of cotton farming also was marked by the steady increase in the number of slaves, the labor force essential to the development of plantations. Tax returns for 1860 showed the number of slaves had grown to 733, with ninety-nine of 312 taxpayers (almost one-third) owning one or more slaves. While total numbers indicated the growing importance of slavery, the expansion of slave holdings in the county pointed even more directly to the creation of larger plantations. Many slave holdings remained relatively small, with thirty slave owners possessing only one slave and eighteen with two slaves. On the other hand, thirty-three slave owners now had between three and nine slaves, eleven had between ten and nineteen, and seven certainly had planter potential with twenty or more.[15]

The landed elite clearly participated in this expanding cotton economy, and the increasing importance of slaves among them marked this shift. As in the past, all of the landed elite did not own slaves, but twenty-four now did. The percentage of the landed elite with slaves had increased to a significant degree, growing from 57 percent to 71 percent. The twenty-four members who owned slave property counted 431 of them as their property. This number represented an actual drop in the overall proportion of the total slaves owned by Brazos County residents to 59 percent, but this can be accounted for by the increase in the number of smaller holdings countywide. Of the seven slave owners with more than twenty slaves at this time, all owned more than a thousand acres of land.

Land and slaves made the local elite an even more powerful economic force in Brazos County. As has been seen, the value of the property of the landed elite was greater than that of all landowners in the county, but for those who owned slaves the difference was even more striking. Only seven members of the landed elite had twenty or more slaves, but the assessed value of their land far outstripped that of the fellow members of their class and also their neighbors. Representing only 4 percent of the taxpaying land owners, they owned 21,778 acres of land or about 16 percent of the overall acreage. On the other hand, this acreage was assessed at $220,769, an amount equal to 35 percent of the total $632,985 assessment for 1860. The average value per acre of their land was $10.13, more than double the countywide average. John Millican, the county's largest landowner and the owner of sixty-seven slaves, continued to have some of the highest priced land in the county, with an assessed value placed at $13.00 per acre. The valuation on the land of Thomas Wilson, who owned ninety-eight slaves and also was part of the landed elite with the possession of 3,400 acres, was $10.00 per acre.

That the tax returns show real changes in the position of the landed elite is confirmed in part by the agricultural census of 1860. That year seventy-one farms reported that they grew cotton. The manuscript returns listed only ten of the landed elite as growing cotton, but that is consistent with the patterns of slave ownership shown in the tax records. While these ten cotton growers represented only 14 percent of producers, they grew 840 bales. This number equaled 38 percent of the total crop grown in the county, showing the increased importance of cotton for this landed class.[16]

The members of the landed elite continued to be a mix of older families and newcomers, with the persistence of those who had been in Brazos County in 1855 and the emergence of new land owners indicating the opportunities presented by the county's expanding economy. The persistence rate of old families was roughly the same in the five years from 1855 to 1860 as it had been during the previous five years. Of the thirty members of the large landowning class in 1855, twelve survived individually into 1860. Eight more appear to have died, but their families continued to hold on to the land. Thus, the persistence rate among the landed elite of 1855 was 67 percent, a rate slightly higher than that of the period from 1850 to 1855. Ten did not persist. Nine of these appear to have left the county, while one, William J. Lewis, had his holdings reduced from 2,040 acres to 150.

As in the past, the local elite was bolstered by the appearance of newcomers within its ranks between 1855 and 1860. Their identities suggest a continuing degree of upward mobility within the county, although most were new arrivals. Four of the fourteen new members of the landed elite had lived in the county in 1855 and acquired additional lands. As in the previous five-year period, these individuals often acquired significant amounts of property. George Higgs increasing his holdings from 369 acres to 1,943; Thomas Green from 996 to 1,838; William McIntosh from no land to 1,375 acres; and H. R. Henry from none to 1,107. Among the individuals who had arrived after 1855, K. Womble, a fifty-one-year-old immigrant to the county from North Carolina, was the largest landowner with 3,419 acres.

The promise that existed in the period 1855 to 1860 faced serious challenges in the years that followed. The growing presence of African-American slaves and the integration of Brazos County into the southern cotton economy ensured that its people were not immune from the growing tension leading up to the Civil War. In August 1860 citizens at Millican met in response to the discovery of an alleged abolitionist plot to cause slave uprisings in northern Texas. Indeed, they believed that they had uncovered a similar plot locally, formed by abolitionist emissaries to "destroy the lives and property of our citizens, and to attempt to encite [*sic*] our negroes to insurrection." As a result they created a committee of vigilance to quell the unrest among the slaves and remove any suspected abolitionists. Among other resolutions passed, the meeting insisted that slave owners not allow slaves to leave their premises without written passes, that ministers not preach to the slaves for the next twelve months, that the slave patrol be strengthened, and that owners not allow slaves to own horses. This meeting showed a community uncertain of its future in a political milieu that threatened the reduction of the South to a slave-owning minority within the nation.[17]

As a slave society and with considerable concern for the implications of the election of Abraham Lincoln as president in 1860, Brazos County residents voted in favor of secession in the state referendum held on February 23, 1861. The vote in fact demonstrated broad support for disunion, with 215 voting in favor of seceding.[18] Their action brought about five years that had the potential for producing revolutionary changes in the county, although few probably understood that possibility at the time. In fact, as the war years passed, many local residents may have little perceived the war's impact. The one exception would be the families of those who departed for service. The census of 1860 showed at least 426 potential enlistees, white men between the age of twenty and fifty, but no precise number of those who actually joined is known. A county history noted that at least two infantry and two cavalry companies included local men: J. W. Mattox's company, raised in August 1861; Seymour C. Brasher's company, part of Company F, 10th Texas Infantry, in October 1861; Captain L. J. Wilson's Company I, 21st Texas Cavalry, the following year, and G. W. Daniels's Company E, 25th Texas Cavalry, also in 1862. This could have been as many as four hundred men, but these units often were not full and some men may have enlisted in several of these units, which limits that number. An examination of the muster roll of Company F of the 10th Texas, for example, shows only forty-eight of its members actually came from Brazos County.[19]

The departure of these men had an inevitable impact on their families. Married soldiers, often coming from families with limited resources, left behind wives and children who quickly faced privation. In his examination of Brazos County court records, Paul R. Scott found that as early as May 19, 1862, the commissioner's court appropriated $2,000 for the support of destitute families of soldiers and created a committee to determine those entitled to support. The following November the court afforded additional aid by purchasing beef for needy families. The following year, attempting to maintain support, the county levied an ad valorem tax of twenty-five cents on each hundred dollars of assessed property, although it allowed individuals a tax credit for donations that they made. By autumn of 1863 county support could be maintained only by borrowing money. Scott estimated that about eighty-two families received some sort of support during the war.[20]

While individual families may have suffered, the broader impact of the mustering of troops on the county is less certain. The departure of many of the local men who joined deprived the community of workers, but their absence did not necessarily undermine the stability of life for most people. An examination of the men who enlisted in Company F, 10th Texas Infantry suggests that most who joined the army came from among the very young, common laborers, and the unmarried. An analysis of the forty-eight members of that company who could be found in the census, revealed that they had an average age of twenty-seven. This older age might suggest that a more mature and propertied class of individuals were involved in the war, but other aspects of their life suggest the contrary. Of the forty-eight Brazos County members of the company, thirty-six were single men who had no familial responsibilities. Eleven of the forty-eight were farmers with land, but the rest were stock drivers, herders, laborers, overseers, tenants, and students. Only one of the enlistees, the fifteen-year-old John E. Womble, came from one of the families of the landed elite. While in some cases families suffered from their absence, overall their departure did little to undermine the basic social and economic order.[21]

At the same time that these men left, the war also was in the process of creating new economic opportunities locally. These favorable prospects hinged to a considerable degree on the arrival of the Houston & Texas Central at Millican. The town's location as a rail terminus made it a logical place to locate a military camp and also a depot through which supplies would move from the coast into the interior. In October 1861, Gov. Edward Clark established a camp at Millican that would be one of the points for the instruction and mustering in of troops.[22] With the military ensconced at Millican, merchants obviously benefited but area farmers also found a ready market for their cattle, other livestock, and foodstuffs in the army and among individual soldiers. Of course the presence of the army camp also presented some problems. A Houston newspaper noted in November 1861 that deserters from the camp had remained in the area and had been "loafing about stealing horses." When five men were captured, a party of vigilantes took them away from their military guards, hung three of them and shot the other two.[23]

Throughout the war years the location of the railhead at Millican also continued to work to the county's advantage in favoring the cultivation of cotton. Despite admonitions that planters should shift from cotton production to corn and wheat, the county's farms never stopped growing cotton. Contemporary newspapers noted that cotton produced locally and further up the Brazos River valley kept on flowing to Millican where it was shipped subsequently to other points and on to Mexico. In turn, supplies from Mexico moved through Millican on the way into the interior of Texas.[24] When Millican was incorporated as a town in 1864, it reported a population of 3,000, reputedly second in size only to Galveston and Houston.[25]

Tax records from 1865 strengthen the argument that while individual soldiers and their families may have suffered, the war little affected the county. Rather than being set back, Brazos County actually grew during the war years. The 1865 tax assessment showed 420 taxpayers, up from the 312 reported in 1860. In addition, people were buying land, as the total number of landowners increased from 199 to 238 and the total of assessed lands increased from 135,261 to 177,583 acres. The overall proportion of landowners to the general population declined, but that may have been caused by the fact that the town population, driven by the rapid growth of Millican, may have been growing even faster than that for the county as a whole.

The tax rolls indicated, further, that the war did little to affect the acquisition of large land holdings as membership in the landed elite actually increased during the war years. By 1865 the number of individuals with more than a thousand acres of land had expanded from thirty-four to fifty-three. At the same time, and suggesting that land was being shifted to farm cultivation, the average amount of property owned by landed elite continued to decrease, to 2,096 acres, but this still amounted to a holding considerably larger than the 746-acre average for landowners throughout Brazos County. This growth through the war years cannot be fully explained, although possible perception of land as an investment that would survive the travails of war encouraged the purchase of large tracts of land.

As to the fate of the antebellum landed elite, the war years actually seem to have promoted greater stability, possibly discouraging individuals in that group from moving. The persistence rate in this period was even greater than in the previous five-year period, with twenty-eight of the thirty-four members of the landed elite of 1860 surviving the war years and hanging on to their status, for a persistence rate of 82 percent. The properties of most of these individuals remained relatively unchanged, although a tendency to acquire even more land was apparent among some. Five actually increased the amount of land they owned significantly. C. C. Seale expanded the land he owned from 3,592 acres to 4,241; Thomas C. Wilson from 3,400 to 4,340; Harvey Mitchell from 1,252 to 4,558; Jeff P. Mitchell from 1,120 to 2,912; and Michael Hardeman from 1,247 to 3,284. How they accomplished this feat in the midst of war is unclear, although the fact that Seale was county assessor, Harvey Wilson a surveyor, Jeff Mitchell a physician, and Hardeman a skilled craftsman suggests they had been positioned to make money during the war and turn their profits into land. Of the 1860 landed elite, only Harriett Spencer lost land, with a decrease from 1,187 to 365 acres, which moved Spencer out of the large landowning class. Others may have wanted to reduce their landholdings. K. Womble, for example, apparently wanted to sell 1,660 acres of his land, including "160 acres in cultivation in Brazos bottom, with comfortable buildings, gin house, &c." He was willing to be paid in Confederate money, but was unsuccessful.[26]

The local elite survived as landowners, but what that meant for the future was uncertain. The war had made one revolutionary change in the local economy. It ended slavery and left unanswered whether or not the economy could continue to prosper using free labor. Because the railroad placed federal posts at Galveston and Houston in close proximity, word of emancipation reached Brazos County quickly. Whites wondered how the former slaves would react to their freedom, but blacks actually had few options. The former slaves emerged from captivity with few skills other than knowledge of farming, few tangible assets, and no place to go. Although they might seek others for whom to work, they had few opportunities other than to go back to work on the county's farms. The future of the county's landed elites depended in large part on exactly how well they could utilize this work force. The uncertain future was shown most clearly in the property assessments of 1865. The value of land in the county dropped to only $2.55 per acre, half of what it had been in 1860.

In addition to their loss of control over labor, emancipation threatened local elites because of the loss of capital that had been invested in slaves. As Randolph B. Campbell has shown, slaves were not only important as workers but they also served as the basis for the credit that sustained the agricultural economy. Planters and farmers could secure credit with their slaves as collateral. Consequently, whites in Brazos County lost, at least in terms of assessed value, a credit base of $597,906 when slavery ended. This was a potentially devastating loss, and only the future would show to what extent economic endeavors could be continued.

Even though the landowners of Brazos County faced considerable uncertainty at the war's end, other factors appeared to be working in their favor. Southern farmers were determined to go back to the cultivation of cotton, and at least initially many observers believed the picture for the future was quite rosy. Above all, the resumed march of the Houston & Texas Central through Brazos County promised the further development of agricultural lands, although it ultimately spelled the doom of Millican as a market town. As early as August 1865, newspapers indicated that the road had begun to lay ties along the eighteen miles graded prior to the war between Millican and Bryant's [*sic*] Station.[27] Reports indicated an almost immediate movement of cotton to market, with a good harvest beginning with the autumn of 1865. That fall the *Galveston News* informed readers that "immense quantities" of cotton were accumulating at Millican and that the road did not have enough engines and cars to get it to market.[28]

Even so, the future of free labor was uncertain. In the years that followed, Brazos County experienced considerable tension between landowners and freedmen, including an outbreak of racial violence that was among the most deadly as well as best documented incident of its sort in the Reconstruction era. Reports beginning with the first arrival of officials of the Bureau of Refugees, Freedmen and Abandoned Lands indicated frequent conflicts between workers and employers. In June 1867, for example, the Bureau agent at Millican reported that the freedmen were not working well, but he attributed that to the fact that they were being treated badly. Few, he noted, had received remuneration for the previous year's work.[29] A subsequent report indicated that employers seldom hesitated to cheat the freedmen and that whites believed it was "no crime to take from a former slave his just earnings."[30] Indeed, that year whites were making efforts to place even greater control over the freedmen through "threats of the Ku Klux Klan."[31]

In July 1868 these tensions devolved into a bloody racial confrontation outside of Millican. When confronted with Ku Klux Klan members attempting to frighten them, blacks responded with gunfire. Klansmen later threatened retaliation. Then, the rumor of a lynching and a confrontation with a deputy sheriff led a local black leader, George Brooks, to call for blacks to arm themselves.[32] Whites concluded that a black uprising against whites was in progress and a sheriff's posse was gathered to reinforce officials at Millican. The Bureau agent at Bryan attempted to reconcile the parties, even bringing in Federal troops, but he could not prevent a confrontation outside of the town when whites scoured the countryside looking for freedmen with arms. In the days that followed Brooks was lynched and an unknown number of blacks were killed. Subsequently, the agent believed peace had returned, but the event clearly indicated the ability of the white community to suppress the blacks, and it probably ensured that the labor practices that had led up to the confrontation remained in place.[33]

Labor difficulties were a major problem in the county's economic life in the years after the war, but a variety of other factors added to the uncertainty for the local economy in the immediate postwar years. In many ways, risks associated with farming that had not presented themselves in the 1850s did so after the war. As planters prepared for the cotton harvest in the autumn of 1867, reports indicated that the cotton worm had been devastating crops from Brazos County down the river. Observers estimated that not more than one-fourth of the crop planted that year would be harvested.[34] In the spring of 1868 heavy rains and serious flooding reduced local crops.[35] In addition, Brazos County was subjected to the ravages of diseases. During the summer of 1867 a yellow fever epidemic hit the entire area along the Brazos River, with newspapers providing daily lists of men and women killed by the fever.[36] Taken as a whole, the rosy picture darkened through the first years after the war.

While the anecdotal material emphasized problems, tax records and the 1870 census indicated that overall things may not have been as bad as they appeared. The 1870 agricultural census marked an actual economic expansion, showing an increase in the cotton produced in the county from 2,209 bales in 1860 to 6,927.[37] Essential to this enhanced productivity was the continuing increase in land ownership. From the end of the war until 1870, the number of landowners listed on the tax rolls doubled to 476 individuals. As the number of landowners increased, other trends also suggested that land was being shifted from grazing to the growing of crops. The size of the average holding continued to decline, reaching 499 acres. Property valuations began to rise from their immediate postwar low, even though not approaching the prewar high.

In the midst of this overall expansion, however, for the first time the position of the landed elites appeared unsettled. Their numbers had steadily increased through the 1850s and the war years, and they continued to do so between 1865 and 1870. At this point fifty-nine taxpayers were part of the elite with more than a thousand acres of land. In addition, after ten years of decline the average number of acres that they owned increased, moving up from 2,096 acres to 2,342. Persistence rates, however, suggested problems among the landed elites. Thirty-nine of the members of the 1865 elite remained in the county in 1870, but their overall well-being was less certain. Nine of the thirty-nine had dropped out of the elite class, either disappearing from the tax rolls or reporting the loss of land. The persistence rate of the elite thus dropped to a low of 57 percent. Again, the tax rolls show a pattern, but in the end do not let us know exactly what was happening to individual landowners. Some obviously had moved, leaving the county and providing little evidence as to why they did so. In other cases land simply had been lost, such as Charles Smith's move from 1,417 acres to 299 acres, but the why is unknown.

Even though the persistence rate was down, thirty members of the elite of 1865 did manage to hang on to their property. Some acquired even more. Wilson Reed was the most successful, emerging in 1870 as the largest land owner in the county with 14,905 acres. Harvey Mitchell also was one of the success stories, adding 7,035 acres to the 4,558 he had owned in 1865. As in the past, suggesting opportunities for success still remained in the county, they would be joined by landowners from within the county who had increased their property to one thousand acres or newcomers who had moved in from outside. Many of the former moved into the bottom of the elite class, with individuals like Henderson Hardy who had supplemented his 518 acres with another 924 acres being typical. L. Edwin, the third largest landowner in the county with 8,870 acres, typified those who had arrived after the war.

The steady expansion of population and landownership and the breakup of larger holdings that had been the major trend in Brazos County for two decades continued into the final years of Reconstruction, the period between 1870 and 1874, but these trends were accompanied by new factors. By 1874 the number of land owners in the county reached 555, up seventy-nine individuals from 1870. For the first time a new pattern in landownership appeared, with forty-seven African Americans comprising the majority of new landowners.[38] At the same time that landownership increased, however, the number of acres assessed by the tax collector declined, dropping to 184,997 acres, a loss that has no easy explanation although in the midst of a taxpayer revolt against the Republican administration at the time individuals may have refused to report their holdings. The increase in landowners and the decline in total assessed lands led inevitably to a decrease in the average size of holdings, although that had been a trend in place since 1850. The average at this time fell to 333 acres per landowner. Ultimately, even though the total acreage reported declined and the county experienced significant problems interfering with agriculture, landowning continued to increase.

As between 1865 and 1870, the period of 1870 to 1874 showed a less secure picture for the county's landed elite even in the midst of a period of economic expansion. For the first time the number of individuals with more than a thousand acres declined, dropping from fifty-three to forty-one. In addition, the average acreage for them dropped as well, decreasing on the average more than 500 acres to 1,841. Their share of the total property in the county also dropped; 7 percent of all property owners now owned only 41 percent of the total property in the county. As in the first years after the war, persistence rates also showed instability, with the percentage of large land owners surviving this four-year period dropping to the lowest point during the period of study, 33 percent. Only twenty of the fifty-nine individuals who had owned a thousand acres in 1870 remained part of that class in 1874. The days of the landed elite in Brazos County appeared on the verge of ending.

As has been noted, an examination of tax assessments cannot account for the fate of each individual taxpayer. Individual biographies, family histories, or a search through land transactions offer the historian tools to potentially answer that question. When it is possible to do so, it is possible to discern something of why they, at least, fit within the particular trend that they did. It often had little to do with larger historical events. The fate of the Millican family is instructive. Their economic demise appears to have resulted more from the lifestyle of a fractious family, whose names often made newspaper headlines in this period. In February 1860 one of the Millicans lost his thumb in a shooting affair in Washington County, an event that showed something of the family's character. The following August, F. M. Millican was killed by his brother after a fight in which the brother had been knifed by F. M. That October, Elliott Millican died when he jumped from a Washington hotel window "in a fit of insanity, caused by hard drinking." In 1871 Robert Meyers killed the brother of J. E. Millican, then killed J. E. when the latter, in a drunken rage, attempted to kill Meyers. In 1872 John E. Millican died at the hands of the children of Robert Meyers, after John killed their father. Not surprisingly, few Millicans remained on the tax rolls by 1874, and all together they owned only 2,700 acres.[39]

As has been shown, however, an analysis of tax assessments does allow us to see patterns of landholding and some characteristics of landowners. Such an examination provides a framework within which the stories of individuals are more understandable. It helps us see whether or not an individual's gain or loss of property is typical or atypical. For Brazos County, these local records clearly show that the period 1850 to 1874 was one of steady growth, at least in terms of population and landownership. Until the very end, these figures also demonstrate that the community was one where at least for the landed elite conditions were very stable and that the broader economic situation allowed their persistence over time. In addition, the records suggest that the war had relatively little real impact on the community. If one were to look only at the period 1860 to 1874 the decline in the size of landholdings might suggest that the war had a major effect on land ownership in the county, but looking at the whole era the steady decline in the size of landholdings shows that trend to have been in place throughout the antebellum years as well. At least in this frontier county in Texas, the end of large land holdings simply marked the passage of the community from a stock raising economy to one centered more on farming. War and Reconstruction may have had little to do with this change.

Notes

1. See, as examples, Randolph B. Campbell, *A Southern Community in Crisis: Harrison County, Texas, 1850–1880 (*Austin: Texas State Historical Association, 1983); Carl H. Moneyhon, *The Impact of the Civil War and Reconstruction on Arkansas: Persistence in the Midst of Ruin* (Baton Rouge: Louisiana State University Press, 1994); Jonathan Wiener, *Social Origins of the New South: Alabama, 1860–1885* (Baton Rouge: Louisiana State University Press, 1978); and "Planter Persistence and Social Change, 1850–1870," *Journal of Interdisciplinary History* 7 (Autumn 1976): 255–57. See also Richard G. Lowe and Randolph B. Campbell, "The Distribution of Wealth in Texas, 1861," *Journal of American History* 63 (Sept. 1976): 316–24; and Campbell and Lowe, *Wealth and Power in Antebellum Texas* (College Station: Texas A&M University Press, 1977).

2. James Roark, *Masters Without Slaves: Southern Planters in the Civil War and Reconstruction* (New York: W. W. Norton, 1977).

3. See Moneyhon, *The Impact of the Civil War and Reconstruction on Arkansas*, 15, fn. 6, for a discussion of the problem of a quantitative definition of the plantation elite.

4. United States Bureau of the Census, *The Seventh Census of the United States: 1850* (Washington, D.C.: Robert Armstrong, 1853), 503.

5. Mark Odintz, "Brazos County," in Ron Tyler, et al., eds., *The New Handbook of Texas* (6 vols.; Austin: Texas State Historical Association, 1996), 1: 712 (hereafter *NHOT*).

6. Bureau of the Census, *Tenth Census, 1880, Part III: Productions of Agriculture* (Washington, D.C.: Government Printing Office, 1883), 88.

7. Eleanor H. Nance, "Richard Carter," *NHOT*, 1: 1,000; Lon F. Curbello, Jr., "Robert Hemphill Millican," *NHOT*, 4: 747; Christina L. Gray, "Millican, Texas," *NHOT*, 4: 747; "The Thomas Bowman Family," in Glenna Fourman Brundidge, ed., *Brazos County History: Rich Past—Bright Future* (Bryan, TX: Family History Foundation, 1986), 194.

8. Brundidge, *Brazos County History,* 200–1.

9. Bureau of the Census, *Seventh Census of the United States: 1850*, 514, 517.

10. Brundidge, *Brazos County History*, 60.

11. *Nacogdoches Chronicle*, May 31, 1853; *San Antonio Ledger*, Sept. 8, 1853; *Austin Texas State Gazette*, Sept. 17, 1853, Sept. 2, 1854; *Houston Telegraph*, June 30, 1858.

12. Subsequently, this survival rate will be referred to as persistence. Persistence rates will be one of the marks of the impact of events on local landed elites.

13. (Clarksville) *Standard*, Mar. 7, 1857; (Austin) *Texas State Gazette*, Apr. 17, 1858; *Houston Telegraph*, Jan. 30, 1858; Gray, "Millican, Texas," 4: 747.

14. The census taken in 1860 showed some 551,774 acres in farms, although only 53,139 were considered improved. The cash value of farms had increased to $1,764,388.

15. Bureau of the Census, *Agriculture of the United States in 1860* (Washington, D.C.: Government Printing Office, 1864), 141; Bureau of the Census, *Population of the United States in 1860* (Washington, D.C.: Government Printing Office, 1864), 484. The census reported 1,063 slaves in the county in 1860, more than were listed on the tax rolls.

16. "Selected U.S. Federal Census Non-Population Schedules, 1850–1880" [http://search.ancestry.com/search/db.aspx?dbid=1276 (accessed Aug. 18, 2011)]; Bureau of the Census, Eighth Census, 1860, Texas, Brazos County, Schedule 4, Products of Agriculture, Record Group 29, National Archives, Washington, D.C. (Microfilm T1134, Roll 3).

17. *Houston Weekly Telegraph*, Aug. 31, 1860.

18. Brundidge, *Brazos County History*, 85.

19. Ibid., 86–87.

20. Paul R. Scott, "From Dilapidated Community to Banner County," in ibid., 90–91.

21. "Texans in the Civil War, 10th Texas Infantry, Company F" [www.texansinthecivilwar.com/10th_Infantry/Company_f.html (accessed Dec. 16, 2011)].

22. *Dallas Weekly Herald*, Oct. 16, 1861.

23. *Washington Ranger* quoted in *Houston Tri-Weekly Telegraph*, Nov. 13, 1863.

24. "MILLICAN, C.S.A." [http://www.brazoscountyhistory.org/node/38 (accessed Dec. 16, 2011)].

25. Gray, "Millican, Texas," 4: 747.

26. *Houston Tri-Weekly Telegraph*, Sept. 26, 1862.

27. *Dallas Weekly Herald*, Oct. 12, 1865.

28. *Galveston News* quoted in *Dallas Weekly Herald*, Nov. 11, 1865; W. L. M. to Dear Herald, Nov. 4, 1865, in *Dallas Weekly Herald*, Nov. 11, 1865, "New Advertisements," *Dallas Weekly Herald*, Dec. 23, 1865.

29. Edward Miller to J. T. Kirkman, June 26, 1867, Letters Received, Records of the Assistant Commissioner for the State of Texas, Bureau of Refugees, Freedmen and Abandoned Lands, RG 105, NA (hereinafter RACST, BRFAL) (M821, Roll 7).

30. Report for Months Ending March 1868, April 4, 1868, N. H. Randlett, Reports of Operations and Conditions, RACST, BRFAL (M821, Roll 25).

31. Report for Months Ending June 30, 1868, July 9, 1868, in ibid. (M821, Roll 26).

32. The basic outline of the confrontation is based on N. H. Randlett's report, unless otherwise noted. Randlett to Charles A. Vernou, July 22, 1868, RACST, BRFAL (M821, Roll 14). See also Report for Months Ending June 30, 1868, July 9, 1868, Randlett, Reports of Operations and Conditions, RACST, BRFAL (M821, Roll 26), for further background on events leading up to the outbreak.

33. Randlett to Vernou, Aug. 30, 1868, RACST, BRFAL (M821, Roll 14).

34. *News Letter*, Sept. 7, 1867, quoted in *Flake's Bulletin*, Sept. 12, 1867.

35. *Flake's Bulletin*, Mar. 26, 1868.

36. Ibid., Oct. 3, 1867.

37. Bureau of the Census, *The Statistics of the Wealth and Industry of the United States* (Washington D. C.: Government Printing Office, 1872), 250–52.

38. Of the forty-seven African-American landowners, seven were women. These taxpayers owned an average of twenty-two acres, but the amount of land held by each individual varied from an acre per person to 100 acres each for Lewis Randall and Peter Brown, and even 398 acres for John Love.

39. *Houston Weekly Telegraph*, Feb. 21, Oct. 27 (quotation), 1860; *Austin Texas State Gazette*, Sept. 15, 1860; *Flake's Bulletin*, Feb. 12, 1870; *Galveston Tri-Weekly News*, May 31, 1871, Sept. 2, 1872.

Pvt. James M. Wood, Mann's Texas Cavalry, organized in 1864 and posted at Galveston. Courtesy of DeGolyer Library, Southern Methodist University

Soldiering on the Texas Coast and the Problem of Confederate Nationalism

Andrew F. Lang

Beginning with the publication of Bell I. Wiley's pioneering works on Johnny Reb and Billy Yank, scholarly literature on Civil War soldiers has been bold and controversial. Historians have long since developed myriad interpretations to recreate the lives and experiences of the countless men who donned the blue and gray. In fact, scholars increasingly and effectively have utilized soldiers' wartime accounts as useful tools to investigate the nineteenth-century's deep cauldron of social, cultural, and political values. Thus, the field has evolved to encompass much more than merely battles and generals, and now underscores the centrality of race, gender, nationalism, and memory. Although the past three decades have witnessed an impressive and unusually perceptive outpouring of scholarship on Civil War soldiers—many of which have duly answered Maris A. Vinovskis's call to integrate social and military history—almost exclusive emphasis has been placed on those Yankees and Confederates who served within the war's principal campaigning armies. Historians have, therefore, crafted diverse explanations for soldier ideology, attitude, and motivation, all generally focused upon the famous eastern and western theaters. Most, however, rarely discuss the effect of the conflict on the "other soldiers" who served behind the lines, in garrisons, or as occupation forces. Such men are significant in number, yet they remain at best a huge mystery and at worst a neglected footnote.[1] This essay seeks to provide a nuanced and textured contribution to the established literature on Civil War soldiers by addressing how those who operated as coastal garrison troops in Texas understood the purpose of their peculiar military missions.[2] These men rarely engaged Union forces while assigned to one of the war's backwaters, which fostered a static environment of boredom and inactivity. Troops stationed in garrisons that stretched from Brownsville to Sabine Pass struggled to maintain cohesion and a sense of purpose. Periodic insubordination, mutinies, and generally low spirits characterized this military existence as men who served in coastal outfits suffered not only from a lack of material goods, but also few inspiring and symbolic leaders. Rather than focusing exclusively on the traditional historiographical paradigms of why soldiers fought, this study primarily reflects how situation, circumstance, environment, and experience overlapped to inform particular cultural responses to the nature of Civil War military service.[3] Therefore, two broad yet interrelated questions are posed.

First, what were the ideological, moral, and tangible effects of war upon Confederate soldiers who rarely saw combat and were largely removed from the war's principal events and armies? The interpretative thrust of this piece revolves around not only the current literature on Civil War soldiers, but also on the development of national identity in the Confederacy. Recent scholarship suggests that many white southerners identified themselves as Confederate citizens committed to the project of nation-building, and they accepted defeat only after their armies in the field were forced to capitulate to a more powerful foe. This argument largely displaced the "loss of will" thesis, which posited that the Confederacy collapsed internally, long before the surrender at Appomattox, because of a failure to establish a cohesive identity, an overbearing government, battlefield defeats, guilt over slavery, and class conflict between elite slaveholders and yeomen.[4] The Confederate soldiering experience fits neatly within this historiographical framework. Many scholars now agree that, in spite of unfathomable physical hardship and battlefield defeats, Confederate troops were dedicated nationalists who believed that they were the true guarantors of an independent southern nation.[5] Thus secondly, how did garrison soldiers fit within this nationalistic mold when stationed in relatively static isolation and prevented from marching, campaigning, and fighting in the war's grand battles?

The Texas Gulf Coast serves as an ideal locale in which to test current scholarly theories about the Confederate soldiering experience and wartime nationalism. The Lone Star State is normally overlooked in Civil War studies primarily due to the lack of any large-scale Union invasion. Indeed, with the exception of the brief Union occupation of Galveston in late 1862 and various other points along the coast in 1863–1864, Texans escaped significant influence from United States armies. Thus, Texas's coastal defenders, who enlisted to protect the gateway to the state's interior, did not experience the war's grand campaigns and rarely interacted with the enemy. Although localized approaches might not be representative of the wider whole, they do allow the historian to complete an intimate and detailed study over particular dynamics that may be invisible in broader examinations. Indeed, hardly any room has been dedicated in the current literature to Confederate garrison soldiers, which can potentially reveal new insights into the republican expectations deeply held by nineteenth-century volunteer citizen-soldiers and the wartime influence on the southern culture of honor. While certainly not displacing, but rather complementing, current historiographical trends, this essay can possibly point toward a more complicated understanding of military service and nationalism during the Civil War.[6]

The first Confederate troops who populated the Texas coast were drawn, naturally, from nearby locales, but also from the state's western communities. These volunteers collectively relished their roles as citizen-soldiers and defenders of Texas's most important region. Scores of volunteers rushed to the coast in service to the incipient nation, and entered the military with carefully defined expectations. They unequivocally trusted that their service as civilian volunteers necessitated combat, which potentially fulfilled long-held cultural visions of battlefield glory and martial grandeur. The Texas frontier tradition, from which many of the state's initial Civil War troops were raised, inspired quests to defend home during times of crisis. Texas's citizen-soldier ideal long centered on the principle that, upon moments of external threat, white male citizens would voluntarily leave their private lives and serve in the military defense of the republic, state, or nation. This trait stressed the belief that men were expected to act individually and spontaneously in their volunteering, fight aggressively against the region's foes, and return home immediately upon a completed mission. Thus, implicit cultural qualifications for citizenship—voluntary fighting, physical prowess, and masculine courage—were placed upon white males considered to be the most reliable and honorable defenders of the republic, and later the state.[7]

Although Texas now faced a new enemy—the Union army and navy—citizens embraced their voluntary military heritage and hurried into the ranks to withstand any potential coastal invasion. The region's first defenders initially enjoyed high morale, born primarily out of a strong sense of Confederate nationalism. Much like their counterparts in the larger Confederate armies, these soldiers crafted their immediate wartime identity on a hatred of perceived Yankee invaders, their confidence as defenders of a slaveholding republic, and the knowledge that they protected both home and nation. And, in concert with their citizen-soldier heritage, coastal Confederates expressed their martial enthusiasm and believed that their present position required fighting and, if necessary, dying. A soldier at Galveston observed that many of his comrades wore "red or blue shirt striped [pants] with a revolver stuck to both right and left side and Bowey knife behind and in thare hand musketts shot guns riffles and all kinds of arms practicing and going through minuvers."

Similarly, Elijah Petty, who served in the 17th Texas Infantry, remarked that "We are making cartridges—moulding bullets, rubbing up guns and pistols and sharpening knives for the purpose of welcoming the Lincolnites 'with bloody hands to hospitable graves.'" He then informed his daughter that "If we fight . . . your father will be found in the front rank, let it cost what it may." And, an officer acknowledged that his men at Indianola "will fight until there are none left to tell the story." Troops were eager to defend the region's strategic and economic importance to the state and Confederacy, even in spite of the woeful state of local defenses, and a volunteer in the 10th Texas Infantry defiantly intended "to make a permanent stand" in his protection of the coastline.[8]

Hailing from locales across the state, the soldiers who served in coastal areas were similar to the countless other volunteers in the United States and Confederacy who were motivated out of a profound sense of patriotism, abhorrence of the enemy, and enthusiasm for adventure. In spite of these collective values, however, the protection of home and hearth assumed supreme importance. Whether their families resided in a coastal town or a community in the interior, Confederate defenders of the Texas coast understood that they functioned as a shield against an impending Union invasion. Some soldiers initially refused to serve elsewhere. They had established livelihoods on the coast and were unwilling to venture away from their antebellum residences. The desire to remain wedded to the coast and form a local defense of the region, however, did not function in isolation. It was instead linked with an acute loyalty to the new southern nation. The very essence of Confederate nationalism required multiple layers of loyalty, including ties between home and country, and coastal soldiers explicitly acknowledged this association. P. C. Woods informed his wife that he "endeavor[ed] to do my whole duty to God and my country. Constant duties I hope will make my absence from my family associations bearable." Coastal Confederates, by virtue of their citizen-soldier philosophy, recognized the mutual obligation to protect their families and defend their new nation.[9]

And so they waited. The war's first year eventually closed with nary a glimpse of Union forces. Of course, coastal Confederates witnessed occasional blockading vessels pass harmlessly along the horizon, yet they rarely drifted into contact with the soldiers who remained anxiously on the shore. Months passed, and as 1862 dawned, and the excitement of secession and military mobilization had long expired, with the prospect of a fight with the enemy growing paler by the day, some volunteers complained of monotony and menial hardship, while others even began to question the rationale of service in such remote locations. Isaiah Harlan, who served in the 10th Texas Infantry at Fort Hebert near Galveston, wrote in February, "We are not doing anything here . . . I have nothing to write [of interest]. I don't know when I'll be home." He also grumbled that he had mastered few drill tactics and blamed his officers for being "such gofers [who] can't learn any thing, scarcely and of course the rest of us get along slowly." Morale along the Texas Gulf Coast thus began to be shaped by the lack of martial activity, and spirits consequently plummeted. Soldiers came to feel unusually detached from the conflict and failed to comprehend their purpose in the Confederate army. Troops typically performed picket duty, strolled along the beach collecting sea shells, or stared at the distant Union blockading fleet. William B. Duncan, an officer in Spaight's Cavalry Battalion, realized that the blockaders posed little threat, so he permitted small, secret furloughs for his men. He recognized that his command's spirits were soured because their only visible enemy operated solely in an economic, and not militaristic, context. Thus, as some Confederate officials similarly deduced, since "[n]o invasion of Texas is deemed probable," coastal soldiers should be uprooted and transferred to Tennessee and Arkansas, where southern military fortunes had endured significant reverses.[10]

Hardly anything in the daily lives of coastal Confederates produced a semblance of national purpose or duty. They had entered the military with clear ambitions and cultural understandings of how victory would be achieved, based almost exclusively on fighting in grand battles. Indeed, James Black, a member of the 1st Texas Heavy Artillery, "dreamed last night the last Battle was fought on Galveston Island. I thought our Regiment fought with desperation driving the enemy into the Gulf. After the battle was over I thought peace was made." Yet, after months of drilling and sitting idly, the likelihood of a fight and perceived contributions to the Confederate cause greatly dissipated. "I am tired of soldiering I assure you," wrote Thomas Jefferson League, "it is far from being the vocation I should select for a constant occupation." Another soldier complained from Velasco, "I can see no reason for [being stationed here] myself, for now that we have got here, we can neither see or hear anything of the Yankees." The Confederacy's entire existence was born out of military events and wartime interaction. The southern soldiers, who volunteered, campaigned, and fought in the conflict's major battles viewed themselves as the principal agents in the quest for national independence. Service in backwater garrisons, however, did not foment the level of morale necessary to buttress an ideological attachment to the southern nation.[11]

Once it appeared likely that the war would not touch the Texas Gulf Coast, numerous regimental and company commanders articulated the depressed sentiments of their men and requested to be transferred to other theaters. Officers petitioned the state government and argued that their commands were ready to march to Richmond, Virginia, and even Washington, D. C., while others suggested that their services were not even needed on the coast. Captain A. C. McKeon acknowledged that many citizens opposed his unit leaving Galveston in the face of the Union naval blockade, but he noted that "I am satisfied that one solitary company leaving Galveston could make but little difference admitting that there is a 'probability' that our services 'might' be required here. I am anxious to be in the fight with my Company and ready to take the field." McKeon's appeal was not "solitary," but rather one in a long line of similar requests. Another captain, John Miller, estimated that "the danger to our Gulf Coast has been much exaggerated." He believed that the potential Union occupation of various coastal locales would not be detrimental to the Confederacy. Arkansas and Missouri, according to Miller, were of greater strategic importance, even to Texas's fate. Cavalry officer George W. Durant likewise admitted that his unit threatened to disband if they were not sent to theaters stretching from Arizona to Virginia. He said that his men were "panting for Glory" and were tired of waiting for any action to develop along the Texas Gulf Coast.[12]

Soldiers' spirited ambitions, which were once grounded in confidence and martial passion, became adversely shaped after the realization that coastal military service did not meet the perceived cultural requirements of volunteer duty. Guarding cotton at the mouth of the Brazos, laboring on fortifications at Corpus Christi, or performing constant drill exercises at Sabine Pass, prevented soldiers from comprehending fully the true meaning of their service. In their minds, they were doing too little to contribute to the war effort. William Kuykendall, a soldier in the 1st Texas Cavalry (Confederate) near Brownsville, considered that "[w]hen we inlisted in the service we expected to be sent to the seat of war where we would at once see active service and thus be able to prove ourselves worthy of the cause we espoused." In fact, these sentiments extended beyond the region's defenders. A pair of responses, divergent in tone, yet cut from the same cultural cloth, reflected the internal and ideological pressures faced by coastal Confederates. Gideon Lincecum, a prominent civilian who lived in Washington County, received a downcast letter from a soldier stationed at Virginia Point who related his displeasure with serving in a distant corner of the Confederacy. Lincecum expressed his genuine sympathy to the "deep-rooted disaffection at the unnecessary inactivity and useless expenditure of the time and means and strength of the common soldier." This reaction stemmed from a long-held understanding that troops became demoralized after their expectations, based on the citizen-soldier philosophy, were not met.[13]

Joseph B. Polley, who served in the 4th Texas Infantry in Robert E. Lee's Army of Northern Virginia, and who campaigned and fought virtually all across the eastern theater, adopted a markedly different perspective. He sarcastically remarked during the summer of 1862, "who, oh who, wouldn't gladly risk his life in arduous service on the Texas coast?" Polley judged that garrison troops were lazy and did not appreciate their quality of life and safety: "With nothing to do and a horse to do it on; with every delicacy to tempt the appetite, and with starched linen to wear; with a servant to wait on him, and, while he takes a post-prandial siesta, fan the flies off his noble brow and away from his soft, white hand; with ladies to look at and walk with, listen to and talk to, and dance with and make love to, and with only a lazy gunboat in the hazy distance to affright his heroic soul by an occasional shell." That type of military life certainly did not meet Polley's approval. "A stern and unaccommodating fate denies the crown to my ambition that such a service would be," he wrote. "It is only here in Virginia I may hope to win laurels."[14] Both Lincecum's and Polley's expressions, although vastly different in attitude, reflected how nineteenth-century contemporaries distinguished the proper roles of citizen-soldiers. And, their statements underscored the negative pronouncements made by coastal garrison troops themselves. Active participation in war, especially one in which national implications were at stake, was required, in their minds, for those who temporarily left their private lives and volunteered their services.

Meanwhile, in July 1862, John Bankhead Magruder was relieved as a field commander in the Army of Northern Virginia. Confederate authorities then ordered him to direct the District of Texas, New Mexico, and Arizona. Magruder's arrival in Houston in November 1862 was met with great celebration as local citizens believed "they had at last found a military leader worthy of their support." Magruder, who was an aggressive fighter, immediately set to work on plans to recapture Galveston, which had been easily occupied by Union military forces nearly a month earlier. Considering that a soldier's morale and subsequent national identification was affected largely by proximity to military events and activity, Galveston's recapture by Confederate forces on January 1, 1863, resulted in soaring spirits. In one of the few instances during the war, these soldiers were called upon to engage in military activity and tactics that resembled acts undertaken by comrades in other theaters. J. H. Russell, a private in the 7th Texas Cavalry, remarked that his captain called for volunteers to retake the city, "and I for one leaped forth with eagerness to respond to the call of my Country." Following the successful takeover, soldiers' sentiments and letters home soared with confidence. Coastal troops referred to the battle as a "brilliant affair," and praised their efforts and commanders. In the battle's immediate aftermath, soldiers were supremely confident that the city would stay in Confederate control for the rest of the war. Russell informed his wife that he and his unit captured scores of Union prisoners and commandeered much-needed provisions and guns. "But the best of all," he concluded, "is we [have] retaken Galveston. Run all the feds out, and now possess the City." Another soldier bragged that "Galveston is now ours & likely to remain." More important, though, the city's recapture allowed soldiers to examine larger wartime events in a more positive light and even express an unequivocal commitment to sacrifice and hardship. Thus in the days following the stunning victory, coastal Confederates celebrated Magruder because he had planned the attack, coordinated the fighting, and was unquestionably victorious.[15]

Galveston's recapture functioned as a hugely symbolic event, especially for its coastal defenders. Indeed, the Houston *Telegraph* proclaimed that the soldiers had affected a great shift in the Island City: sentiments markedly improved and the region's defenses rapidly progressed, as Galveston prepared to become "the Vicksburg of Texas." Magruder and his men received celebrated praise from the highest levels of the Confederate government, including personal congratulations from Jefferson Davis. Sam Houston also acknowledged that Magruder "breathed new life into everything; you have illustrated to [Texas's troops] what they can do." Galveston's defenders had, in their minds, reconfirmed themselves as citizen-soldiers.[16]

Nevertheless, the static nature of coastal military life eventually came once more to define the garrisons that dotted the Texas Gulf Coast. With the exception of the stunning victory at Sabine Pass, sentiments quickly resembled the more characteristic tones of indifference, boredom, tedium, and monotony. Whereas troops' spirits were lifted temporarily in Galveston, those stationed at other coastal locales seemed completely immune to the inspiring news. A soldier wrote from the fortifications at Brazoria County, the same day on which the battle occurred, "We are entirely isolated here . . . and you can see nothing around but soldiers. You have no idea how dull it makes it appear. We have [only] to drill,

drill, drill, from 7 o'clock in the morning until 9." And, an officer in the 8th Texas Infantry near Port Lavaca admitted days later that his men were on the verge of severe demoralization. William H. Neblett, who served in the 20th Texas Infantry, likewise acknowledged in April 1863, "This is an extremely monotonous and tiresome life. We do not drill any and have nothing to do but answer to our name at roll call which is done at morning and evening and [then] go on dress parade." These collective responses marked a dearth of military responsibility and aversion to service, which led ultimately to dangerously depressed spirits.[17]

Life for communities with Confederate garrisons constituted a miserable existence for both civilians and soldiers. Residents who fled Galveston, for instance, at the beginning of the war slowly started to repopulate the city, which led to a tenuous and conflicted relationship with local soldiers. Galveston was, in every sense, an occupied city: martial law was declared, civilians were subjected to the rules of war, and habeas corpus was suspended per Magruder's authorization. Beginning in the summer of 1863 reports surfaced about troop depredations in which goods and produce were stolen from local merchants, alcohol and tobacco forcibly commandeered at gunpoint from local saloons, and, in one case, a private citizen being hanged for defending himself against a renegade soldier. Meanwhile, troops stationed in garrisons just outside the Island City were arrested for desertion after refusing to perform routine work. Finally, rampant drunkenness and gambling supplied the necessary ingredients for a deteriorating military life. One soldier despondently wrote from Galveston, "I can safely say I do not like [garrison] life. It is true our fate is bad and our living is hard. But that is not the worst. It is the wickedest place I ever saw. It is useless for me to try to describe what sort of wickedness is practiced here. The Devil himself can only do it."[18]

These, however, were relatively minor episodes. Morale among the coast's military population finally reached its nadir by the late summer of 1863, and erupted into a series of mutinies. Dozens of soldiers at Galveston revolted against their officers, and complained incessantly about the quality and quantity of their food, which was reportedly "sour, dirty, weevil-eaten, and filled with ants and worms." Moreover, troops were demoralized about seemingly useless drill on hot summer afternoons, late wage payments by the Confederacy, and especially the recent news of Vicksburg's surrender. Private James Black reported in August that "There is a great deal of disaffection among the troops here. Many of them are whipped since the fall of Vicksburg." Consequently, members of the 3rd Texas Infantry and 1st Texas Heavy Artillery refused to drill or obey their superiors' orders. One officer attempted to quell the uprising by ordering other soldiers to surround the dissidents with loaded rifles and artillery pieces. Eventually, under the threat of military incarceration and even death, the mutineers hesitantly gave up. This brand of insubordination stemmed not only from soldiers' obvious disgust with poor provisions. A. Q. Clements, a member of the 3rd Texas, cited another cause. He reported to his sister a month after the mutiny that he no longer could tolerate "seeing the destruction of my country and the misery and destruction of war which prevails throughout the land." The realization that they could not combat the loss of Vicksburg, combined with their lack of faith in Confederate authorities to provide for their material and financial interests, led these men to act out of their perceived alienation from both the war effort and their government.[19]

A pair of similar episodes occurred in September 1863. Scores of soldiers from Terrell's Texas Cavalry Regiment deserted their unit following Magruder's order for dismounted garrison service at Galveston. "Under this last order, quite a number of men abandoned the [unit] and returned to their homes," reported the unit's captain. The appellants believed that they possessed a right to active field service, which they regarded as an essential component to their enlistment. The captain added that this conviction "may be regarded as the only palliation for desertion," rather than a pronounced disloyalty. Indeed, the soldiers judged that, unless their definitions and understandings of military service were met, their time was better spent at home with their families. Meanwhile, soldiers at Sabine Pass intended "to leave their colors and go to their homes" due to rumors of invasion by Federal forces and Indians on the northern frontier. Some garrison officers, who allegedly "[spoke] disparagingly of the war," convinced these men that their position on the coast rendered their families vulnerable and defenseless.[20]

Reports of large-scale Union incursion indeed informed soldiers of their precarious station. Coastal Confederates understood that their homes were left relatively undefended as stories increasingly drifted into their camps about enemy forces possibly entering Texas. Troops realized that, if the news ultimately proved accurate, there simply were too few Confederates to protect the coast as well as the interior. Magruder found it almost impossible to establish the "relative importance of the different sections of Texas to be defended," because of the shortage of troops to garrison all of the coast's vital locales. The region was much too large to defend completely. He eventually selected only a few strategic beachheads, including Fort Esperanza, Sabine Pass, and Galveston, which he concluded were the most important areas to secure. Men and materiel were, therefore, constantly shifted, moved, and repositioned along the coast to meet the threat of a possible Union invasion. This resulted, however, in mutinous sentiments already prevalent in some units: soldiers, who knew they were outnumbered, were loath to be stationed at coastal points which they deemed secondary to the safety of their families.[21]

The problems were exacerbated when Union Maj. Gen. Nathaniel P. Banks launched his Rio Grande expedition against Texas in November 1863. Long-held fears of invasion were finally realized when United States forces landed at Brazos Santiago and proceeded northward along the coast. Banks's campaign, which lasted until the spring of 1864, effectively occupied Brownsville, Corpus Christi, Saluria, Matagorda Island, Indianola, and Port Lavaca. The Confederates retained only Velasco, Galveston, and Sabine Pass. Combat rarely occurred as Union forces, which easily outnumbered the coastal defenders, effortlessly established their presence. Confederate Brig. Gen. Hamilton P. Bee, for instance, commanded fewer than two hundred men at Brownsville, which was hurriedly evacuated upon first sight of the Union army. Fort Brown, protecting the town, was burned, resulting in mass chaos, confusion, and mutiny. Bee later argued that similar episodes would be commonplace as Confederates were forced constantly to retreat from approaching Union troops. Magruder agreed. He continued to receive reports that coastal soldiers, whose morale had declined rapidly, could not be relied upon to remain at their posts. Troops were especially concerned about the increasing number of Union beachheads that could be used to launch invasions into the interior, and thus quit their units.[22]

Throughout the winter of 1863–1864, a host of coastal Confederates spread across the region responded explicitly to this disconcerting situation. Jeff Morgan informed his wife that "I have no good news . . . for every thing look[s] very gloomy at this time." He warned of a potential invasion as far north as Houston, from where he wrote, and admitted that he would not be able to return home any time soon. "There is a good deal of uneasiness here [in Galveston] about the Yankees," wrote William H. Neblett, who feared that "we have not enough troops to defend the place against a strong force." Rudolf Coreth, a soldier in the 32nd Texas Cavalry, sent to his family a series of letters which captured the "absolute demoralization" among his comrades. "Confidence in this war has now sunken very much," he opined. "I talked yesterday with several and they were all in accord with one another that they would rather have mules than Negroes and Confederate money." These depressed spirits emanated from a collection of sources, many of which had defined the totality of the coastal soldiering experience. The Rio Grande expedition pushed local Confederates into a string of retreats and countermarches, which prevented outright fighting and adequate defense of the region. Because of shortages in manpower and weaponry, coastal soldiers watched as towns fell harmlessly to Union forces.[23]

Men who had enlisted expressly to guard the coast at all costs were now forced into capitulating or facing the Union military in pseudo-siege warfare. William Neblett again wrote from Galveston, "I think it is the intention of Gen Magruder to prepare the place for a siege . . . This gives us some uneasiness for fear that we may be cut off and starved after a long time into surrender." Soldiers at Matagorda Bay especially endured a miserable existence as United States gunboats pounded the beachside garrison. "The Feds shell us nearly every day," related John Claver Brightman, who recorded that infantry and cavalry units were prevented from venturing outward to resist the enemy's presence. Edward Pye admitted to his wife that the constant shelling sapped his comrades' morale. It was a "bloodless Campaign," he noted, yet the men were "mighty gloomy & out of spirits—the most of them—abuse old *Magruder & the war*—each one considering himself the *worst off* of any man in *The Confederacy*."[24]

Soldiers simply felt increasingly helpless in a war that they considered was spiraling out of their control. These responses, though, did not function in isolation. Rather, they were compounded, as Edward Pye acknowledged, when some coastal Confederates began to blame John B. Magruder for their despondent condition. Although Magruder had genuinely attempted to remedy the Trans-Mississippi Department's lack of supplies and inadequate food, his men had become alienated from him. The coastal Confederates under his command hailed largely from rural and frontier portions of Texas, and were noticeably troubled by Magruder's ostentatious and urbane personality. He had a long-standing reputation for being easily tempted by the bottle, egotistical in his personal appearance, and arrogant to the point of sheer annoyance. In most situations, Magruder stubbornly carried out what he deemed to be correct, regardless of decorum, tradition, or law. Edmund Kirby Smith, the commander of the Trans-Mississippi Department, privately acknowledged that Magruder "has an utter disregard for the law" and that "no reliance [can] be placed upon his obedience to an order unless it chimed in with his own plans and fancies." He was forced to spend most of his time in seemingly far-away Houston, where he was consumed by administrative and logistical matters for the Trans-Mississippi Department. Thus was partly the nature of garrison life: men were alienated from their commanding general's presence, which largely eliminated the possibility to be inspired by his potential leadership and example. In reality, quite the opposite was true. Magruder was accused of turning Texas into "a great military camp, subject to military rules," as he ordered his subordinates to shoot deserters and govern their districts with autocratic authority.[25]

As the war dragged on, coastal troops became further estranged from their commanding general. One soldier, H. C. Medford, complained that "My life [stationed near Galveston] is but damned little pleasure . . . . This war is beggaring me." In the early spring of 1864, Medford, like many of his comrades who served along the coast, again became painfully aware that their provisions and food were deteriorating. He criticized the poor quality of beef rations that he and his companions were given and wrote, "[i]t is an outrage that confederate soldiers should be compelled to live upon what we live upon." He did not necessarily support the idea of an armed uprising, although tersely noted that "if there are any justifiable causes for such things, it is here in our army." Men under Magruder's command were manifestly dispirited, and believed that Confederate authorities, including Magruder, actively mistreated soldiers in coastal garrisons. "I am afraid our country will never prosper," Medford concluded, "when there [is] so much fraud and perfidy practiced upon the private soldier by the functionaries of the government."[26]

Indeed, the situation had grown increasingly worse, and in March 1864 the military population's morale declined sharply, and resulted in another mutiny. Soldiers were particularly distressed because they did not believe that their superiors shared in their wants and hardships. For example, several of Galveston's prominent socialites hosted a dinner and ball for General Magruder and his staff. News of the event traveled quickly among the various units scattered around the city, and many soldiers became outraged when they learned of the merriment and food to be enjoyed by their officers. One soldier estimated that nearly 500 of his comrades stormed the house where the party was taking place, "approaching with arms, and two pieces of artillery, and preparing to raze the house to the ground." Magruder agreed to talk with the dissidents who demanded that he not enjoy the feasts or dances while they, as well as their families at home, suffered. The general pleaded with the mob to disband on the conditions that they would receive better rations and furloughs. The soldiers reluctantly complied, and probably assumed that Magruder would uphold his word. Later in the night, however, he and his guests enjoyed their party anyway.[27]

Coastal Confederates served in a static environment in which they were powerless to remedy an increasingly grim military situation, intensified by a commanding general with whom they could not associate. Soldiers had all but erased the memories of Magruder's laudable actions during the recapture of Galveston; instead, they viewed their leader with detached skepticism. These dynamics forged within the soldiers a negative and restless mindset by which martial passions could not be explored. L. D. Bradley noted that his post at Mud Island reflected the "dullness and apathy consequent upon Garrison duty," which encompassed serious consequences. Sentiments remained severely downcast along the coast as continued clashes between soldiers and civilians underscored the stresses of war within occupied garrisons. Discipline declined rapidly as coastal Confederates comprehended their inability to resist defeat and many departed for home, while others plundered remnants of local garrisons. Robberies, fights, and even murders were common throughout the war's final months, weakening relations between soldiers and local civilians. Some troops in Galveston, for instance, raided local stores and saloons, stealing whatever goods remained in the vicinity. Even though Magruder had promised to remedy some of the soldiers' complaints, and expressed soaring patriotic rhetoric in hopes of rallying his command, many deserted, plundered, and evaded service between late 1864 and May 1865. Soldiers' actions undertaken late in the war, which reflected their approach to the vast majority of the conflict, signified that they had little control over the environment that dictated their actions.[28]

Four broad conclusions can be drawn from this examination of wartime garrison culture along the Texas Gulf Coast. First, coastal Confederates initially celebrated their positions as volunteer citizen-soldiers who functioned within the nineteenth-century republican tradition. Temporarily suspending one's self-interested private life and voluntarily bearing arms in defense of home and nation operated centrally within the web of republican citizenship. Even those who rushed to defend Texas's coast in 1861 appreciated the immediacy of duty and service. They recognized the critical national predicament and understood that they would return to private life as soon as the crisis was resolved. One coastal defender wrote in November 1861, "my Country needs my services and I would be worse than no man and unworthy . . . if I refused or failed to respond to her call." The process of volunteering signified the perpetuation of republican identity, yet it did not perform in isolation. Rather, it functioned in concert with fighting, the very act which furthered the quest of obtaining broader national objectives. Thus, as one soldier acknowledged upon reaching Galveston, "we expect to engage in a hand to hand struggle for the defence of our Country."[29]

The evolution of garrison life, however, greatly challenged these conceptions of republican duty and expectations of military service. Soldiers stationed in backwater outfits were largely prevented from temporarily sacrificing self-interest for the sake of the nation's cause. Confederates in the large campaigning armies and coastal units both endured unfathomable physical hardships, yet only active service, in their minds, met the necessary demands of republican duty. Indeed, early in the war, several junior officers notified the governor that their coastal units threatened to desert if they were not deployed to the front lines. A soldier in the 20th Texas Infantry likewise wrote, "things go on in the same uninterrupted course leaving us here as mere spectators of that great drama of the war[,] with now and then some stirring report of our going into active service[,] but so far it has all been mere idle rumor." Personal interest soon surpassed the citizen-soldier philosophy once garrisoned Confederates realized that they were not being used to advance a national objective. In the spring of 1863 one soldier opined that, because he was not doing anything of military value, "[m]y honest opinion is that I ought to be discharged from the Confederate service," while another acknowledged the difficulty of being "confined in camps for years when [we] should be at home to assist [our] familys & instruct [our] children." The stagnant milieu of garrison life precluded these men from seeing beyond their poor provisions, lack of pay, and concern for home; they came to believe that their role as citizens could be used more effectively to further private and domestic interests.[30]

Second, and directly related, the static conditions of garrison service eliminated the opportunity to participate in the Civil War's grand campaigns, which prevented soldiers from establishing an authentic *esprit de corps* and an ideological attachment to the Confederacy. Confederate soldiers' exposure to the war, in the form of mobilization, campaigning and fighting, and collective sacrifice in the field, served as essential ingredients within the cauldron of national dedication. One soldier, William Neblett, wrote just after the 1863 mutiny, "[t]here is a great amount of demoralization in the Regiments here. From what I can hear such is not the case with the troops East of the Mississippi or those who have been in active service." His statement reflected the diverging nature of military duty experienced by Confederate soldiers. Active participation in the war stimulated a mindset among troops in the principal southern armies that they were the true guarantors of an independent Confederacy.

Confederates who fought and campaigned in Virginia, Tennessee, and Georgia, maintained endurance and cultivated an enthusiasm for Confederate independence through interaction and fighting with Union forces in which battlefield victories, and even defeats, superseded revolting hardships, mass bloodshed, bad food, inclement weather, little pay, and periods of dull camp life. Those who were assigned to garrisons along the Gulf Coast, however, rarely echoed these sentiments due to uninspiring feelings of uselessness and ill worth.[31]

Even John B. Magruder recognized these influences when, following the 1863 Galveston mutiny, he admitted shockingly that his own soldiers would "be so unmindful of their high obligations and so unjust to themselves and the fair fame of their regiments as to exhibit a spirit of insubordination from such petty motives as dissatisfaction with their rations and indisposition to drill or a desire for furloughs." He then declared that fellow Confederate soldiers on distant battlefields, who had suffered the same hardships as those on the coast, "will hear with incredulity, and then believe with anguish, the tale which reflects such dishonor and disgrace upon their comrades left behind to defend their beloved State." Although Magruder's words were characteristically flamboyant, he understood the inherent disparities between garrison and campaigning service. Nonetheless, the dynamic and static forces of garrison life were much too strong for Magruder's men to overcome.[32]

Third, service in backwater garrisons conflicted with notions of antebellum honor. The principles of defending home, nation, or simply procuring battlefield valor induced countless northerners and southerners to volunteer, yet the idle customs of coastal military life prevented the realization of such expectations. Honor was, in many cases, a key concept that inspired enlistment and was tied directly to views of courage and masculinity. However, these deeply cherished traits simply could not be explored or tested within wartime garrisons. This broad dynamic was not only reserved for the Civil War; rather, it reflected striking continuity across the longer nineteenth century. For example, in 1847, a volunteer during the Mexican War wrote of the long-term occupation of Mexico City: "[t]here is neither honor or prospect in a garrison life . . . If there was any likelihood of an engagement I do not believe that a single man in our company would wish to return until the fight was over, but the question is asked, 'Supposing this war should continue 5 or 8 years, are we to be kept doing garrison duty?'" This question helped link the Mexican and Civil War generations, both of which were deeply concerned with the maintenance of wartime honor and martial ambition.[33]

Once the prized attachments to honor were stripped away by the strictures of garrison life, soldiers often reverted to another determinant of antebellum culture: violence. Southern society especially inculcated violence as a mechanism by which to right wrongs or remedy fallen expectations. Indeed, Confederate soldiers stationed in remote garrisons who had originally enlisted to fight, and subsequently sat on their arms, watched as the war exploded around them. Their restlessness turned into petty misbehavior, then to mutiny, and ultimately into outright violence against fellow soldiers as well as civilians. Garrison culture was devoid of battlefield combat, which pushed soldiers to enact their bellicose tendencies upon their immediate surroundings. The internal pressures of garrison life thus created the dark setting in which unorganized violence flourished.[34]

Finally, because they operated within an environment that was detached from republican military expectations, ultimately absent a nationalistic ideology, and removed from conceptions of antebellum honor, garrisoned Confederates were forced into an ideological ambivalence both to the southern nation and its wartime cause. The culture of coastal garrison life offers a significant departure from recent Confederate historiography which emphasizes that many white southerners possessed the will to win *despite* low morale, disgust with the Confederate government, or battlefield reverses. The vignettes and episodes cited in this essay appear, at first glance, to be in stark contrast to this mode of inquiry. Indeed, a look at the lives and experiences of coastal Confederates opens a window onto the war's often-forgotten underside. However, garrison soldiers in Texas did not call for the Confederacy's demise nor yearn for a Union victory in spite of their immense distaste with military life and desperate hope for the war's conclusion. Coastal troops became disaffected largely by uncontrollable circumstances within a style of military service that did not conform to particular cultural understandings, but overt disloyalty rarely influenced their actions. Even during the 1863 mutinies, in which soldiers defiantly resisted their superiors and abandoned their units in droves, official reports routinely claimed that "we do not believe those who have deserted the ranks are disloyal to the Government or unfriendly to our cause."[35]

Coastal Confederates' peculiar position within the broader wartime landscape forced them into a middle-ground of ambivalence in which they reconciled their military assignments against concerns for family and home. It simply was not worth the sacrifice, in their minds, to perform mindless picket duty and execute seemingly pointless drill maneuvers when they could do nothing simultaneously to contribute to the cause of Confederate independence. These sentiments remained fixed throughout the totality of the war. Aaron Estes penned from Galveston in 1862 that "We are getting tired of sitting here without a fight. It is hard that a man must stay away from his family and all, and no fighting going on." A soldier in the 20th Texas Infantry later complemented this perspective, when he wrote during the summer of 1863, "the life we lead here could hardly be considered camp life at all except for the galling and damnable military restraint which calls all a man['] s patriotism in to reconcile him to it." Thus, the absence of consistent engagement with Union military forces served as the centerpiece to this brand of ambivalence. A growing chorus of prominent historians has recently advised scholars to investigate the depths of Confederate ambivalence and to move beyond the current intellectual binary which pits diehard nationalists against internal defeatists. Perhaps further investigations into the culture of military service behind the lines can promote this objective.[36]

Notes

1. Bell Irvin Wiley, *The Life of Johnny Reb: The Common Soldier of the Confederacy* (Indianapolis: Bobbs-Merrill, 1943), and *The Life of Billy Yank: The Common Soldier of the Union* (Indianapolis: Bobbs-Merrill, 1952); Aaron Sheehan-Dean, "The Blue and the Gray in Black and White: Assessing the Scholarship on Civil War Soldiers," in Aaron Sheehan-Dean, ed., *The View from the Ground: Experiences of Civil War Soldiers* (Lexington: University Press of Kentucky, 2007), 9–11; Maris A. Vinovskis, "Have Social Historians Lost the Civil War?: Some Preliminary Demographic Speculations," *Journal of American History* 76 (June 1989): 34–58. Kenneth W. Noe recently acknowledged that many of the most recent soldier studies "clearly favored the men who enlisted at the beginning of the war and battled as long as they could in the so-called fighting regiments." He thus called upon historians to begin focusing on the war's conscripts, deserters, men who enlisted long after the war began, and those who served as garrison troops. See Kenneth W. Noe, *Reluctant Rebels: The Confederates Who Joined the Army after 1861* (Chapel Hill: University of North Carolina Press, 2010), xii, *passim.*

2. This study analyzes only those soldiers who served in Confederate units. Texas State Troops, while important and prevalent on the coast, were technically not in service to the Confederate nation, but rather to the state.

3. This approach contributes to recent scholarly trends which emphasize the evolution of culture within the ranks, instead of underscoring the motivations for enlistment or the reasons for which men remained in the military. See, for example, Charles E. Brooks, "The Social and Cultural Dynamics of Soldiering in Hood's Texas Brigade," *Journal of Southern History* 67 (Aug. 2001): 535–72; Jason Phillips, *Diehard Rebels: The Confederate Culture of Invincibility* (Athens: University of Georgia Press, 2007); Joseph T. Glatthaar, *General Lee's Army: From Victory to Collapse* (New York: Free Press, 2008); James M. McPherson, *For Cause and Comrades: Why Men Fought in the Civil War* (New York: Oxford University Press, 1997).

4. For a cogent summary of this historiographical debate, see Gary W. Gallagher, "Disaffection, Persistence, and Nation: Some Directions in Recent Scholarship on the Confederacy," *Civil War History* 55 (Sept. 2009): 329–53. For the purposes of this study, nationalism is defined as the "level of commitment—whether it was through sentiment, expression, action, or deed—that an individual directed toward the Confederate cause," associated with "an intricate combination of local and state loyalties that functioned simultaneously and were fused together with adherence to the actual nation." Identity is defined as "the inward and psychological manifestation of the multiple loyalties that Confederate nationalism required. Identity is a unique sense of one's self combined with the characteristics that distinguish one person or group from another." See Andrew F. Lang, "' Upon the Altar of Our Country: Confederate Identity, Nationalism, and Morale in Harrison County, Texas, 1860–1865," *Civil War History* 55 (June 2009): 280.

5. Gary W. Gallagher suggests that Robert E. Lee and the Army of Northern Virginia "functioned as the principle focus of Confederate nationalism for much of the war," and that southerners used "Lee and his men . . . as the preeminent symbol of the Confederate struggle for independence and liberty." See Gary W. Gallagher, *The Confederate War* (Cambridge: Harvard University Press, 1997), 63, 85.

6. For works on the principal military campaigns in Texas, see Edward T. Cotham Jr., *Battle on the Bay: The Civil War Struggle for Galveston* (Austin: University of Texas Press, 1998); Edward T. Cotham Jr., *Sabine Pass: The Confederacy's Thermopylae* (Austin: University of Texas Press, 2004); Stephen A. Townsend, *The Yankee Invasion of Texas* (College Station: Texas A&M University Press, 2006); Stephen A. Dupree, *Planting the Union Flag in Texas: The Campaigns of Major General Nathaniel P. Banks in the West* (College Station: Texas A&M University Press, 2008).

7. Mark E. Nackman, "The Making of the Texas Citizen Soldier, 1835–1860," *Southwestern Historical Quarterly* 78 (Jan. 1975): 231–53. These dynamics, of course, were not necessarily unique only to Texas; these very qualities reflected the broader American citizen-soldier ideal throughout much of the nineteenth century. See Ricardo A. Herrera, "Guarantors of Liberty and Republic: The American Citizen as Soldier and the Military Ethos of Republicanism, 1775–1861" (Ph.D. diss., Marquette University, 1998), xiv, 215–20; Ricardo A. Herrera, "Self-Governance and the American Citizen as Soldier, 1775–1861," *Journal of Military History* 65 (Jan. 2001): 21–52.

8. John Johnson to Dear Cousin, Apr. 25, 1861, Johnson (John) Letter, Pearce Civil War Collection, Navarro College, Corsicana, Tex. (hereafter cited as PCWC); Elijah P. Petty to Wife, Dec. 5, and to Daughter, Dec. 8, 1861, in Norman D. Brown ed., *The Civil War Letters of Captain Elijah P. Petty, Walker's Texas Division, C.S.A.* (2 vols.; San Antonio: University of Texas Institute of Texas Cultures, 1982), 12–13; D. M. Stapp to Paul O. Hebert, Oct. 17, 1861, *War of the Rebellion: A Compilation of the Official Records of the Union and Confederate Armies*, 128 vols. (Washington: GPO, 1880–1901), Series 1, Vol. 4, Pt. 1, p. 124 (hereafter cited as *OR*. All citations refer to Series 1 unless otherwise noted); Aaron Estes to Deare Wife, Nov. 29, 1861, Aaron Estes Letters, 10th Texas Infantry File, Texas Heritage Museum Historical Research Center, Hill College, Hillsboro, Tex. (hereafter cited THM); Isaiah Harlan to Dear Ma, Nov. 10, 1861, Harlan Letters, 10th Texas Infantry File, THM; C. G. Collings to Unknown, Dec. 14, 1861, Amerman-Collings Collection, Houston Metropolitan Research Collection, Houston, Tex. (hereafter cited as HMRC); T. A. Harris to Edward Clark, Sept. 25, 1861, Governor Edward Clark Papers, Box 301-38, Folder 31, Texas State Library Archives Commission, Austin (hereafter cited TSLAC). On the poor condition of coastal defenses, see Lester N. Fitzhugh, "Saluria, Fort Esperanza, and Military Operations on the Texas Coast, 1861–1864," *Southwestern Historical Quarterly* 61 (July 1957): 66–100; and Alwyn Barr, "Texas Coastal Defense, 1861–1865," *Southwestern Historical Quarterly* 65 (July 1961): 1–31.

9. P. C. Woods to Dear Wife, Mar. 26, 1862, P. C. Woods Letters, 32nd Texas Cavalry File, THM; *Bellville Countryman*, Oct. 2, 1861; Charles David Grear, *Why Texans Fought in the Civil War* (College Station: Texas A&M University Press, 2010), 47–51; McPherson, *For Cause and Comrades*, 8, 13, 18–21, 27–28; Sheehan-Dean, *Why Confederates Fought*, 1–10; Lang, "' Upon the Altar of Our Country,'" 278–306; David M.

Potter, "The Historians' Use of Nationalism and Vice Versa," in Potter, *The South and the Sectional Conflict* (Baton Rouge: Louisiana State University Press, 1968), 34–84, esp. 48–49.

10. Isaiah Harlan to Dear Ma, Feb. 19, 1862, Harlan Letters, 10th Texas Infantry File, THM; Judah P. Benjamin to Paul O. Hebert, Feb. 24, 1862, OR, 9: 700; M. S. Townsend to Dear Wife, Apr. 11, 1862, Moses Townsend Papers, Nesbitt Memorial Library Archives, Columbus, Tex.; Estes to Deere wife and children, Jan. 5, and Feb. 14, 1862, and to Deere Brother Jan. 29, 1862, and to Dear Friend, Jan. 29, 1862, Estes Letters, 10th Texas Infantry File, THM; Petty to Dear Margaret, Apr. 7 and 8, 1862, in Brown, ed., *Journey to Pleasant Hill*, 48; Galveston *Weekly News*, Apr. 15, Nov.19, and June 24, 1862; Philip Caudill, *Moss Bluff Rebel: A Texas Pioneer in the Civil War* (College Station: Texas A&M University Press, 2009), 46, 34, 40; James A. Irby, *Backdoor at Bagdad: The Civil War on the Rio Grande* (El Paso: Texas Western Press, 1977), 21–24.

11. James Black to Dear Patience, Sept. 26, 1862, James Black Correspondence, 1860–1865, Civil War Times Illustrated Collection, United States Army Military History Institute, Carlisle Barracks, Carlisle, Penn. (hereafter cited USAMHI); Thomas Jefferson League to Mary D. League, Nov. 6, 1862, Thomas Jefferson League Papers, Galveston and Texas History Collection, Rosenberg Library, Galveston, Tex.; L. D. Bradley to Little Honey, Dec. 8, 1863, Bradley (L. D.) Papers, PCWC; William Melton, "A Veteran of the Civil War Gives Some Unpublished History: A Reminiscence," 13th Texas Infantry File, THM; Cotham, *Sabine Pass*, 41.

12. A. C. McKeon to Clark, July 11, 1861, Clark Papers, Box 301-37, Folder 22, TSLAC; John Miller to Clark, Aug. 4, 1861, Clark Papers, Box 301-37, Folder 25, TSLAC; George W. Durant to Clark, Sept. 3, 1861, Clark Papers, Box 301-38, Folder 29, TSLAC; See also Hal G. Runnels to Clark, May 10, 1861, Clark Papers, Box 301-35, Folder 13, TSLAC; Petty to Dear Wife, Jan. 13, 1862, in Brown, ed., *Journey to Pleasant Hill*, 36; R. R. Garland to Samuel Boyer Davis, Dec. 6, 1861, *OR*, 4: 153; Fitzhugh, "Military Operations on the Texas Coast," 72, fn. 13.

13. William Kuykendall, Civil War Diary, Kuykendall Family Papers, 1821–1891; Gideon Lincecum to J. Hawkins Lewis, Feb. 2, 1862, in Jerry B. Lincecum, et al., eds., *Gideon Lincecum's Sword: Civil War Letters from the Texas Home Front* (Denton: University of North Texas Press, 2001), 163.

14. Joseph B. Polley, *A Soldier's Letters to Charming Nellie: The Correspondence of Joseph B. Polley, Hood's Texas Brigade*, ed. Richard B. McCaslin (Knoxville: University of Tennessee Press, 2008), 33 (quotation), 114–15, 143, 152.

15. Cotham, *Battle on the Bay*, 99, 105–39; Robert L. Kerby, *Kirby Smith's Confederacy: The Trans-Mississippi South, 1863–1865* (New York: Columbia University Press, 1972), 18; Thomas M. Settles, *John Bankhead Magruder: A Military Reappraisal* (Baton Rouge: Louisiana State University Press, 2009), 158–251; J. H. Russell to Dear father and Mother, Dec. 8, 1862, J. H. Russell Civil War Letters, 7th Texas Cavalry File, THM; James Reily to Dear Sir, Jan. 8, 1863, Starr (James Harper) Papers, 1796–1905, Dolph Briscoe Center for American History (hereafter cited as CAH); J. E. Harrison to My Dear Ballinger, Jan. 3, 1863, Ballinger (William Pitt) Papers, 1815–1909, CAH; Diary entry, Jan. 1, 1863, and W. R. Howell to Miss Sallie, Jan. 19, 1863, Howell (W. Randolph) Papers, 1861–1879, CAH; John Claver Brightman to William Brightman, Jan. 1, 1863, Brightman (John Claver) Papers, 1859–1865, 1933, CAH; W. S. Alexander to J. H. Starr, Jan. 7, 1863, James Harper Starr Papers, CAH; E. C. Ritchie to My dear Cecilia, Jan. 12, 1863, J. E. Wallis to Dear Kate, Jan. 28, 1863, Tucker Family Papers, Rosenberg Library; L. D. Bradley to Little Honey, Jan. 8, 1863, Bradley Papers, PCWC..

16. "Letter from Galveston," Houston *Telegraph*, Jan. 6, 1863; Jefferson Davis to John B. Magruder, Jan. 28, 1863, *OR*, 15: 211; Sam Houston to Magruder, Jan. 7, 1863, *OR*, 15:933–34.

17. Brightman to Dear Brother and Sister, Jan.1, 1863, Brightman Papers, CAH; D. D. Shea to A. G. Dickinson, Jan. 3, 1863, 8th Texas Infantry General File, THM; William H. Neblett to Dear Lizzie, Apr. 9, 1863, in Erika L. Murr, ed., *A Rebel Wife in Texas: The Diary and Letters of Elizabeth Scott Neblett, 1852–1864* (Baton Rouge: Louisiana State University Press, 2001), 81–83; E. J. Wright to Dear Sister, Mar. 20, 1863, Alley Family Papers, CAH; M. K. Hunter to Dear Mother, Feb. 19, 1863, Hunter Family Papers, CAH; John W. Lockhart to My Dear Wife, Feb. 14, 1863, Lockhart Papers, Rosenberg Library; "Letter from Galveston," Houston *Telegraph,* June 5, 1863; Cotham, *Battle on the Bay*, 148, 157; Settles, *Magruder*, 271–72. The battle of Sabine Pass took place on Sept. 8, 1863. For a detailed study of the engagement, see Cotham, *Sabine Pass*.

18. Simon Kuykendall to Dear Wife and Children, Mar. 11, 1863, Kuykendall Papers, Rosenberg Library; Galveston *Weekly News*, June 24, 1863; J. W. Wallis to Dear Kate, Apr. 3, 1863, Tucker Family Papers,

CAH; James Pitman Saunders Diary, in "Saunders of Virginia and Texas," *Historical Southern Families* 7 (1963): 178; Charles W. Hayes, *History of the Island and the City of Galveston* (2 vols. Cincinnati, 1879 [set in type but not released]; Austin: Jenkins Garrett Press, 1974), 2: 621, 625–26; Ashbel Smith to J. D. McAdoo, Nov. [?] 1863, Smith (Ashbel) Papers, 1823–1926, CAH; E. J. Wright to Dear Sister, Mar. 20, 1863, Alley Family Papers, CAH; M. K. Hunter to Dear Mother, Feb. 19, 1863, Hunter Family Papers, CAH; John W. Lockhart to My Dear Wife, Feb. 14, 1863, Lockhart Papers, Rosenberg Library; X. B. Debray to Samuel Boyer Davis, Oct. 19, 1862, OR, 15: 836; Neblett to Dear Lizzie, Apr. 6, 9, 17, and 28, 1863, in Murr, ed., *Rebel Wife in Texas*, 81–83, 88–89, 98–99; Alwyn Barr, "The 'Queen City of the Gulf' Held Hostage: The Impact of the War on Confederate Galveston," *Military History of the West* 27 (Fall 1997): 119–38; Cotham, *Battle on the Bay*, 148, 157; Settles, *Magruder*, 271–72.

19. James Black to Dearest Patience, Aug. 22, 1863, James Black Correspondence, USAMHI; A. Q. Clements to Kind and Affectionate Sister, Sept. 15, 1863, "Hardships of Army Life in Texas During the Civil War Told in Letter by Soldier to Relatives," A. Q. Clements Letters, 3rd Texas Infantry File, THM; E. F. Gray to R. M. Franklin, Aug. 4, 1863; Debray to A. N. Mills, Aug. 11, 1863; Debray to Edmund P. Turner, Aug. 12, 1863; Debray to Mills, Aug. 12, 1863, P. N. Luckett to Turner, Aug. 13, 1863; John B. Magruder, General Orders No. 139, Aug. 24, 1863—all cited in *OR*, 26, pt. 1, pp. 241–46. See Gallagher, *Confederate War*, 20–21, 24, for the impact of Vicksburg's surrender on the broader Confederate population.

20. Officers of Terrell's Regiment to Turner, Sept. 30, 1863, and Magruder, General Orders No. 264, Sept. 30, 1863, *OR*, 26, pt. 2, pp. 277–79.

21. Magruder to W. R. Boggs, Sept. 4, 1863, *OR*, 26, pt. 2, pp. 203–5; Neblett to Dear Lizzie, May 15, 1863, in Murr, ed., *Rebel Wife in Texas*, 112; Fitzhugh, "Military Operations on the Texas Coast," 89–93; Townsend, *Yankee Invasion of Texas*, 14, 16, 18.

22. Ibid., 14–63; Kerby, *Kirby Smith's Confederacy*, 192–93; Irby, *Backdoor at Bagdad*, 28–30; H. P. Bee to Turner, Nov. 8 and 21, 1863, *OR*, 26, pt. 1, pp. 434–35, 437–38. At the onset of the Rio Grande expedition, Magruder had only nine thousand men to defend the entire state. Official returns reported that Confederate troop strength along the coast fluctuated approximately between five thousand and ten thousand men active and present for duty between November 1862 and December

1864. See *OR*, 15: 883, 884, 946; 26, pt. 2, pp. 98, 129, 194, 280–81, 376; 41, pt. 4, pp. 1,084–85, 1,137–40.

23. Jeff Morgan to Dear Wife, Dec. 7, 1863, Jeff Morgan Letters, 35th TX Cavalry File, THM; Neblett to Dear Lizzie, Dec. 22, 1863, in Murr, ed., *Rebel Wife in Texas*, 254; Rudolf Coreth to family, Feb.4, 1864, and Dec. 24, 1863, in Minetta A. Goyne, ed., *Lone Star and Double Eagle: Civil War Letters of a German-Texas Family* (Fort Worth: Texas Christian University Press, 1982), 118–19, 114–15; Townsend, *Yankee Invasion of Texas*, 62–64; Kerby, *Kirby Smith's Confederacy*, 193.

24. Neblett to Dear Lizzie, Dec. 22, 1863, in Murr, ed., *Rebel Wife in Texas*, 254; Brightman to Dear Mother, Nov. 28, 1863, to Dear Brother and Sister, Jan. 20, 1864, to Dear Brother, Jan. 21, 1864, Brightman Papers, CAH; Frank E. Vandiver, ed., "Letters from the Confederate Medical Service, 1863–1865," *Southwestern Historical Quarterly* 55 (Jan. 1952): 384.

25. Settles, *Magruder*, 259, 271–72; E. Kirby Smith to R. W. Johnson, Jan. 15, 1864, *OR*, 34, pt. 2, p. 870; Vandiver, ed., "Letters from the Confederate Medical Service," 384; Caudill, *Moss Bluff Rebel*, 36–49; Townsend, *Yankee Invasion of Texas*, 58–72.

26. Diary entry, Feb. 14, 1864, in Rebecca W. Smith and Marion Mullins, eds., "The Diary of H. C. Medford, Confederate Soldier, 1864," *Southwestern Historical Quarterly* 34 (Oct. 1930): 120–21.

27. Diary entries, Feb. 15, and Mar. 12, 1864, in Smith and Marion Mullins, eds., "Diary of H. C. Medford," 111, 128, 129; Neblett to Dear Lizzie, Mar. 12, 1864, in Murr, ed., *Rebel Wife in Texas*, 343; Houston *Daily Telegraph*, Mar. 8, 1864; Cotham, *Battle on the Bay*, 162; Barr, "Texas Coastal Defense," 30.

28. Bradley to Little Honey, Aug. 25, 1864, Bradley Papers, PCWC; Galveston *Weekly News*, Jan. 6, Apr. 27, 1864, and Jan. 4, 1865; Hayes, *History of Galveston*, 612–21; Cotham, *Battle on the Bay*, 160–67; Brad R. Clampitt, "The Breakup: The Collapse of the Confederate Trans-Mississippi Army in Texas, 1865," *Southwestern Historical Quarterly* 108 (Apr. 2005): 499–534; Kerby, *Kirby Smith's Confederacy*, 424.

29. Herrera, "Guarantors of Liberty and Republic," xiv, 215–20; Petty to Wife, Dec. 5, 1861 in Brown, ed., *Journey to Pleasant Hill*, 12; H. W. McLeod to Clark, May 19 and 21, 1861, and E. B. Nichols to Clark, July 27, 1861—both in Clark Papers, TSLAC; Johnson to Dear Cousin, Apr. 25, 1861, Johnson (John) Letter, PCWC.

30. George W. Durant to Clark, Sept. 3, 1861, Clark Papers, Box 301-38, Folder 29, TSLAC; Neblett to Dear Lizzie, Nov. 22, 1863, in

Murr, ed., *Rebel Wife in Texas*, 98–99; Simon Kuykendall to Wife, Mar. 11, 1863, Kuykendall Papers, Rosenberg Library; Petty to Wife, Apr. 6, 1862, in Brown, ed., *Journey to Pleasant Hill*, 47; Settles, *Magruder*, 271.

31. Neblett to Dear Lizzie, Aug. 18, 1863, in Murr, ed., *Rebel Wife in Texas*, 138; Diary entry, Mar. 12, 1864, "Diary of H. C. Medford," 132; J. Tracy Power, *Lee's Miserables: Life in the Army of Northern Virginia from the Wilderness to Appomattox* (Chapel Hill: University of North Carolina Press, 1998), 46; Susannah U. Bruce, "The Fierce Pride of the Texas Brigade," *Civil War Times Illustrated* 46 (Sept. 2007): 32–39; Gallagher, *Confederate War*, 73–74; McPherson, *For Cause and Comrades*, 94–102; Phillips, *Diehard Rebels*, passim; Henry M. Trueheart to Dear Tom, Feb. 6 and Apr. 14, 1864, in Edward B. Williams, ed., *Rebel Brothers: The Civil War Letters of the Truehearts* (College Station: Texas A&M University Press, 1995), 187; Diary entries, Apr. 21 and May 6, 1864, McCarty (Thomas L.), Papers, 1864–65, CAH; George Lee Robertson to Dear Julia, Apr. 15, 1864, Robertson (George Lee) Papers, 1839–69, CAH. These negative dynamics were especially pronounced during the fall of 1863 when Confederates on the Texas coast were forced constantly to move, retreat, and scatter at various locales for defense. See Fitzhugh, "Military Operations on the Texas Coast," 93.

32. General Orders No. 139, Aug. 24, 1863, *OR*, 26, pt. 1, p. 246.

33. M. K. Hunter to Dear Mother, Feb. 19, 1863, Hunter Family Papers, CAH; Diary entry, Nov. 26, 1847, in Richard Coulter, ed., *Volunteers: The Mexican War Journals of Private Richard Coulter and Sergeant Thomas Barclay, Company E, Second Pennsylvania Infantry* (Kent, OH: Kent State University Press, 1991), 216; Diary entry, Nov.14, 1847, in Nathaniel Cheairs Hughes Jr., and Timothy D. Johnson, eds., *A Fighter from Way Back: The Mexican War Diary of Lt. Daniel Harvey Hill, 4th Artillery, USA* (Kent, OH: Kent State University Press, 2002), 141; Richard Smith Elliott to Editors of the Reveille, Apr. 29, 1847, in Mark L. Gardener and Marc Simmons, eds., *The Mexican War Correspondence of Richard Smith Elliott* (Norman: University of Oklahoma Press, 1997), 185; McPherson, *For Cause and Comrades*, 22–29; R. Bruce Winders, *Mr. Polk's Army: The American Military Experience in the Mexican War* (College Station: Texas A&M University Press, 1997), 70–71; Bertram Wyatt-Brown, *Southern Honor: Ethics and Behavior in the Old South* (New York: Oxford University Press, 1982), 39, 156–59, 164–70; Earl J. Hess, *The Union Soldier in Battle: Enduring the Ordeal of Combat* (Lawrence: University Press of Kansas, 1997), 96–97. Honor, however,

was not nearly as important to Confederate soldiers who enlisted after 1861. See Noe, *Reluctant Rebels*, 38–40.

34. Wyatt-Brown, *Southern Honor*, 165; Linderman, *Embattled Courage*, 35–47; John Hope Franklin, *The Militant South, 1800–1861* (Cambridge: Harvard University Press, 1956), 4–13, 34–36, 90–91; R. Don Higginbotham, "The Martial Spirit in the Antebellum South: Some Further Speculations in a National Context," *Journal of Southern History* 58 (Feb. 1992): 3–26, esp. 13–15.

35. Officers of Terrell's Regiment to Turner, Sept. 30, 1863, *OR*, 26, pt. 2, pp. 278–79, 277. One of the colonels who helped suppress the 1863 Galveston mutiny wrote that it was "[t]he opinion of a large majority of the officers being given that there was really no disloyal sentiment amongst the men," and was rather "an expression of disaffection at the quality of their food, and the amount of duty required of them during the extreme hot weather, and was not prompted by any disloyalty to our cause." See Report of Col. P. N. Luckett, Aug. 13, 1863, *OR*, 26, pt. 1, p. 245; Emory M. Thomas, *The Confederate Nation: 1861–1865* (New York: Harper and Row, 1979), 223; William Blair, *Virginia's Private War: Feeding Body and Soul in the Confederacy, 1861–1865* (New York: Oxford University Press, 1998), 140–50; Jacqueline Glass Campbell, *When Sherman Marched North from the Sea: Resistance on the Confederate Home Front* (Chapel Hill: University of North Carolina Press, 2003), 71–74; Anne Sarah Rubin, *A Shattered Nation: The Rise and Fall of the Confederacy, 1861–1868* (Chapel Hill: University of North Carolina Press, 2005), 1, 50–52, 90, 127–31, 138, 146, 204; Peter S. Carmichael, *The Last Generation: Young Virginians in Peace, War, and Reunion* (Chapel Hill: University of North Carolina Press, 2005), 121–78; Gallagher, *Confederate War*, 5–12, 50, 63, 73, 75–80; Phillips, *Diehard Rebels*, 9–75; Sheehan-Dean, *Why Confederates Fought*, 1–10, 132–37, 190–91.

36. Aaron Estes to Dear Friend Ed, Jan.29, 1862, Aaron Estes Letters, 10th Texas Infantry File, THM; Neblett to Dear Lizzie, Apr. 28, 1863, in Murr, ed., *Rebel Wife in Texas*, 98–99; Caudill, *Moss Bluff Rebel*, 44; Gallagher, "Disaffection, Persistence, and Nation," 351–52. Kenneth W. Noe convincingly argues that Confederates who enlisted later in the war expressed far less nationalism than those who enlisted at the beginning of the conflict. However, the moment of enlistment seems not to have been of foremost importance to those soldiers who served on the Texas coast, primarily because the cultural challenges to the republican citizen-soldiering tradition outweighed the timing of enlistment. See Noe, *Reluctant Rebels*, 23–37.

Cartoon by Thomas Nast, *Harper's Weekly*, August 5, 1865

North Texans and Civil War Amnesty: Helpless Instruments in the Hands of Rebellion?

Bradley R. Clampitt

At the end of the Civil War, President Andrew Johnson pursued a lenient plan of Reconstruction designed to return the former Confederate states to their proper relationship with the Union as swiftly as possible. His plan included amnesty proclamations intended to restore full legal and political rights to ex-Confederates, in most cases, in exchange for an oath of allegiance to the United States and a pledge to obey emancipation legislation. Johnson's first and most important proclamation affected the greatest number of southerners but excluded from general amnesty fourteen classifications of individuals (see Table). Any person who fell within one or more of the fourteen categories could not secure amnesty simply by swearing an oath. Instead, Johnson required those individuals to write directly to him to request a pardon.[1]

Those letters of application, and in some cases attached letters of recommendation, contain a wealth of information with regard to the applicants' identities, political beliefs, wartime activities, and often, explanations for why they thought they deserved a pardon. A study of the applications filed from North Texas counties provides an opportunity to examine those issues within a specific community and to place the local findings within a statewide context. Moreover, the meaningful opposition to secession present in North Texas presents an intriguing twist to the study of Civil War amnesty. How did anti-secession sentiment factor into the pursuit of amnesty and did it affect the results? Were certain North Texas applicants simply "helpless instruments in the hands of rebellion," as one applicant claimed, or were the pardon applications from the region representative of Texas overall? The files of the forty-two North Texas applicants reveal significant insight into the applicants' identities, their views on the sectional crisis and the Civil War, their strategies for securing amnesty, and the evaluation process employed by Johnson and his administration. Ultimately, the amnesty process in North Texas and the

Johnson administration's handling of it proved consistent with statewide trends.[2]

Table: Exceptions to Andrew Johnson's First Amnesty Proclamation[28]

Exception	*Explanation*
1st	Confederate civil or diplomatic officials
2nd	Individuals who vacated U. S. judicial positions to aid the rebellion
3rd	Confederate Army officers above the rank of colonel and Navy officers above the rank of lieutenant
4th	Individuals who left seats in the U. S. Congress to aid the rebellion
5th	Individuals who resigned commissions in the U. S. Army or Navy and afterward served the rebellion
6th	Individuals who treated black prisoners of war or their white officers unlawfully
7th	Individuals who absented themselves from the U. S. in order to aid the rebellion
8th	Confederate military personnel who were educated at the U. S. Military Academy or the U. S. Naval Academy
9th	Former Confederate governors
10th	Individuals who left homes in U. S. jurisdiction to aid the rebellion
11th	Individuals who engaged in the destruction of U. S. commerce on the high seas or conducted raids into the U. S. from Canada
12th	Individuals in federal custody
13th	Voluntary participants in the rebellion who held taxable property worth at least $20,000
14th	Individuals who broke oath of allegiance issued December 8, 1863

North Texas in 1865 comprised the counties of Collin, Cooke, Dallas, Denton, Ellis, Fannin, Grayson, Hunt, Johnson, Kaufman, Montague, Parker, Tarrant, and Wise. On the eve of the Civil War, the population of those fourteen counties stood at 68,757 free whites, a single free black resident, and 8,424 slaves, who were only 11 percent of the region's total population. Statewide, slaves constituted approximately 30 percent of the population in 1860. Given the relatively small slave population in the region, it is not surprising that the voters in Collin, Cooke, Fannin, Grayson, and Montague counties rejected secession from the Union in 1861. In three others, Denton, Hunt, and Wise, at least 40 percent of the voters opposed separation. Unlike many counties in East Texas, north central Texas abounded in small scale, even subsistence, farmers. Thus, relatively few residents depended on slave labor. Additionally, because several of those counties stood in frontier locations on the border of Indian Territory to the north and unsettled land to the west, residents there depended on the United States Army for protection against Indian raids. According to one historian, the insecurity of that frontier existence served as the primary explanation for many North Texans' rejection of secession.[3]

Forty-two North Texas residents applied for amnesty under Johnson's first proclamation. Thirty-eight North Texans applied under the first or thirteenth exception, while one applied under both. Consistent with the results of my previous study of 746 Texas applicants statewide, all North Texas applicants under the first or thirteenth exception (or both) received pardons. Individuals who applied under any combination of exceptions that included a military component (third, fifth, or eighth) were pardoned at a rate of 33.3 percent, again consistent with the statewide rate of 35.2 percent. My statewide study, which grew out of a county-level study in Professor Randolph B. Campbell's local history research seminar, demonstrated that Johnson more closely scrutinized applications from high-ranking Confederate military officials, individuals educated at the United States Military Academy at West Point or the United States Naval Academy at Annapolis, and individuals who had resigned United States military commissions in order to serve the Confederacy. Those individuals, respectively, had led the rebellion on the battlefield, had been trained and educated at public expense, and had sworn an oath to defend the nation, only to take up arms against the United States. In accordance with the policy he and his cabinet established early in the amnesty process, Johnson rejected the majority of those applicants, while he forced most civil officials and the southern elite to ask him directly for a pardon. My statewide study logically focused primarily on the rejected applicants. This study briefly examines the two rejected North Texas applicants, but more important, scrutinizes the pardoned applicants, something the larger study could not accomplish because of the sheer number of applications.[4]

Only three North Texans applied for amnesty under the military related exceptions (third, fifth, or eighth), and Johnson rejected two of them. An applicant under the eighth exception, Connecticut native Roswell W. Lee migrated to Texas in 1839, approximately six years after his graduation from West Point. Lee served briefly in the United States Army before his migration to Texas and listed his occupation as civil engineer or surveyor. Like a number of other North Texas applicants, he insisted that he had opposed secession and even voted against it. Lee's file includes a letter of recommendation from a longtime friend to support the applicant's claim with regard to secession. Despite his professed opposition to the rebellion, however, Lee enlisted in the Confederate service and held the rank of colonel at the war's conclusion. Though it was not unusual for an individual to oppose secession but then support the Confederacy, amnesty applicants who did so typically attempted to explain their actions. Lee offered no explanation for his decision to enlist in the Confederate military, and the West Point graduate failed to secure a pardon.[5]

The only other rejected North Texas applicant, William Hugh Young of Grayson County, also claimed to have opposed secession, and a letter of recommendation in his file describes the applicant as a "young man of no political influence" who had been drawn "into the whirlpool of secession by surrounding circumstances." A student at the University of Virginia when the war began, Young left his studies to enlist in Confederate military service in Texas at the age of twenty-three years. He climbed the officers' ranks in the Army of Tennessee, ultimately serving as a brigadier general. Federal forces captured Young in October 1864 and imprisoned him at the Johnson's Island prisoner-of-war camp in Lake Erie, near Sandusky, Ohio, where he remained at the time of his application for amnesty. Thus Young applied under the third exception because of his rank as a brigadier general and under the twelfth exception because he remained in federal custody at the time of his application. Though the individual who recommended him for amnesty pointed to Young's youth and the force of circumstances to explain the applicant's Confederate service, Young himself offered no explanation. For an applicant under almost any non-military related exception, that would have likely proven insignificant. But for a high-ranking Confederate officer still in federal custody, this omission almost certainly hindered Young's chances to secure a pardon.[6]

Only one other North Texan applied for a pardon under any exception other than the first and/or thirteenth. W. H. Hord of Dallas County applied for amnesty under the third exception, having served as brigadier general for the 13th Brigade Texas State Troops, beginning in December 1861. His service consisted of enrolling and organizing militia, and he insisted that he never left the area or served in the Confederate military itself. Fifty-six-years-old at the time of his application, he had resided in Dallas County for more than twenty years, had served as county judge from 1848 to 1850, and again briefly occupied that post after the war in 1865. Provisional Governor Andrew J. Hamilton appointed Hord chief justice during the early days of Presidential Reconstruction but removed him from office as a result of Unionist protests, one of which decried Hord as "one of the first mobocrats of the county." Area residents informed the governor of Hord's ardent support of secession and insisted that Republicans or former Union men could never receive justice in his court. Hord, of course, neglected to mention his secessionist past in his pardon application. Several residents and county officials vouched for Hord and signed a recommendation judging him a "worthy and highly esteemed citizen" and "one of the oldest & first settlers of this portion of the States." Strong recommendations and the relatively limited nature of his military service helped Hord secure his pardon.[7]

All thirty-nine other North Texas applicants also received pardons, and each applied under the first and/or thirteenth exception. Those under the first exception served the Confederate government in capacities that included an Indian agent, one congressman, and numerous minor offices such as postmasters, tax assessors, and tax collectors. Predictably, multiple applicants professed no support for the Confederacy, or in some cases, expressed genuine opposition to secession and the rebellion in hopes of influencing Johnson and his subordinates in the amnesty process. Considering the political climate in North Texas in 1861 and the meaningful opposition to secession in those counties, most of the applicants probably described their sentiments truthfully. But some applicants who claimed to have opposed secession, or at least professed no support for the Confederacy, applied for pardons under the first exception. Thus the question arises: how did those individuals find themselves not only in support of the Confederacy, but in a capacity that disqualified them from general amnesty? Individuals under the first exception held government offices in the Confederacy, so an argument that they simply conformed under pressure from the pro-Confederate majority would prove a difficult sell. Still, a few such applicants offered exactly that explanation.[8]

George F. Marchbanks, for example, served as a tax assessor and mail carrier in Ellis County despite a professed opposition to secession. According to his letter of application for pardon, Marchbanks had always opposed secession until the day of the election, at which time he voted in favor of the ordinance because he "thought it best for all southern people to go together in such a movement." Marchbanks insisted that "the movement was at no time in conformity with his feelings" and that he supported the rebellion "from a conviction that it was his duty to abide the decision of the majority." Similarly, in Cooke County, Jeremiah E. Hughes initially resigned his position as United States postmaster at the time of secession but "was compelled by the circumstances that surrounded me and being a poor man with a Family, to go with the majority and remain at this place." In addition to his stint as postmaster, however, Hughes also served the Confederate government as county clerk and tax collector. Meanwhile, postmaster H. R. S. Rose of Grayson County maintained that he "has always been a union [*sic*] man at heart," voted against secession, and accepted his position only as a matter of "self defense," while Fannin County resident James Galbraith, identified as "one of the best union men in the county," allegedly accepted the position of tax assessor strictly to avoid Confederate military service. A fellow Fannin County resident, postmaster James K. Blair, also insisted that he had opposed the rebellion and accepted the position in order to avoid military service.[9]

Galbraith's brother Samuel processed other Fannin County applications as county clerk and, according to a letter of recommendation in James Galbraith's file, had been publicly known as a Union man for some time. James Galbraith's claim the he accepted his office strictly to avoid Confederate military service is likely true, but either way, choosing a minor civil office over Rebel military service made for a potentially compelling argument for amnesty. Blair's claim that he had "used every exertion in my power to suppress" the rebellion proves more problematic. In November 1865 Blair received an appointment as county judge under the Texas provisional state government and won election to that office in June 1866. In the summer of 1867, however, Congress authorized United States military officers to remove southern public officials whom they deemed impediments to Reconstruction, and soon thereafter, Federal officers deemed Blair such an impediment. Although his removal from office does not confirm that Blair lied about his opposition to the rebellion, he clearly failed to convince Federal officers in charge of Congressional Reconstruction in North Texas of the validity of the claims that he made in his 1865 amnesty petition.[10]

A prominent Grayson County applicant also averred that he had been compelled to serve the Confederacy despite his personal convictions, though his account portrays pressure of an entirely greater dimension. Matthew Leeper served as a federal Indian agent for certain Comanche bands and other affiliated groups in Indian Territory and occupied a similar position for the Confederacy. Early in the war, according to Leeper's amnesty application letter, Confederate troops near Fort Smith, Arkansas, confronted him and seized all government property in his possession. Despite his predicament, he somehow managed to maintain possession of the money allotted to the tribes and attempted to find Federal forces. Before he reached Fort Smith, however, he learned that Confederate units had occupied that post after the Federals had abandoned it. Again he found himself surrounded "by men opposed to the government." Faithful to his obligations, he elected to spend the money for the benefit of the area Indians rather than turn it over to Confederate officials. While at Fort Smith, however, Leeper met the new Confederate Commissioner of Indian Affairs, David Hubbard of Alabama.[11]

At that point Leeper made the decision that ultimately disqualified him from general amnesty. Hubbard asked him to continue in his capacity as Indian agent but on the payroll of the Confederacy. Leeper explained, "He requested me to return to the Agency, and take charge of the Indians, try to keep them quiet, and satisfied, and still endeavor to learn them something of the habits and customs of civilized men." After accepting the proposal, Leeper found himself "surrounded by Confederate soldiers" (Indians). He claimed that at that point he advised them, "If they thought proper to go North, that I had no doubt that the Federal Government would still provide for them, and if they remained, the Southern people were pledged to do so; but in any event by no means to take up arms against either party." On October 23, 1862, Leeper made a dramatic escape from Fort Cobb, Indian Territory, when a band of Union-affiliated Delaware and Shawnee Indians attacked the post occupied by the Confederate-allied tribes of the Wichita Agency. Only partially clothed, he fled the chaotic scene in the middle of the night and traveled south to avoid his would-be killers. Confederate officials considered him dead until, with the help of some Comanche allies, he made his way to his family in Sherman, Texas.[12]

Clearly attempting to prove his loyalty to the United States, Leeper informed Johnson that his "humblest efforts to the fullest extent were exerted in opposition to the rebellion." Of course, that proved at least a mild exaggeration. After all, Leeper had directed the Wichita Agency for the Confederates for more than a year before his dramatic flight to Texas, and only the Indian raid terminated his service. In summation of his antebellum political views, he informed Johnson that he had "insisted that the Southern people wait until some of their rights were violated under the laws and Constitution of the United States before they took up arms, and if their rights were violated they had their remedy in the courts of the country." He stated that no republican form of government would last twenty years if secession were legitimate and concluded that every disgruntled office seeker would opt for separation and the establishment of a new government. Finally, Leeper maintained that, "If the people did madly plunge themselves" into war, "the first gun would sound the death knell of Negro slavery in these United States." He maintained that he had stood firm in his beliefs "until the rebellion assumed such gigantic dimensions, that no man could use them and live in the southern country." Leeper ultimately blamed the southern people for causing "devastation of the country, by the wildest fanaticism." In the face of such "ruin and destruction," he acted for himself and his family and could not have left the area without endangering himself. That last statement may have been true, but it seems hardly likely that fleeing Confederate service would have presented any danger greater than what he faced during his tenure in Indian Territory.[13]

A fellow Grayson County applicant under the first exception also pointed to pro-Confederate community pressure and a desire to avoid conscription to explain his status as a Confederate officeholder. Christopher C. Binkley voted against secession and resisted the forces of rebellion until what he described as the "unprecedented reign of terror" swept his region. Indeed, Binkley, whose Unionism is well documented, once fled his home with a pro-Confederate mob on his heels. He described the position he ultimately accepted as a "petty" office known as Confederate States Commissioner for Texas. He secured the position through the aid of influential friends rather than flee the region and leave his family. After the war, during Presidential Reconstruction, Unionist Binkley joined others in a call for the presence of Federal troops to restore order in North Texas and publicly opposed the gubernatorial campaign of former Confederate general James W. Throckmorton, who described Binkley as among the class of individuals who had "skulked from danger and drew no sword in defense of either belligerent and who now flock around the slain carcass like filthy beasts and vultures."[14]

The argument that uncontrollable circumstances dictated wartime behavior also proved a common thread among six North Texans who sought amnesty under the thirteenth exception. Three of those men insisted that they had voted against secession, while all six denied providing voluntary support for the rebellion, thus making their only "offense" the fact that they lived in a former Confederate state and possessed taxable property worth more than $20,000. Fannin County resident Thomas R. Williams complained that Confederate authorities had impressed his property without his permission. Williams described himself as a miller and millwright by trade and insisted that he was probably not worth half of the $20,000 after the war. He applied for amnesty because he believed that "It is not the wish or the policy of the Government to punish those who have been the helpless instruments in the hands of the rebellion." Three thirteenth exception applicants who claimed to have opposed the rebellion performed military service, they insisted, because they had no choice. M. H. Wright yielded "a physical obedience to the powers and authority then over Texas, both state and Confederate," but served militia duty in Hunt County only. Grayson County resident James P. Dumas, who described himself as "a firm & decided Union man," served in the militia involuntarily but secured the duty of providing beef for the families of Confederate soldiers. Dallas County resident Walter Caruth served in the regular Confederate military as a captain but reiterated that "He was opposed to the War." A relative, William Caruth, also a thirteenth exception applicant from Dallas County, wrote an almost identical letter, including the underlined statement about his opposition to the war. William Caruth, however, avoided military service by hiring a substitute when drafted into the Confederate military and again when conscripted by the state. He might have wondered whether Johnson, whose grudge against the southern elite was well known, would appreciate his avoidance of military service to the rebellion or cringe at his obvious display of wealth.[15]

The other thirteenth exception applicant who pointed to uncontrollable circumstances to explain his involuntary support of the Confederacy, Abraham Freeman of Dallas County, contended that his participation in the rebellion "was the result of the force of the circumstances that surrounded him" and "consisted only in such contributions as the duty & honor of a patriot would at all times demand in support of his struggling country . . . be this cause right or wrong." The fifty-one-year-old Ohio native insisted that he had voted against secession and assisted Confederates because of his "natural sympathy for those involved in the great misfortune & not of reason & the better judgment." Freeman's claim of "natural" sympathies echoed the explanations offered by many southern women who applied for presidential pardons.[16]

Three other pardon applicants pointed to extenuating circumstances to explain the apparent contradiction between their lack of Confederate sentiment and status as Confederate office holders. In those cases, however, the individuals pointed not to politics or pressure, but rather to community need. Sinclair Stapp, for example, served as Honey Grove postmaster in Fannin County because, he contended, his friends and neighbors asked him to serve and because no other man in the area was exempt from military service. Similarly, Henry Pinney attributed his service as a postmaster in Hunt County to a desire to serve his neighbors and community, not to "commit treason." Another Hunt County postmaster, W. J. Sorelle, also claimed that he held the position because there was no other man left to do it. Moreover, Pinney and Sorelle both held their respective positions under the United States government before the war and simply continued their duties under Confederate auspices. Stapp, Pinney, and Sorelle, each more than sixty years old, professed no staunch anti-secession sentiments, simply that they had served the rebellion only in their capacities as postmasters.[17]

At the other end of the political spectrum, eight North Texas amnesty applicants admitted pro-Confederate sentiments and acknowledged their support of secession. Even among those eight, however, the relative strength of their dedication to the rebellion varied, or perhaps the extent to which the applicants acknowledged that dedication varied. Charles A. Warfield, for example, implied his true sentiments without an explicit statement when he wrote of himself, "Whatever may have been his opinions of Slavery or the right to Secede, he now believes, those questions have been settled by the power of the Government." The sixty-six-year-old former tax collector in Hunt County made his position clear without accepting blame or acknowledging wrongdoing. Similarly, George Piguese of Collin County and Thomas F. Crutchfield of Dallas County, both former Confederate postmasters, each admitted that they had considered secession proper at the beginning of the war but offered no further insight into their beliefs.[18]

Two other applicants also wrote little with regard to their wartime contributions to the Confederacy, but elaborated on their support for secession. Joseph C. Rushing of Ellis County identified himself as a

"Conservative Democrat" but insisted that he had not followed politics closely for the five years immediately prior to the war. He supported secession, he stated, because other southern states had already taken the step and because he thought the South should be united in such a momentous act. Thus, he considered it his "duty to go with his countrymen in such a crisis." Rushing operated a successful law practice before the war but maintained that he accepted a minor civil office in part to support himself and his family and in part because he thought every man would be called to serve, and he preferred civil service. Former Fannin County tax collector Barney L. Johnson voted in favor of the Texas Ordinance of Secession because he thought it represented a "constitutional remedy for wrongs he was led to believe were inflicted by the United States. He has now surrendered that supposed right for the future." The fifty-five-year-old Tennessee native made clear his endorsement of secession without offering details on his wartime activities, without accepting blame for his actions, and without admitting the illegality of secession, acknowledging only that force of arms had settled the question.[19]

Thomas V. Toler also detailed his support for secession but, unlike those described above, chronicled his wartime sentiment and activities. A Virginia native, Toler had lived in Kentucky and Illinois before settling in Texas in 1853. He spent most of those years as a school teacher and "was never a politician, certainly not a violent one . . . ." Though never politically active, Toler certainly followed sectional politics and developed powerful sentiments on the subject. He explained, "From my youth, I believed in the doctrine of States' rights, and consequently felt indignant at all the acts of the Northern States or people, that I considered aggressive upon the rights of the South." He initially opposed secession because he considered it an inappropriate avenue to redress southern grievances, but he changed his mind when Texas called for a vote on secession. At that point, Toler "believing that the die was cast, and that every true friend of the South ought to unite heart and hand in maintaining her rights . . . gave up all opposition and voted for secession as cheerfully as any of my fellow citizens."[20]

When the war began, Toler "was governed in my conduct by the same views and feelings, and though too old and feeble for military service, I gave all the assistance I could lawfully to the cause of the South." In spring 1864 he joined what he described as a "Military Committee" under the direction of Major William Quayle. According to Toler, the committee comprised Hunt County's "oldest and most prominent" citizens and resolved to restore order in the region, then plagued with lawlessness. He also served as a tax collector and county clerk and held the latter position until Provisional Governor Andrew J. Hamilton named his successor in September 1865. Toler more than once insisted upon his honesty and assured Johnson that he intended to honor his amnesty oath "in letter and in Spirit."[21]

Former Confederate Congressman William B. Wright also detailed his pro-secession sentiments and his wartime service. Wright practiced law in Georgia, Alabama, and Texas before the war and wrote that he had been "born, reared, and educated in the South and indoctrinated in the belief that the states were sovereign and independent in their action, and that the first and highest allegiance of the Citizen was first due to his state it is not surprising that my destiny was irrevocably fixed and determined by my state." The learned lawyer thus admitted his support for secession but essentially considered that position predetermined for him by the circumstances of his birth and education. Elected to represent the Sixth Congressional District, the Fannin County resident served on several congressional committees, including that on Indian Affairs, and proposed amendments to existing bills, including legislation that exempted from the draft militia units engaged in frontier defense. He failed to win reelection in 1863 and served at the rank of major in the Confederate Trans-Mississippi Army until its surrender in 1865. In his letter of application, Wright acknowledged no wrongdoing but also made no attempt to diminish his role in the rebellion, with the exception of his claim that he had made every effort to prevent the persecution of Unionists.[22]

Wright's application and those of the other North Texans examined here reinforce the conclusion that the content of the applicants' letters made little difference to Johnson and his subordinates in their decision to grant amnesty unless the individual applied under certain exceptions. Johnson and his staff closely scrutinized those applications from individuals who applied under military related exceptions (third, fifth, eighth) and granted almost blanket amnesty to others. Among those he examined closely, Johnson considered factors such as the applicants' wartime service, attitude, letters of recommendation, and actions since the war. For most others, however, and in Texas for all who applied under the first and/or thirteenth exceptions, none of those factors mattered. The mere act of taking the oath and applying for the pardon proved sufficient.[23]

Southerners of course knew none of that when they applied for amnesty. They knew that any ex-Confederate who failed to secure amnesty was legally considered guilty of treason, a crime punishable by heavy fines, imprisonment, disfranchisement, confiscation of property, or death. Those who applied under the thirteenth exception likely knew of Johnson's lifelong grudge against the elite of southern society and thus had every reason to take the amnesty application seriously. No one yet knew that Johnson intended to pardon first and thirteenth exception applicants across the board, content to consider their direct application to him adequate repentance. Johnson ultimately showed no interest in remaking southern society beyond emancipation, and he certainly never entertained the idea of disfranchising significant numbers of white southerners or redistributing white-owned property to freedmen.[24]

The application of Hunt County resident and former postmaster Elbert Pinney reveals just how little the public knew of Johnson's true intentions. A physician by profession, the Connecticut native served as a surgeon for the 1st Chickasaw Battalion and later performed the same function for the 1st Battalion Texas Cavalry. Two individuals who recommended Pinney for a pardon wrote to Illinois Congressman Elihu Washburne for help with the matter and described the applicant's family as "among the most influential (Radical if the Administration will allow the word) Republicans in your district." Those letters, written in October 1865, accompanied Pinney's application for amnesty. If the writers knew that those letters would make their way to Washington, they clearly failed to grasp that emphasizing an applicant's connections to the Republican Party would hardly win over Andrew Johnson. Within one year, no politically aware individual would have made such a mistake because Johnson's views had become clear and his battle with Congress for control of Reconstruction was well underway.[25]

Because North Texas amnesty applicants knew nothing of Johnson's intentions and because of the severity of the potential punishments, the forty-two individuals examined here took the process seriously and employed what they considered the wisest strategies to secure pardons. Predictably, among those who commented on secession, most claimed that they had opposed the movement, though several admitted their support. A few individuals pointed to community pressure or an attempt to avoid conscription to explain their Confederate civil service or their ineligibility for general amnesty. Others simply summarized why they met the requirements of their respective exception and offered no further explanation.

In light of the political climate of North Texas at the time of secession, most applicants likely wrote truthfully. However, a few of the applications examined here demonstrate that in the pursuit of a pardon, honesty was not always the best policy. One prominent applicant certainly secured his pardon despite a misleading, if not dishonest, application letter. James G. Bourland of Cooke County applied under the thirteenth exception and correctly wrote that no other exception applied to him. A wealthy former member of the state legislature and the county's second largest slaveholder in 1860, he neglected to mention his leading role in the infamous "Great Hanging" in Gainesville, Cooke County, in which he and other Confederate Texans hanged forty suspected Unionists. Though none of the exceptions to general amnesty specifically applied to Bourland's role in the mass execution, those actions could hardly be considered irrelevant. Additionally, individuals who served with Bourland later accused him of wartime atrocities, including the summary execution of prisoners of war. Bourland's role in the hanging also betrayed the spirit of his application letter in which he claimed to have advanced the Confederate cause only in the capacity of frontier defense against Indians. Moreover, Bourland's presidential pardon later assisted his successful effort to avoid conviction for his part in the hanging.[26]

Almost certainly others omitted important information from their applications, or simply lied, but the point remains that for the vast majority of amnesty applicants it rarely mattered. Ultimately, Johnson's handling of North Texas pardon requests proved consistent with his treatment of applications statewide. The presence of anti-secession sentiment in North Texas made no difference in the process, nor did persecution of Unionists in actions such as the Great Hanging in Gainesville. In most cases, Johnson's decision was made before he or his staff even read the application, whether the applicant admitted secessionist sentiment or identified himself as one of the "helpless instruments in the hands of rebellion."[27]

Notes

1. Bradley R. Clampitt, "' Not Intended to Dispossess Females': Southern Women and Civil War Amnesty," *Civil War History* 56 (Dec. 2010): 326–27; Clampitt, "Two Degrees of Rebellion: Amnesty and Texans after the Civil War," *Civil War History* 52 (Sept. 2006): 255–58; Jonathan T. Dorris, *Pardon and Amnesty under Lincoln and Johnson: The Restoration of the Confederates to Their Rights and Privileges, 1861–1898* (Chapel Hill: University of North Carolina Press, 1953), 53–57, 95–107, 240–41, 308–11, 340–44; James D. Richardson, ed., *A Compilation of the Messages and Papers of the Presidents, 1787–1897* (10 vols.; Washington, D. C.: Government Printing Office, 1896–1899), 6: 311–12;

Application of Thomas R. Williams (Texas), Case Files of Applications from Former Confederates for Presidential Pardons, 1865–1867, United States Department of War, Records of the Adjutant General's Office, 1780s–1917, Record Group 94, National Archive, Washington D. C. (hereafter cited as Amnesty Papers). Andrew Johnson's fourteen exceptions to general amnesty included seven exceptions initially adopted as part of Abraham Lincoln's amnesty plan.

2. Applications of Christopher C. Binkley, James K. Blair, James G. Bourland, Walter Caruth, William Caruth, Phillip D. Crume, Thomas F. Crutchfield, J. D. Dumas, James P. Dumas, Abraham Freeman, James Galbraith, Joel W. Hagee, W. H. Hord, Jeremiah E. Hughes, Barney L. Johnson, Middleton T. Johnson, Hugh Kirkpatrick, Roswell W. Lee, Matthew Leeper, George Marchbanks, Joseph B. Meredith, William B. Miller, E. W. Newton, Josiah Nichols, Elbert Pinney, Henry Pinney, George H. Piguese, H. R. S. Rose, Joseph C. Rushing, Junius W. Smith, Thomas M. Smith, W. J. Sorelle, Sinclair Stapp, E. J. C. Thompson, Thomas V. Toler, Charles A. Warfield, John G. Williams, Thomas R. Williams (quotation), Wade H. Witt, M. H. Wright, William B. Wright, and William Hugh Young in Amnesty Papers.

3. United States Census Bureau, *Population of the United States in 1860* (Washington, D. C.: Government Printing Office, 1864), 472–86; Randolph B. Campbell, *An Empire for Slavery: The Peculiar Institution in Texas, 1821–1865* (Baton Rouge: Louisiana State University Press, 1989), 55–56; Joe T. Timmons, "The Referendum in Texas on the Ordinance of Secession, February 23, 1861," *East Texas Historical Journal* 11 (Fall 1973): 15–16; Ralph A. Wooster, "Civil War," in Ron Tyler et al., eds., *The New Handbook of Texas* (6 vols.; Austin: Texas State Historical Association, 1996) (hereafter cited as *NHOT*), 2: 121; Walter L. Buenger, *Secession and the Union in Texas* (Austin: University of Texas Press, 1984), 15, 66–68. The east-west boundaries of the sample counties selected here coincide with Buenger's geographic divisions of Texas in 1861.

4. Clampitt, "Two Degrees of Rebellion," 262–80; Amnesty Papers.

5. Application of Roswell W. Lee, Amnesty Papers; United States Census Bureau, Eighth Census, 1860, Texas, Fannin County, Schedule 1 (Free Inhabitants), NA.

6. Application of William Hugh Young, Amnesty Papers.

7. Application of W. H. Hord, Amnesty Papers; Randolph B. Campbell, *Grass-Roots Reconstruction in Texas, 1865–1880* (Baton Rouge: Louisiana State University Press, 1997), 66, 67 (second quotation).

8. Applications of Christopher C. Binkley, James K. Blair, James G. Bourland, Walter Caruth, William Caruth, Phillip D. Crume, Thomas F. Crutchfield, J. D. Dumas, James P. Dumas, Abraham Freeman, James Galbraith, Joel W. Hagee, Jeremiah E. Hughes, Barney L. Johnson, Middleton T. Johnson, Junius W. Smith, Hugh Kirkpatrick, Matthew Leeper, George Marchbanks, Joseph B. Meredith, William B. Miller, E. W. Newton, Josiah Nichols, Elbert Pinney, Henry Pinney, George H. Piguese, H. R. S. Rose, Joseph C. Rushing, Thomas M. Smith, W. J. Sorelle, Sinclair Stapp, E. J. C. Thompson, Thomas V. Toler, Charles A. Warfield, John G. Williams, Thomas R. Williams, Wade H. Witt, M. H. Wright, and William B. Wright in Amnesty Papers.

9. Applications of George F. Marchbanks, Jeremiah E. Hughes, H. R. S. Rose, James K. Blair, and James Galbraith in Amnesty Papers. Joel W. Hagee served as a postmaster in Grayson County, applied under the first exception, and claimed to have voted against secession. He offered no explanation for his status as an office holder in his application for pardon.

10. Application of James K. Blair in Amnesty Papers; Texas Secretary of State, Election Register, 1865–1870, Texas State Library and Archives, Austin; Campbell, *Grass-Roots Reconstruction*, 14–15.

11. Application of Matthew Leeper, Amnesty Papers.

12. Ibid.; Jeanne V. Harrison, "Matthew Leeper, Confederate Agent at the Wichita Agency, Indian Territory," *The Chronicles of Oklahoma* 47 (Autumn 1969): 242–57.

13. Application of Matthew Leeper, Amnesty Papers; David La Vere, *Contrary Neighbors: Southern Plains Indians and Removed Indians in Indian Territory* (Norman: University of Oklahoma Press, 2000), 167–76.

14. Application of Christopher C. Binkley, Amnesty Papers; Election Register, 1865–1870; Richard B. McCaslin, *Tainted Breeze: The Great Hanging at Gainesville, Texas, 1862* (Baton Rouge: Louisiana State University Press, 1992), 163, 169–70 (third quotation), 185; Clampitt, "Two Degrees of Rebellion," 277.

15. Applications of Thomas R. Williams, M. H. Wright, James P. Dumas, Walter Caruth, and William Caruth, Amnesty Papers.

16. Application of Abraham Freeman, Amnesty Papers; Clampitt, "Southern Women and Civil War Amnesty," 340–42. William B. Miller of Dallas County also applied under the thirteenth exception and claimed to have voted against secession but offered no further relevant discussion of his wartime activities.

17. Applications of Sinclair Stapp, Henry Pinney, and W. J. Sorelle, Amnesty Papers.

18. Applications of Charles A. Warfield, George Piguese, and Thomas F. Crutchfield, Amnesty Papers.

19. Application of Joseph C. Rushing and Barney L. Johnson, Amnesty Papers.

20. Application of Thomas V. Toler, Amnesty Papers.

21. Ibid.

22. Application of William B. Wright, Amnesty Papers; Clampitt, "Two Degrees of Rebellion," 268–69; Ezra J. Warner and W. Buck Yearns, *Biographical Register of the Confederate Congress* (Baton Rouge: Louisiana State University Press, 1975), 264; Thomas W. Cutrer, "William B. Wright," *NHOT*, 6:1,092.

23. Clampitt, "Two Degrees of Rebellion," 255–81.

24. Clampitt, "Southern Women and Civil War Amnesty," 328, 346–47; Clampitt, "Two Degrees of Rebellion," 278; Eric McKitrick, *Andrew Johnson and Reconstruction* (Chicago: University of Chicago Press, 1960), 146–49; Brooks D. Simpson, *The Reconstruction Presidents* (Lawrence: University Press of Kansas, 1998), 74–75, 129–30; Hans L. Trefousse, *Andrew Johnson: A Biography* (New York: Norton, 1989), 227.

25. Application of Elbert Pinney, Amnesty Papers.

26. Application of James G. Bourland, Amnesty Papers; Clampitt, "Two Degrees of Rebellion," 275–76; Eighth Census of the United States, 1860, Texas, Cooke County, Schedule 2 (Slave Inhabitants), NA.; Richard B. McCaslin, "James G. Bourland," *NHOT*, 1: 662–63; McCaslin, *Tainted Breeze*, 18, 184.

27. Application of Thomas R. Williams, Amnesty Papers (quotation).

28. Table based on information in Clampitt, "Two Degrees of Rebellion," 257–59.

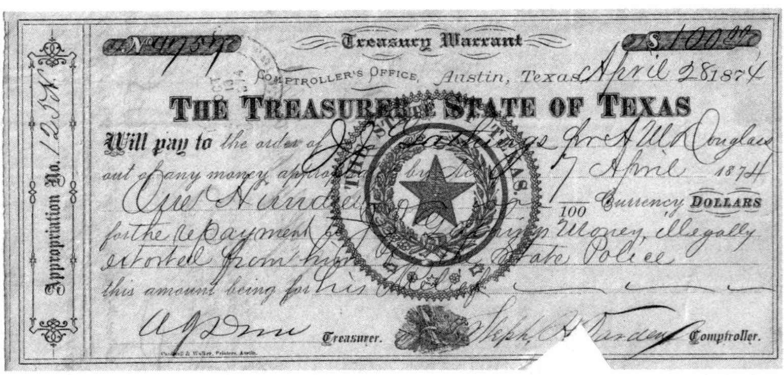

Texas treasury warrant issued to James J. Gathings in 1874. Personal Collection of Richard B. McCaslin

Texas Reconstruction in Popular Memory: What Really Happened in Hill County in 1871

Richard B. McCaslin

Texas legislators in 1874 righted a terrible wrong, or so they claimed. It had already become part of Democratic lore that Republican governor Edmund J. Davis was an oppressive dictator. The same idea was quickly becoming embedded in popular memory in the Lone Star State as conservative Democrats "redeemed" it from Reconstruction by beating the Republicans at the ballot box. Perhaps the most persuasive evidence in the portrayal of Davis as an oppressor was his use of martial law in 1871 after a series of brutal incidents, one of which involved James J. Gathings Sr. in Hill County. Gathings was arrested by Davis's hated State Police and compelled to pay a large fine by Republican Adjutant General James Davidson. This sparked an angry controversy, and the Democratic majority in the legislature, just months after vanquishing Davis and his allies, made amends by reimbursing Gathings for his entire loss. At least one treasury warrant he received in 1874 declared that the money was "for the repayment of J. J. Gathings's money, illegally extorted from him by the State Police." But in fact Gathings was guilty of several crimes, all of which were connected to his effort to help two murderers avoid justice. And at least one of the killers, his son, remained at large. The true story behind the affair for which Gathings was compensated by the legislature, which became a vital issue in the political reconquest of Texas by conservative Democrats, reveals just how damaging the abandonment of Reconstruction was at what Randolph B. Campbell has called the "grassroots" level in Texas. Gathings and his partners in crime remained in power, and Texas missed an opportunity to secure real reform by the enforcement of its laws. Instead, Texas leaders and writers condoned what later generations would condemn as a "hate crime," and their excuses for that transgression became enshrined in popular memory for almost a century.

The political controversy began with a heinous felony at Clifton, in Bosque County, Texas, on December 26, 1870. Freedman Joe Willingham was traveling with the wife of Lewis Willingham, who was also black. The two travelers were "quiet persons" and "long resident about Meridian," and they were on their way to Waco for Christmas when they stopped at a grocery store in Clifton. Groceries often served as a source of alcohol in nineteenth-century Texas towns, and Joe Willingham got into a confrontation with "some drunken men," who "whipped" him. The Willinghams continued on their journey, but men followed them. Later, her body was found three miles from Clifton, shot through the head and heart. Joe was found three more miles away, "shot several times through the body." It was not hard to guess who had committed the murders; as a newspaper noted soon afterward, the persons who were responsible for the killing were "well known" and openly stayed in Clifton "all next day." A coroner's jury, convened that same day or the next, declared that the guilty parties were in fact James J. Gathings Jr., a Confederate veteran of the 12th Texas Cavalry from Hill County, and Soltolla Nicholson, about whom little more is known.[1]

Among those who attended the coroner's inquest at Clifton was W. T. Pritchett. He had been a State Police lieutenant for fewer than four months, appointed soon after the Twelfth Legislature created the agency in July 1870, and had only arrived in the area in October, but he decided to act. Gathering six other State Police officers, two white and four black, Pritchett rode for the Hill County home of James J. Gathings Sr., where he apparently expected to arrest the younger Gathings and Nicholson. The State Police covered the almost fifty miles between Clifton and the Gathings's house by traveling through the night, arriving about dawn on December 28. Having learned that the two fugitives had been there only an hour earlier, Pritchett asked the elder Gathings, who confronted the State Police at the door of his residence, to allow them to search the premises. Gathings demanded to see a search warrant, and when Pritchett said that he did not have one, refused to let the officers enter his home. When Pritchett insisted, Gathings brandished a shotgun and—with a string of ugly racial epithets—made it clear he would not admit blacks into his house. Pritchett ultimately prevailed, but he prudently had two of his white officers conduct the search. Finding no one to arrest, Pritchett and his party left to find breakfast, the three white State Police riding to a place where they could buy a meal, while their four black colleagues went to a nearby home where they could eat for free.[2]

With only an escort of two fellow officers, Pritchett became an easy target for a Gathings counterattack. The three State Police, after they ate, resumed their pursuit of the younger Gathings and Nicholson, but they were surrounded by at least a dozen armed men before they could rejoin their black comrades. Outgunned, Pritchett and his two companions surrendered and were escorted back to Gathings's house. Their captors claimed to have writs to arrest them for unlawful entry, but they did not. After a wait of several hours, during which time the other State Police were captured, writs were obtained from a justice of the peace, Alexander M. Lawrence. Pritchett for some reason did not want to be tried by Lawrence, perhaps because he knew that the justice was a neighbor and possible friend of Gathings, so he asked that he and his men be arraigned before Richard R. Booth Jr., the justice of the peace in the county seat of Hillsboro. Booth was too young to have served in the Confederate Army; perhaps more important, he and his father were outspoken Republicans and supporters of Governor Davis. Lawrence agreed, and Gathings and his comrades delivered the seven State Police to Booth. Armed men stood glowering as Booth heard the case, but the justice stood his ground. He dismissed all of the charges against Pritchett's comrades because Lawrence's writs were faulty, and he required an appearance bond of only $500 for the lieutenant. Gathings angrily demanded that Booth set a higher bond for Pritchett and, when Booth failed to comply, secured more arrest warrants, probably from Lawrence. Pritchett, who inexplicably lingered in Hill County after signing his appearance bond, was arrested again, but he escaped and hurried to report to Adjutant General Davidson at Austin.[3]

Davidson and his colleagues in the Davis administration probably were not surprised with the news from Hill County. The residents had overwhelmingly voted in favor of secession in 1861, and at least three companies of Confederate cavalry were raised there. Murders of blacks were commonplace in Texas during Reconstruction, and Bosque and Hill counties were especially notorious for violence. According to the Austin *State Journal*, no fewer than two people were killed in Bosque County each week in 1870. During June 1870, at least two freedmen were murdered in adjacent Hill County. That same month, in response to a request from the Texas Senate for a report on the violence in the state, Davidson described Hill County as living under a "reign of violence." He explained that "Gangs of lawless men" threatened blacks there, while local residents either did nothing or even helped the murderers. The murder of two white men in Hill County during April 1870 had led to official calls for action, but the killing of two blacks in June apparently met with silence. Events in the late summer of 1870 seemed to confirm Davidson's denunciation. William O. and George H. Cox were arrested in Hill County for several murders they had committed in North Texas, but a party of men helped them escape when they were being escorted northward by William Hooper, a State Police officer assigned to Hill County. Perry Kincheon "Kinch" West, the Coxes' brother-in-law and fellow outlaw who traveled with them to Hill County, allegedly led the rescue party, and then organized another attack on the Hill County jail in September 1870, during which one guard was killed and another injured.[4]

What Davidson and Governor Davis must have realized was that the affair in Hill County marked a defining moment for the Republicans. They considered the maintenance of order to be essential for establishing the credibility of Republican rule. After the creation of the State Police, Davidson asked for and got reports from 108 sheriffs detailing the violence in their counties, and he personally inspected the State Police posts in three dozen counties. Hill County quickly emerged as a particular challenge. State Police officer Pierce Nagle, who served at the Waco post in McClennan County, was wounded by West and his comrades when he attempted to serve warrants in the late summer of 1870. Sheriff Evan Beauchamp of Hill County in mid-September begged for enough State Police to arrest West. Davidson sent Lt. Thomas H. Williams with fifteen men, but they only exchanged gunshots with the outlaws as the latter fled into the woods. After Pritchett took charge, he met with Beauchamp and offered to send five men, but the sheriff declined the offer, saying that a handful was not enough. Beauchamp also refused to have a letter from Governor Davis, given to him by Pritchett, read aloud at a meeting. This declared that if the people of Hill County did not end the reign of terror by West and his allies, the Governor would declare martial law and send State Police and militia to impose order. Furthermore, the people of the county, or "such of them as are to blame in this respect," would have to pay the expenses of such an operation. To support this message, and stung by rebukes from Davidson for moving slowly, Pritchett sent Sgt. William E. Evans to Hill County with five men on October 29, despite Beauchamp's declaration that they would not be effective. These riders arrested five men, one of whom had been with West, and killed another who drew his revolver.[5]

Two days before Pritchett sent the State Police into Hill County, Beauchamp reported that West and his men had left the area, and Davis responded by telling him that plans to send the militia into his county had been "suspended." But the governor remained suspicious, and when reports surfaced that Beauchamp was inept or even supported the violence, Davis had him removed and appointed John P. Grace, another Republican, in his place. Interestingly, some of the same sources also condemned Richard R. Booth and his brother Charles L. Booth, who served as attorney for Hill County, but they remained in office. When Sheriff Grace reported in early December that the Hill County jail had again been raided and another prisoner freed, it must have been clear to the governor and his adjutant general that peace had not been established with either the departure of West or the removal of Beauchamp, and that earlier plans to send the State Police and militia might have to be reactivated. The killing of the Willinghams, and Pritchett's confrontation with the Gathings, convinced the governor that drastic action was necessary not only to preserve order, but to establish the authority of his administration.[6]

The fact that the Gathings were prominent, and very pro-Confederate, may have intensified emotions on both sides in December 1870. James J. Gathings Sr. had come from Mississippi to Texas in 1849, then moved to Hill County about 1853 and platted his own town, which he named Covington in honor of his in-laws. By 1860 he owned more slaves and land than anyone else in the county, including his brother Philip, who arrived about 1854. They both raised livestock, and James was one of the settlers who introduced Durham cattle into the region. James also diversified his investments, establishing a brick yard, tannery, grist mill, sawmill, machine shop, textile mill, and a plant that made shoes, saddles, and harness. He served as postmaster of Covington from its founding through the Civil War and as a road overseer, while Philip was elected as a justice of the peace. The two of them established Gathings Male and Female College, which operated from 1863 until 1885, while James's wife Martha helped to establish a Methodist church for their community. James allegedly declined a commission from Sam Houston at the outset of the Civil War, but his eldest sons, James J. Gathings Jr. and William C. Gathings, enlisted in Company A of the 12th Texas Cavalry. Their brother-in-law, Joseph P. Wier, a delegate to the Secession Convention, led their company and later their regiment until he was killed at Yellow Bayou in May 1864. After surrendering in 1865, William recovered Wier's body from its battlefield burial site and brought it to the family cemetery at Covington. Philip's oldest son, Philip W. Gathings, who also served in the 12th Texas Cavalry, survived the war but died soon afterward, which may well have intensified the Gathings' emotions about people such as Davis and Davidson who did not share their commitment to the cause they had lost. And the death of James J. Gathings Sr.'s wife in 1870 certainly did not improve his mood.[7]

The Gathings had already come under official suspicion for violence in Hill County prior to their confrontation with the State Police. Lt. Harrison Holt of the 6th United States Cavalry, as the military commissioner for Hill and Johnson counties, mentioned them in his September 1869 report on violence in his district. Fresh from a similar assignment in Bell County, where he and his troopers had chased outlaws in August 1869, Holt recounted a bizarre series of incidents in which a band of ten white men wearing "masks Gowns and tall hats" had terrorized blacks in Hill County one night. Surrounding two black men on the road between Hillsboro and Cleburne, they forced the pair to whip each other at gunpoint. Riding to the home of another freedman, they repeated this scene with several other blacks, and then stole six dollars. Apparently at least one freedman may have defied them, because they shot a black man in the foot at their third stop. Holt could name the perpetrators, although he misspelled their names. On his list were three of James J. Gathings Sr.'s adult sons: William, George, and Benjamin Gathings, all of whom he identified as "Gathans." Among the other seven men were three of James J. Gathings Jr.'s brothers-in-law, James T. DeMumber, Merritte A. Sedberry, and Alexander Rush Sedberry. Holt had no doubts about what kind of men had conducted this spree: "It is a fact that an organization exists in Hill County and composed of citizens thereof styling themselves the Ku Klux Klan." He would have arrested all of them forthwith, but he was called away to muster elsewhere.[8]

Upon receiving a report from Pritchett, Davis declared Hill County to be under martial law on January 10, 1871, and ordered Adjutant General Davidson to lead a company of State Guards, a militia organization created to support the State Police, to Hillsboro. Because the State Guards had apparently never organized in Hill County, Davidson mustered Capt. Edward H. Napier and his Company H of the 6th Regiment of the State Guard, which was composed of about fifty men from Williamson County. James C. Wooters, a Confederate veteran, was officially in command of the 6th Regiment, but J. M. Gibbs, the colonel of the 4th Regiment of the State Guard, was put in charge of the militia operation in Hill County. Gibbs, like Napier, had apparently never served in a Confederate unit. Furthermore, he was serving as sheriff of Grimes County, having taken office under a federal military directive in 1869, and Davis trusted him enough that he would be assigned to oversee martial law in Walker County in February 1871. While Gibbs served as the overall leader, Napier became the post commander at Hillsboro, and Davidson directed the military commission that he established in the local courthouse. With everyone and everything in place by mid-January, Davidson ordered the arrest of the men who had detained Pritchett. Sheriff Grace, accompanied by members of the State Guard, quickly returned with the accused felons. He later protested this assignment to Davis, but the governor sharply retorted that all of this would not have been necessary if Grace had properly enforced the law. [9]

Davidson's dragnet snared eleven men. James J. Gathings Sr. was brought before the military commission, along with his sons Benjamin C., George W., and David A. Gathings. None of these three men had served in the Civil War—the latter two were too young—but all were now young adults who still lived with their father and apparently participated in the capture of Pritchett. Philip Gathings was also arrested. Two detainees were sons-in-law of James J. Gathings Sr.: Astyanax M. Douglass, a twice wounded veteran of the 6th Mississippi Infantry who had come to Texas in 1866 and married Charlotte Ann Gathings Wier, the widow of Joseph P. Wier; and James T. DeMumber, who had married Mary Jane Gathings in 1860 before joining the 8th [12th] Texas Infantry and being wounded in combat in Arkansas. Henry Strong, like Douglass, had served in the 6th Mississippi Infantry for the duration of the war before coming to Texas, while William L. Towner came to Texas during the war, and re-enlisted, after serving briefly as the captain of a company in the 6th Mississippi Infantry. Henry Williams, at the age of twenty-two, was too young to be a Confederate but was a neighbor of the Gathings. Finally, Frank T. Wier, a native of Mississippi, must have been related to Joseph P. Wier, the late husband of Gathings' daughter. There were, of course, three notable suspects not brought before Davidson: Soltolla Nicholson and James J. Gathings Jr. remained at large, and the latter's older brother, William C. Gathings, was also not arrested. William still lived with his father, unlike James, but he was often assigned the task of chasing those who had stolen livestock, and so he may well have been absent.[10]

Davidson, certainly wary of having to confront a mob, allowed only members of the State Guard and State Police, and the arrested men, into the room where the military commission met. Many angry words were exchanged, but the intent of the proceeding was clear from the start. Once arraigned, and having posted bond, the detainees would become a matter for the local civil authorities. Davidson and the State Guard would depart, and the law would be allowed to take its course. Perhaps Gathings, who emerged as the leader of his group, understood this, for much of his argument with Davidson focused on how much their bond would be. Davidson declared the amount had to be $3,000, saying that was what the cost of his operation had been. And he insisted that not only would Gathings sign bonds for $3,000, he would in fact pay that amount at once or undergo a trial by Davidson's military commission, with the almost certain threat that he and his colleagues would be sent to the state prison in Huntsville. Davidson may have expected Gathings and his colleagues to never appear in court, thus forfeiting the bond and in effect paying a heavy fine. Or perhaps he thought that Gathings could not raise the money and all would go to jail. Either way, Davidson would have made his point. Gathings initially balked at a bond six times higher than that set for Pritchett, but when Davidson told him he had fifteen minutes to pay or go to prison, he began to gather the money. In short order he presented the military commission with one thousand dollars in gold coins and $1,765 in "United States currency," presumably a mixture of silver coins and paper notes. Under the law establishing the State Guard, the governments of counties in which martial law was declared had to pay all of the costs of such operations, but Governor Davis had given Davidson the option to levy "either upon the county, or upon the parties implicated in the recent outrages." Davidson, by collecting the money from Gathings, settled the issue in favor of the Hill County authorities. Whether Gathings and his fellow prisoners were ever tried, and there is no record that they ever were, they had paid a hefty fine, and their detention had cost Hill County nothing.[11]

Having completed their business in two days, Davidson and the State Guard left Hill County, and the angry controversy began. Governor Davis submitted a report to the Texas Senate in February 1871, and it was sent to the Committee on Militia. Just eight days later, a majority of the members endorsed a response that declared Davis had committed "no excess" regarding martial law in Hill County. George R. Shannon did submit a minority dissenting report, arguing that the governor could not declare martial law while the legislature was in session nor delegate the power to enforce martial law to anyone else. Furthermore, the governor could not fine just a portion of the people in a county to pay the expenses of martial law; the cost had to be paid by all or none of the people. This was apparently ignored by the rest of the senators. After all, the argument was both excessively technical and specious, and Shannon had already become notorious for his opposition to the State Guard. When a Hill

County grand jury in March demanded a legislative investigation, after failing to indict the Gathings men for any of their excesses, the Senate took no further action. Similarly, Davis ignored a gentle suggestion from District Judge J. P. Wood that he should return Pritchett to Hill County for a trial, which Wood assured him would be fair and impartial.[12]

Meanwhile, a heated debate erupted in the public forum. The Waco *Examiner* declared that Davidson's operation was a "Daring Robbery" and that the elder Gathings should have shot Pritchett. The Houston *Union* countered that the Gathings were "old and notorious offenders," having in 1866 twice blocked the arrest of another member of the family who stole a mule. The Austin *Daily State Journal* repeated the story about the mule and declared that the Gathings were "jail birds and lawless offenders." Not to be outdone, the *Union* included the Gathings, father and sons, on a lengthy list of "murderers" that included former Confederate General Samuel Bell Maxey. The San Antonio *Herald* published a long letter from Gathings's son-in-law, Douglass, who condemned Davis for "robbery" and called for his imprisonment. The Douglass letter was accompanied by declarations from Sheriff Grace and justices Lawrence and Booth that they had not been "coerced" to act as they had, and Grace added that Gathings Sr. was "strictly honorable and law abiding." In September 1871, when Rep. John W. Robertson, a former Confederate colonel, introduced a resolution into the Texas House demanding that Davidson explain what he had done with Gathings's bond money, the *Union* derided it as "buncombe" and happily reported that, although the House passed the measure, Robertson's "insulting" preamble was deleted. Robertson's resolution mirrored the denunciations of Davis issued that same month by the Tax-Payer's Convention at Austin. Andrew J. Hamilton chaired the committee that produced the anti-Davis resolutions, and he declared that when he thought of how a defenseless "old gentleman" in Hill County had been forced to pay $3,000 in gold, he "hung his head in shame." The "old gentleman," Gathings Sr., attended the Convention as a delegate, which prompted the *Union* to denounce him as a "red hot Ku-Klux Democrat." Elsewhere in the state, the San Antonio *Express* joined the *Union* in supporting Davis, while the Dallas *Herald* condemned him.[13]

Robertson failed in his bid to humiliate Davidson, but his effort raised the issue of compensation for Gathings. The adjutant general soon complied with the House resolution by submitting an expense report for the martial law operations in both Hill and Walker counties. His records clearly showed that of the money taken from Gathings, all but $9.33

had been spent on the pay and expenses of the State Guard dispatched to Hill County. This information was submitted to a special committee comprised of Robertson and two of his fellow state representatives. Unfortunately for Robertson, both of the latter were Republicans: Charles W. Gardiner, who chaired the Republican Party in Brazos County, and Carroll P. D. Harn, who had served as a staff officer under Maj. Gen. J. E. B. Stuart before relocating to Texas after the Civil War and earning much notoriety as a Radical. Interestingly, Harn commanded the 8th Regiment of the State Guard, and he chaired the special House committee that included Robertson and Gardiner. The two Republicans signed a report that declared the charges against Davidson had been "made from malicious motives" and were "totally without foundation." Robertson could only add his own weak minority report that admitted Davidson was without blame but insisted someone had clearly done something wrong. He also joined with twenty-four of his colleagues in voting against a resolution that exonerated Davidson, while forty-eight state representatives approved the measure. Undeterred, Texas Representative L. E. Gillette, who had commanded Confederate cavalry in the Trans-Mississippi, introduced the first bill for the repayment of Gathings in early 1873. The House committee to which the measure was referred unanimously approved it, but the proposal failed by a narrow margin.[14]

While the *Union* did its best to belittle Gathings, and the Republican-led legislature refused to reimburse him, a more enduring perspective on the Hill County affair emerged from newspapers allied with Democrats. For example, a writer for the Galveston *Tri-Weekly News* declared that even Napoleon III "never did an act of despotism like that Davis committed in Hill County." Gathings was in fact "An old gentleman, of character, probity and property; one of the weighty men of his section; a man of blameless life and spotless morals; one regarded with respect by his neighbors; a gentleman occupying the most respectable position that God assigns to man—the head of an honorable household." To make his position even clearer, the writer added, "God has created places of greater note, but none of greater respectability than this." There followed a romanticized version of the clash with Pritchett: "A company of armed men stood before his gate and demanded admission, alleging that they were in pursuit of fugitives. He asked for the process of law; they had none. 'Then,' said he, 'you cannot enter. I have been educated in that good old English doctrine established at Bunker Hill and San Jacinto; a man's house is his castle; if you have legal process, come in; if you have not, stay out.'" To reinforce his legal point, the writer explained: "Were the Queen of England and all her Prime Ministers to stand before the gate of her meanest subject, she would not dare to enter without process of law; but these policemen—these armed myrmidons—rush[ed] where royalty dare not tread. They entered the house and grounds; they searched them." And so "Mr. Gathings did what every man has the right to do. He pursued and arrested those who had violated his premises and carried them before a justice of the peace for punishment. He appealed to the law which had been violated and for this he was fined three thousand dollars." The writer concluded, "This is a wrong and an outrage, the like of which has never before been perpetrated in any government professing to be free." And lest anyone not understand his purpose, he added one final growl at Davis, insisting that "innumerable" instances "of tyranny and oppression . . . might be named."[15]

Charles B. Pearre, a Waco lawyer whose brother was a federal Circuit Court judge in Maryland and whose nephew served in Congress, included his version of the Hill County affair in an exhaustive diatribe against Davis published in 1872. Addressing his fellow Democrats, he described the State Guard as "Composed in part of gamblers, drunkards, fugitives from justice, escaped convicts, many of whom have the mark of Cain upon them; of such men as are capable of committing crimes of the darkest dye." Black members of the State Guard were particularly vile: "vindictive against the white race, ignorant, lazy, and totally destitute of honesty." And the State Police were even worse. As his sole example of the oppression of Davis, he claimed that two black State Police kept their pistols trained on Gathings while Pritchett and others searched his home, "even the ladies' rooms." Gathings had been outraged, but he sent Douglass to secure writs before sending his friends in pursuit of Pritchett. Thus it was the State Police, not Gathings and his group, who violated the well-known provisions against illegal search and seizure in the United States Constitution. The ensuing arrest and fining of Gathings was "oppressive Executive robbery," a violation of the laws not only of men but of God. Of course, Pearre did not ever mention the murder of the Willinghams in Bosque County, which might have obscured his point about legality among those not completely blinded by racism. In May 1873, when the legislature discussed a continuation of funding for the State Police, Representative Josiah W. Kemble declared that he knew of three outrages committed by them in his part of the state, including when they came to "rob" Gathings and to murder Jack Mitchell. Even the Galveston *Tri-Weekly News* had attributed Mitchell's murder to unknown men, but Pearre had declared he was killed by State Police, providing persuasive evidence that Kemble, like other Democrats, had read his screed. And newspapers across Texas repeated Kemble's accusations.[16]

The defeat of Davis and his allies in the election of 1873 set the stage for the Gathingses' triumph. Despite the declarations of the San Antonio *Herald* that Gathings Sr., who had been "robbed by a negro State Policeman of $3,000 in gold," would run for the legislature "to show the powers that be that an innocent man cannot be outraged in his district with impunity," he in fact did not campaign. But among the many new legislators who took their seats was Douglass, who worked closely with James T. Ratcliff, a conservative Democratic attorney from Hillsboro who had served in the legislature in 1866, to secure compensation for Gathings. His father-in-law must have been pleased with the amount acquired by Douglass, for the legislature decided that the $1,000 in gold he had surrendered in 1871 was now worth $1,150 in currency. The state treasury on April 7, 1874, was directed to issue twenty-eight warrants for $100 and another for $115 to Gathings, for a total of $2,915. To underscore the intent of the legislative appropriation, Comptroller Stephen H. Darden added his own endorsement on the back of at least one of the notes: "Receivable in payment of any demands in favor of the state." At least one warrant, and probably all, went to the financial operation of James H. Raymond and Charles H. Whitis in Austin, with yet another endorsement from Gathings reminding state employees that Raymond and Whitis could use the note to pay state debts. A cut cancellation by a Treasury clerk indicates that this was indeed done.[17]

The story of Gathings's violation by State Police refused to die, primarily because, as interpreted by Democratic partisans, it provided clear evidence of how oppressive Davis' Republican administration had been. A boilerplate history of Hill County, published in 1892, claimed that Gathings was a "distant relative" of the man who killed the Willinghams in Bosque County. Furthermore, Pritchett's detail had threatened Gathings with pistols, and an angry Pritchett, after he had been released on bond, declared that he would "mob" Gathings's house. Armed men had to guard Gathings's home to deter such an attack. This threat was repeated in a second history of the area printed in 1895. Walter P. Webb, in his history of the Texas Rangers published in 1936, wrote that Pritchett's officers "ransacked" Gathings's home, and Davidson literally extorted money from Gathings. Webb agreed with Pearre, who referred to what Davidson did as "robbery." Almost two decades later, Otis Singletary, in an article for the *Southwestern Historical Quarterly,* presented a version of the affair that clearly reflected the prejudices of Pearre and Webb.

William C. Nunn repeated the same biased account in his oft-quoted history of Reconstruction in Texas, the popularity of which can only be explained by the acceptance of the Democratic perspective in popular memory. Ellis Bailey took it to another extreme in his 1966 book on Hill County, declaring that "an army officer with a group of Col. Gathings's former slaves tried to arrest Col. Gathings at his home." It was not until 1969 that a more scholarly account of the event, written by Anne P. Baenziger, appeared in the *Southwestern Historical Quarterly*. Carl H. Moneyhon, in his history of Reconstruction in Texas published in 2004, included a more balanced but not very detailed narrative, moving one step further from the poisoned perspective of the Democrats who opposed Republican efforts to reform the Lone Star State. He added more information in a biography of Davis published in 2010, placing the event within the context of the governor's overall efforts to quell violence. Most recently, Barry A. Crouch and Donaly E. Brice, in their history of the State Police, fairly recount the event and circumstances leading to it, but they stop short of tracing its incorporation into popular memory.[18]

And what of the people at the center of the controversy? Governor Davis, of course, lost the election of 1873 and left office, but before that his Adjutant General, Davidson, fled the state after allegedly embezzling thousands of dollars in state funds. Pritchett disappears from the public record, as does one of the murderers he intended to arrest, Soltolla Nicholson. James J. Gathings Jr. stayed in Hill County, where he had three more daughters with his wife, the former Laura A. Sedberry, before he died in 1877, at the age of thirty-four. His father remarried, and then died in 1880 after being injured at a cotton gin. Most of their relatives, including both of their wives, Philip Gathings, and the numerous siblings of James J. Gathings Jr., enjoyed long lives before joining the father and son in the family cemetery at Covington. Little more has been found about Henry Strong or Henry Williams, but Frank T. Wier won a race for tax assessor in Hill County in 1876 and four years later lived with Alexander Rush Sedberry and his widowed sister, Laura Gathings, while working as a druggist. One of their neighbors was Henry Williams. William L. Towner, Strong's former comrade in the 6th Mississippi Infantry, lost his race for district clerk in Hill County in 1876, but he later served as a county clerk, district clerk, sheriff and tax collector in Runnels County, where he also joined the United Confederate Veterans and is buried. The elder Gathings's sons-in-law, Astyanax M. Douglass and James T. DeMumber, became the most prominent members of his ersatz posse. Douglass, who named his son James Gathings Douglass in 1874, served three terms in the Texas House and two in the state Senate, and then chaired the Texas Board of Health. DeMumber became a Populist and lost a Texas Senate race to Douglass in 1892, but he stayed active in Hill County politics for at least another decade. Like the rest, they are buried with family members at Covington.[19]

Douglass, as a Texas legislator, was prominent in the 1874 ouster of Superintendent of Public Instruction Jacob C. DeGress, the last "Radical" appointee of Davis to be removed from office. One of the first to enter Degress's office after he vacated it, Douglass pointed dramatically to the fireplace, where some burned papers lay, and emotionally announced that the ashes covered "a multitude of sins." Perhaps a more modest gentleman would have refrained from such an outrageous statement in light of his own past transgressions, but Douglass had little to worry about. The State Police had been abolished in 1873, after the State Guard was reorganized into a more passive militia.[20] Democratic leader and newsmen alike had raised a verbal smokescreen to obscure any clear understanding of what happened in Hill County in 1871, when Douglass had helped his brother-in-law avoid arrest for murder. In so doing, they joined Douglass and his Hill County colleagues in undermining Republican efforts at real reform in Texas. Hundreds of blacks died violently during Reconstruction in Texas, but the deaths of Joe and Elizabeth Willingham became a pivotal moment in Texas history, thanks to the open defiance of one of their killers, his family, and their supporters. The histrionics of many conservative Democratic editors and politicians, including Douglass, warped popular memory, helped to vanquish the Republicans, and added several layers of dirt on the coffin in which Texas's progressive future lay for nearly a century.

Notes

1. Houston *Union*, Jan. 5, 18, 19, 1871; James Davidson to Edmund J. Davis, Feb. 1, 1871, Letterpress Book, Adjutant General's Correspondence, Texas State Library and Archives, Austin [hereinafter cited as TSLA]; *Message of Gov. Edmund J. Davis* (Austin: J. G. Tracy, 1871), 3, 7 [This is extracted from *Senate Journal of the Twelfth Legislature of the State of Texas* (Austin: J. G. Tracy, 1871), 187–203 on Hill County]; Ann Patton Baenziger, "The Texas State Police During Reconstruction: A Re-Examination," *Southwestern Historical Quarterly* 72 (Apr. 1969): 482–83; Ron Tyler et al., eds., *The New Handbook of Texas* (6 vols.; Austin: Texas State Historical Association, 1996), 3: 621 [hereinafter cited as

NHOT]. I have used the last name "Willingham" for the victims because that is how they are identified in contemporary newspapers. Their correct names may be Joseph and Elizabeth Willis, both of whom are listed in the 1870 census for Bosque County. Elizabeth, age twenty-three, was the wife of Lewis Willis, age twenty-four. Joseph, a twenty-five-year-old single man, lived with them and presumably was Lewis' brother. All were from Alabama. None of the three can be found in the 1860 or 1880 censuses. Perhaps they had been slaves of Brooks Moon Willingham or A. Willingham, both of whom had slaves in 1860 near Meridian. See United States Department of the Interior, Bureau of the Census, Eighth Census, 1860, Texas, Bosque County, Schedules 1 and 2 (Record Group 29, National Archives, Washington, D.C.). For James J. Gathings Jr., see Ninth Census, 1870, Texas, Hill County, Schedule 1, and Department of War, Compiled Service Records of Confederate Soldiers Who Served in Organizations from Texas (RG 109, NA) [hereinafter cited as CSR], 12th Texas Cavalry: J. J. Gathings. Nicholson's first name appears differently in various sources, but Soltolla is used by contemporary newspapers. He was a "Native American," and James J. Gathings Sr. was his "guardian," according to Barry A. Crouch and Donaly E. Brice, *The Governor's Hounds: The Texas State Police, 1870–1873* (Austin: University of Texas Press, 2011), 63, 72.

2. Houston *Union,* Jan. 5, 9, 1871; Davidson to Davis, Feb. 1, 1871, Letterpress Book, Adj. Gen. Corr., TSLA; *Message of Gov. Edmund J. Davis,* 5–6; H. P. N. Gammel, comp., *The Laws of Texas, 1822–1897*, 10 vols. (Austin: Gammel Book Company, 1898–1902), 6: 19–21; Baenziger, "Texas State Police," 482–83; Crouch and Brice, *Governor's Hounds,* 64–65, 286; Carl H. Moneyhon, *Texas After the Civil War* (College Station: Texas A&M University Press, 2004), 141–42; *History of Texas, Together with a Biographical History of Tarrant and Parker Counties* (Chicago: Lewis Publishing, 1895), 100; *A Memorial and Biographical History of Johnson and Hill Counties, Texas* (Chicago: Lewis Publishing, 1892), 224; *NHOT, 6: 75*. The Houston *Union*, on Dec. 29, 1870, named William E. Evans as one of the State Police with Lt. W. T. Pritchett; he was a white sergeant who worked at Belton in Bell County. Pritchett was assigned to the Waco post in McClennan County, where the men who served under him in the late fall of 1870 were General Bell, Charles Barker, Richard Castello, Captain Harrison, George W. Hillyard, Joseph Kennedy, Pierce Nagle, and Anthony Rucker. Harrison and Barker's pay records end respectively on Nov. 30 and Oct. 31, 1870, and Crouch and Brice corroborate that they were dismissed at this time. Pierce

Nagle was seriously wounded in October and resigned on Dec. 21, 1870; while he was reinstated later, it is doubtful that he accompanied Pritchett. Bell, Kennedy, and Rucker were black privates who served through the Hill County conflict. Castello, who was commissioned on Dec. 21, 1870, and Hillyard also served through this period, but their race is unknown. William Hooper (Hoopper in some records_ and George Stephens were the State Police assigned to Hill County. Their pay records end respectively on Nov. 30 and Dec. 12, 1870. Crouch and Brice write that this was when both were dismissed from the State Police. There were no State Police assigned to Bosque County. See Crouch and Brice, *Governor's Hounds,* 255, 256, 260, 265, 270, 271, 272, 276, 288, 283, 291; *Texas State Almanac, 1871* (Galveston: Galveston News, 1871), 227; *Message of Gov. Edmund J. Davis,* 10; Dallas *Herald,* Oct. 1, 1870; "Texas Adjutant General Service Records," http://www.tsl.state.tx.us/arc/service/index.php [accessed Feb. 1 to 9, 2011]; Ninth Census, 1870, Texas: Hill County, Walker County, schedule 1; Tenth Census, 1880, Texas, Williamson County, Schedule 1. Most accounts say that Pritchett had six men with him, but Charles B. Pearre says he had seven, three white and four black, in *A Review of the Unconstitutional Laws of the Twelfth Legislature of Texas, and the Oppressions of the Present Administration Exposed* (Baltimore: J. B. Lippincott, 1872), 87 [http://quod.lib.umich.edu/cgi/t/text/ text-dx?c=moa&cc= moa&sid= 95e3f6e828 e116b80d4cccd93c80 6bc1&view=text&rgn=main&idno= AJR4047.0001.001 (accessed Feb. 3, 2011)].

3. Houston *Union*, Dec. 30, 1807, Jan. 5, 9, 1871; Galveston *Tri-Weekly News*, Jan. 13, 1871; San Antonio *Daily Herald*, Jan. 5, 1871; *Message of Gov. Edmund J. Davis*, 6–7; Davidson to Davis, Feb. 1, 1871, Letterpress Book, Adj. Gen. Corr., TSLA; Eighth Census, 1860, Texas, Hill County, Schedule 1; Ninth Census, 1870, Texas, Hill County, Schedule 1; Pearre, *Review of the Laws and Oppressions,* 88; Crouch and Brice, *Governor's Hounds*, 65–66; Baenziger, "Texas State Police," 482–83; *Memorial and Biographical History of Johnson and Hill Counties*, 295–96; Walter P. Webb, *The Texas Rangers: A Century of Frontier Defense* (Boston: Houghton Mifflin, 1935), 223–24. It is intriguing to note that while Richard R. Booth Jr. was too young to be a Confederate, his older brother, William L. Booth, served in Company A of the 12th Texas Cavalry with James J. Gathings Jr. (CSR, 12th Texas Cavalry: William L. Booth). On the other hand, Dale Baum, in *The Shattering of Texas Unionism* (Baton Rouge: Louisiana State University Press, 1999), 213, credits William Hooper and William L. Booth with tampering with the

ballots in Hill County in 1871 to ensure a victory for Edmund J. Davis in the Texas governor's race. Interestingly, Richard R. Booth Sr. before the Civil War led a mob in blocking the arrest of Josephus M. Steiner when the Army tried to arrest him for killing his commanding officer at Fort Graham, Texas. See *NHOT,* 6: 81.

4. Houston *Union*, June 23 and 29, Sept. 1, 1870; Galveston *Flakes Bulletin*, May 1, 21, June 23, July 2, Aug. 20, Sept. 3, 1870; San Antonio *Express*, June 8, 1870; Galveston *News,* Aug. 31, Sept. 23, 1870; *Message of Gov. Edmund J. Davis*, 10–11; Ninth Census, 1870, Texas, Hill County, Schedule 1; Crouch and Brice, *Governor's Hounds,* 53–55; Carl H. Moneyhon, *Edmund J. Davis of Texas* (Fort Worth: TCU Press, 2010), 189; A. Y. Kirkpatrick, *Early Settlers Life in Texas and the Organization of Hill County* (Waco: Texian Press, 1963), 82–83; "Kinch West Research Page," http://freepages.genealogy.rootsweb. ancestry.com/ ~cspowell/ researchpages/ Kinch.html (accessed June 15, 2011); *New York Times*, Oct. 21, 1889; *NHOT,* 3: 620.

5. *Report of the Adjutant-General of the State of Texas* (Austin: Tracy, Siemering & Company, 1870), 9–11; Galveston *Flakes Bulletin*, Oct. 15, Nov. 9, 1870; Dallas *Herald*, Oct. 1, 1870; *Message of Gov. Edmund J. Davis*, 3, 9, 10, 12 [quote], 15–17; Crouch and Brice, *Governor's Hounds,* 28–29, 37–38, 51, 56–61, 283; Moneyhon, *Edmund J. Davis*, 187–88, 189–90. Kinch West, who claimed to have ridden with William Quantrill, was eventually arrested in the Indian Territory by Sheriff John P. Cox of Hill County for the murder of A. D. Martin. Ironically, West had already served four years in prison for killing a man in the Indian Territory, where he had remained after his release in 1881. Cox secured a new indictment in 1889 and captured West, but he was acquitted after claiming Martin initiated the fight that ended with his death. According to Crouch and Brice, Sheriff Cox shot West to death in Fort Worth. See *New York Times*, Oct. 21, 1889; Vinita (OK) *Indian Chieftain*, Oct. 24, 1889, June 18, 1896; Dallas *Morning News*, Aug. 28, 1886, Apr. 5, 1890; Brenham *Banner*, Apr. 10, 1890, St. Louis *Republic,* Apr. 6, 1890; Crouch and Brice, *Governor's Hounds,* 53–55.

6. *Message of Gov. Edmund J. Davis*, 14, 15 [quote], 17; J. P. Wood to Davis, Nov. 10, 1870 Executive Record Book, Oct. 10, 1870 to May 30, 1871, Governor's Office Papers, TSLA; John A. Purnell to Davis, Nov. 28, 1870, Governor's Office Papers, TSLA; Crouch and Brice, *Governor's Hounds,* 61; James V. Reese, "A History of Hill County, Texas, to 1873" (M.A. Thesis, University of Texas at Austin, 1961), 136–39. Davis also removed John A. Purnell as the county clerk in Hill County. James V.

Reese in his thesis claims that John P. Grace was a moderate Republican, while Purnell, Evan Beauchamp, Charles L. Booth, and Robert R. Booth were Radicals. In fact, he declares that the latter four "represented the worst that the terms 'carpetbaggers' and 'scalawags' signify." See Reese, "History of Hill County," 136.

7. *Memorial and Biographical History of Johnson and Hill Counties,* 231, 256, 393, 422, 423, 464, 457–458; Kirkpatrick, *Early Settlers Life*, 82– 83; Crouch and Brice, *Governor's Hounds,* 63–64; Ellis Bailey, *A History of Hill County, Texas, 1838–1965* (Waco: Privately Printed, 1966), 40–42; *The Texas Almanac for 1865* (Austin: State Gazette, 1864), 21, 54; Gammel, *Laws of* Texas, 5: 744; CSR, 12th Texas Cavalry: William C. Gathings, J. J. Gathings; "The Gathings Family," http://www.ncgenweb.us/anson/people/gathings.htm (accessed Feb. 2, 2011); Baenziger, "Texas State Police," 471–73; "The Stevens & Gathings Families of Hill County, TX Home Page," http://familytreemaker. genealogy. com/users/s/t/e/John-D-Stevens/ index. html (accessed Feb. 2, 2011); "Descendants of Robert Jackson-554," http://www.jacksonfamilygenealogy.com/pafn60.htm (accessed Feb. 2, 2011); "Covington, Texas: The Unofficial Site," http:// covingtontexas. com/index.php? p=1_6_History (accessed Feb. 2, 2011); "Gathings College," http://www.stoppingpoints .com/texas/sights.cgi?marker=Gathings+College&cnty=hill) (accessed Feb. 1, 2011); "Jim Wheat's POSTMASTERS & POST OFFICES OF TEXAS, 1846–1930," http://www.rootsweb.ancestry.com/~txpost/postmasterindex. html (accessed Feb. 2, 2011); "Covington Cemetery," http://www.rootsweb.ancestry.com/~txhcgs/covington_pg5.htm (accessed Feb. 2, 2011); *NHOT, 2: 377,* 3: 116–17, 6: 961–62. William H. Parsons, who led the 12th Texas Cavalry until he was promoted to command a brigade, was among the Texas Senators who discussed the Hill County affair in 1871, and he commanded the 1st Division of the State Guard that year. He had a brother, Albert, who was an advocate of black rights and allegedly married Lucy, who was probably a former slave of either James J. Gathings Sr. or Philip Gathings. See Paul Avrich, *The Haymarket Tragedy* (Princeton: Princeton University Press, 1984), 3–12; James R. Green, *Death in the Haymarket* (New York: Pantheon Books), 57–58; Carolyn Ashbaugh, *Lucy Parsons: American Revolutionary* (Chicago: Charles H. Kerr Publishing Company, 1976), 6; *Texas Almanac 1871*, 242; *NHOT*, 5: 74–75.

8. Lt. Harrison Holt to Capt. John B. Johnson Sept. 3, 1869, Records of United States Army Continental Commands, 1821–1920, RG 393, NA (copy in Barry Crouch Papers, Victoria Regional History Center, Victoria

College, Victoria, Texas); Galveston *Tri-Weekly News*, Aug. 6, 13, and 30, 1869; San Antonio *Express*, Aug. 18, 1869. The four other names on Holt's list were John Hammond, P. Kirkpatrick, "Mr. Martin," and D. Matthews. James T. DeMumber was a wounded veteran of the 8th [12th] Texas Infantry (see Footnote 10 on him and the Gathings brothers). Merritte A. Sedberry, who lost his arm while serving with the 15th Texas Infantry, and Alexander Rush Sedberry, who was too young to serve in the Civil War, were two brothers of Laura A. Sedberry, who married James J. Gathings Jr. Their father, William R. Sedberry, was a prominent local leader who worked a farm with slaves near Clifton, in Bosque County, before he died while serving as a lieutenant with the 15th Texas Infantry. See Eighth Census, 1860, Texas, Bosque County, Schedules 1 and 2; CSR, 15th Texas Infantry: Merritte A. Sedberry and William R. Sedberry; "Merritte A. Sedberry," http://www.findagrave.com/cgi-bin/fg.cgi?page=gr&GSln=Sedberry&GSiman=1&GSst=46&GSsr=121&GRid=31693288& (accessed Oct. 26, 2011); "Alexander Rush Sedberry," http://www.findagrave.com/cgibin/fg.cgi?page= gr&GRid=16491635 (accessed Oct. 26, 2011) "William Rush Sedberry Sr.," http://www.findagrave.com/cgi-in/fg.cgi?page=gr&GRid=73240229 (accessed Oct. 26, 2011).

9. Houston *Union*, Jan. 28, 1871; Davis to John P. Grace, Jan.19, 1871, Letterpress Book, Jan. 3, 1871 to Mar. 16, 1871, Governor's Office Papers, TSLA; Davidson to Davis, Feb. 1, 1871, Letterpress Book, Adj. Gen. Corr., TSLA; Davis to B[enjamin]. F. Yerby et al., Mar. 3, 1871, Executive Record Book, Oct. 10, 1870 to May 30, 1871, Governor's Office Papers, TSLA; *Message of Gov. Edmund J. Davis*, 6, 17–18; Gammel, *Laws of Texas*, 6: 11–16; "Texas Adjutant General's Department: An Inventory of Military Reconstruction Rolls," http://www.lib.utexas.edu/taro/tslac/30074/tsl-30074.html (accessed Feb. 3, 2011); *Texas Almanac, 1871*, 243; Pearre, *Review of the Laws and Oppressions,* 88; *Journal of the House of Representatives of the Twelfth Legislature, Adjourned Session, 1871* (Austin: J. G. Tracy, 1871) 157; Webb, *Texas Rangers*, 223–24; Moneyhon, *Texas After the War*, 141; Baenziger, "Texas State Police," 483; Kirkpatrick, *Early Settlers Life,* 82–83; Crouch and Brice, *Governor's Hounds,* 66, 67; Moneyhon, *Edmund J. Davis,* 188. Yerby, who came to Texas from Mississippi with his family in 1866, chaired the grand jury in Hill County that demanded that Davis order the legislature to investigate the Gathings affair. See Houston *Union*, Mar. 17, 1871; Galveston *Tri-Weekly News*, Mar. 13 and 15, 1871; "The Crivarelli and Related Families," http://wc.rootsweb. ancestry.com/cgi-bin/igm.cgi?op=GET&db= mccriv&id=I2294 (accessed Feb. 2, 2011).

10. Houston *Union*, Jan. 28, 1871; "Descendants of Robert Jackson-554;" *Memorial and Biographical History of Johnson and Hill Counties*, 393, 638–40; CSR, 8th [12th] Texas Infantry: James T. DeMumber, and 6th Mississippi Infantry: Astyanax M. Douglass, Henry Strong, and William L. Towner; Houston *Telegraph*, May 13, 1864; Ninth Census, 1870, Texas, Hill County, Schedule 1; Tenth Census, 1880, Texas, Hill County, Schedule 1; "126 Biographical Sketches of Confederate Soldiers—Coke & Runnels Counties, TX," http://files.usgwarchives. net/tx/coke/military/civilwar/csa/126bios.txt (accessed Feb. 2, 2011); Baenziger, "Texas State Police," 483; Crouch and Brice, *Governor's Hounds,* 67. For Frank T. Wier, see Ninth Census, 1860, Mississippi, Noxubee County, Schedule 1, and *NHOT*, 6: 961–62. James J. Gathings Sr. lived with his family for several years in Mississippi before moving to Texas, so this may explain those apparent connections among his colleagues and family members.

11. Houston *Union*, Jan. 20, 28, 1871; Gammel, *Laws of Texas*, 6: 16, 8: 299; *Message of Gov. Edmund J. Davis*, 7–8, 19 [quote]; Webb, *Texas Rangers*, 223–24; Baenziger, "Texas State Police," 483; Davidson to Davis, Feb. 1, 1871, Letterpress Book, Adj. Gen. Corr., TSLA; Davis to Yerby et al., Mar. 3, 1871, Executive Record Book, Oct. 10, 1870 to May 30, 1871, Governor's Office Papers, TSLA; Pearre, *Review of the Laws and Oppressions,* 91; Crouch and Brice, *Governor's Hounds,* 67. In Walker County during February 1871, a man was sentenced to the state penitentiary by a military commission directed by James Davidson. The sentence was later reversed, and the prisoner was remanded to a civil court, but Walker County officials did pay a heavy cost for the operation of martial law. See Moneyhon, *Texas after the Civil War*, 141–42. It is interesting to note that the editor of the Waco *Examiner* claimed that, while Davidson forced Gathings to pay his bond, he also had Sheriff Grace return the bond money paid by Pritchett. See Austin *Tri-Weekly Gazette*, Jan. 25, 1871.

12. Davis to Yerby et al., Mar. 3, 1871, J. P. Wood to Davis, Mar. 12, 1871, Executive Record Book, Oct. 10, 1870 to May 30, 1871, Governor's Office Papers, TSLA; *Message of Gov. Edmund J. Davis*, 8; *Senate Journal of the Twelfth Legislature of the State of Texas* (Austin: J. G. Tracy, 1871), 211, 270 [quote], 282–84, 337, 338; Houston *Union*, Jan. 19, 1871; Patsy M. Spaw, ed., *The Texas Senate: Civil War to the Eve of Reform, 1861–1889* (College Station: Texas A&M University Press, 1999), 112; Crouch and Brice, *Governor's Hounds,* 67–69, 213.

13. Austin *Tri-Weekly State Gazette,* Jan. 25, 27, 1871; Houston *Union*, Feb. 16, Mar. 9, 17, 22, Sept. 25, 30, 1871; Austin *Daily State Journal*, Mar. 2, 1871; San Antonio *Herald*, July 21, 1871; Galveston

Tri-Weekly News, Mar. 8, 13, 15, Aug. 8, Oct. 9, 1871; San Antonio *Express*, Mar. 31, 1871; Dallas *Herald*, Mar. 11, 1871; *Journal of the House of Representatives of the Twelfth Legislature, Adjourned Session,* 84; Francis W. Johnson, *A History of Texas and Texans,* 5 vols. (Chicago: American Historical Society, 1914), 4: 1,867; Crouch and Brice, *Governor's Hounds,* 70, 72; Baenziger, "Texas State Police," 483.

14. *Journal of the House of Representatives of the Twelfth Legislature, Adjourned Session,* 155–56, 774–75; *Journal of the House of Representatives of the State of Texas, Thirteenth Legislature* (Austin: John Cardwell, 1873), 110, 137, 470–71; *Texas Almanac, 1871*, 227, 245; *The Texas Almanac for 1870* (Galveston: Richardson & Company, 1870), 197; Houston *Union,* July 20, 1871; Britney Jeffrey, "HARN, CARROLL PRATHER DUVAL," *Handbook of Texas Online* (http://www.tshaonline.org/handbook/online/ articles/fhagh), accessed July 25, 2012. Published by the Texas State Historical Association.

15. Galveston *Tri-Weekly News*, Apr. 12, 1871.

16. Pearre, *Review of the Laws and Oppressions,* 14–21, 87, 89, 93–95; Dallas *Herald*, May 10, 1873; Austin *Standard*, May 10, 1873; Galveston *Tri-Weekly News*, Nov. 11, 1870, Apr. 4, 1873; Thomas J. C. Williams and Folger McKinsey, *History of Frederick County, Maryland, 2* vols. (Frederick: L. R. Titsworth, 1910), 1: 945. Ironically, Jack Mitchell was shot and killed by Sgt. William E. Evans, who had accompanied Lt. W. T. Pritchett to the Gathingses' house. See Crouch and Brice, *Governor's Hounds*, 178.

17. San Antonio *Herald*, Jan. 6, 1872; *Memorial and Biographical History of Johnson and Hill Counties*, 225; *History of Texas, Together with a Biographical History of Tarrant and Parker Counties*, 100; Gammel, *Laws of Texas,* 8: 299; *Special Laws of the State of Texas, Passed at the Session of the Fourteenth Legislature, January 13, 1874* (Houston: A. C. Gray, 1874), 33; Austin *Democratic Statesman,* Apr. 5, 7, 1874; Johnson, *History of Texas and Texans*, 3: 1,412; Joseph B. Thoburn, *A Standard History of Oklahoma*, 5 vols. (Chicago: American Historical Society, 1916), 4: 1,421; "My Whitehurst/Whitis Line," http://verlee.tripod.com/ whitis.htm (accessed Feb. 6, 2011); *NHOT,* 2: 510–11, 680–81, 5: 460. The warrants for James J. Gathings Sr. were signed by Andrew J. Dorn as treasurer and Stephen H. Darden as comptroller. Gathings Sr. did run for the Texas Senate in the fall of 1871 and placed fourth. See Crouch and Brice, *Governor's Hounds,* 244.

18. *Memorial and Biographical History of Johnson and Hill Counties*, 224; *History of Texas, Together with a Biographical History of*

Tarrant and Parker Counties, 100; Webb, *Texas Rangers*, 223–24; Otis Singletary, "The Texas Militia During Reconstruction," *Southwestern Historical Quarterly* 60 (July 1956): 28–29; Ellis Bailey, *A History of Hill County, Texas, 1838–1965* (Waco: Privately Printed, 1966), 42; Baenziger, "Texas State Police," 482–83; Moneyhon, *Texas After the War*, 142–43; Moneyhon, *Edmund J. Davis*, 190–91; Crouch and Brice, *Governor's Hounds,* chapter 3 *passim*. A county history published in the late nineteenth century includes the same perspective on the Gathings affair: *A History of Texas, Together with a Biographical History of Milam, Williamson, Bastrop, Travis. Lee, and Burleson Counties* (Chicago: Lewis Publishing Company, 1893), 100. Ricky F. Dobbs offers an intriguing comparison in his"' A Slow Civil War': Resistance to the Davis Administration in Hill and Walker Counties, 1871" (M.A. Thesis, Baylor University, 1989), and he used this to write the entry on the Hill County clash for the *New Handbook of Texas*. Interestingly, Charles W. Ramsdell, in his conservative history of Reconstruction Texas published in 1910, did not directly mention the Hill County affair, and his remarks on the State Police were rather restrained. See Charles W. Ramsdell, *Reconstruction in Texas* (New York: Columbia University Press, 1910), 201–302.

19. *Memorial and Biographical History of Johnson and Hill Counties*, 220, 638–40; Dallas *Morning News*, Sept. 25, Nov. 10, 1892, May 6, Nov. 10, 1894, Aug. 25, 1896, Nov. 12, 14, 1898, Apr. 1, 1900, Aug. 5, 1902; Ninth Census, 1870, Texas, Hill County, Schedule 1; Tenth Census, 1880, Texas, Hill County, Schedule 1; *NHOT*, 2: 522, 526–27; "Descendants of Robert Jackson-554;" "The Stevens & Gathings Families of Hill County, TX Home Page;" "Covington Cemetery;" "Old Runnels Cemetery, Runnels City, Runnels County, Texas," http://www.rootsweb.ancestry.com/~txrunnel/cemeteries/ old_runnels.htm (accessed Feb. 2, 2011); "126 Biographical Sketches of Confederate Soldiers—Coke & Runnels Counties." Many burial records and images can also be found at "Find a Grave: Covington Cemetery," http://www.findagrave.com/cgi-bin/fg.cgi?page=cr&CRid=943021 (accessed Feb. 10, 2011). Crouch and Brice, in *Governor's Hounds* (p. 286), wrote that W. T. Pritchett left Texas for Tennessee in February 1871 and never returned. As for the State Police who were with him at the Gathings house, Joseph Kennedy was "dismissed" in January 1871, Sgt. William E. Evans resigned and General Bell was killed by a prisoner in February 1871, George W. Hillyard was "dropped" from the rolls in April 1871, Anthony Rucker was "discharged" in June 1871, and Richard Castello was discharged in January 1872. See Crouch and Brice, *Governor's Hounds*, 256, 260, 265,

271, 276, 288; "Officer Down Memorial Page" [http://www.odmp.org/officer/19657-private-general-bell (accessed Mar. 16, 2012)].

20. Waco *Daily Examiner*, Feb. 21, 1874; Moneyhon, *Texas After the War*, 189; *NHOT,* 6: 75.

PART IV:

Texas and the New South

RENTERS, SHARE-
CROPPERS, LABORERS!

Will You Vote Yourselves Slavery?

If so, Vote for Swann and Mc-
Anally, authors and intro-
ducers of the infamous

LABORING MAN'S PEON
ACT

If not, go to the Polls Saturday
and Vote against them.

Headline in Rockdale *Reporter*, March 2, 1902. Courtesy of Rockdale *Reporter*

The Roots of Southern Progressivism: Texas Populists and the Rise of a Reform Coalition in Milam County

Gregg Cantrell

In the introduction to his 1997 book, *Grass-Roots Reconstruction in Texas*, Randolph B. Campbell noted that although Reconstruction had been the subject of intense academic scrutiny at the state and national levels, few scholars had "sought to determine how the issues of the era came home to people at the local level." Campbell's point about Reconstruction holds true for the subject of this essay: the political circumstances that gave rise to southern progressivism. In the past half-century, scholars have thoroughly delineated the contours of the region's progressive movement from a policy standpoint. They have pointed out that while southern progressivism shared many features with its national counterpart, the movement in the South possessed certain regional characteristics that limited the scope of its reform, most notably that it took place within the newly solidified one-party system and that it would be, in the famous phrase of C. Vann Woodward, progressivism "for whites only."[1]

Although we know a great deal about what southern progressivism looked like, persistent questions remain about who southern progressives really *were*, and how the movement arose from the chaotic political environment of the 1890s. Scholars continue to disagree over a number of fundamental issues: What role did the recently defeated Populists play in the rise of progressivism? Who really supported disfranchisement, and were poor whites as much a target as African Americans? Was the movement, as Woodward claimed, fundamentally "urban and middle-class," or did "the most potent force for southern reform," as Jack Temple Kirby argued, "lie in the frustrations and yearnings of the rural and small town masses?"[2]

Because these questions have yielded so many conflicting answers, perhaps a return to the local level can shed welcome light. No local study can provide definitive answers that are universally applicable to the state or region, but definitiveness has never been the true goal of social history.

As Campbell has argued, the significance of a local case study lies not in its perfect representativeness of some larger whole, but rather in the way that it "explodes facile generalizations" and illuminates subtleties that broader studies may overlook.[3] The following essay, then, offers a case study of how a progressive coalition emerged in one Texas county following one of the most tumultuous decades in the state's political history, the 1890s. By closely examining this county, we shall see how conflict among Democrats, Republicans, and Populists divided the county's citizens along lines of race, class, economic interest, and ideology, as it did in many other places throughout Texas and the South. The essay will also analyze the internal struggles that took place *within* all three political parties, and in the process of doing so, reveal the roles that local leaders, conditions, and issues played in the county's politics. The result will be a more nuanced understanding of the process by which progressivism emerged at the local level. It will also provide a model against which other locales can be compared, as historians continue to investigate the complex politics of the turn-of-the-century South.[4]

The site for this study is Milam County, situated on the west bank of the Brazos River in the heart of the southeast-central Texas cotton belt. Like so many places in the South, Milam County's economy after the Civil War was dominated by cotton, which farmers and planters grew with varying degrees of success in every precinct. By the century's end, tenancy reached alarming proportions, with nearly two-thirds of Milam's farmers working someone else's land. A significant number of these tenants were African-American, as ex-slaves and their descendants comprised about a quarter of the population.[5]

Like other southerners, the cotton farmers of Milam County were hit hard by the agricultural depression of the late nineteenth century. The county had been a stronghold of the Grange during its heyday, and many of the same men had later responded enthusiastically to the Farmers' Alliance. By the late 1880s the Alliance had fifty local chapters, or suballiances, in the county. In 1887 the Alliance established a cooperative store and cotton yard in the county seat, Cameron, and by the mid-1890s this had become the largest and most successful mercantile enterprise in Milam County.[6]

Just as the county's Alliancemen embraced economic cooperation, so they also championed the political demands formulated by the Alliance. Anti-monopoly measures, such as the innovative Subtreasury Plan designed to stabilize crop prices and give debt-ridden farmers affordable credit, appealed to the impoverished cotton growers of central

Texas. They were probably better-educated in the specifics of the Alliance demands than any comparable group of farmers in the nation, for the national leader of the Alliance in the late 1880s, the brilliant if erratic author of the Subtreasury Plan, was a local man, Charles W. Macune.[7]

The county's geography greatly influenced the economic status and thus the voting patterns of its inhabitants. Milam is divided into two major geographic regions. The northern and northwestern two-fifths of the county (corresponding roughly with justice precincts 1, 2, 5, 6, and 7) possessed rich black clays that were ideal for the cultivation of cotton; most of the remainder of the county was sandy.[8] Sandy-land farmers also grew cotton, but on poorer farms.[9] The broad bottom lands along the Brazos River were the location of large estates worked by black tenants. Although almost a quarter of the adult male population worked in non-farm occupations, practically all were in some way tied to the cotton economy. Urban dwellers in the two principal towns, Cameron and Rockdale, practiced trades and professions, kept stores, worked for the three railroads that traversed the county, or were absentee landowners.[10]

On the surface, county politics seemed to epitomize the "Solid South" at the beginning of the 1890s. Since Reconstruction, the Democratic Party had held every local office and carried the county in state and national elections. African Americans, who continued to vote in significant numbers, remained loyal to the Republican Party but posed little threat to the white majority. Beneath this apparently placid surface of white Democratic solidarity, however, whites were bitterly divided. On one hand was the conservative right wing of the Democratic Party, which was dominated by large landowners on the best lands and by business interests in Cameron and Rockdale. They were challenged from the left by progressive Democrats in the Alliance, with its strong power base among the smaller landowners in the sandy parts of the county. In 1892 many of Milam County's Alliancemen broke with their traditional party, the Democrats, and joined the People's Party. When that happened, the Alliance itself became divided between those who chose Populism and others who remained in the Democratic Party. The Alliancemen who remained Democrats came to constitute a large proportion of the progressive wing of that party. Thus another element—agrarian discontent leading to third-party insurgency—contributed to the southernness of Milam County.[11]

The 1892 elections saw all three white factions represented in state-level races, and the campaign established patterns that generally held for the remainder of the 1890s. Conservative Democrats used their considerable economic power to champion traditional causes: pro-business governmental policies, the gold standard, and white supremacy. The progressive Democrats championed moderate reform measures such as the monetization of silver and the Railroad Commission, all the while urging the Populists to surrender their heresies and rejoin the old party. The People's Party, having drawn its core constituency and most of its leaders from the ranks of the Alliancemen, preached the new gospel of the Omaha Platform with its far-reaching program of reform, including the Subtreasury Plan, government ownership of the railroads, and protections for organized labor.[12] The Populists' main tasks at election time were to mobilize that constituency and convince reluctant Democrats to leave the Democratic Party. And all factions had to wrestle with the vexing problem of race, for with whites so divided the plain reality was that blacks now potentially held the balance of power in the county.[13]

In the 1892 campaign the Populists' main theme was the betrayal of the people by the Democratic Party. At a debate in Milano in early June, a local Populist opened his speech by "charging the democratic party with being untrue to the people in advocating . . . the remonetizing of silver, abolishing the national banks, etc., in their platforms, [and then] voting against the measures in congress." Sensitive to the emotional attachment of white southerners to the Democratic Party, the Populists' strategy was to portray the move into third-party politics as having been forced on them by the corrupt leaders who had gained control of the old party.[14]

The Populists knew that Democrats would appeal to voters in the name of southern patriotism and the Lost Cause. In mid-July more than five thousand people attended a Confederate veterans' reunion in Cameron. Although the speeches and activities at the reunion were supposed to be nonpartisan, the press noted that there had been much discussion about "the refusal of the third party people to participate." In some parts of the county, it was reported, "the third party people even give barbecues to keep away any of their folds from the reunion." Why would the Populists go to such lengths to keep voters away from a Confederate reunion? Most likely they were afraid that the Democrats would use the occasion to keep veterans in the Democratic camp with powerful reminders of the South's Democratic heritage.[15]

The Populists displayed a spirit of camaraderie and enthusiasm in the 1892 campaign that the Democrats, divided into feuding factions and complacent after years of electoral dominance, lacked. Local Populist clubs met regularly to hear their party's principles explained. In June the Populists of Rockdale constructed a brush arbor with seating capacity for a thousand people for a party rally in which James H. "Cyclone" Davis would be the featured speaker. The following month twelve hundred people attended a Populist barbecue south of Rockdale. The *Galveston Daily News* reported that "Bounteous provision was made in the way of eatables and drinkables. Between the speech-making, the feeding, the music and the dancing all who attended returned to their homes pleased with the results of the day." A few weeks later, fifteen hundred attended a Populist camp meeting on the San Gabriel River.[16]

Democrats found themselves on the defensive. Speaking in Rockdale, Democratic leader Thomas S. Henderson claimed "that the form of government that the people's party was advocating was a new thing and not thoroughly understood by the people and that if they understood it they would not want it." Forced by the obvious economic distress around him to admit the need for reform, Henderson could only contend "that all remedy for wrongs must be sought for and found inside the Democratic Party, as the only party that had given the people relief in the past." All too often Democrats simply resorted to ridicule, calling the Populists "malcontents and soreheads."[17]

Perhaps the most difficult, but necessary, aspect of the Populist campaign was the effort to capture the black vote.[18] In mid-June the press reported "that the negroes were organizing with the third party." Capt. Ben Arnold, a white Union army veteran who moved to the county in 1867 and had been a Republican leader since, advised black voters that "in county and state affairs . . . considering the fearful democratic majority, if [the Populists] were willing to join issue with the colored voter, admit him into their councils and give him representation on their ticket, he might consistently join them." To Arnold's surprise, he later learned that African Americans had in fact participated in the Populist county convention and had elected a black delegate to the state convention. Whether or not this gesture on the part of the Populists would win the support of the black masses remained to be seen.[19]

Efforts by the Populists to woo black voters intensified in August 1892. A three-day Populist rally in Cameron featured "activities for whites" at the courthouse and for blacks at the city park pavilion, featuring speeches "by eminent colored orators." Ten days later the brick warehouse of the International & Great Northern Railroad in Rockdale was "filled with white and colored people's party folks, democrats, republicans and prohibitionists, to listen to the people's party speakers." John B. Rayner of neighboring Robertson County, a powerful black orator who would later become a statewide Populist leader, delivered an hour-and-a-half speech which was reported by the *Galveston Daily News* as being "conservative, sensible and logical, and . . . well received by all present." In September Rayner again spoke in Milam County to a mixed audience of black and white Populist "sympathizers." Ultimately, however, the only Populist candidate formally endorsed by the county's black Republicans was congressional hopeful Isaac Newton Barber. Progressive Democratic governor James S. Hogg's denunciation of lynching, and the endorsement of conservative Democratic gubernatorial candidate George Clark by the state's black Republicans, held many African Americans in one Democratic camp or the other.[20]

Despite Populist efforts, most of the Democratic candidates carried the county in 1892 by a narrow two-hundred-vote margin out of nearly five thousand cast. Although their political differences had led conservative and progressive Democrats to nominate different candidates at the state level, in county and precinct races the two Democratic factions had wisely put aside their differences. At the precinct level, the People's Party did elect a county commissioner and two justices of the peace. And in the congressional race—the one countywide contest in which the black Republicans had formally endorsed a People's Party candidate—the Populist carried the county by almost three hundred votes.[21]

Geographically the Populist strongholds were in the poorer, sandier farming regions in the southern part of the county, while Democrats ran much better in the richer black lands in the north and along river bottoms. These are trends that generally held true in 1892 and throughout the Populist revolt. Voting allegiance was also associated with the tenancy rate in rural precincts. The Democrats generally did best in areas with the highest tenancy rates, apparently reflecting the influence that Democratic landlords exercised over black and white tenants, while the heavily Populist precincts had somewhat lower rates of tenancy.[22]

From even a cursory examination of the 1892 results, it is obvious that two factors prevented a Populist sweep of the county. First, and most glaring, was the party's inability to attract urban voters. In the two major towns, Cameron and Rockdale, the Populist presidential ticket ran dead last with only 11 percent of the vote, compared to the 62 percent recorded by the Democrats and 28 for the Republicans. Results were similar in state races. If the two towns are excluded from the county totals, the Populists would have swept the county. Even in three-way races the Populists could win in the countryside, but in town they were slaughtered by the Democrats and ran far behind the Republicans.[23]

The black Republicans were the other major obstacle for the Populists. The 1892 elections underscored the necessity of winning black votes, either by converting individual black voters to the People's Party or, more likely, by gaining the formal endorsement of Populist candidates by black Republican conventions. By the time the 1894 campaign began, black Populist clubs had been organized at Maysfield and Jones Prairie in the black-majority second precinct near the Brazos River. In August of that year the black Republicans of the Rockdale area held a mass meeting at a local church to debate their strategy for the upcoming elections. Attendance was heavy, "but outside of speeches nothing was done."[24]

The Democrats scored a major victory on September 23, 1894, when Milam County's Republicans met in Cameron and endorsed the county-level Democratic ticket "by an overwhelming vote." Local Populists were "rather blue" about this, for they had placed high hopes on a Republican endorsement. It was rumored, however, that some Republicans were unhappy with their party's actions and "that an attempt will be made to break the indorsement [*sic*]."[25]

That effort came in early October when S. S. Brewer, an African American who had been converted to Populism, called a "mass meeting of the colored people" in hopes of swinging the black Republicans into the Populist camp. Black Republicans who wished to endorse the local Democratic ticket called a similar meeting, and the two gatherings were scheduled for the same day in Rockdale. The events of that day illustrate the extraordinary importance of the African-American vote to both parties, and the abiding interest of blacks in local political affairs.[26]

African Americans from all over the county began to arrive in Rockdale throughout the morning, and at one o'clock in the afternoon both factions met separately. The Springfield Baptist Church was "packed" with African Americans who came to hear Populist speakers. Meanwhile, the main body of the black Republicans met at the Methodist Church to discuss the wisdom of endorsing the county Democratic ticket. Deliberations continued all afternoon, until a recess was taken at six o'clock. At seven-thirty the Rockdale Silver Cornet Band, "headed by leading Populists," paraded through the streets, followed by a procession of white and black supporters. The march ended at the Springfield Baptist church, where the Populist meeting was resumed. Several white and black Populists spoke, with the prominent Dallas Populist Harry Tracy keynoting. The pro-Democratic African Americans also resumed their meeting at the Methodist church, resulting in a confirmation of their decision to back the county Democratic ticket. As the vote was being taken, members of the pro-Populist faction began to arrive, and as the *News* put it, "the fun began." The Populists moved to reconsider the Democratic endorsement, "and for a short time pandemonium reigned supreme. Every negro in the hall was on his feet gesticulating and wildly calling to Mr. Speaker, and Mr. Speaker and the secretary were both trying to hold the floor at once." The motion to reconsider was defeated, and "the objectionists" then gave up and rejoined the Populist gathering at the Baptist church. The carnival atmosphere was made complete by the attendance of a large number of African-American women, who set up stands outside both meeting places and sold food and refreshments. The white press apparently deemed it of little importance to report on the actual debates, but the result was that blacks remained divided in their loyalties. Nevertheless, the local correspondent reported that it "could not be denied" that "the third party made a good impression." "Consequently," he added, "as the time grows shorter the fight waxes hotter."[27]

The results of 1894 showed significant gains for the third party. Populist gubernatorial and congressional candidates carried Milam County, and the party again elected one commissioner and one justice of the peace. Most significant, the Populists finally won a countywide race, electing W. A. Nabours county treasurer by a 112-vote margin. Geographically, the Populists recorded major gains in the countryside and a small improvement in the towns, though they still lost the urban vote by an overwhelming margin.[28] Overall, the Populist gubernatorial candidate, Thomas L. Nugent, polled pluralities in twenty-two of the county's thirty-four voting boxes. But among black voters the Populists' success was, at best, mixed. The Democrats easily carried the black-majority Second Precinct with 54 percent of the vote, while the Populists and Republicans tied with 23 percent each. If the Populists had hoped to attract African Americans away from the other parties en masse, they were surely disappointed.[29]

The Populists' biggest failures lay in the countywide races, where Democrats won every contest except that of county treasurer. Although Milam County's Populists could now muster majorities in state and precinct races, the Democrats still won by five hundred votes in most county-level races (sheriff and county judge, for example). The most likely explanation for this phenomenon is the personal popularity of local leaders like Sheriff John H. Bickett and County Judge Sam Streetman. Party loyalty and ideology were important to the Populists of Milam County, but in these local races, many Populists put friendship, personal loyalty, and competence before party loyalty, and they considered Populist ideology far less significant when deciding who would sit in the sheriff's office or preside over the commissioners' court. The same personal loyalties also account for the success of Populist treasurer Nabours, a respected Confederate veteran.[30]

Indeed, the Populists had never won the hearts and minds even of all reform-minded voters in Milam County. The progressive Democrats had always had a strong following in the county, and in the mid-1890s, as their disagreements with the conservatives grew more pronounced, they intensified their efforts to coax the Populists back into the Democratic Party. Some Populists, such as Macune, enjoyed warm relations with local progressive Democrats, no doubt hoping to lure them into the People's Party, instead of the reverse. Macune even briefly operated an independent newspaper in the county in 1895 with both Populist and progressive Democratic partners. Progressive Democratic speeches during the summer of 1895 sounded increasingly Populistic in their criticism of "capitalists" and "millionaires," who monopolized the nation's money and credit. Populists, however, labored to remind third-party faithful that silver coinage was "of minor importance" in the overall Populist program.[31]

The agrarian revolt reached its high point in the 1896 elections. As the Democrats carried on their family feud over silver and gold, the Populist campaign continued with enthusiasm.[32] African-American Republicans once again were the wild card in the political deck. If anything, they were even more factionalized than two years earlier, with one wing endorsing the local Democrats and the other supporting the Populists. At one point in late July a near-riot broke out during the county Republican convention at the courthouse in Cameron. In an attempt to have their respective leaders seated as convention chairman, four hundred Republicans engaged in "the wildest scene of confusion ever witnessed" in the county. A *News* reporter described the events:

> Over 400 negroes were on the floor of the court house, and they all made a grand rush for the platform. Some were trying to throw the opposing chairman off the platform, while others were trying to protect their chairman. The entire 400 became one surging, crushing and howling mob. Some weapons were drawn and canes were used freely. The whole inner space of the bar was crowded with the combatants. Some were pulled down, trampled on and belabored; others were thrown over the judge's stand into the pit below. How they escaped without fatal injuries is remarkable. The scene was one impossible to describe.

After half an hour of this, someone in the back of the room began singing "an old, familiar camp meeting song," and soon a chorus of four hundred voices was swaying to the melody of "The Sweet By and

By." "The effect," according to the reporter, "was marvelous." When the singing ended, Sheriff Bickett mounted the podium and advised the Republicans to proceed peacefully, which they did. However, the smaller, pro-Populist, faction still bolted the convention rather than acquiesce in an endorsement of the county Democratic ticket.[33]

As the 1896 elections neared, the *Houston Post* accurately reported that "confusion prevails" in Milam County. National and state politics had thrown an enormous wrench in the Populist works. The national People's Party convention "fused" with the Democrats, nominating Democrat William Jennings Bryan for president and Populist Tom Watson for vice president. Furious over such a sellout, Texas Populist leaders struck a deal with state Republican bosses, promising Populist votes for William McKinley in return for Republican support of the Populist state ticket. Milam's two delegates to the national Populist convention were dismayed over both developments. They were willing to accept Bryan *if* the Democratic Party would recognize Watson as his running mate—which, of course, the Democrats would not do. The outspoken Macune no doubt expressed the sentiments of many Populists when he announced that Populism had been betrayed and severed his ties with the People's Party.[34] The two county Republican factions finally reached an uneasy truce, endorsing the Populist-Republican fusion deal in state and national races but leaving voters free to choose between the Populists and Democrats in county races.[35] When the votes were counted, the national Democratic ticket had carried the county with 54 percent of the vote. Enough Populists had united with the Republicans to give McKinley 32 percent of the vote.[36]

The effects of the Populist fusion deals at the national and state levels were obvious in other Milam County races. Many Populists were so disgruntled over these trades with Democrats and Republicans that they simply gave up on Populism. In the gubernatorial race between Democrat Charles A. Culberson and Populist Jerome C. Kearby, in which the Republicans supported Kearby, the Democrats carried the county by more than three hundred votes. The popular treasurer W. A. Nabours again was the only Populist to win a county office.[37]

There can be little doubt that the national Democratic Party's nomination of Bryan and its adoption of a platform endorsing silver coinage, a federal income tax, and other minor Populist reforms hurt the Populist cause at the local level. As the national party became more progressive, a growing number of local Democratic leaders could now plausibly persuade Populists that nothing was to be gained by their continued political revolt. In races for county judge and state representative, progressive, pro-silver

Democrats recorded sweeping thousand-vote majorities over two of the most prominent Populists in the county.[38] The message for Milam County's Populists was clear: The day of the People's Party had passed.

Although fusion with the Democrats destroyed the People's Party as a viable party in 1896, the battle for reform, and for political supremacy in Milam County, was far from finished. The split in the Farmers' Alliance and the emergence of the Populists in 1892 had weakened, but by no means destroyed, the progressive wing of the Democratic Party. Many established political leaders of the 1880s who were reform-minded stayed with the Democratic Party's progressive wing. They were led by Cameron's Monta J. Moore, a lawyer, editor, and professional politician who was not yet thirty when he worked for Hogg's reelection.[39] The Populists were led by longtime county chairman J. D. Shelton. In contrast with the youthful, urbane Moore, Shelton was a grizzled veteran of Indian warfare on the Texas frontier and as a Confederate soldier had been wounded three times. For thirty years he worked as an itinerant Baptist preacher, farming on the side. His ministerial career had come to an end when, to use Shelton's own words, "they kicked me out of the [missionary] association" for calling certain local preachers a "devil called, soft place hunting, high salary grabbing, contemptible, modern priesthood." Shelton was among the most radical of Populists, but to many voters he must have seemed like a relic of a bygone era and not the sort of progressive politician suited to the era of telephones and electric lights.[40]

The conservative wing of the county Democratic Party was always smaller numerically than the progressive forces, but its members' economic power helped compensate for their smaller numbers. Most of the county's real wealth supported the conservative faction, and its leadership came from among the banking, railroad, and mercantile interests in Cameron and Rockdale, who often were also large absentee landowners. Dominating the conservative Democrats was the Hefley family of Cameron. The Hefleys sat on railroad boards, practiced law, sold insurance, operated hardware and furniture establishments, and owned extensive commercial and residential real estate. Two family members boasted a combined landholding of some 10,000 acres, which surely gave them sizable political influence over their numerous tenants, many of whom would have been African Americans.[41]

The exodus of poor farmers into the People's Party forced the progressive Democrats to share power with the conservatives in the early and mid-1890s. But in 1898 the conservatives flexed their muscles, electing Oscar F. McAnally to the Texas House of Representatives. McAnally was the outspoken editor of the *Cameron Herald,* the mouthpiece of the conservative Democrats, and he faithfully represented the planting, banking, railroad, and mercantile interests of the Hefleys and other elite families. His presence in the state legislature was an affront to progressive Democratic leader Moore, who had previously held the seat.[42]

Although whites of all parties had tried to woo African-American voters throughout the 1890s, persuasion was not the only tool they used. No evidence survives to implicate Populists in fraud or manipulation of the black vote, but the story was quite different with the Democrats. No matter which faction won, charges and countercharges of fraud flew—not so much between Populists and Democrats, but among the Democrats. When progressive Democrats won, the conservatives cried foul. When conservative Democrats won, progressives bitterly complained. Many Democrats disliked the vote-buying used by both factions, but it had become a way of life in the county's Democratic politics. In the spring or summer primaries it determined which faction's candidates would be nominated; in the fall, vote-buying was absolutely necessary in order to defeat the Populists. After the 1896 county Democratic primary, which produced a number of progressive victories, a conservative described the election. The primary, he wrote, "developed into one of the grandest farces ever perpetrated on the Democratic Party in Milam County. Practically no test was required. Republicans, Populists, negroes and Mexicans voted, regardless of politics and pledges." Despite the fact that his side had done well in the election, a progressive editor from Cameron echoed the same sentiments: "It is a shame," he wrote, "There being no test, negroes, Republicans and Populists voting in the primaries without question, I consider the primaries a rape on the Democratic Party in Milam County." Some of this cross-voting of non-Democrats in the Democratic primary may have been a calculated attempt on the part of Populists and Republicans to send the weakest possible Democrat against them into the general election. However, most of it—especially among African Americans—was simply the result of Democratic chicanery. In any case, Milam's progressive Democrats knew that if the county party barred returning Populists from voting in Democratic primaries, conservatives would retain the upper hand. Consequently, unlike neighboring Brazos County and many other counties, Milam's progressives kept their Democratic primaries open in 1896, 1898, and 1898 to all voters regardless of past political affiliation.[43]

Vote-buying, however, continued to be a problem, and the problem appears to have escalated after 1896, with the conservatives as beneficiaries. One source placed the price of African-American votes in the

1898 county Democratic primary at fifty cents a head. Following the 1900 primary, the Populist press reported that on election afternoon "the price of votes advanced and we were told by good democrats that as high as $6 [apiece] was paid for votes. . . . Negroes were voted like sheep."[44] Fraud notwithstanding, the biggest question facing Milam County politicians of all parties at the turn of the century was the future of the Populists. Although there were no *legal* impediments to Populists returning to the Democratic Party, many of them still hesitated to surrender their crusade. And as long as the Populists remained outside the Democratic Party, the conservative Democrats would maintain their powerful position and would continue to elect conservative candidates such as State Representative McAnally.

The Democrats had openly courted the Populists as early as 1895. In January of that year, Macune assumed editorship of the *Milam News,* published in Cameron. He officially claimed the *News* to be nonpartisan, but he nonetheless openly supported the People's Party. By mid-1895 Macune's paper was on shaky financial footing, and several investors—including at least two prominent progressive Democrats—became partners in the venture. Soon thereafter Macune reemphasized his own personal political position by enrolling in Milam's Populist club. When conservative editor McAnally of the rival *Cameron Herald* castigated both Macune and his progressive Democratic partners for consorting with each other across party lines and betraying their respective parties, none other than Progressive leader Monta Moore stepped in and publicly defended the deal.[45] After the 1896 elections, progressive Democrats stepped up their appeals to the Populists to return to the Democratic fold. Facing hopeless odds on their own, many Populists responded positively. The only countywide Populist officeholder—County Treasurer W. A. Nabours—severed his Populist ties to seek reelection in 1898 as an independent. Since his opponent was a prominent conservative Democrat, Nabours no doubt hoped to poll the votes both of Populists and progressive Democrats.[46]

Even more significant for the progressives was the gradual conversion of local Populist newspaper editor William M. Ferguson of the *Rockdale Messenger*. Immediately following the 1898 election, Ferguson began trying gently to convince fellow Populists that nothing more could be accomplished by maintaining the local Populist organization. Progressive Democrats had embraced a number of the less radical Populist programs, including free silver and direct legislation. "[I]f the Bryan democracy makes as great a stride toward us in 1900 as it did in 1896," Ferguson argued, "We may shake hands . . . across the bloody chasm." Ferguson's increasing receptiveness to progressive overtures was particularly significant because in 1898 he was serving on the Populist state executive committee.[47]

As the 1900 campaign season drew nearer, Populist moderates such as Ferguson and progressive Democrats such as Moore stepped up efforts to engineer a return of the Populists to the Democratic Party. In January 1900 Ferguson urged his party not to nominate a ticket for county and precinct offices. Another prominent local Populist agreed, saying, "Among the democrats we have some preference. Let it be a democratic fight in the county. Let us get our forces as near together as possible and the least objectionable man put him in the office."[48]

Despite such pleas, not all Populists agreed. County chairman Shelton spoke for the radical Populists who refused to compromise any part of the third-party platform. Never one to mince words, he described a Populist returning to the Democratic Party as a "suck-egg dog . . . whining back to the [Democrats] who . . . pat him on the head, only . . . to see him wag his tail and get down on his belly and crawl up to them like a lick-spittle, and lick the nasty political democratic snot off their feet." "I may go down to h—l," he thundered at his opponents, "but I'll never go back to you."[49]

Shelton managed to persuade his fellow Populists to field a slate of county candidates in the 1900 general election, but his task grew increasingly difficult. During that election local progressive Democrats would openly appeal for Populist support against conservative opponents.[50] After the spring Democratic primary resulted in the nomination of more conservatives, Populist editor Ferguson editorialized bitterly about the methods the conservative V. B. Hudson used to defeat progressive Democrat Moore in his campaign for district attorney. In his praise of Moore and his criticism of the conservatives' fraudulent methods, the Populist editor did everything short of actually endorsing the progressive Democrat for an independent race in the general election.[51]

With the conservatives' considerable financial resources and superior control over the black vote, it appeared they would continue defeating progressives in the primaries. What the progressive Democrats needed most was a way to clean up their party's spring elections. Securing fair elections would also play a key role in luring the obstinate Populists back into the fold. Texas Populists were so embittered over the widespread fraud used by Democrats against them that electoral reform had become one of their paramount concerns. Reforming the election process would thus serve as a show of good faith on the part of progressive Democrats that they were serious about according the former Populists an honored place in the Democratic Party.[52] During the 1900 spring campaign, a local Populist explained why his hopes for reform were dim: "[I]f you have got plenty of money and whisky . . . you can run for office . . . [but] no man can get an office in Milam County without plenty of money."[53]

Both progressive Democrats and Populists realized that this state of affairs could be changed by eliminating black voting. Populist appeals to blacks had mostly failed, and Populists with some justification believed that the purchasable black vote had been the key to their defeat both in county and statewide elections. Although the progressive Democrats had themselves apparently profited in the mid-1890s from fraudulently cast black ballots, they, like the Populists, had increasingly suffered defeat at the hands of their own party's conservative faction through these corrupt methods. With the Populist threat now safely behind them, the progressives could lure wavering Populists back into the Democratic Party with promises of fair play and strike a blow at the conservatives by mounting a campaign to end black voting.

Populist editor Ferguson began calling for adoption of a nonpartisan white man's primary at the county level in 1898. He renewed the agitation in 1900. "A white man's union, in which any man can enter the lists and run a clean fair race without fear of boodle and boodlers [vote-buying] . . . is the solution of a long unsolved question," Ferguson argued. It would "place the expressed will of the people in the ascendancy, thereby robbing the professional schemer and politician of his power on election day."[54] That spring the progressive Democrats took up the cause of whites-only local elections and managed to place a white primary referendum on the countywide Democratic primary ballot. That was good enough for many old Populists, and with considerable help from Populists crossing party lines to vote in the Democratic primary, blacks were officially barred from participating in future primaries by a vote of 3,042 to 1,564. Only three of the ten precincts polled majorities in favor of black voting. Not surprisingly, two of these were black-majority Precinct 2 and the city of Cameron. More than any other areas, these were strongholds of conservative Democrats who stood to lose the most by the disfranchisement of blacks. With only one exception, in every precinct where Populists won or ran close races throughout the 1890s, the margin of victory for the white primary was better than two to one.[55]

Although progressive Democrats spearheaded the drive to exclude blacks from the Democratic primary, there can be no doubt that many

Populists joined the effort. Ferguson gave this account of the 1900 primary: "The best joke on the Democrats occurred in precinct No. 3. . .; the populists of that beat declared they would go in and vote the negro out. And they did so. . . . At Hamilton Chapel and Sandy Creek [two heavily Populist voting boxes in Precinct 4] almost every Populist participated." In two other Populist strongholds the editor had "heard populists say beforehand that many, if not all were going into the primaries." As it turned out, Populists in these precincts not only voted to purge future Democratic primaries of black voters but also succeeded in nominating several ex-Populists to run for local offices as Democrats in the general election. The Populist return to the Democratic Party had begun in earnest.[56]

The adoption of the white primary in 1900 had signaled the start of a new era of cooperation between Populists and progressive Democrats, but that beginning had not been strong enough to break the hold of the conservatives on most countywide offices. Now that the progressives had invited the Populists back into the reform coalition by purging blacks from the primaries, those same Democrats would have to show they were still serious about reform. In 1900 about one-third of the Populists remained actively loyal to the third party, and they still put out their own ticket in the general election.[57] Since the white primary would not go into effect until 1902, the conservatives had again managed to profit from fraud in the black precincts.

The most obvious symbol of the conservative Democrats' continuing strength in 1900 was the reelection of conservative McAnally as Milam County's representative to the legislature, a situation that galled the progressive Democrats. McAnally and progressive leader Moore had been at each other's throats since 1895, when McAnally condemned Moore for his friendship with Macune. In early 1902, with the county's first whites-only Democratic primary approaching, Moore and his allies mounted a major campaign to defeat McAnally for reelection to the House. McAnally himself provided the reform forces with the ammunition they needed. In January 1902 he introduced a bill in the legislature establishing heavy fines for farm tenants or sharecroppers who violated their written or verbal contracts with landlords. If a farmer could not pay the fine, a jail term was possible.[58]

When the bill was made public, the progressive Democratic press in Milam County exploded in anger. "It is the most henious [*sic*] monster I believe I ever saw," wrote an incensed farmer. "The measure at once establishes a class in this country." The progressive press bristled with words like "slavery," "peonage," and "serfdom" in describing the bill.

Moore harshly criticized McAnally's bill in public. On the eve of the Democratic primary, headlines asked:

> "RENTERS, SHARECROPPERS, LABORERS!
> WILL YOU VOTE YOURSELVES SLAVERY?
> LABORING MAN'S PEON ACT
> If no, go to the Polls Saturday and
> Vote against them."[59]

In the first all-white primary that March, the coalition of progressive Democrats and ex-Populists buried McAnally by a nearly two-to-one margin, electing progressive Democrat G. S. Miller.[60] And in the clearest sign yet of the successful Populist-progressive Democratic rapprochement, former Populist county treasurer W. A. Nabours won the Democratic nomination for his old office. Considering that some several hundred of the Populists (led by the obstinate radical Shelton) still opposed the dissolution of the People's Party, the turnout in the primary was a remarkable 67 percent. This was true even in the old Populist strongholds. For example, in the staunchly Populist eighth precinct, where in 1894 only 25 percent of voters had cast Democratic ballots, 65 percent of the eligible (white) voters now participated in the Democratic primary. Clearly large numbers of Populists—probably a majority—returned to the Democratic Party.[61]

That fall's general election erased any lingering doubts about the new coalition's viability. When a corporal's guard of hard-core Populists ran prominent third-party leader B. F. Williams against progressive Democrat G. S. Miller for the state representative's seat, Miller destroyed the old Populist, carrying every justice precinct and winning thirty-eight of the forty-three individual voting boxes. Even in the bastions of Populism, rural Precincts Four and Eight, Miller handily won. The Populists were able to muster only about 700 votes out of 3,500 cast.[62]

At the same time that the progressive Democrats were orchestrating a rapprochement between themselves and the Populists via the local white primary, Democrats in Austin were pressing a poll tax amendment through the legislature. Although progressive Democrats in the legislature spearheaded the drive for the poll tax—and even some Populist leaders viewed it as a reform that would purify the ballot—Milam's poor white farmers broke with their leaders and opposed it, recognizing that while it would indeed eliminate the "corrupt" black vote, it would also eliminate many impoverished whites from the electorate. Why run the risk of disfranchising poor whites, they reasoned, when those voters who "deserved" to be disfranchised—African Americans—had already been eliminated by the county's white primary rule?[63]

In the 1902 general election the poll tax amendment was placed before voters for approval. When the vote was tallied in Milam County, it was clear that voters had perceived a huge difference between the white primary and the poll tax. Whereas the vote on the white primary two years earlier had carried easily by a two-to-one margin, the poll tax referendum had divided the county almost evenly, winning approval by a mere fifty-three votes out of 3,461 cast. Predictably, the poll tax had met its strongest opposition in those areas where Populists had done well in the nineties. Moreover, a majority of the precincts that approved the poll tax had just as strongly opposed the adoption of the white primary two years earlier.

This is best demonstrated by looking at a typical Populist voting box, the New Salem box in Justice Precinct Four. At New Salem (which had voted for Populist gubernatorial candidate Thomas Nugent 142–27 over his two opponents in 1894), the vote against the poll tax was an overwhelming 64–8. New Salem was so staunchly Populist that many voters had stayed home in the Democrats' white primary referendum two years earlier, but of those Democrats and Populists who did participate, the vote had been a decisive 29–11 in favor of the white primary. Obviously some of these were old Populists, since the Democrats had never been able to poll forty votes on their own. But the 64–8 vote against the poll tax can best be assessed by comparing it to the other significant vote that took place the same day: the state representative race between the Populist Williams and the progressive Democrat Miller. In that contest, New Salem's seventy-two voters—who agreed almost unanimously on their distaste for the poll tax—gave Williams a narrow 39–33 victory over Miller. The lessons from this are clear: in an isolated, poor white farming community like New Salem, where Populism dominated in the 1890s, many Populists who remained in the electorate after the turn of the century returned to the progressive wing of the Democratic Party, voted the black man out of it, and then joined forces with the few remaining Populists to resist the poll tax.

No doubt many poor white men who had viewed the purging of African Americans from the Democratic primary as an avenue toward reform now felt betrayed by the party's attempt to exclude poor whites from the restored Democratic reform coalition. The poll tax referendum results from the black-majority Second Precinct illustrate this point; in this conservative Democratic precinct where voter turnout (with a large black vote) had consistently been more than seven hundred during the 1890s, the vote in 1902 was 292–52 in favor of the poll tax. At two of the Second Precinct voting boxes in the Brazos bottom—Jones Prairie and Baileyville—the combined vote for the poll tax was 166–0. Now that the conservative white Democrats of the Second Precinct no longer had a bloc of black votes to manipulate, they were not about to surrender whatever power they had left to an unbeatable majority controlled by Populists and progressive Democrats.

Despite the opposition of many voters in the old Populist strongholds to the poll tax, and the correspondingly heavy support given to it by black-belt planters, the results of the poll tax referendum should not be read exclusively as an elitist counterrevolution by conservative Democrats against their more reformist neighbors. The conservatives alone could never have mustered the slender majority that the poll tax received in Milam County. They enjoyed the assistance of at least a minority of the progressive Democrats, who saw the amendment as yet further insurance against fraud from whatever source. Realizing that many in the new reform coalition (the ex-Populists at New Salem, for example) were against the poll tax, the editor of the *Rockdale Reporter,* a progressive Democratic paper, denounced as a "heretic" any Democrat who refused to support the tax. He contended that "by requiring a tax receipt secured six months or more before election, fraudulent voting can be prevented almost entirely. No sharp candidate will buy tax receipts for purchasable voters six or eight months in advance. . . . The amendment will prevent fraudulent voting. There is no reasonable doubt as to that."[64]

In all likelihood, conservative planters and reform-minded farmers alike recognized that the poll tax would only prevent the return to the electorate of the poorest of tenant farmers, black and white, and not significantly change the existing political equation. Voter turnout figures from the mid-1890s to the mid-1900s in the county certainly bear out such a conclusion. Voter participation had reached all-time highs in the mid-nineties. From 5,589 votes cast in the 1894 gubernatorial election, turnout peaked at 7,119 in 1896. Thereafter the decline in turnout had been steady: 5,646 in 1898; 4,570 in 1900; and 3,461 in 1902, when voters approved the poll tax. Thus the total number of votes cast in the last election before the poll tax went into effect was almost exactly half of what it had been in 1896. Rather than beginning a sharp decline in actual voter turnout, passage of the poll tax actually marked a stabilization in the number of citizens who voted. To be sure, the turnout in the general election continued to plummet after 1902 (2,641 in the 1904 gubernatorial race; 1,360 in 1906), but that was because almost all meaningful political decisions now took place in the Democratic primaries; the general election simply elicited little interest. On the other hand, turnout in the Democratic primaries actually increased in the first two elections after the poll tax went into effect (3,451 voted in the 1902 general election's poll tax referendum; 4,026 in the 1904 Democratic primary; 3,674 in the 1906 primary). Likewise, the number of poll taxes paid in 1904 exceeded by nearly eight hundred the turnout in the 1902 referendum that approved the tax. And by 1907 the number of men paying the poll tax had increased, despite a decline in the county's population.[65]

The white primary had eliminated black voters; the destruction of Populism had caused many whites to drop from the electorate. In other words, disfranchisement—at least measured in terms of voter turnout before and after the enactment of the poll tax—had clearly been a *fait accompli* in Milam County; the poll tax only helped to solidify and institutionalize what had already happened.[66]

The effective campaign for the white primary and the successful courting of Populist voters by the progressive Democrats set in motion the progressives' final drive to supremacy in Milam County. In the race for attorney general, the most important statewide race of 1904, the county's voters overwhelmingly supported progressive R. V. Davidson. In countywide races, the conservative McAnally, who championed the "nefarious" landlord and tenant bill and incurred the wrath of progressive Democrats two years earlier, again ran for representative in a three-man contest and finished third. A year after the election, an employee of McAnally's cut the politico's throat in broad daylight on a Cameron street (it was eventually ruled justifiable homicide). The conservative district attorney V. B. Hudson, whose corrupt electioneering in 1900 had inspired so much criticism in the progressive press, also went down to defeat. Progressive Democrat Jeff D. Kemp, one of Macune's partners in the *Milam News* in 1895, was elected county clerk. And former Populist Nabours was now so popular with Democratic voters that he ran unopposed for another term as county treasurer.[67]

In 1906, the day that Milam's progressive coalition had long awaited finally arrived. Thomas M. Campbell won the governorship and swept the progressive wing of the Democratic Party to power in Texas. In the spring primary, four candidates had run for governor. All four claimed credentials as reformers, but only two—Campbell and Oscar B. Colquitt—were original Hogg supporters; they clearly were the most progressive. The results of the election were an unequivocal statement of the county's political sentiments. With widespread support from the old Populists who were still in the electorate, Campbell and Colquitt together polled 79 percent of all votes cast in Milam County. The most conservative candidate, C. K. Bell, who ran with the endorsement of Gov. S. W. T. Lanham, ran dead last in the county with 9 percent of the vote.[68]

The legislature elected in November 1906 has been called "the most reform minded legislature in Texas history." It outlawed speculation in agricultural futures; eased taxes on farmers while increasing the burden on banks, railroads, and other corporate interests; and passed the so-called "Hogg Amendments" prohibiting insolvent corporations from doing business in Texas, outlawing corporate contributions to political campaigns, and banning railroads from distributing free passes to politicians. Populists had played no small part in these achievements.[69]

After 1906, Populism was just a memory in Milam County. But from the ruins of Populism emerged a coalition of progressive Democrats and former Populists that triumphed over all challengers. Progressivism may have owed much of its character to urban, middle-class influences, but Milam County's experience suggests that it also enjoyed strong support from farmers, including many of those who had once supported the People's Party. Disfranchisement played a key role in the rise of the local progressive coalition. Progressive Democrats extended an offer of fair play to Populists in the guise of a whites-only Democratic primary, and many white Populists who had never been entirely comfortable with their party's overtures toward African Americans—and who blamed Populism's defeat on black voting—responded positively to that offer. They helped vote blacks out of the primaries and then returned in sizable numbers to the Democratic Party, where their desire to rein in the power of railroads, banks, furnishing merchants, and landlords found new expression in the progressive legislation of the Campbell administration and its successors. Meanwhile, the relatively small body of Populists who could not countenance a surrender of Populism's most radically egalitarian measures either drifted into the Socialist Party or quit the electorate in frustration and disillusionment. Progressivism in Milam County, like its counterparts at the state, regional, and national levels, would be a relatively tame affair compared to the rambunctious agitation of the Populist era, and it would come at considerable cost to democracy—as Milam's African-American citizens would surely have attested.

In his conclusion to *Grass-Roots Reconstruction in Texas*, Randolph B. Campbell urged his readers to "Be very careful in generalizing about events and developments . . . in so large and varied a state." This caveat holds true for the preceding study. Milam County should not be assumed to be a perfect microcosm of a whole state or region, although there are reasons to believe that much of what happened there was repeated in many other places. If that proves to be the case, then future studies may sustain the contention that Populists played a significant role—both for good and for ill—in shaping the politics of southern progressivism in the twentieth century.[70]

Notes

1. Randolph B. Campbell, *Grass-Roots Reconstruction in Texas* (Baton Rouge: Louisiana State University Press, 1997), 1; C. Vann Woodward, *Origins of the New South,* 1877–1913 (Baton Rouge: Louisiana State University Press, 1951), esp. Chap. 14. Overviews of southern progressivism include Jack Temple Kirby, *Darkness at the Dawning: Race and Reform in the Progressive South* (Philadelphia: Lippincott, 1972); Dewey W. Grantham, *Southern Progressivism: The Reconciliation of Progress and Tradition* (Knoxville: University of Tennessee Press, 1983); Edward L. Ayers, *The Promise of the New South: Life after Reconstruction* (New York: Oxford University Press, 1992); William A. Link, *The Paradox of Southern Progressivism, 1880–1930* (Chapel Hill: University of North Carolina Press, 1997).

2. Woodward and Kirby quoted in Samuel L. Webb, "Southern Politics in the Age of Populism and Progressivism: A Historiographical Essay," in John B. Boles, ed., *A Companion to the American South* (Malden, MA: Blackwell, 2002), 330.

3. Campbell, *Grass-Roots Reconstruction,* 6.

4. State and local studies that specifically examine the relationship between Populism and progressivism include: Sheldon Hackney, *Populism to Progressivism in Alabama* (Princeton: Princeton University Press, 1969); Michael Magliarai, "What Happened to the Populist Vote? A California Case Study," *Pacific Historical Review* 64 (1995): 389–412; Samuel L. Webb, *Two-Party Politics in the One-Party South: Alabama's Hill Country, 1874–1920* (Tuscaloosa: University of Alabama Press, 1997); Webb, "From Independents to Populists to Progressive Republicans: The Case of Chilton County, Alabama, 1880–1920" *Journal of Southern History* 59 (1993): 707–36; Jeffrey J. Crow, "Populism to Progressivism in North Carolina: Governor Daniel Russell and His War on the Southern Railway Company," *Historian* 37 (1975): 649–67; Gene Clanton, "Populism, Progressivism, and Equality: The Kansas Paradigm," *Agricultural*

History 51 (1977): 559–81; Robert W. Cherny, *Populism, Progressivism, and the Transformation of Nebraska Politics, 1885–1915* (Lincoln: University of Nebraska Press, 1981). For Texas, see Alwyn Barr, *Reconstruction to Reform: Texas Politics, 1876–1906* (Austin: University of Texas Press, 1971); and Worth Robert Miller, "Building a Progressive Coalition in Texas: The Populist-Reform Democrat Rapprochement, 1900–1907," Journal of Southern History 52 (1986): 163–82.

5. I have taken the 1900 manuscript population census for Milam County and put into digital form the race, occupation, ethnicity, and land-owning status (whether land is rented or owned, and if it is owned, whether it is mortgaged or not) for every adult (age twenty-one and over) male in the county (9,071 total). Of those who were listed as "farmers," 63 percent rented their farms. This figure excludes those who were listed as "farm laborers," for many of these were sons and other relatives of farm owners who lived and worked on their families' farms. When farm laborers are added to renters, the proportion of people who worked on farms they did not own is 73 percent. Broken down by race, this figure was 68 percent for whites and 88 percent for blacks. African Americans comprised 26 percent of the adult males in the county. The Census Office's published figures on tenancy differ somewhat from my figures, because the census's published figures for each county are based upon numbers of *farms* that are operated by renters or owners, rather than the number of adult male *individuals* (i. e., eligible voters) who farm for a living. However, the numbers are very close: for 1900, the published percentage of Milam County farms operated by non-owners was 61 percent, compared to my 63 percent of adult male "farmers" who worked other people's land. The Census Office's published percentage of farms operated by tenants was 10 percent lower for 1890 than for 1900. See United States Census Office, *Statistics of Agriculture, Eleventh Census, 1890* (Washington, D.C.: Government Printing Office, 1895), 186–87; United States Census Office, *Twelfth Census, 1900, Agriculture, Part I* (Washington, D.C.: United States Census Office, 1902), 128–29.

6. List of Granges compiled by the late Robert A. Calvert of Texas A&M University from master list, National Grange Headquarters, Washington, D.C., in possession of the author; *Rockdale Messenger,* June 20, 1889; *Cameron Herald,* Apr. 11, 1895. There were twenty-three subordinate Granges in Milam County during the 1870s and 1880s. On the Farmers' Alliance in Texas, see Donna A. Barnes, *Farmers in Rebellion, The Rise and Fall of the Southern Farmers Alliance and People's Party*

in Texas (Austin: University of Texas Press, 1984); Lawrence Goodwyn, *Democratic Promise: The Populist Moment in America* (New York: Oxford University Press, 1976); Robert C. McMath Jr., *Populist Vanguard: A History of the Southern Farmers' Alliance* (Chapel Hill: University of North Carolina Press, 1975); Theodore Mitchell, *Political Education in the Southern Farmers' Alliance,* 1887–1900 (Madison: University of Wisconsin Press, 1987).

6. On Macune's career see Charles W. Macune Jr., "The Wellsprings of a Populist: Dr. Charles W. Macune before 1886," *Southwestern Historical Quarterly* 90 (1986): 139–58; Goodwyn, *Democratic Promise;* Charles Postel, *The Populist Vision* (New York: Oxford University Press, 2009), 33–38.

8. William T. Carter, *et al., Soil Survey of Milam County, Texas* (Washington, D.C.: United States Department of Agriculture Bureau of Chemistry and Soils, 1925).

9. I have taken a 20 percent sample of landowners (excluding those who owned only town lots) from the Milam County tax rolls for 1900 and calculated average farm size, average value of farmland, average total taxable property, and other data for each commissioner's precinct (or "beat," as they were commonly called). The best way to gauge the differential in land values between the two major geographical regions is to compare data for Beat Two, which lay almost entirely in the black-prairie region and also contained rich alluvial land along the Brazos River, and Beat Four, which lay primarily in the sandy soil of southwest Milam County. The average landowner in Beat Two owned 192 acres valuated at $7.97 per acre on average. The average landowner in Beat Four owned 157 acres valuated at $4.11 per acre. The commissioners' beats were not identical to the justice precincts described later in this essay (see FN 22), as one beat could be composed of multiple precincts.

10. Seventy-six percent of the adult males in the county were listed on the 1900 census as farmers or farm laborers.

11. For a treatment of these divisions at the state level, see Barr, *Reconstruction to Reform*. In this study I have chosen to identify the two Democratic factions by the names which are descriptively the most accurate if somewhat anachronistic: "conservative" and "progressive" Democrats. Contemporary Texans most often referred to the conservative faction as "Sound Money Democrats," "Gold Democrats," the pejorative "Goldbugs," and occasionally "Bourbon Democrats." The progressive faction was variously known as the "Silver Democrats," "Reform Democrats," or "Silverites." Despite identification of the factions with

gold or silver, it should be understood that the two factions disagreed over railroad regulation, tenant farmer legislation, and many other issues of state and local importance, and not just over federal monetary policy.

12. Major studies of Populism at the national level include John D. Hicks, *The Populist Revolt: A History of the Farmers' Alliance and the People's Party* (Minneapolis: University of Minnesota Press, 1931); Gene Clanton, *Populism: The Humane Preference in America, 1890–1900* (Boston: Twayne, 1991); Robert C. McMath Jr., *American Populism: A Social History, 1877–1898* (New York: Hill and Wang, 1993); Postel, *Populist Vision*, and Goodwyn, *Democratic Promise*. For Texas Populism, see Roscoe Martin, *The People's Party in Texas: A Study in Third-Party Politics* (Austin: University of Texas Press, 1933; rpt. ed., 1970); and Barnes, *Farmers in Rebellion.* Surveying a wide range of sources, I have been able positively to identify ten Populist candidates in Milam County who were previously leaders in the Alliance. They are: J. M. Alexander, I. N. Barber, B. C. Barrett, C. N. Fokes, J. B. Gilliland, J. A. Kirkman, Antone Lesovsky, J. A. Lincoln, R. S. Murff, and W. A. Nabours. No doubt many, if not most, other Populist leaders also were Alliancemen before the formation of the People's Party.

13. For examples of other states where similar divisions existed and where African Americans held the balance of power, see Jane Dailey, *Before Jim Crow: The Politics of Race in Postemancipation Virginia* (Chapel Hill: University of North Carolina Press, 2000); and James Beeby, *Revolt of the Tar Heels: The North Carolina Populist Movement, 1890–1901* (Jackson: University Press of Mississippi, 2008).

14. *Galveston Daily News,* May 9, June 5, 1892.

15. Ibid., July 22, 1892.

16. *Galveston Daily News,* May 24, June 3, 8, July 17, 20, Aug. 2, 5, 14, 1892.

17. Ibid., Aug. 2, 1892, Oct. 29, 1894; *Austin Statesman,* July 29, 1892.

18. There is a voluminous literature on African Americans and Populism. Major works include Lawrence Goodwyn, "Populist Dreams and Negro Rights: East Texas as a Case Study," *American Historical Review* 76 (1971): 1,436–56; Goodwyn, *Democratic Promise;* Woodward, *Origins of the New South*; Gregg Cantrell and D. Scott Barton, "Texas Populists and the Failure of Biracial Politics," *Journal of Southern History* 60 (1989): 662–63; William H. Chafe, "The Negro and Populism: A Kansas Case Study," *Journal of Southern History* 34 (1968): 402–19; Gerald H. Gaither, *Blacks and the Populist Revolt: Ballots and Bigotry in the "New*

South" (University: University of Alabama Press, 1977); Robert M. Saunders, "Southern Populists and the Negro, 1893–1895," *Journal of Negro History* 54 (1969): 240–61; Herbert Shapiro, "The Populists and the Negro: A Reconsideration," in August Meier and Elliott Rudwick, eds., *The Making of Black America: Essays in Negro Life and History* (2 vols.; New York: Atheneum, 1969), 2: 27–36; R. Jean Simms-Brown, "Populism and Black Americans: Constructive or Destructive?," *Journal of Negro History* 65 (1980): 349–60; Omar H. Ali, *In the Lion's Mouth: Black Populism in the New South, 1886–1900* (Jackson: University Press of Mississippi, 2010); Steven Hahn, *A Nation under Our Feet: Black Political Struggles in the Rural South from Slavery to the Great Migration* (Cambridge, MA: Harvard University Press, 2003): 431–40; Postel, *Populist Vision*, 173–220.

19. *Galveston Daily News,* June 16, 1892.

20. Ibid., Aug.14, 26, Sept. 13, 21, 1892. On Rayner's career, see Gregg Cantrell, *Kenneth and John B. Rayner and the Limits of Southern Dissent* (Urbana: University of Illinois Press, 1993); Postel, 188–93.

21. Milam County Election Returns, Volume 2, Milam County Courthouse, Cameron, Tex. All of the subsequent election returns, unless otherwise noted, are from Volume 2 (1890–1898) or Volume 3 (1900–1908) of the county election returns and will not be cited individually.

22. The eight justice precincts formed the basic political units of Milam County. The Census Bureau fortunately based its enumeration districts on these precincts. In some cases, one precinct comprised one enumeration district. In other cases, up to four enumeration districts were contained in one precinct. However, each of the twenty enumeration districts lay entirely within the boundaries of one of the eight precincts. Using the 1900 manuscript census of population, I compiled a data set for each precinct containing the race and occupation of each of the county's 9,071 eligible voters (males age twenty-one or over). Enumeration districts are described in the Census Enumeration District Descriptions, Twelfth Census, 1900 (Tenth Supervisor's District, Texas), Record Group 29, National Archives, Washington, D.C. Within each justice precinct there were between two and twelve voting precincts. County commissioners were responsible for establishing sites for voting boxes and defining boundaries. New precincts were established or old ones abolished virtually every year. However, like the enumeration districts, each of the voting precincts lay entirely within the boundaries of one of the eight justice precincts. In order to match election returns with census data, the election returns from each voting box in a given justice precinct were

added together to provide justice-precinct-level returns. For purposes of analysis, the towns of Cameron and Rockdale have been considered separately from their respective precincts (1 and 4). It is possible to analyze them separately because each town had its own enumeration districts and voting boxes. Throughout this essay, therefore, when voting patterns in Precincts 1 and 4 are mentioned, unless otherwise specified I will be referring to those precincts *exclusive* of their respective towns. Essentially, this paper will divide Milam County into ten units of analysis: Precincts 1 (excluding Cameron), 2, 3, 4 (excluding Rockdale), 5, 6, 7, 8, Cameron, and Rockdale. Unless otherwise stated, in this paper the word "precinct" will mean the justice precincts plus the two towns. Descriptions of voting precinct boundaries and justice precinct boundaries can be found in the Commissioner's Court Minutes, Milam County Clerk's Office, County Courthouse, Cameron, Tex. The most consistently Populist precincts were 4 (52 percent tenancy) and 8 (53 percent tenancy), both well below the county average (63 percent). The most consistently Democratic precincts (excepting the two urban precincts, Rockdale and Cameron) were 2 (73 percent tenancy) and 7 (69 percent tenancy), both well above the county average.

23. The results of the presidential vote in Cameron and Rockdale (combined) were: Democratic, 62 percent; Republican, 28 percent; Populist, 11 percent. In the gubernatorial contest between James S. Hogg, George Clark, and Thomas L. Nugent, Hogg received 47 percent of the urban vote to Clark's 42 percent and Nugent's 11 percent. The Populists did better in two-way races where there was no Republican ticket, but they still lost by substantial margins in the towns.

24. *Galveston Daily News,* Aug. 20, 1894.

25. Reportedly only seven votes were cast in favor of endorsing the Populist county ticket; see *Galveston Daily News,* Sept. 24, 26, 1894.

26. Ibid., Sept. 26, Oct. 5,1894.

27. Ibid., Oct. 14, 16, 1894.

28. In 1892 the Populists won 11 percent of the town vote and 45 percent of the country vote; in 1894 they polled 13 percent of the town vote and 53 percent of the country vote (these comparisons are of 1892 presidential race and 1894 gubernatorial race—the only major races in which all three parties placed tickets in the field).

29. Even more distressing for the Populists was their failure to carry Precinct 2 in any of the two-way races between Democrats and Populists. If black Republicans were voting Populist in those races, it was not in large enough numbers to affect the outcome.

30. W. A. Nabours won election to the county treasurer's office in 1894 by a narrow 112-vote margin. The following year, the Milam County Bank, in which Nabours had deposited a large sum of the county's funds, went broke. Rather than leave his bond-signers to pay the bill, Nabours and his brother sold their farms and repaid the county out of their own pockets. In acknowledgement of this extraordinary gesture, the voters re-elected the Populist treasurer with a staggering 89 percent of the vote. I am grateful to two relatives of Nabours, Frances Baldwin of Cameron and Shirley Z. Gall of Gage, Okla., for sharing biographical information on him. Also see *Cameron Herald,* Apr. 11, 1895.

31. *Cameron Herald,* July 11, 25, Aug. 1, 1895; *Galveston Daily News,* Aug. 5, 6, 30, 1895.

32. The two Democratic factions of Milam County were badly divided in 1896, holding separate primaries and nominating conventions and engaging in much harsh rhetoric. See, for example, *Galveston Daily News,* Aug. 5, 6, 31, 1895, May 9, June 20, July 17, Aug. 6, Sept. 3, 1896; *Houston Post,* Oct. 28, 1896.

33. *Galveston Daily News*, July 27, 1896.

34. Ibid., Aug. 10, 1896.

35. Ibid., Sept. 22, Oct. 1, 28, 1896.

36. Fourteen percent of the county's voters stayed with the Bryan-Watson Populist ticket, even though it had no chance of winning.

37. At the precinct level, the Populists elected one justice of the peace, two constables, and either one or two county commissioners (the party affiliation of the victorious commissioner in Precinct 3 is unclear from the records).

38. In the county judge race, progressive Democrat W. M. McGregor defeated Populist L. N. Barber, 4,044 to 2,970; in the 62nd District State Representative race, progressive Democrat Nat H. Tracy defeated Populist A. C. Isaacs, 4,013 to 2,949.

39. For a biographical sketch of Moore, see L. E. Daniell, ed., *Personnel of the Texas State Government, with Sketches of Distinguished Texans* (Austin: Press of the City Printing Co., 1887), 202; *Cameron Herald,* Apr. 11, 1895. Perhaps more influential, but less active in progressive Democratic affairs, was Rockdale's Nat H. Tracy, a lawyer, farmer, and merchant who had also been a Confederate captain. For a biographical sketch of Tracy, see *History of Texas Together with a Biographical History of Milam, Williamson, Bastrop, Travis, Lee and Burleson Counties* (Chicago: Lewis Publishing, 1893), 843–46. Tracy was the brother of prominent Populist leader Harry Tracy of Dallas.

40. Shelton's account of his life appears in the *Rockdale Messenger,* Nov. 3, 1898. Despite his stature in the Alliance, C. W. Macune rarely played a leading role in Populist politics in his home county, even though he returned to Cameron in the mid-1890s and for a while publicly supported Populism. The other major Populist leader was A. C. Isaacs, a gray-bearded Tennessean in his seventies who had practiced medicine with mixed success before eventually becoming a prosperous farmer. Isaacs had served one term in the state legislature in the 1880s. For a sketch of Isaacs, see *History of Texas Together with a Biographical History,* 759–80. Also important in Milam Populist circles was William M. Ferguson. Ferguson never sought public office but as the editor of the *Rockdale Messenger* and member of the Populist state executive committee in 1898 he wielded considerable influence. Ferguson was an old Greenbacker from the 1870s and a Grange lecturer. His role in county politics will be discussed later in this study.

41. One Hefley brother, John M., was president of Cameron's First National Bank. Another, James S., was described in this manner by a contemporary: "The subject of this sketch is a money-maker. His right to be so designated is unquestioned." See *History of Texas Together with a Biographical History,* 375–76, 423–26, 501; *Cameron Herald*, Apr. 1, 1895.

42. The progressive faction managed to elect Monta Moore and Nat Tracy to represent the county in the state House of Representatives in 1894 and 1896, respectively. Conservatives held a number of county and precinct offices. Among these was the important post of county sheriff, which was held by John H. Bickett from 1893 to 1897. In 1895 Bickett served as chair of the eleventh senatorial district's "Sound Money" (i.e., conservative) Democrats. See *Galveston Daily News,* Aug. 31, 1895.

43. In some Texas counties after 1896 conservative Democrats prevented a return of the Populists to the Democratic Party by passing test oaths that barred anyone who had not voted Democratic in the past from voting in future Democratic primaries. This was done in adjacent Robertson County; see *Kosse Cyclone,* Sept. 23, 1897. Such an oath was never passed in Milam County. In 1896, 1898, and 1900 no tests were required for voting in the primaries. After the adoption of the white primary in 1900, the county Democratic Party required the following oath: "I am a white man and a Democrat, and I hereby pledge my honor that I will support the nominees of the Democratic Party from Constable to Governor." This would not have been satisfactory to either Democratic faction before 1900. The conservatives would have opposed it because

it eliminated critical black votes; progressives would have opposed it because it would have eliminated wavering Populists who might want to vote for some progressive Democrats in the primary while reserving the right to vote for some Populists in the general election. See *Rockdale Reporter,* Jan. 23, 1902.

44. *Rockdale Messenger,* Apr. 12, May 10, 1900.

45. *Cameron Herald,* July 11, 25, Aug. 1, 1895.

46. Ibid., Nov. 3, 1898; *Galveston Daily News,* Aug. 31, 1895, June 4,1896. W. A. Nabours lost the county treasurer's race in 1898 to the conservative Democratic ex-sheriff John H. Bickett, but by 1902 Nabours rejoined the Democratic Party and won three more consecutive terms as county treasurer. *See Rockdale Reporter,* Mar. 27, 1902, July 21, 1904, Aug. 9, 1906, all from original editions in the *Reporter* offices, Rockdale, Texas.

47. *Rockdale Messenger,* Nov. 17, 1898.

48. Ferguson and the *Messenger* also began to support those wings of the state and national People's Party that advocated fusion with Bryan Democrats. See *Rockdale Messenger,* Feb. 15, 22, 1900.

49. Ibid., December 15, 1898. J. D. Shelton and a corporal's guard of diehard Populists still maintained the party organization as late as 1904; see *Rockdale Reporter,* June 2, 1904.

50. See announcements by A. J. Lewis, L. C. McBride, and W. J. Porter in *Rockdale Messenger,* Mar. 1, 8, Apr. 12, 1900. After 1900 the Democrats would be opposed in general elections only by a Populist-dominated Independent ticket, which never won.

51. *Rockdale Messenger,* May 31, 1900.

52. Miller, "Building a Progressive Coalition," 172–73.

53. *Rockdale Messenger,* Apr. 12, 1900.

54. *Rockdale Messenger,* June 29, 1898, Mar. 8, Apr. 12, May 17, 1900. The precedent for an all-white primary had already been established in Milam County. Cameron and Rockdale had recently established a white primary for municipal elections. Significantly, the white primary in Rockdale in 1900 resulted in the election of progressive Democrat Nat H. Tracy as mayor.

55. The third precinct to support black voting was the small, isolated, staunchly Populist Precinct 8. In this precinct, 71 percent of those who voted chose to continue allowing blacks to participate in the primary. Several possible scenarios could account for this anomaly. Perhaps the few Democrats in the overwhelmingly Populist precinct were afraid of a Populist resurgence if the Democrats' black "allies" were disfranchised.

It is also possible that the ninety-nine votes against disfranchisement came from Populists who crossed party lines to vote in the Democratic primary. Precinct 8 was one of the most solidly Populist precincts and these voters might have harbored such resentment against progressive Democrats that they wished to see the progressives continue to be cheated by the conservatives. Finally, it is always possible that someone, for some reason, fraudulently manipulated the returns. Whatever the case, only 140 of 640 eligible voters in the precinct actually voted (a turnout of 22 percent), and this minuscule turnout seriously reduces the statistical significance of the pro-suffrage vote there. For the returns of the 1900 Democratic primary, see *Rockdale Messenger,* May 17, 1900.

56. *Rockdale Messenger,* May 10, 1900. To give a better indication of Populist support for reentry into the Democratic Party, it is useful to examine more closely the Hamilton Chapel and Sandy Creek voting boxes. In the 1894 congressional race between Populist L. N. Barber and Democrat George C. Pendleton, Pendleton polled a total of forty-five votes at the two boxes. In the 1900 Democratic primary vote on disfranchisement, the combined vote of the two boxes was 108–65 in favor of the white primary. While this does not prove conclusively that significant numbers of Populists in these precincts entered the Democratic primary in 1900 and voted for disfranchisement, it is highly suggestive of that result. (Note: this 108–65 figure includes returns from a third voting box—known as the Hord box—carved out of the Hamilton Chapel precinct between 1892 and 1900.) Significantly, Populist crossover votes only seemed to affect the white primary referendum; conservative Democrats still won most of the party's nominations in the primary. Apparently Populists were willing to help progressive Democrats exclude blacks from primaries, but they were not yet prepared to vote for candidates of the progressive Democrats. Returns are from the *Rockdale Messenger,* May 17, 1900.

57. The Populist ticket in 1900 was led by Allen Lewis, the party's candidate for sheriff. Lewis polled 1,188 votes; other Populist candidates polled somewhat fewer votes. In 1894 and 1896 the People's Party had polled about 3,000 votes in Milam County.

58. The text of the bill can be found in the *Rockdale Reporter,* Feb. 13, 1902.

59. *Rockdale Reporter,* Feb. 13, Mar. 6, 1902; *Cameron Herald,* Feb. 13, 1902.

60. Oscar F. McAnally received 36 percent of the votes cast. In Cameron, Rockdale, and the black-majority Precinct 2, he polled 58

percent of the votes. His combined total for all other precincts was a mere 26 percent. For election returns see *Rockdale Reporter.* Mar. 8, 1902. Progressive G. S. Miller of Gause won the race with 55 percent of the vote. A third progressive candidate, T. V. Weir, received 9 percent. McAnally charged that Monta Moore and Paul Keith, editor of the *Rockdale Reporter,* had conspired to defeat him. "The plan," wrote McAnally, "appears to be (Monta managing) . . . to keep one of these candidates at home and out of view of the voters, while the other is to make a still hunt in the southern portion of this county, with instructions to say all the mean things possible about me." Whether or not this was indeed the plan, the result was a resounding defeat for McAnally. See *Cameron Herald,* Mar. 6, 1902.

61. The 25 percent figure for Precinct 8 was the Democratic share of the vote in the 1894 gubernatorial election. There were approximately 6,757 eligible white voters in the county, of whom 67 percent voted in the 1902 Democratic primary. In each of the three precincts that consistently returned Populist majorities in the mid-1890s, the turnout was greater than 50 percent (of eligible white voters). Turnout was, of course, greater in the traditionally Democratic precincts, suggesting the Populist return to the Democratic Party was far from complete. Clearly, some Populists were still heeding chairman J. D. Shelton's pleas to Populists to stay out of the Democratic primaries. Estimates of the number of eligible voters (and hence voter turnout) in each precinct for 1892–1898 were derived in the following manner: first, the total population for each precinct and the two towns was taken from the 1890 and 1900 censuses. Then a straight-line interpolation was used to produce an estimate of total population per precinct for the years 1892, 1894, 1896, and 1898. Using these figures, the population of each precinct for these four years was expressed as a percentage of the 1900 population [e.g., the population of Precinct 2 was 6,974 (in 1900) and 6,592 (interpolated estimate for 1898), so the 1898 population figure was 95 percent (or .95) of the 1900 figure]. These percentages (for each precinct, 1892–1898) were then multiplied by the actual number of eligible voters per precinct in 1900 to obtain the estimated of eligible voters per precinct for 1892–1898 [e.g., using the .95 figure in the example above, .95 was multiplied by 1,605 (the estimated number of eligible voters in Precinct 2 in 1900) to produce an estimated 1,517 estimated eligible voters in Precinct 2 in 1898]. Thus the accuracy of the estimates of eligible voters for each precinct for the years 1892–1898 is subject to two assumptions: the estimates assume a constant rate of population growth in each precinct between 1890 and

1900, and they assume a constant ratio of eligible voters/total population. The first of these assumptions will have relatively little bearing on the years closest to 1890 and 1900 (i.e., 1892 and 1898) but will make middle-year estimates (1894 and 1896) somewhat less accurate. The second of these assumptions is very valid and should have little effect on the accuracy of the estimates. Overall, this method should produce very accurate estimates of the number of eligible voters in each precinct for each year between 1890 and 1900. For 1902, the 1900 figures have been used. The population of Milam County changed only slightly between 1900 and 1910 (there was a 7 percent decline in the population), and this change was not dramatic enough to affect significantly the analysis conducted in this study.

62. Even in the five voting boxes that B. F. Williams carried, the vote was close. Four of those boxes were in the sandy, isolated countryside outside of Rockdale, the candidate's home.

63. Miller, "Building a Progressive Coalition," 173–74; Michael Perman, *Struggle for Mastery: Disfranchisement in the South, 1888–1908* (Chapel Hill: University of North Carolina Press, 2000), 272–81.

64. *Rockdale Reporter,* Oct. 30, 1902.

65. For poll tax payment figures see *Rockdale Messenger,* Feb. 9, 1905; *Cameron Herald,* Feb. 7, 1907.

66. J. Morgan Kousser has analyzed the post-disfranchisement turnout in the eleven ex-Confederate states, comparing turnout in the primaries with that of the general election, and has found very little overall difference between the two. Generally speaking, the primaries brought out more voters than the general elections in the Lower South states while the general elections continued to attract the most voters in the Upper South and Texas. Kousser thus concludes that the "substitution of intra- for inter-party competition after institution of the Democratic primary amounted to much more than a mere change of name." This generalization does not hold for Milam County, where by 1906 the turnout in the primary was nearly three times that of the general election. Milam's experience more closely resembles that of the Deep South states such as Georgia and Mississippi, where the primaries attracted many more voters than the general elections. This significant difference between Milam County and the state of Texas as a whole underscores the tremendous regional variations in disfranchisement patterns. See Kousser, *Shaping of Southern Politics*, 226–27 (esp. Tables 8.1 and 8.2).

67. R. V. Davidson polled almost a thousand more votes than his nearest opponent. The 1904 Democratic primary returns can be found

in the *Rockdale Reporter,* July 21, 1904. Positive identification of individual candidates with one faction or the other is very difficult at the county level. However, the races mentioned in this paragraph unquestionably resulted in conservative defeats. On Davidson's progressive credentials, see Barr, *Reconstruction to Reform,* 225–26, 234. For Oscar F. McAnally's murder, see Dallas *Southern Mercury,* Jan. 4, 1906; *Bartlett (Tex.) Tribune*, May 4, 1906, May 24, 1907; *Dallas Morning News*, May 12, 1907. Events at the state level paralleled those in Milam County. The composition of the legislature shifted dramatically as a result of the 1902 elections, as counties like Milam replaced conservative legislators with more progressive ones. Of 125 House members who took office in 1901, only 43 returned in 1903. These changes soon bore fruit. In 1903 and 1905 the Texas legislature approved the Terrell Election Laws, which reformed the state's corruption-prone election machinery. The legislature enacted much-needed tax reforms aimed at making corporations shoulder a more equitable share of the tax burden, and the Standard Oil monopoly was effectively barred from the state. See Miller, "Building a Progressive Coalition," 178; and Barr, *Reconstruction to Reform,* 229–36.

68. In Milam County, Oscar B. Colquitt polled 43 percent of the vote to Thomas M. Campbell's 36 percent. This division of votes between two progressives probably reflects a disagreement in the county over an increasingly important issue: prohibition. Campbell's prohibitionist sentiments were well known, although he publicly declared liquor to be a non-issue. Colquitt was equally well known as a foe of prohibition. Of the two more conservative candidates, Micajah M. Brooks was an avowed prohibitionist while C. K. Bell, like Campbell, tried to avoid the issue. Thus the massive majority polled by Campbell and Colquitt cannot be attributed to prohibition sentiment in the county, for the two losing candidates' stands on the measure mirrored the two winners' positions. Election returns for the 1906 Democratic primary can be found in the *Rockdale Reporter,* Aug. 9, 1906. For discussions of the candidates and the statewide campaign, see Barr, *Reconstruction to Reform,* 236–40; Miller, "Building a Progressive Coalition," 178–81. For information on the 1906 gubernatorial race in Milam County, see *Gause Gazette,* June 8, 22, Aug. 11, 1906; *Cameron Herald,* July 5, 19, 1906.

69. Miller, "Building a Progressive Coalition," 164, 181.

70. Campbell, *Grass-Roots Reconstruction*, 220.

Black Tenant Farmer's Home, Little Rock, Arkansas. Courtesy of Library of Congress

African-American Housing and Health Patterns in Southwestern Cities, 1865–1900

Alwyn Barr

After the Civil War, many African Americans in southwestern cities, including some former urban slaves and all new migrants into the towns, faced an immediate need for housing. The resolution of that problem would influence their lives and the nature of the cities in several ways. It could perpetuate integrated antebellum residential patterns, when domestic slaves lived in the houses of their owners or in quarters nearby. Or it could enhance the residential segregation that had begun on the fringes of older cities in the Southeast, with free blacks and hired-out slaves living away from the slaveholders. If new urban migrants settled in areas near the heart of these towns, their presence could foreshadow the development of ghettoes similar to the ones that resulted from black migration into northern cities in the early twentieth century. Since most ex-slaves left their bondage penniless and few free blacks lived west of the Mississippi River, not many of them could afford good housing. Furthermore, the quality and location of that housing became a major influence on the health of black populations in southwestern towns.

Some scholars have suggested that segregated neighborhoods emerged quickly in cities of the South that experienced most of their growth during the post-Civil War period, which would include those west of the Mississippi River. Other studies conclude that separate black settlements arose on the edge of southeastern cities in the years from 1865 to 1880. That has been attributed to the availability of cheap land, especially in less healthy areas, a preference to live close to employment, white desires for separation, and the location of black institutions. To understand housing patterns in southwestern towns, it is important to determine the relative influence of these factors and whether they caused the cities to fit one of the proposed models or to form another variation.[1]

Table 1: Population by Wards, 1870

	Total	*White*	*Black*	*Black %*
Little Rock	12,380	7,101	5,279	42
First Ward	3,180	2,063	1,117	35
Second Ward	2,603	1,714	889	34
Third Ward	3,715	1,662	2,053	55
Fourth Ward	2,882	1,662	1,220	42
Houston	9,382	5,691	3,691	39
First Ward	38	488	250	34
Second Ward	1,638	1,164	474	29
Third Ward	2,812	1,737	1,075	38
Fourth Ward	3,055	1,741	1,314	43
Fifth Ward	1,139	561	578	51
San Antonio	12,256	10,299	1,957	16
First Ward	3,173	2,790	383	12
Second Ward	2,957	2,472	485	16
Third Ward	3,055	2,544	511	17
Fourth Ward	3,071	2,493	578	19

Some former slaves who continued as domestic servants remained in quarters with or near their white employers, who apparently continued to separate themselves from African Americans by social status rather than geographical distance. In each of the southwestern cities this practice appeared, usually concentrated by 1870 in one or two wards that contained more upper and middle class whites. For Little Rock that distinction developed for the Second Ward in the southwestern quadrant of the city away from the Arkansas River. In Houston, the Second and Third wards, which extended southwest away from downtown and Buffalo Bayou, had such housing arrangements. The Fourth and Fifth wards, residential areas south and west of downtown, held most Shreveport domestic servants. In San Antonio the pattern is less clear because of the smaller black population, but more African-American servants apparently lived with the predominantly native born Anglos of the Third Ward, in the northeastern quarter of the city east of the San Antonio River.[2]

In each city a second pattern emerged as new migrants concentrated on the edges of town where less expensive land could be found. A Little Rock newspaper editor noted "about the outskirts" of the primarily African-American Third Ward in the southwestern part of town "the cabins put up for temporary use by the colored people who have taken up residence here since the war." A United States soldier named the area "Lick Skillet" because of the poverty he observed among its black residents. Other African Americans created "Blissville," apparently in the First Ward, in the northeastern portion of the city along the Arkansas River. Atop Hanger's Hill on the eastern edge of Little Rock arose another group of huts known as "Hard-Scrabble." "The city of Houston will soon have its 'Africa'," noted a reporter, "Near the New Orleans Depot there is already a considerable settlement of negroes, whose numbers are constantly increasing." The area "on the outer edge of the Fourth Ward," south of Buffalo Bayou and west from the center of town, became known as "Freedmantown." "Vinegar Hill, on the north side of the bayou," reported the Houston *Post,* reflecting white racial and class views, "has been noted for the disreputable characters that congregate there, where none reside save negroes of the very lowest class." That concentration gave the Fifth Ward an African-American majority in 1870. In San Antonio "the negroes were in the small villages and settlements . . . one . . . called Lincolnsville and the other Newcombsville," in honor of a local Republican Party leader. One developed in the Second Ward west of the San Antonio River and north of Commerce Street and the other in the Fourth Ward east of the San Antonio River and south of Commerce. The greatest residential concentration of African Americans in Shreveport seems to have been in the Second and Third wards, which may have had black majorities. They lay just west of the business district, a variation from the pattern of suburban settlement in the other southwestern towns. Heavy black settlement also extended out into the Sixth Ward to the southwest.[3]

When an index of residential segregation by wards is applied to the southwestern cities in 1870, Little Rock showed the greatest separation with a 15.5 index, followed by Houston with 11 and San Antonio with 7.5. Lack of comparable figures for Shreveport does not allow the calculation of its index. Because of the rapid rate of black population growth in the towns west of the Mississippi River, one might expect the development of African-American ghettoes similar to those that emerged in northern cities in the early twentieth century. Yet the population distribution by wards and the segregation indexes for the southwestern cities suggest they contained no greater concentrations of black population than southeastern cities, which had segregation indexes in 1870 that ranged from 3 in Richmond, Virginia, to 24 in New Orleans and 28 in Louisville. Certainly the segregation indexes fell well below those of mid-twentieth-century cities, which ranged from 30.7 to 74.6 in three southern cities and from 68.5 to 86.6 in ten northern cities.[4]

The impression of integrated residential areas reflected in part the distribution of servants throughout the southwestern cities. The population figures for wards, however, fail to reveal the new concentrations that developed primarily on the outskirts of towns. While 1870 census takers did not include street addresses, they found African Americans in several neighboring dwellings in each of the southwestern towns. The concentrations were more numerous in the First and Third wards of Little Rock, the Fourth and Fifth wards in Houston, the Third and Sixth wards of Shreveport, and the Second and Fourth wards in San Antonio. This may be because, to limit travel time and costs, some African Americans settled close to their jobs. Since most held working-class positions, black neighborhoods developed around train depots, wharves, and cotton compresses.[5]

Geography influenced the location of other black neighborhoods, because land in low areas that might flood or be less healthy would be available at lower prices. In Houston, many African Americans lived on Buffalo and White Oak Bayous. One black area in San Antonio lay just west of San Pedro Creek. Town Branch ran through the Third and First wards of Little Rock, where many freedmen settled. In Shreveport some African Americans found housing in the downtown near the Red River and Cross Bayou, while others lived in Silver Lake Bottom and St. Paul Bottom as the town expanded. Yet this pattern seems less dominant than in some southeastern cities. African Americans in the Third Ward of Little Rock also occupied high ground around the black colleges there. The elevated Allendale section of Shreveport also included numerous black inhabitants. East of the San Antonio River, African Americans lived on ground that rose gently from that stream. In Houston, whites and blacks alike searched in vain for higher ground.[6]

Some historians have suggested that the placement of educational and religious institutions advanced the process of residential segregation. In Little Rock, Howard School in 1870 stood "right in the midst of what is generally termed Negro town, near Bethel (colored) church" and Mt. Holly Cemetery. The five black churches established in Little Rock by 1873 stood in the First and Third wards. New churches during the 1880s appeared on the outer edge of the Third Ward. That trend continued in the 1890s, but new churches also sprang up in the old Second Ward and beyond the original wards. In Houston the earliest black churches founded outside of downtown stood in the Fifth Ward and "Freedmantown," which helped solidify those residential concentrations. New churches established in the 1890s reflected the creation of black neighborhoods around the business district on the west and south sides in the Second and Third wards. The African-American churches of Shreveport in 1882 stood close together, with two in the Third Ward and four in the bordering streets of the Fifth Ward. By 1900 the church locations remained generally the same, with a slight shift westward into the Allendale section. In San Antonio, where black neighborhoods evolved more slowly, one early African-American church stood in the northwestern Second Ward, while three others were built in the northeastern Third Ward, close to the Fourth Ward with its slightly larger black population. By the 1890s, the churches in the old Second and Third wards had been joined by two new congregations in the old Fourth Ward southeast of the business district.[7]

Schools followed population growth more slowly than churches. In Little Rock two black schools stood in the Third Ward and one in the First Ward continuously from the 1870s. The founding of Philander Smith College and Arkansas Baptist College in the Third Ward during the 1880s reinforced that population concentration. Only in the 1890s did the school board create a new school for the old Second Ward in response to the outward movement of African Americans into that area. The one black school in San Antonio during the 1870s stood in a central location just north of the business district. The school board established a second school in the 1880s on the east side, where the Third and Fourth wards came together. The west side received a third school in the late 1880s because of the continued concentration of blacks in the First and Second wards near downtown. In other towns, schools did not shift with populations. Shreveport maintained its three black public schools in the Third, Fourth, and Fifth Wards through the 1880s and 1890s. The Houston school board established a black school in each ward during the 1870s and continued that pattern through the 1890s. Thus educational and religious institutions in the southwestern cities seem to have had only a limited impact on population shifts. Some churches, but only a few schools, acted to encourage residential changes by their location.[8]

Table 2: Population by Wards, 1890

	Total	*Whites*	*Blacks*	*Black %*
Houston	27,548	17,178	10,370	38
First Ward	1,980	1,203	777	39
Second Ward	3,339	2,079	1,260	38
Third Ward	7,363	4,705	2,658	36
Fourth Ward	8,757	5,079	3,678	42
Fifth Ward	6,109	4,112	1,997	33
San Antonio	37,673	32,854	4,720	13
First Ward		2,342	127	5
Second Ward		5,374	466	8
Third Ward		4,220	819	16
Fourth Ward		5,534	637	10
Fifth Ward		3,878	304	7
Sixth Ward		5,623	1,385	20
Seventh Ward		3,656	850	19
Eighth Ward		2,227	132	6

As southwestern towns expanded, several factors might contribute to increased residential segregation. The development of streetcar lines allowed the cities to spread in the 1880s, with the white middle class moving to the edges of the cities, where they built new and more spacious houses. To further that process, Anglos who controlled most of the land created building associations with no black members. Many African Americans could not afford to join the outward movement. Yet the small black middle class did respond through its fraternal groups that organized their own building associations by 1890. Even those organizations, however, were forced to operate in restricted areas. As R. C. Childress, a black educator in Little Rock, explained: "It has been my privilege to work with some of the leading banks engaged in selling the Negroes lots in certain sections of the city . . . . He is encouraged to segregate and to have property with other Negroes." In Houston that took the form of a separate African-American suburb, Independence Heights, established in 1899 on the northern fringe of the Fifth Ward.[9]

Despite some concentrations of black population, the application of an index of residential segregation by wards in 1890 and again in 1910 reveals only limited changes from 1870. Houston declined from an index of 11 in 1870 to 5.5 in 1890, and climbed only to 7 by 1910, although it had one additional ward. San Antonio expanded its wards from four to eight by 1890, which more clearly revealed ethnic concentrations. Thus its index increased from 7.5 in 1870 to 23.5 in 1890 but showed no further change by 1910. Southwestern towns, despite their more rapid growth, continued to compare favorably in segregation indexes with the cities of the Southeast. There the indexes in 1910 stood at 15 in New Orleans, 16.8 for Charleston, 35 in Louisville, 39.4 for Jacksonville, and 40 in Richmond. For ten northern cities in 1910 the indexes ranged from 31.6 in Columbus to 66.8 in Chicago.[10]

Tables 2 and 3 indicate the population distribution by wards for Houston and San Antonio. In the latter, the black population in the various wards ranged from 2.2 to 20.2 percent in 1910, but half of African Americans lived in the adjacent Sixth and Seventh wards on the east side. Black population in Houston wards ranged from 20 to 38 percent in 1910, also with a concentration of over half the African Americans in the bordering Third and Fourth wards on the southeast side of town.[11]

Little Rock alone of the southwestern cities had city directories at the end of the nineteenth century that listed people by addresses. From such listings it is possible to determine whether each city block was segregated or integrated. The more tedious process of locating people by address from earlier alphabetical directories allows a comparison to determine change over a period of time. An analysis of Little Rock blocks in 1871 reveals that 29 percent were integrated and 71 percent segregated, with 61 percent entirely white and 10 percent completely black. While black or integrated blocks existed in every ward of the town, a majority lay in the Third Ward in the southwestern quadrant. In 1900 Little Rock blocks remained 28 percent integrated and 72 percent segregated—60 percent were all white and 12 percent all black. Most of the black or predominantly African-American blocks could be found in the Third Ward in the south central part of the city and in the Seventh Ward—the former First Ward in the northeast along the river. The percentages are misleading to some extent, however, because several of the integrated blocks in the older areas contained large numbers of people, while some of the all white or black blocks on the edge of town had few residents. A notable degree of segregation had developed with the influx of black population after the Civil War, and it changed little over the next thirty years.

Table 3: Black Population by Wards, 1910

	Total	*Blacks*	*Black %*
Houston	78,800	23,929	30.4
First Ward	6,954	1,390	20.0
Second Ward	7,572	2,335	30.8
Third Ward	24,705	7,662	31.0
Fourth Ward	16,772	6,366	38.0
Fifth Ward	16,854	4,967	29.5
Sixth Ward	5,943	1,209	20.3
San Antonio	96,614	10,716	11.1
First Ward	10, 132	227	2.2
Second Ward	14,864	1,052	7.1
Third Ward	11,766	1,495	12.7
Fourth Ward	16,569	1,335	8.1
Fifth Ward	7,773	931	12.0
Sixth Ward	14,885	3,013	20.2
Seventh Ward	14,787	2,513	17.0
Eighth Ward	5,838	150	2.6

About 30 percent of the African Americans living on integrated blocks in Little Rock served as domestics, roughly 50 percent were laborers or skilled workers, and 20 percent pursued business, professional, or white collar occupations. Whites living on integrated blocks included about 45 percent business, white collar, and professional people, approximately 40 percent laborers or skilled workers, and about 15 percent widows. Foreign-born whites formed roughly 20 percent of those on integrated blocks. Grocers and barkeepers who probably served African Americans comprised almost half of the businessmen in these areas. Widows without additional income could not move out of integrated neighborhoods as easily as others. Yet neither black servants nor white who could not move appear to have dominated the population in those integrated residential areas to the degree they did in older southeastern cities.[12]

Comments by African Americans and Anglos bear out the continuing residential integration in Little Rock. A prominent white Democrat, John R. Frazier, said of black Republican leader John E. Bush, "for a great many years he live a neighbor to me." Black composer William Grant Still reminisced that "there was segregation in Little Rock during my boyhood, but my family lived in a mixed neighborhood and our friends were both white and colored. So were my playmates."[13]

Census and city directory statistics are unavailable for Shreveport. Yet impressionistic evidence suggests similar patterns of both integrated and segregated blocks. A newspaper article in 1887 spoke of the concentration of "colored people, in Mugginsville and Allendale," but later commented that "this neighborhood is rather thickly settled by white and colored people and is one of the most orderly in this community." Later historians speak of residential segregation as a result of the new commission government in the early twentieth century.[14]

The image of segregation also should be tempered to some extent by an awareness of the residential mobility that existed for all citizens of southwestern cities. Persistence rates for those urban dwellers from 1870 to 1880 reveal that only 20 to 42 percent of native whites, 17 to 39 percent of immigrants, and 24 to 36 percent of blacks remained in the towns after ten years. The especially low persistence rates among unskilled white workers—7 to 14 percent among native whites and 8 to 18 percent for immigrants, except in Houston—raise questions about the view that whites in integrated neighborhoods remained only because economic limitations trapped them there.[15]

To attempt to clarify the issue, one must consider migration patterns within the towns. From Table 4 it is clear that San Antonio constituted the most stable community. Among its 1870 residents, from 17 to 23 percent of its European immigrants, African Americans, and native whites remained at the same address in 1880. Only 8 percent of its Mexican Americans still lived in the same place. Little Rock and Shreveport reflected greater internal migration. Among the 1870 residents of Little Rock only 9 to 14 percent of the European immigrants, native whites, and blacks remained at the same address in 1880, while those groups in Shreveport had an even lower range of 3 to 7 percent from 1870 to

1882. In each community European immigrants moved less frequently than native whites, although the differences generally were limited. More important, African Americans moved in about the same percentages as whites when the native white and immigrant figures are combined. Furthermore, blacks moved outward from the center of the towns at slightly higher rates than did whites. Finally, while the skilled workers and the business, professional, and white collar groups moved less frequently among whites, the black laboring class remained at the same address as often as did African Americans with more skilled occupations. In Little Rock and Shreveport, black laborers also moved outward at slightly higher rates than skilled workers or business and professional people, although the reverse was true in San Antonio. From these figures one may conclude that most whites who remained in integrated neighborhoods probably could afford to move if they desired to do so.

From 1880 to 1900, African Americans continued to move outward from the center of the towns at about the same rates as before in Little Rock and Shreveport, and at an even higher rate in San Antonio. Whites continued to move outward at roughly the same rate in San Antonio and at increased rates in Little Rock and Shreveport. Both the persistence rates and the economic levels of the remaining whites suggest at least some toleration of integrated residential areas. Since black persistence rates in residential areas do not seem to differ greatly from white rates, it does not appear that African Americans found themselves unable to seek new housing opportunities. Blacks actually moved outward from older parts of the towns at slightly higher rates than did whites. Although some new residential areas remained closed to blacks, they did retain a degree of outward mobility that would become less common in the twentieth century.[16]

Table 4: Emigration From and Migration Within Cities

	Emigrated (or died)	Did not move	Moved short distances	Moved outward
Shreveport, 1870–1882				
Native whites	80%	3%	13%	4%
Laborers	100	0	0	0
Skilled workers	84	0	12	4
Business, professional, white collar	76	5	15	4

Table 4: Emigration From and Migration Within Cities *(continued)*

	Emigrated (or died)	Did not move	Moved short distances	Moved outward
European immigrants	84%	7%	6%	3%
Laborers	96	0	2	2
Skilled workers	91	3	3	3
Business, professional, white collar	76	11	10	3
African Americans	79%	7%	9%	5%
Laborers	76	8	10	6
Skilled workers	88	5	4	3
Business, professional, white collar	61	8	31	0
Little Rock, 1870–1880				
Native whites	76%	12%	8%	4%
Laborers	80	10	3	7
Skilled workers	82	8	6	4
Business, professional, white collar	67	17	11	5
European immigrants	75%	14%	4%	7%
Laborers	91	3	3	3
Skilled workers	85	8	2	5
Business, professional, white collar	53	28	7	12
African Americans	79%	9%	4%	8%
Laborers	73	11	6	10
Skilled workers	89	5	2	4
Business, professional, white collar	85	11	4	0

Table 4: Emigration From and Migration Within Cities *(continued)*

	Emigrated (or died)	Did not move	Moved short distances	Moved outward
San Antonio 1870–1880				
Native whites	71%	17%	8%	4%
Laborers	78	14	8	0
Skilled workers	75	22	3	0
Business, professional, white collar	60	15	15	10
European immigrants	63%	23%	7%	7%
Laborers	68	18	7	7
Skilled workers	67	24	5	4
Business, professional, white collar	62	20	9	9
Mexican Americans	84%	8%	2%	6%
Laborers	87%	7%	2%	4
Skilled workers	82%	9%	4%	5
Business, professional, white collar	61%	17%	0	22
African Americans	64%	20%	7%	9%
Laborers	63	26	10	1
Skilled workers	89	8	0	3
Business, professional, white collar	80	0	0	20

During the Civil War and immediately afterward, most African Americans found themselves limited to poor housing because of their working class economic status. Freedmen in Houston "erected little shanties, just sufficient to protect them from the weather, all packed and jammed as closely as they can be," according to the *Tri Weekly Telegraph*. "Large numbers of contrabands are huddled together," explained a Little Rock newspaper; "small huts in great numbers are built in close proximity to each other." In Shreveport, some blacks lived in an abandoned church building until a portion of the structure collapsed. The United States Army forced others from a former Confederate arsenal.[17]

Similar conditions continued throughout the nineteenth century for some African Americans. The Vinegar Hill section of Houston appeared to one white observer as "a settlement of one- and two-room box-shaped, dilapidated structures, occupied by negro women and children, and scattered over the surface of the ground with no semblance of regularity or system, with no fences or dividing lines." Another black section in the Fourth Ward during the 1870s included sheds, small cottages, and houses in need of repair. In the 1880s a prominent white leader of San Antonio rented out "negro shanties on Avenue E." An 1899 fire in Shreveport burned several small tenant houses rented by African Americans, which were valued at $150 to $500 each. New black migrants to Little Rock at the beginning of the twentieth century "crowd into houses with no sanitation and no ventilation."[18]

During the same period, however, some African Americans with skilled occupations found it possible to save money and begin to improve their dwellings. One year after emancipation a Freedmen's Bureau officer reported that at least 125 homes, some worth $500, had been erected by African Americans in Houston. As early as 1869, a reporter in San Antonio observed that freed people there "make money enough to purchase, from time to time, little tracks of land and build homesteads." A black foundry foreman could testify by the 1870s: "I have a nice residence in Shreveport at the north end." By that period the Third Ward of Little Rock also appeared to contain several black home owners. In the 1890s an African-American newspaper noted that "the colored people of Houston own many homes. Homes are cheap, ranging from $100 upwards, on easy payments." Similar advances had been achieved in Little Rock, where the *Arkansas Gazette* announced: "the negroes of this city in large numbers are owners of the homes they occupy, ranging from the three-room cottage to the two-story pretentious residence." A black community leader estimated at least 1,500 home owners had holdings valued at $1,600,000 early in the twentieth century.[19]

Despite the improvements in housing by a growing black middle class, inadequate housing, based upon limited economic opportunities for the larger black working class, resulted in poor health for many African Americans in southwestern cities. In the summer of 1865, a Little Rock newspaper already attributed an increased number of deaths among blacks to unhealthy dwelling situations. When smallpox appeared in Shreveport during December of that year, a Freedmen's Bureau officer reported "the unemployed Freedmen by reason of great exposure and suffering are the ones that will suffer the most." When the sickness also struck Houston African Americans, the Bureau agent there commented: "Their being crowded together as they generally are in all sorts of hovels tends to spread the disease." The problem of poor housing may have been a factor in other illnesses. A Houston reporter observed black "shanties" in 1866 and predicted: "These buildings are crowded with tenants, and, we fear, they will cause mortality to be very great should the cholera visit this continent next summer." The San Antonio board of health reported: "The crowded condition of many of the tenement houses, occupied by negroes and others, is such as to ensure a widespread and malignant prevalence to the cholera or other epidemic . . . Ten or twelve persons sometimes occupy a single small room."[20]

Such conditions did not disappear during the late nineteenth century. A black leader in Little Rock early in the twentieth century described new migrants to the city who "crowd into houses with no sanitation and no ventilation, and it is not long before they are stricken with that dread disease, consumption." In a discussion of hygiene, a black doctor admonished his readers to choose housing locations away from stagnant water and to install sewers if possible.[21]

The mortality rate among African Americans in southwestern towns generally seems to have been higher than for whites throughout the late nineteenth century. In Shreveport black deaths outnumbered white deaths in almost every year, just as blacks generally outnumbered whites. Black mortality rates per 1,000 population, however, also ranged higher than white mortality in most instances. The margin of difference actually widened in 1900, but this may have resulted from better accounting procedures. The black rate usually ran four to six deaths more per 1,000 population, although the gap widened to more than twenty more deaths per 1,000 population in some years.[22]

Houston usually suffered more white deaths than black, which paralleled the population percentages. But in most years the black mortality rate per 1,000 population stood above the white rate. Although the typical difference appears to have been only between one and four more deaths per 1,000, it could range up to nine more deaths per 1,000 population in some years.[23]

During the early years after the Civil War in Little Rock, black deaths seem to have outnumbered white deaths, with a much higher rate of mortality per 1,000 population. That situation apparently reversed by the mid-1870s as deaths fell more into line with population percentages. By the early twentieth century, African Americans suffered about two more deaths per 1,000 population than did whites.[24]

In San Antonio, black deaths always fell well below the white figures, as did the black population percentage. The mortality rate per 1,000 population also indicated one to eight fewer black deaths than white deaths. When the limited available statistics are employed to separate Mexican Americans from Anglo Americans, however, it appears that both minority groups had higher death rates per 1,000 population than did Anglo Americans. For African Americans the figures ranged from one to six deaths more per 1,000 population, while Mexican-American deaths varied from two to over twenty higher per 1,000 population.[25]

When death rates for blacks in the southwestern towns are compared with those for the larger cities of the Southeast, they appear to be lower except for Shreveport.[26] The difference probably reflects slightly less crowded living conditions in the smaller western communities and perhaps fewer old dwellings with sanitation problems.

Spectacular epidemics struck each of the southwestern towns at different times. Yellow fever hit Shreveport in 1867 and caused more deaths among whites than blacks—an unusual result for that community. In 1873 a second epidemic of yellow fever devastated the town from August to November. During that period the disease killed 639 Anglo Americans and 120 African Americans out of the 2,600 persons who became ill. Shreveport temporarily lost a high percentage of its population as people fled to avoid the epidemic. Cholera appeared in Little Rock and Houston during 1866 and in San Antonio during 1867–1868, although the number of deaths seems to have been more limited. In Houston, African Americans felt the impact of the illness to a greater extent than other ethnic groups. Smallpox struck down citizens of Houston during 1867 and 1874, Little Rock in 1870, and Shreveport in 1884. It, too, appeared to have affected more blacks than whites. Of the forty-one cases in Little Rock from February to April 1870, African Americans formed three-fourths. The cases reported in Houston during 1874 seemed to have been primarily in the black neighborhoods. For the epidemic period from January to March 1884 in Shreveport, black deaths outnumbered white deaths by at least forty to eight. Smallpox appeared again in Shreveport as late as 1900, but the epidemics seem to have declined after the mid-1880s.[27]

African Americans died in larger numbers from other diseases and health problems that persisted in the southwestern towns. Tuberculosis ranked first among the threats to life for blacks in each community during most time periods. Pneumonia and dysentery seem to have followed closely as deadly diseases in all four. Tuberculosis in particular struck African Americans more frequently than whites. In 1900 blacks suffered 83 percent of the cases in Shreveport, compared to their 53 percent of the population. For San Antonio they comprised 17 percent of the cases but were less than 12 percent of the population in a city famous for attracting whites seeking a healthy climate to treat such diseases. In patterns of disease, the southwestern cities conformed to national trends.[28]

Still births and other illnesses resulted in a high infant mortality rate for each of the cities. Children accounted for almost half of the black deaths in San Antonio during the 1870s and 1880s. In some months of the 1880s, children formed a majority of the deaths among African Americans in Little Rock. In Shreveport, roughly one-third of the African Americans who died in the 1890s were children. Of the black children born in Shreveport in 1900, three out of ten died before they reached one year of age, compared to two out of ten white children. For San Antonio that same year, two of ten black children died during their first year, while the rate for white children was 1.74 out of ten, although the inclusion of Mexican-American children with Anglo Americans may have kept the gap from being greater. In comparison to the larger cities of the Southeast, African-American infant mortality rates in the southwestern towns generally were lower, probably for the same reasons that led to a lower overall death rate.[29]

In addition to poorer housing, the quality of medical care received by African Americans who fell ill probably influenced the death rates of the southwestern towns. The white press frequently blamed black health problems on the African Americans themselves. Some newspapers suggested blacks did less than they might have to assist their own sick. A Little Rock paper charged an "utter disregard of sanitary laws by the mass of colored people." Yet African Americans contributed to most efforts aimed at controlling epidemics and aiding the ill. Isaac Harn cared for black cholera victims in San Antonio when the epidemic struck in 1867. When yellow fever hit Shreveport in 1873, Gus Level spent hours nursing those who were stricken. Four squads with a membership of 152 African Americans helped patrol Shreveport during the yellow fever scare of 1878 to enforce a quarantine against persons from New Orleans and other infected towns along the Mississippi River. To limit smallpox in the Red River community during 1884, the Colored Knights of Pythias, a fraternal group, organized efforts to care for its members who became ill. Black fraternal groups in each city generally collected funds for that purpose. When Houston experienced worries over yellow fever in 1897, a black political leader "had colored men on the streets cleaning up."[30]

Initial efforts to provide more permanent care for sick persons in the free black community came from the Union Army during the Civil War and from the Freedmen's Bureau immediately after the conflict. In Little Rock, captured by Federal forces in 1863, an army doctor and a hospital assistant offered some aid during the following year. Yet a northern observer commented: "the idea that anything is good enough for a 'nigger' has an abiding place still in the minds of not a few connected with the freedmen." By July 1865 the military had assumed direction of St. John's Hospital in the Arkansas capital. The institution operated on a segregated basis, with separate kitchens and dining rooms for blacks and whites. The Freedmen's Bureau then provided hospital facilities during the late 1860s in Little Rock.[31]

The assistant superintendent of the Freedmen's Bureau for Shreveport opened a hospital with forty patients in July 1865. "This is a necessary as well as a charitable institution," he explained, "as the city authorities have as yet taken no measures to provide for the indigent sick." Since those conditions continued to exist, the Bureau maintained its medical services until May 1868. During the first ten months of 1866, the hospital staff provided assistance for 599 persons. When the Bureau closed the hospital, it sent several of the ill to New Orleans and sought families for orphans. Yet some patients remained in Shreveport rather than be separated from their relatives. Although available to indigent whites, the hospital staff apparently found their services accepted only by blacks from Shreveport and the surrounding area. In Houston, the Freedmen's Bureau operated a hospital with thirty beds during 1866 because the local governments failed to provide such services.[32] The smaller black population of San Antonio did not include enough cases of illness to stimulate Bureau action in that community.

City and county governments, dominated by conservative southern whites, overcame their early reluctance to extend medical services to African Americans by 1867 or 1868. That change in attitude probably resulted from a growing desire to control the spread of sickness and eliminate the necessity of a continued federal presence by the Freedmen's Bureau. By 1867 the city of Houston had agreed to enlarge its hospital, while the Harris County medical facility began to accept persons who could not pay for services. Thus both institutions reported black and white patients. In February 1868 the Shreveport city council agreed to pay a dollar a day per person for the Shreveport Infirmary "to treat all indigent sick (white and black)."[33]

Local Republican parties that developed after the Reconstruction Acts of 1867 expressed somewhat greater interest in providing medical care for African Americans. And for three years, beginning in fall 1868, the Louisiana state government came to the assistance of Shreveport by paying two-thirds of the expenses for the local hospital, with Caddo Parish providing the other third. After a two-year lapse, the state renewed its financial support. In 1869 local political leaders and others also urged the founding of a state charity hospital. The Republican majority in the state legislature responded in 1870 by authorizing $100,000 for such a medical facility, on a site to be acquired by the local government. The hospital board included Republican officials of the city and county, as well as C. C. Antoine, the black state senator from Shreveport, and William Harper, a black state representative. Despite opposition from white Democrats, the city offered two and a half acres of land in 1871. The state government issued a charter for the hospital in 1876. A small building served limited numbers of patients until another appropriation in 1884. With the completion of a new building, the hospital began to provide services in 1889 to increased numbers of patients, half of whom were from outside the town. By 1895 the hospital had 200 beds, divided into four wards segregated by race and sex.[34]

Medical care in the decades after the Civil War often depended on cooperation between government and private or religious organizations, some of which welcomed black patients. In Little Rock the city government by the 1870s subsidized the Ladies Benevolent Association Hospital, which cared for blacks and whites into the 1880s. The Catholic Church opened the Little Rock Infirmary in 1888 that accepted "the 'sick poor' of all classes, creeds and colors." The city constructed a new hospital in the 1890s that presumably served both races on a segregated basis. The Catholic Church also founded the initial medical facility in San Antonio during the winter of 1869–1870. Santa Rosa Hospital served the entire community "without regard to religion." Although one African American was among the persons immediately accepted into the hospital, its arrangement with small rooms probably allowed for segregation. San Antonio and Bexar County did not build a public hospital until the late 1880s. An early report indicated that the facility would treat Mexican Americans but made no mention of African Americans. By 1885 the Houston Infirmary, founded by three doctors, had a separate "Colored Ward."[35]

African-American efforts to provide medical services for the southwestern black communities generally achieved success in the 1880s. A black doctor, Thomas Harris, opened an office in Little Rock briefly in the mid-1870s. Black physicians or dentists became permanent residents of Little Rock in 1883, Houston in 1884, and San Antonio in 1885. By the end of the century, Houston counted seven black doctors and dentists, Little Rock five, and San Antonio and Shreveport each had three. J. H. Smith, an African-American physician, sought both black and white support in 1886 to create a small hospital that would serve the African Americans of Little Rock. His efforts seem to have been unsuccessful. Black medical men also spoke publicly and wrote about the need for careful ventilation, good sewers, pure water, and proper diet. In San Antonio a Home for Aged Colored Persons and Orphan Children existed by 1899 under African-American direction. A black nurse established modest Feagan Hospital in Houston at the turn of the century. African Americans in Texas rallied behind J. D. Davis, a black physician in Houston, during 1903 to urge a state supported hospital that would also house elderly former slaves in the bayou city. A committee solicited funds to purchase land as a means of attracting public financial aid.[36] Despite these efforts, most African Americans in the four southwestern cities still found themselves forced to rely on segregated medical facilities under white supervision as the twentieth century began.

Some African Americans in southwestern cities from 1865 to 1900 resided throughout the towns as servants, but others began to concentrate in scattered enclaves on the outskirts. Despite the rapid growth of these cities, segregated neighborhoods emerged more slowly than in older southeastern communities and northern cities. As in the older urban areas, concentrations resulted from black interest in living close to employment, the greater availability of less expensive land in low lying areas, and white preference for separation. The locations of some black churches probably reinforced such patterns, but schools had only a limited impact, unlike older southern cities. Although segregation emerged in the southwestern cities by 1870, it increased very little by 1900. Furthermore, each community experienced a high rate of population turnover in which over 75 percent of the 1870 residents did not remain in 1880. Among those who continued to live in the cities, African Americans found themselves excluded from some new suburbs, but moved outward from the older sections at about the same rate as whites. Whites living in integrated neighborhoods do not appear to have been trapped there to the degree suggested in older southern cities.

Freedmen in the southwestern cities generally could afford only small cabins for housing, and large numbers of people often lived in these huts in crowded conditions. The more skilled and educated African Americans began to acquire land and construct larger homes, yet the poor housing available to most African Americans remained one cause of health problems. Black mortality rates per 1,000 people generally ranged higher than white rates in all of the Trans-Mississippi towns. Except for Shreveport, however, those rates compared favorably with the mortality rates of blacks in southeastern cities. Less crowding and fewer old buildings in the newer southwestern cities probably explain the difference. Yellow fever epidemics hit whites harder than blacks, who suffered more from cholera and smallpox. Of the constant threats to health, tuberculosis, pneumonia, and dysentery felled the most in these black communities as they did in the southeast. Children accounted for a high percentage of African-American deaths in the Trans-Mississippi towns, although the rate was less than in cities east of the Mississippi River. The Freedmen's Bureau provided the first hospitals for blacks in each town except San Antonio. Local governments or private organizations took over by 1870, with segregated facilities. The emerging black middle class contributed to health care as individuals, through organized groups, and beginning in the 1880s as dentists and doctors. Thus African Americans in southwestern cities of the late nineteenth century faced problems similar to those in southeastern cities. Yet black communities in southwestern towns created a variation of the patterns in the older cities that involved less segregation and crowded housing as well as lower mortality rates.

Notes

1. Richard C. Wade, *Slavery in the Cities: The South, 1820–1860* (New York: Oxford University Press, 1964); Allan H. Spear, *Black Chicago: The Making of a Negro Ghetto, 1890–1920* (Chicago: University of Chicago Press, 1967), 11–27, 142–46; Paul A. Groves and Edward K. Muller, "The Evolution of Black Residential Areas in Late Nineteenth-century Cities," *Journal of Historical Geography* 1 (Apr. 1975): 169–91; John Kellogg, "Negro Urban Clusters in the Postbellum South," *Geographical Review* 47 (July 1977): 310–21; Howard N. Rabinowitz, *Race Relations in the Urban South, 1865–1890* (New York: Oxford University Press, 1978), 97–151. Segregation had developed to a limited extent in Trans-Mississippi towns before the Civil War as slaves sought more independence by living apart from their owners. See Paul D. Lack, "Urban

Slavery in the Southwest," *Red River Valley Historical Review* 6 (Spring 1981): 13.

2. United States Census Bureau, Ninth Census, 1870, Schedule 1: Population, Arkansas: Pulaski County, Louisiana: Caddo Parish, Texas: Bexar and Harris counties, National Archives, Washington, D.C.

3. *Morning Republican* (Little Rock), Mar. 24, 1868; Ira Don Richards, *Story of a River Town: Little Rock in the Nineteenth Century* (Benton, Ark.: Privately printed, 1969), 82, 136; Adolphine Fletcher Terry, *Charlotte Stephens: Little Rock's First Black Teacher* (Little Rock: Academic Press of Arkansas, 1973), 45; Houston *Tri-Weekly Telegraph*, Mar. 23, 1866; Houston *Telegraph*, July 1, 1876; Houston *Post*, Sept. 11, 1883; William J. Knox, "Early History of San Antonio as Related to his Son Frank Arnold Knox" (Typescript, Aug. 10, 1961, San Antonio School District Office), 6; *Mooney and Morrison's General Directory of the City of San Antonio for 1877–78* (Galveston, 1877), 185; *House Reports* 261, 43rd Cong., 2nd Sess., Pt. II, 462 (Serial No. 1,660); Shreveport *Times*, May 24, 1879; Cary D. Wintz, "Blacks," in Fred R. Von der Mehden, ed., *The Ethnic Groups of Houston* (Houston: Rice University Studies, 1984), 16; Kenneth Mason, *African Americans and Race Relations in San Antonio, Texas, 1867–1937* (New York: Garland Publishing, 1998), 28, 104.

4. Zane L. Miller, "Urban Blacks in the South, 1865–1920," in Leo F. Schnore, ed., *The New Urban History* (Princeton: Princeton University Press, 1975), 201; United States Census Office, *The Statistics of the Population of the United States . . . Ninth Census 1870* (Washington, D.C.: Government Printing Office, 1872), 87, 270, 272. The segregation index used in this study is an "index of dissimilarity." In these cities it reveals how evenly the black and white populations are distributed in wards compared to black and white populations in the city as a whole. Higher numbers reflect greater segregation. For a detailed explanation, see Karl E. Taeuber and Alma F. Taeuber, *Negroes in Cities: Residential Segregation and Neighborhood Change* (New York: Aldine Publishing, 1969), 29–30, 45–47, 50, 53, 54, 236–37; or University of Michigan Population Studies Center, "Racial Residential Segregation Measurement Project," http://enceladus.isr. umich.edu/race/calculate.html (accessed July 21, 2012).

5. Houston *Tri-Weekly Telegraph*, Mar. 23, 1866; Knox, "Early History of San Antonio," 6; *Baptist Vanguard* (Little Rock), Oct. 15, 1896; *Sanborn Fire Insurance Maps, Texas, Houston, 1885, 1896* (Microfilm, Southwest Collection, Texas Tech University); Mason, *African Americans and Race Relations in San Antonio*, 27.

6. *Arkansas Gazette* (Little Rock), Aug. 1, 1884; Richards, *Story of a River Town*, 57; Shreveport *Times*, Nov. 1, 1899.

7. Rabinowitz, *Race Relations in the Urban South*, 101; *Arkansas Gazette* (Little Rock), June 11, 1870; *Beasley's Little Rock Directory, 1873–74* (Little Rock, Ark., 1873), 175; *Commercial and Statistical Review of Little Rock, Arkansas, 1883* (Little Rock, Ark., 1883), 30–31; *Little Rock City Directory, 1900–01* (Little Rock: Arkansas Democrat Company, 1900), 68–70; *Mooney and Morrison's Directory of the City of Houston, 1877–78* (Houston, Tex., 1877), 38; *Morrison and Fourmy's Houston Directory, 1892–93* (Houston, Tex., 1892), 51–52; *Morrison and Fourmy's General Directory of the City of Shreveport, 1882–83* (Houston, Tex., 1882), 50; *Brueggerhoff and Baird's 1900 Shreveport City Directory* (Shreveport, La., 1900), 13–14; *Morrison and Fourmy's General Directory of the City of San Antonio, 1881–82* (Houston, Tex., 1881), 76; *Jules A. Appler's General Directory of the City of San Antonio, 1899–1900* (San Antonio, Tex., 1899), 4–5; See also Cary D. Wintz, "The Emergence of a Black Neighborhood: Houston's Fourth Ward, 1865–1915," in Char Miller and Heywood T. Sanders, eds., *Urban Texas: Politics and Development* (College Station: Texas A&M University Press, 1990), 105.

8. *Little Rock City Directory, 1872–73* (Little Rock, Ark., 1872), 12; *Little Rock City Directory, 1900–01*, p. 93–94; *Morrison and Fourmy's General Directory of the City of San Antonio, 1879–80* (Houston, Tex., 1879), 73, *Morrison and Fourmy's General Directory of the City of San Antonio, 1885–86* (Houston, Tex., 1885), 47, *Morrison and Fourmy's General Directory of the City of San Antonio, 1889–90* (Houston, Tex., 1889), 48; *Morrison and Fourmy's General Directory of the City of Shreveport, 1882–83*, p. 51; *Brueggerhoff and Baird's 1900 Shreveport City Directory*, 11; Galveston *News*, July 23, 1879; Houston *Post*, Sept. 17, 1895. The question of whether black churches and schools advanced housing segregation is discussed in John Kellogg, "The Evolution of Black Residential Areas in Lexington, Kentucky, 1865–1887," *Journal of Southern History* 48 (Feb. 1982): 49–51.

9. W. N. Hartshorn, ed., *An Era of Progress and Promise, 1863–1910* (Boston: Priscilla Publishing Co., 1910), 51; *Arkansas Gazette* (Little Rock), Dec. 4, 1881, Dec. 12, 1890, Oct. 17, 1899; Houston *Post*, Sept. 17, Oct. 17, 1893, Apr. 20, 1899; Julia Jones, *Houston—1836–1940* (Houston: J. Jones, 1941), 17; William Corner, ed., *San Antonio de Bexar* (San Antonio: Bainbridge and Corner, 1890), 35; Mason, *African Americans and Race Relations in San Antonio*, 32–33.

10. United States Census Office, *Report on Population of the United States at the Eleventh Census: 1890* (Washington, D.C.: Government Printing Office, 1895), Pt. I, 482; United States Bureau of the Census, *Negro Population, 1790–1915* (Washington, D.C.: Government Printing Office, 1918), 107; United States Bureau of the Census, *Thirteenth Census of the United States, 1910: Abstract of the Census with Supplement for Texas* (Washington, D.C.: Government Printing Office, 1913), 657; Miller, "Urban Blacks in the South, 1865–1920," 201; Taeuber and Taeuber, *Negroes in Cities*, 47, 52, 54. The segregation indexes for Richmond, New Orleans, and Louisville are based on black-native white comparisons. The indexes for black-foreign white comparisons are New Orleans 19, Louisville 26, and Richmond 30.

11. Census Office, *Population at the Eleventh Census: 1890*, Pt. I, 482; Bureau of the Census, *Negro Population, 1790–1915*, p. 107; Bureau of the Census, *Thirteenth Census, 1910: Abstract,* 657. See also John William Graves, *Town and Country: Race Relations in an Urban-Rural Context, Arkansas, 1865–1905* (Fayetteville: University of Arkansas Press, 1990), endpaper map.

12. *Little Rock City Directory, 1871* (Little Rock, Ark.: Henderson and Albertson, 1871); *Little Rock City Directory, 1900–01*. For the use of city directories to analyze housing segregation, as well as the view that most whites on integrated blocks could not move, see Rabinowitz, *Race Relations in the Urban South*, 106–14.

13. A. E. Bush and P. L. Dorman, eds., *History of the Mosaic Templers of America—Its Founders and Officials* (Little Rock: Central Printing Co., 1924), 31–32; William Grant Still, "My Arkansas Boyhood," *Arkansas Historical Quarterly* 26 (Autumn 1967): 285.

14. Shreveport *Times*, Apr. 23, 1887; Maude Hearn O'Pry, *Chronicles of Shreveport* (Shreveport: Journal Publishing, 1929), 187; Louisiana Writers' Project, *Louisiana: A Guide to the State* (New York: Hastings House, 1941), 366–67.

15. See Tables 4–7 in Alwyn Barr, "Black Migration into Southwestern Cities, 1865–1900," in Gary W. Gallagher, ed., *Essays on Southern History: Written in Honor of Barnes F. Lathrop* (Austin: University of Texas, General Libraries, 1980), 27–30.

16. Samples of 1870 residents of the southwestern cities were traced through city directories for 1880, 1890, and 1900, except for Shreveport, where only the 1882 and 1900 directories were available. The basic concept for analyzing migration patterns is set forth in Howard P. Chudacoff, *Mobile Americans: Residential and Social Mobility in Omaha,*

1880–1920 (New York: Oxford University Press, 1972). Statistics on Houston have not been included because of problems in data collection.

17. Houston *Tri Weekly Telegraph*, Mar. 23, 1866; *Arkansas Gazette* (Little Rock), July 1865; *Southwestern* (Shreveport), July 19, 1865, Mar. 24, 1869. See also Wintz, "Blacks," 15–16.

18. Charles D. Green, *Fire Fighters of Houston, 1838–1915* (Houston: Dealy-Adey Co., 1915), 137; Houston *Telegraph*, July 1, 1876; San Antonio *Express*, Aug. 18, 1882; Shreveport *Times*, Mar. 3, 1899; Hartshorn, *Era of Progress and Promise*, 52.

19. Byron Porter to William H. Sinclair, Sept. 1, 1866, Letters Sent, Sub Assistant Commissioner, Houston, Vol. 100, Records of the Bureau of Refugees, Freedmen and Abandoned Lands, Record Group 105, NA; San Antonio *Express*, Mar. 26, 1869; *House Reports* 261, 43rd Cong., 2nd Sess., Pt. II, 460 (Ser. 1,660); Edward King, *The Great South* (Hartford: American Pub., 1875), 282; Indianapolis *Freeman*, July 29, Sept. 16, 1893; *Arkansas Gazette* (Little Rock), Dec. 28, 1898; J. E. Bush, "Afro-American People of Little Rock," *Colored American Magazine* 8 (Jan. 1905): 42. See also Wintz, "Blacks," 8; Graves, *Town and Country*, 103.

20. *Arkansas Gazette* (Little Rock), July 8, 1865; [D. H. Reese] to D. G. Fenno, Dec. 17, 1865, Letters Sent, Sub Assistant Commissioner, Shreveport, Vol. 439: p. 29; W. B. Pease to J. T. Kirkman, Mar. 8, 1867, Letters Sent, Sub Assistant Commissioner, Houston, Vol. 101: p. 121; Houston *Tri Weekly Telegraph*, Jan. 31, 1866; San Antonio *Herald*, Sept. 30 1866, in Pat Ireland Nixon, *A Century of Medicine in San Antonio: The Story of Medicine in Bexar County, Texas* (San Antonio: P. I. Nixon, 1936), 135.

21. Hartshorn, *Era of Progress and Promise*, 52; E. M. Woods, *Blue Book of Little Rock and Argenta, Arkansas* (Little Rock: Central Printing Co., 1907), 152–54.

22. Minutes of the Board of Trustees of the City of Shreveport, City Hall, Book B: 591, 592, 599, 606, 610, 618, 627, 631, 637, Book C: 45, 60, 66, 72, 81, 82, 95, 103, 107, 112, 120, 129, 601–9; *Southwestern* (Shreveport), Nov. 6, 13, 20, 27, Dec. 4, 11, 1867, Jan. 5, Feb. 9, Mar. 9, Apr. 6, May 11, June 15, July 6, Aug. 3, Sept. 7, Oct. 5, Nov. 2, Dec. 7, 1870, Jan. 11, Feb. 8, Mar. 3, Apr. 5, May 3, July 5, 1871; Shreveport *Times*, Nov. 15, 1873, Feb. 6, 1890, Jan. 28, 1898, Jan. 27, 1899; United States Census Office, *Twelfth Census of the United States, Taken in the Year 1900: Vital Statistics* (Washington, D.C.: Government Printing Office, 1902), Pt. I, 344–45.

23. Death Records, City of Houston, 1886–1900; B. H. Carroll, *Standard History of Houston, Texas* (Knoxville: H. W. Crew, 1912), 131.

24. *Arkansas Gazette* (Little Rock), May 1, 1869; *Daily Republican* (Little Rock), Dec. 31, 1874; Woods, *Blue Book of Little Rock*, 159–60.

25. James L. Rock and W. I. Smith, *Southern and Western Texas Guide for 1878* (St. Louis: A. H. Granger, 1878), 167–68; *Morrison and Fourmy's General Directory of the City of San Antonio, 1879–80*, p. 54; Steven Gould, *Alamo City Guide, San Antonio, Texas* (New York: Macgowan & Slipper, 1882), 80, 81; United States Census Office, *Report on Vital and Social Statistics in the United States at the Eleventh Census: 1890* (Washington, D.C.: Government Printing Office, 1896), Pt. I, 646; Census Office, *Twelfth Census, 1900: Vital Statistics*, Pt. I, 536.

26. *Arkansas Gazette* (Little Rock), July 6, 1884; *Mortality Among Negroes in Cities* (Atlanta: Atlanta University, 1896), 8; W. D. Weatherford, *Negro Life in the South* (1915; reprinted Miami: Mnemosyne Pub., 1969), 71–72.

27. *Southwestern* (Shreveport), Nov. 6, 13, 20, 27, Dec. 4, 11, 1867; Shreveport *Times*, Oct. 1, Nov. 15, 1873, Jan. 13, Feb. 3, 10, 24, Mar. 2, 9, 1884, Jan. 25, 1900; City Council Minutes, Little Rock, Book C: 154; San Antonio *Express*, Dec. 2, 1867, Jan. 6, 14, 1868; Carroll, *Standard History of Houston, Texas*, 138; W. B. Pease to J. T. Kirkman, Mar. 8, 1867, Letters Sent, Sub Assistant Commissioner, Houston, Vol. 101: p. 121; *Morning Republican* (Little Rock), May 6, 1870; Galveston *News*, Jan. 15, 28, 1874.

28. *Southwestern* (Shreveport), Jan. 5, 1870, May 3, 1871; Shreveport *Times*, Jan. 28, 1898; Register of Deaths, Shreveport Health Department, 1880, 1890, 1900; Houston *Tri-Weekly Telegraph*, Feb. 6, 1866; Death Records, City of Houston, 1874–1900; *Arkansas Mansion* (Little Rock), Aug. 11, 18, 25, Sept. 8, Oct. 20, Nov. 10, 24, 1883, Feb. 2, 16, 23, Mar. 15, Apr. 19, 1884; Woods, *Blue Book of Little Rock*, 159–60; Death Records, San Antonio City Health Department, 1873–98; Census Office, *Twelfth Census, 1900: Vital Statistics*, Pt. I, 344–45, 536–37; *Mortality Among Negroes in Cities*, 18.

29. *Southwestern* (Shreveport), Jan. 5, 1870, May 3, 1871; Shreveport *Times*, Jan. 28, 1898, Jan. 27, 1899; Register of Deaths, Shreveport Health Department, 1880, 1890, 1900; Death Record, City of Houston, 1890, 1900; *Arkansas Gazette* (Little Rock), Aug. 5, 1883; Death Records, San Antonio City Health Department, 1873–98; Census Office, *Twelfth Census, 1900: Vital Statistics*, Pt. I, 344–45, 536–37; Weatherford, *Negro Life in the South*, 73.

30. Houston *Tri-Weekly Telegraph*, Feb. 6, 1866; *Arkansas Gazette* (Little Rock), July 6, 1884; Shreveport *Times*, Aug. 18, 22, 23, Sept. 15, 1878, Feb. 3, 13, 1884, Jan. 31, 1889; San Antonio *Express*, Dec. 2, 1867; Indianapolis *Freeman*, Oct. 2, 1897.

31. United States Army, Department of the Tennessee, General Superintendent of Freedmen, *Extracts from Reports of Superintendents of Freedmen* (Vicksburg, Miss.: Freedman Press, 1864), 17; *Arkansas Gazette* (Little Rock), July 29, 1865; F. P. Gross to Henry Page, Jan. 31, 1867, Narrative Reports of Operations from Subordinate Officers, 1866–68, Assistant Commissioner, Arkansas, RG 105, NA; *Evening Republican* (Little Rock), Dec. 24, 1867; Mason, *African Americans and Race Relations in San Antonio*, 180.

32. Report of W. B. Stickney, Aug. 1, 1865, in *Senate Executive Documents* 2, 39th Cong., 1st sess., 89–90 (Ser. 1,237); Report of P. H. Sheridan, Oct. 31, 1866, and Report of J. B. Kiddoo, Freedmen's Bureau, Texas, Oct. 1866, in *Senate Executive Documents* 6, 39th Cong., 2d sess., pp. 79–81, 153 (Ser. 1,237); A. H. Fish to Caleb W. Hamer, June 19, 1866, Special Orders No. 26, Freedmen's Bureau, Louisiana, Apr. 7, 1868, C. C. Radmon to Martin Flood, May 4, 1868, Freedmen's Bureau Hospital, Shreveport, Letters Sent, Vol. 410, RG 105, NA; [Martin Flood] to William Thatcher, Feb. 6, 1867, Sub Assistant Commissioner, Freedmen's Bureau, Shreveport, Vol. 439: p. 37; Minutes, City of Houston, 1865–1869, pp. 144, 156, 171; John Cornelius Engelsman, "The Freedmen's Bureau in Louisiana," *Louisiana Historical Quarterly* 32 (Jan. 1949): 172–73.

33. W. B. Pease to J. T. Kirkman, Mar. 8, 1867, Letters Sent, Sub Assistant Commissioner, Houston, Vol. 101: pp. 121–22; Houston *Daily Telegraph*, Mar. 3, 1867; *Southwestern* (Shreveport), Feb. 19, 1868.

34. *Southwestern* (Shreveport), Jan. 20, 1869, May 11, 1870, Jan. 25, May 10, 1871; Shreveport *Times*, Feb. 15, 1884, Aug. 9, 1889, Aug. 5, 1894, Illustrated Edition, Oct. 1894, Women's Edition, July 1895; *Morrison and Fourmy's General Directory of the City of Shreveport, 1882–83*, 20; Charles Vincent, *Black Legislators in Louisiana During Reconstruction* (Baton Rouge: Louisiana State University Press, 1976), 179.

35. Minutes, Little Rock City Council, July 12, 1877, Book F: 483; *Arkansas Gazette* (Little Rock), Jan. 4, 1880, Jan. 1, 1882, Jan. 5, 1886, Nov. 2, 1897; *Arkansas Mansion* (Little Rock), Feb. 16, 1884; San Antonio *Express*, Jan. 6, 1870, July 10, 1888; *Sanborn Fire Insurance Maps, Texas, Houston, 1885.*

36. *C. K. Caron and Co.' s City Directory of Little Rock, Pine Bluff and Hot Springs for the Year 1876–77* (Little Rock, Ark., 1876), 202; *Sholes' Directory of the City of Little Rock, and Argenta, 1883–84* (Little Rock, Ark., 1883), 101; *Little Rock Directory, 1886* (Little Rock, Ark., 1886), 388; *Morrison and Fourmy's General Directory of Houston, 1884–85* (Houston, Tex., 1884), 330; *Morrison and Fourmy's General Directory of the City of San Antonio, 1885–86* (Houston, Tex., 1885); *Little Rock City Directory, 1900–01*, pp. 603, 629–30; *Morrison and Fourmy's General Directory of Houston, 1900–01* (Houston, Tex., 1900), 437, 455; *Appler's General Directory of San Antonio, 1899–1900*; *Brueggerhoff and Baird's Shreveport 1900 City Directory*, 278–79; *Arkansas Gazette* (Little Rock), Nov. 17, 1886; San Antonio *Express*, Dec. 12, 1899; Houston *Post*, July 20, 1903; W. E. B. DuBois, ed., *Efforts for Social Betterment Among Negro Americans* (Atlanta: Atlanta University, 1909), 92; Woods, *Blue Book of Little Rock*, 153–54. For a comparison with health care east of the Mississippi River, see Rabinowitz, *Race Relations in the Urban South*, 128–38.

Familiar sight in Texas under the Terrell Election Laws. Courtesy of Library of Congress

Populism and the Poll Tax in Cooke County, Texas

Mark Stanley

Generally, poll taxes are considered in terms of their role within the Jim Crow system— laws formulated to limit the political influence of blacks. These taxes, however, also served to reduce the political power of poor whites, as exemplified by the Populist movement at the turn of the century. Rural Populists, most of whom were poor farmers, advocated the abolition of the national banking system, an increase in the money supply, and a commodity credit system. Another radical reform supported by the Populists was government regulation of the telephone, telegraph, and railroad industries. By 1896, the Populists had made significant inroads into mainstream politics only to be derailed by the fusion presidential candidacy of William Jennings Bryan for both the Populist and Democratic parties. Though some elements of their program were later implemented by others, Populism had run its course by 1900. But the Populists' often radical message, and the degree to which they were successful in disseminating it, still posed a danger to the political hegemony of conservative Democrats in Texas, who implemented a series of electoral reforms, including poll taxes, to disfranchise former Populists.[1]

Conservative Democrats, mindful of growing Populist political power, and fearful of a coalition between blacks and Populists that would erode their own political power, used the poll tax, which had been collected sporadically on heads of households in Texas for many years, as a tool to limit their opponents. Fredric D. Ogden noted that in Texas, "the Populist Party not only caused a demand for Negro disfranchisement but also evoked a desire on the part of conservative Democrats to disfranchise poor and illiterate whites." He added, "adoption of the poll tax and Populism were related. Most of the opposition to the 1902 amendment came from the remnants of the Populist Party." Farmers who lived in the less fertile and relatively isolated "Cross Timbers" region of North Texas tended to be strongly Populist. These hardscrabble farmers sympathized with the Populist message, while their "geographic location away from the social, cultural, and political hubs . . . fostered skepticism of authority exhibited in opposition to the Democratic disfranchising methods." Such attitudes prompted conservative Democrats to press even harder for franchise restriction. Historian J. Morgan Kousser has explained that, though the time of immediate political danger from Populists had passed by 1902, as long as the voting franchise remained relatively unrestricted, the conservative Democratic hegemony was threatened. According to Kousser, "Excluding Negroes from politics did have partisan as well as racial consequences; it deprived any anti-Democratic [Party] group of the hope of attracting the votes of those most persecuted by the political and economic status-quo." The push for the poll tax by conservative Democrats was a form of political insurance, a legal means of denying the possibility of a coalition forming against them.[2]

Poll taxes have a long history in the United States. Prior to the post-Civil War era, they were regarded primarily as a means of raising revenue to provide for public services. As Ogden notes, "The poll tax as a revenue measure is an ancient and obsolete device." But historically the tax on heads of households was not a voting requirement. Ironically, poll taxes were initially used to increase the number of voters, rather than limit it. According to Ogden, "in the early republic period poll taxes were used to widen the electorate by making payment of the tax a substitute for property requirements." The poll tax as a method to restrict suffrage, Ogden writes, "dates back primarily to the period from 1890 to 1908." It is important to observe that the years between 1890 and 1908 correspond neatly with the period in which Populism was at the height of its power and influence, especially in Texas. Though poll taxes had been used in Texas as a means of raising revenue, particularly for schools, for many years, it was only after the passage of the constitutional amendment of 1902 that proof of payment was actually required at the polling site. Thus, those who could not, or would not pay the tax, were restricted from voting once it passed.[3]

The architect of franchise restriction in Texas was Alexander W. Terrell, best known for the so-called Terrell Election Law. Terrell first suggested the poll tax as a means to restrict black suffrage in 1879 during the Sixteenth Texas Legislature. The measure passed in the Senate but failed in the House, partly due to the understanding that the proposed law would affect not only blacks, but poor whites as well. Terrell remained active in Texas political life for many years. But in 1893 President Grover Cleveland appointed Terrell as his minister to the Ottoman Empire. Terrell served in that capacity from 1893 to 1897, the very period during which Texas Populists exercised their greatest political influence. When

Terrell returned to Texas, he found its politics even more divisive than usual. In 1901 the state legislature passed a measure to place a poll tax amendment before the voters in the fall of 1902. At about the same time, Terrell won a seat in the Texas House of Representatives. He supported the poll tax amendment as "the first step toward purifying the ballot box." When Terrell re-entered the House in early 1903, he sought to cement the gains made by the voters' acceptance of the poll tax by shepherding through legislation that mandated primaries for all parties that received significant numbers of votes in campaigns for state offices. These became known as "white primaries," because blacks were excluded from participating in party primaries. The new laws also provided for secret ballots and forbade payment of poll taxes by any one other than the actual voter. On the surface, the Terrell election laws offered reform by reducing the "buying" of votes by party machines and taking politics out of the smoke-filled rooms of party conventions, but the laws strengthened the status-quo by limiting the electorate, to the benefit of conservative Democrats who dominated Texas.[4]

In Texas, the institution of a poll tax as a suffrage restriction necessitated a change in the state's fundamental law, and thus required placing a proposition on the ballot to amend the Texas Constitution. Obviously for such a proposition to pass, those holding power would have to convince a majority of Texas voters of the efficacy of and necessity for changing the state's election laws. Historian Donald S. Strong has stated the main arguments of the poll tax's proponents: "Three standard and time-honored arguments support the retention of the poll tax as a voting prerequisite. They are: that it is necessary to maintain 'white supremacy,' that it is essential to the support of the schools, and finally, that it is useful in keeping government in the hands of 'the better class of people.'" In Texas, clearly these arguments appealed to a wide range of voters, particularly to their insecurities and prejudices. Several of the arguments, such as the need to fund schools, sounded rational. Others appealed to the basest of human sentiments, including class issues and racism. Related arguments, such as the need to end the buying and selling of votes, were less convincing. In the final analysis, the arguments used would have to be strong and wide-ranging in order to convince a substantial percentage of the electorate—especially those in the lower middle class and lower class who would be disfranchised—to surrender their own right to vote by making the poll tax a suffrage requirement.[5]

The case of Cooke County, Texas, offers an opportunity to understand, on a small scale, the adoption of the poll tax as a suffrage restriction and the consequences of that action. This paper will analyze the results of five elections in Cooke County—the 1896 presidential and gubernatorial races, the 1900 and 1904 presidential races, and the 1902 poll tax proposition itself. Analysis of these elections provides answers to two questions. First, did significant numbers of people who would be disfranchised accept the arguments for the poll tax and vote for the amendment? Second, did the poll tax actually reduce the voter turnout in heavily Populist precincts? To do this, each of the previously mentioned elections will be analyzed on a precinct-by-precinct basis. Cooke County is located just south of the Red River and just north of the Dallas-Fort Worth area. The central portion of the county lies in the fertile Grand Prairie. The eastern and western portions of the county consist of less fertile Cross Timbers lands. In 1900, the county's population totaled 27,494. Of those, 796 were "foreign born," mostly Germans settled in the towns of Muenster and Lindsay. The county's African-American population was 1,875, or 7.6 percent of the total population.[6] The ethnic makeup of Cooke County, of course, as well as its location, had generated strong support for the Populists, and thus made the county a prime target for the poll tax.

To gauge how voters were courted on the poll tax, a look at local newspapers is in order. Unfortunately, Cooke County's major newspaper, *The Daily Hesperian*, is not extant for the necessary time period, but other area newspapers are helpful. These also provide an excellent representation of the arguments used by proponents of the tax in the region. In an editorial, the *Dallas Morning News* favored the proposition. The paper's editors gave not just one of the arguments cited by Strong, but all three, and even added a few others for good measure: "one of the strongest arguments in favor of the amendment is found in the frauds often perpetrated by repeaters, imported voters, vote buyers, and other brokers in corrupt politics . . . it will be in order to provide by statute that the tax must be paid and the receipt taken some months before the primary or the regular election . . . for safeguarding the ballot box." To make the point clear, the editors repeated, "One of the main objects of the amendment is to prevent fraudulent voting." They also wrote, "The tax is small and the returns are correspondingly large in Texas. The free school is of itself quite enough argument in favor of a change which is quite sure to add more than $100,000 to the education fund." The paper derided those who had previously refused to pay the poll tax for not doing their civic duty. The editors noted, "It is now claimed that as many as 100,000 men now refuse to pay even a poll tax . . . they patronize liberally and criticize eloquently the public schools to which they contribute no support . . . It goes without saying they should at least pay the poll tax." One wonders how those who had previously refused to pay the tax on principle, attempting to undermine the conservative Democrats by boycotting state elections, would have reacted to being accused of being irresponsible as citizens.[7]

One of the more interesting and dubious arguments for the passage of the poll tax amendment was addressed to Texas's black population and appeared as a letter to the editor of the *Dallas Morning News.* G. J. Grasty of Dallas declared "To the Colored Race of Texas" that: "There is a movement on foot to prejudice your minds against the poll tax amendment." He explained, "This law [that] you are asked to oppose by your vote means that every man, white or black, must pay a poll tax of $1.50 before he can vote. Does that cut the black man out any more than the white? One dollar of that tax goes to the school fund, which you share in equally with the whites." Concerning suffrage, he added, "These parties say it will disfranchise the black voter. To which I reply it will not disfranchise any honest, self-respecting colored or white man; but if you are a worthless, unreliable, dishonest fellow, with no desire to uplift your race, then you will and ought to be disfranchised. Grasty also addressed the issue of race: "What do these people say to you and about you? Not that they desire to elevate your race. No, no; but simply that they need you . . . . Now, see what they say about you: The colored race can be depended on to vote for the man who buys their votes, and the colored race can be depended on to vote against the poll tax, so they can sell out their ballots."[8] It does not seem likely that black voters would have been swayed by such arguments. In the days of Jim Crow laws, blacks knew better than anyone that their schools were only "separate," not "equal." Furthermore, it seems more likely that many in Grasty's target audience would have long been dissuaded from voting through harassment and threat, as was common in the day.

The Populist Party leadership was aware of the political ramifications of the poll tax. Ogden described a circular issued by the Populist Party State Headquarters in Dallas just two days before the 1902 vote. It asked readers to: "Read this—Lincoln's warning to the American people—'I bid the laboring people beware of surrendering a power which they already have, and which, when surrendered, will close the door of advancement to them and fix new disabilities upon them till all of liberty will be lost.'" The handbill added, "Lincoln saw the coming evil, and with prophetic eyes he saw what would result. His prophecy is now being fulfilled. On Tuesday next, the laboring people will be called upon to vote for an amendment to our Constitution, which, if carried out will rob them of their liberties at the ballot box. Every laboring man who loves liberty, who believes in freedom of suffrage, who prizes his rights of citizenship should vote against the poll tax amendment." The circular was signed by Milton Park, who had been the party's presidential candidate in the previous election, and by J. D. Johnston, the party's state chairman. Their warning went mostly unheeded, however, by many of the party's own members. The most remarkable aspect of the whole Populist movement was how its leaders opposed racism despite the leanings of their members in order to create a spirit of cooperation between black and white for achieving common goals. This proved to be the party's Achilles' heel. C. Vann Woodward wrote that, "Racism was exploited in the South with fantastic refinements and revolting excesses in the Populist period." The issue of race split the Populists at a time when they needed to be united to survive. The poll tax presented a means of both disfranchising blacks, while capitalizing on racial tensions in order to eliminate the party as a political force.[9]

Perhaps the *Dallas Morning News* coverage of the poll tax issue was more in line with the views of its urban, more liberal readers. More rural newspapers may have more accurately reflected the coverage that Cooke County residents would have seen. In January 1902, readers of the *Decatur News*, published in neighboring Wise County, read a story on a recent meeting of the Texas State Federation of Labor. The writer included an excerpt from a resolution of the federation that read: "Resolved, that we urge organized and unorganized labor throughout the state . . . to defeat the proposed amendment . . . making franchise rights dependent upon a poll tax receipt." In nearby Fannin County, readers of the *Bonham News* could review the full text of the proposed amendment reprinted in the paper in mid-August. Interestingly enough, the proposal made no mention of exactly how much the intended tax might be. One week later, the *Bonham News* printed a racially and politically charged editorial on the issue: "Republican politicians are certain to oppose the poll tax amendment . . . because it would deprive thousands of worthless negroes of the voting privilege . . . . Not one of them will go on the stump against the amendment because they know it is a righteous measure and cannot be successfully attacked." The editors appealed to the civic mindedness of its readers with, "The man who refuses to support the government has no moral right to a voice in its affairs . . . It is the duty of every honest, debt-paying, tax-paying citizen to work for the passage of the amendment." The *Bonham News* editorial probably offered a good representation of the views of both the newspaper editors and the voting public in North Texas.[10]

For good measure, some North Texas newspapers also reprinted the opinions on the topic of leading statesmen. The editors of the *Bonham News* noted, "We are certain we could not use our editorial space today for a better purpose than to present the views of Judge A. W. Terrell." Terrell's views as presented proved to be as succinct as they were racist: "Give Texas a pure ballot; give her this and all of the needed reforms will quickly follow . . . . We must place the elective franchise in the hands of those only who appreciate a free government . . . . The lazy and depraved element of every race, who will not pay even a poll tax for education, must be kept from the ballot box." Terrell made it plain that his intention with the poll tax amendment was not aimed only at blacks, but poor "wandering white men, Mexicans, and vagrants." The *Bonham News* also reprinted an article from the *Sherman Register* in Grayson County, which borders Cooke County on the east. The article contained an interview with former governor John H. Reagan on the poll tax. Reagan stated, "As I understand it, the citizen pays a poll tax as the price of the protection of his person and personal rights by the government . . . . A failure to comply . . . is a breach of his duty . . . . What right has anyone to enjoy the protection of the law and the privileges of the citizen who refuses . . . to contribute to the support of the government and the school fund? The law applies equally to the whites and the blacks."[11]

Reagan thus reiterated the same point on proper citizenship made earlier by Terrell, and others followed suit. In a letter to the editors of the *Bonham News*, published just a few days before the vote on the poll tax amendment, a "Cornfield Democrat" wrote, "Eternal vigilance is ever the price of liberty . . . five political parties are in the field with state tickets . . . It is known that every Socialist and Republican always votes when he hasn't been dead over three days. Let Democrats show the same diligence." This excerpt from his letter, "Just Before the Battle," is revealing, because it refers to the conservative Democratic perspective on the crowded political field of the time, which lay at the heart of the effort to limit the franchise.[12] Sadly, many of those they sought to disfranchise shared the same sentiments, and thus voted for a bill that ultimately restricted their rights.

At first glance, it may appear that poll taxes were so small that they could not have constituted a significant restriction on voting, but that is not the case. In Texas in 1902, the state levied a poll tax of $1.50, while the counties could levy a maximum of twenty-five cents and cities could levy a maximum poll tax of $1.00. In Cooke County, the Commissioner's Court approved a tax "for county poll, twenty-five cents per capita" on

May 15, 1902. Gainesville, the largest city in the county, was not incorporated until 1913, so there was no city poll tax. Thus in 1902, citizens of Cooke County faced a total poll tax of $1.75. On the surface, a $1.75 tax does not seem excessive. However, the aptly named T. F. Farmer provides an example of taxes Cooke County residents paid in 1902. Farmer owned 85 acres at an assessed value of $450.00, or $5.29 per acre. In addition, Farmer owned three horses assessed at $100.00, four head of cattle assessed at $40.00, and three hogs assessed at $5.00. On this property, Farmer paid a total of $7.04 in state and local taxes. The poll tax constituted $1.75 of those taxes or nearly 25 percent of Farmer's total taxes.[13]

To illustrate further the value of $1.75 in North Texas in 1902, one need only look at retail advertisements in the *Dallas Morning News* from that time. A luxury item such as an Eastman Kodak folding camera could be bought for $4.80. Grocery prices also provide comparisons. A grocery company advertised the following prices: twenty pounds of granulated sugar for $1.00, ten pounds of lard for $1.00, one pound of coffee for ten cents, five pounds of preserves for $1.35, and seven sacks of table salt for twenty-five cents. Clearly, $1.75 could buy several months' supply of food for a family. Obviously these poor farmers, when faced with the choice of feeding their families or voting, probably chose to feed their families with that amount of money.[14]

Feeding their families was much on the minds of Cooke County farmers as they voted in 1896, 1900, 1902, and 1904. In 1896 difficult economic circumstances led farmers to support Populist candidates. Falling farm prices and increasing debt had made times hard, and farmers were attracted to the Populist platform that promised help. The presidential election that year is significant, because William Jennings Bryan led the tickets of both the Populist and Democratic parties. Less widely known, but more telling of the political situation at that time, was the Texas governor's race. The candidates were Democrat Charles A. Culberson and Populist Jerome C. Kearby, with no Republican in the race. Analyses of these national and state elections in Cooke County reveal much about both the political mood of the time as well as the level of political participation in each precinct. The two races also provide a baseline of comparison with later elections in Cooke County.

What is immediately apparent in analyzing returns from the two races in 1896 is the growing strength and support for the Populists. The Populist presidential ticket led by Bryan out-polled the Republican ticket headed by William McKinley, 875 votes to 664. Of course, the Democratic ticket led by Bryan won the county by a wider margin, with 3,502 votes. The Texas governor's race of 1896 was even more indicative of strong Populist sentiment. In this election, Democrat Culberson received 3,404 votes, while Kearby, the Populist, received 1,764 votes or 34 percent. Clearly, in Cooke County, the Populist Party was a force to be reckoned with. The results of these two elections in certain precincts, as seen in Table 1, reveal even more about the magnitude of the challenge to the conservative Democrats.[15]

Table 1: Cooke County, Texas Precinct Analysis
Precincts with High Percentage of Populist Votes
Presidential and Governor's Race, November 3, 1896

Precinct	*Presidential*	*Governor's*
Burton	46%	60%
Mountain Springs	60%	71%
Burns	46%	64%
Bloomfield	37%	64%
Bulcher	41%	62%
Woodbine	32%	51%

Because the 1896 races created a lot of public interest and high voter turn-out, they are a good representation of the Cooke County electorate. As seen in Table 1, a precinct-by-precinct analysis of the governors' race indicates that while Populist candidate Kearby won 34 percent of the county-wide vote, he received clear majorities in six of Cooke County's twenty-five precincts. Analysis of the presidential race at the county level indicates strengths in the same precincts, although not as strongly because of vote splitting due to Bryan's presence on two tickets. The Populist presidential ticket received 20 percent of the vote in the average precinct and 17 percent countywide. Close examination of both of these races also indicates the changing political picture in that Populist Kearby received more votes for governor than the Republican presidential candidate McKinley by a margin of three to one. Thus, Populists enjoyed considerable support in the precincts of Burton, Mountain Springs, Burns, Bloomfield, Marysville, Bulcher, and Woodbine, enough to concern conservative Democrats.[16]

In Cooke County the election of 1900 did not generate as much interest as did that of 1896, and consequently voter turnout was lower. As far as presidential candidates are concerned, this election was a rematch of the previous election, with Democrat Bryan pitted against Republican McKinley. And there was no credible Populist candidate. The analysis of precinct results of the presidential election, presented in Table 2, is useful in two ways. First, since this election was mainly a contest between Republicans and Democrats, and the Populists did not split votes as they had in 1896, it is possible to identify those precincts with high Republican preference. Second, since this was the last national election before the institution of the poll tax, it provides the basis for a direct comparison of the effect of the tax in the next election. Analysis of the results of the 1900 presidential election reveals that the Republicans polled 20 percent of the vote in the county. As seen in Table 2, nine of thirty precincts in the county voted Republican at near or above the average rate. Of those, Mountain Springs, Bloomfield, Bulcher, and Woodbine had also voted heavily Populist in the previous election. It is likely that two of them, Bloomfield and Woodbine, as well as Gainesville's Ward 3, had substantial black populations as both voted Republican well above the county average in 1900. Exact identification of electoral precincts with substantial black populations is difficult as census date for 1900 was based upon the county's eight Justice of the Peace precincts rather than the thirty electoral precincts, making comparisons impossible.[17]

Table 2: Cooke County, Texas Precinct Vote Analysis
Precincts with High Percentage of Republican Voters
Presidential Election, November 6, 1900

Precinct	*Percentage*
Gainesville, Ward 1	17%
Gainesville, Ward 2	19%
Gainesville, Ward 3	29%
Gainesville, Ward 4	15%
Gainesville, Ward 5	23%
Mountain Springs	19%
Bloomfield	38%
Bulcher	20%
Woodbine	30%

When the people of Cooke County went to the polls on November 4, 1902, it seems that many of them would have had good reason to vote against the poll tax proposition, and thus against a conservative Democratic initiative, yet they did not. In fact, the proposition carried the county by a wide margin of 79 percent to 21 percent. As seen in Table 3, only five of twenty-nine precincts voted against the proposition, and only two by a significant margin. Of the five voting "against," Mountain Springs, Bloomfield, Bulcher, and Leo were among those that had voted heavily Populist in the 1896 election. Strangely enough, Lindsay, the precinct with the highest percentage "against" vote in the county, at 81 percent, was among the most conservative, voting strongly Democrat in the three elections analyzed. For example, in Lindsay, every single vote cast for governor or president in the 1896 elections was for the Democratic Party candidates. When the poll tax was passed, Lindsay was among those precincts suffering the least reduction in voter turn-out in the 1904 presidential election, with a 16 percent decline. This fact poses an interesting question that has no obvious answer—why would these people have voted "against" the poll tax? What is most striking, however, about the results of the poll tax vote in Cooke County is that many of the people who should have been most opposed to the tax–those who were ostensibly its targets–apparently voted for it. For example, the people of Burns and Burton precincts voted 83 percent and 86 percent, respectively, for the poll tax. These former Populist stronghold precincts were among those hardest hit by the tax.[18]

Table 3: Cooke County, Texas Precinct Analysis
Adopting the Poll Tax, November 4, 1902
Precincts that Voted Against

Precinct	*Percentage*
Mountain Springs	50%
Bloomfield	62%
Bulcher	51%
Leo	51%
Lindsay	81%

The presidential election of 1904 was the first following the institution of the poll tax. This election pitted Democrat Alton B. Parker against the incumbent Republican president, Theodore Roosevelt. Although the election was not particularly noteworthy, the decline in voter turn-out was significant and much greater than can be explained by mere apathy. Countywide, voting for that election was down 37 percent from 1900 and, by a stunning 52 percent, from the baseline 1896 election. In addition, the average precinct in the county saw a decline in voting of 44 percent from 1900 to 1904, which suggests that not just blacks and former Populists were affected by the poll tax. As shown in Table 4, thirteen of the county's precincts saw voting in the election drop by about half to three-quarters between 1900 and 1904. Every precinct in the county showed such significant declines in voting; in fact, only five precincts showed a decline of less than 30 percent. Among the precincts hardest hit by the poll tax were almost all those that had previously voted either heavily Populist in 1896 or Republican in 1900. The lone exception was the precinct of Woodbine that was about average with a 43 percent decline in voting. Clearly, the poll tax cut a wide swath across the electorate of Cooke County. As was probably the intention of its proponents, many of the former Populists and blacks of the county were disfranchised by the tax—as were many others.[19]

Table 4: Cooke County, Texas Precinct Vote Analysis Precincts with High Decline in Voting from 1900 Presidential Election, November 8, 1904

Precinct	*Decline*
Dexter	74%
Coesfield	60%
Burton	69%
Mountain Springs	63%
Burns	60%
Bloomfield	60%
Rosston	52%
Leo	62%
Bulcher	62%
Sivell's Bend	62%
Valley View	54%
Hemming	56%
Tyler Bluff	57%

One of the most puzzling aspects of the poll tax in Texas is its passage. Why would anyone vote in the affirmative to give up their right to vote without penalty? But in many cases, that is exactly what happened. In Cooke County, voting in presidential elections declined by 37 percent between 1900 and 1904, yet only 21 percent voted against the poll tax in 1902. Clearly, a substantial portion of the electorate voted for the tax either thinking it would not affect them or failing to care that it would. It is obvious that, although the poll tax preserved the political power of the conservative Democrat elite, they could not have secured its passage on their own. They had to have the support of the middle and lower classes. Again, why would these people have voted for the poll tax?[20]

Historians have offered several answers. The first is most often cited and refers to the role of the poll tax within the Jim Crow system. The basic argument is that white people at that time were so racially prejudiced against blacks that they were willing to forgo their own right to vote in order to deny the same to blacks. Correspondingly, some whites were willing to abdicate their own power and influence to the stewardship of the upper classes that could pay the tax. The second answer is an offshoot of the previous one, based on human nature. Those who were interested in limiting the voting rights of others realized that a bad harvest or a decline in the economy would mean that they could not pay their poll tax. But, as people are often inclined to do, they probably dismissed that possibility by thinking it "will never happen to me," and voted for the tax. The third is related to the poll tax's long history in the South and its use as a source of tax revenues to fund schools. Many people were accustomed to the tax and thought it was their civic duty to pay it, failing to think of the poll tax as franchise restriction.[21]

One of the more interesting arguments to explain the passage of the poll tax is that of historian J. Morgan Kousser, who contends that it was simply the product of the social and political beliefs of southerners at that time. He wrote: "Modifications in suffrage laws merely formalized changes produced by such extralegal forces as violence, intimidation, the growing hegemony of socioeconomic elite, and the decline in party competition." At the same time, he adds that "changes in electoral laws and procedures did in themselves have very substantial impact on both the scope of political participation and the mode of political activity in the South." Kousser's explanation for why people voted for the poll tax is thus relatively simple. Suffrage restriction, including the poll tax itself, fit a belief system held by the majority of the southern electorate that accepted and encouraged the disfranchisement of a substantial portion of society for the perceived good of the whole. This is the simplest explanation, and it does not exclude the possibility that people used the previous rationales to justify their votes for the poll tax.[22]

In the end, conservative Democrats were successful at eliminating the political threat posed by blacks and poor whites in Cooke County. Voter turnout decreased in every precinct—but especially in the Populist and Republican precincts. Clearly, many voters disfranchised themselves by voting for the poll tax amendment—only five of the twelve hardest hit precincts voted against the tax. The poll tax, first suggested by Terrell in 1879, could have been instituted at that time if it was merely to restrict black suffrage. But, the tax failed then because many legislators feared it would disfranchise their own constituents. The measure languished only to be revived following the successes of the Populists in the mid 1890s. The poll tax effectively guaranteed the continued domination of the social and political elite. Thus, the poll tax was much more than just an effort to disfranchise blacks. In fact, blacks, who comprised only 7.6 percent of the population, were already out-voted and had little political influence. To a large extent, conservative Democrats were able to harness the political and social beliefs of the electorate to secure a less competitive, and thus more favorable, political environment. Furthermore, with voter turnout in the 1904 presidential election down by nearly 40 percent from 1900, many who were not necessarily targets of the tax were disfranchised as well.

The mandatory poll tax proved greatly effective at limiting the electorate of Cooke County, Texas—and numbers reflect this. Data in the form of statistics are one of the most dependable yet least used tools of historians. Political scientist V. O. Key's use of quantitative analysis in *Southern Politics in State and Nation* provided a sociopolitical snapshot of the American South at the time of its publication in 1949. Key noted that there had as yet been no "comprehensive" analysis of southern politics and likened historians' understanding of the subject to "caricature." The work is still cited more than sixty years after its publication. Historians Randolph B. Campbell and Richard G. Lowe used quantitative analysis to reveal the realities of slaveholding in Texas in their works, *Planters and Plain Folks* and *Wealth and Power in Antebellum Texas*. They found that Texans, no matter what their social class, were prosperous and united by both agriculture and support for the institution of slavery. They also found that the majority of wealth in the state was concentrated in the hands of less than 10 percent of the people. Moreover, Texas' political leaders were more likely to be wealthy. Following in their footsteps, this quantitative analysis of voting records in Cooke County, following imposition of the poll tax, suggests that a similar pattern of racism and class division persisted well into the twentieth century, reinforced by the passage of laws that preserved the hegemony of conservative Democrats for many years to come.[23]

Notes

1. Alwyn Barr, *Reconstruction to Reform: Texas Politics, 1876–1906* (Austin: University of Texas Press, 1971), 143–45. For a discussion of the Populist movement's effect on Texas politics, see Randolph B. Campbell, *Gone to Texas: A History of the Lone Star State*, 2nd ed. (New York: Oxford University Press, 2012), 320–31.

2. Fredric D. Ogden, *The Poll Tax in the South* (University: University of Alabama Press, 1958) 18, 20; James T. Carawan, "Populism and the Poll Tax: The Politics and Propaganda of Suffrage Restriction in North Texas, 1892–1904" (Master's Thesis, University of North Texas, 1997), 80; J. Morgan Kousser, *The Shaping of Southern Politics: Suffrage Restrictions and the Establishment of the One Party South* (New Haven: Yale University Press, 1974), 7.

3. Ogden, *Poll Tax in the South,* 2, 18, 20.

4. Lewis L. Gould, *Alexander Watkins Terrell: Civil War Soldier, Texas Lawmaker, Diplomat* (Austin: University of Texas Press, 2004), 74, 123, 149–52.

5. Donald S. Strong, "American Government and Politics: The Poll Tax; the Case of Texas," *The American Political Science Review* 38 (Aug. 1944): 695.

6. Ron Tyler, et al., eds., *New Handbook of Texas*, 6 vols. (Austin: Texas State Historical Association, 1997), 2: 308–9; United States Bureau of the Census, Twelfth Census of the United States, 1900, Texas, Cooke County, Schedule 1, National Archives, Washington, D.C.

7. *Dallas Morning News*, Sept. 28, 1902, p. 16.

8. Ibid., Nov. 2, 1902, p. 6.

9. Ogden, *Poll Tax in the South,* 18–19; C. Vann Woodward, *The Burden of Southern History* (Baton Rouge: Louisiana State University Press, 1968), 156–57.

10. *Decatur News*, Jan. 17, 1902; *Bonham News*, Aug. 15 and 22, 1902.

11. Ibid., Oct. 10, 1902.

12. Ibid., Sept. 5, Oct. 10 and 31, 1902.

13. Ogden, *Poll Tax in the South,* 33, 46; Commissioner's Court Records, County Clerk's Office, County Courthouse, Gainesville, Texas, Vol. 6, p. 510; Assessment of Property Tax for 1902, Cooke County, Texas, 14 (Microfilm: University of North Texas, Willis Library). Although the poll tax did not become a suffrage requirement until 1903, taxes were the same as in 1902, thus the use of T. F. Farmer's tax records for that year gives an accurate view of the poll tax's portion of his total tax burden.

14. See advertisements in *Dallas Morning News,* Sept. 28, 1902, p. 9.

15. Election Returns, County Clerk's Office, County Courthouse, Gainesville, Tex., Vol. 2, pp. 110–13.

16. Ibid., Vol. 2, pp. 110–16.

17. Ibid., Vol. 3, pp. 1–5.

18. Ibid., Vol. 2, p. 39, and Vol. 3, pp. 64–69.

19. Ibid., Vol. 3, pp. 64–69.

20. Ibid., Vol. 3, pp. 64–69.

21. The first argument in this passage is a statement of common thought on the subject with some influence by J. Morgan Kousser on the last point. The third argument in the passage is influenced by Fredric D. Ogden.

22. Kousser, *Shaping of Southern Politics,* 3, 5. Ironically, this supports the assertion of Randolph B. Campbell that the history of Texas is essentially southern.

23. V. O. Key Jr., *Southern Politics in State and Nation* (New York: Alfred Knopf, 1949), 1; Richard G. Lowe and Randolph B. Campbell, *Planters and Plain Folk: Agriculture in Antebellum Texas* (Dallas: Southern Methodist University Press, 1987), 189–90; Randolph B. Campbell and Richard G. Lowe, *Wealth and Power in Antebellum Texas* (College Station: Texas A&M University Press, 1977), 135–36.

PART V:

Texas and the Twentieth Century

Ladies Pavilion dominates the Corpus Christi waterfront in this postcard. Courtesy of Corpus Christi Public Library

Investing in Urban: The Woman's Monday Club and the Entrepreneurial Elite of Corpus Christi, Texas[1]

Jessica Brannon-Wranosky

Newly urban areas in the South, around the turn of the twentieth century, promised opportunity to thousands of people looking to make their mark. Spread across the region, cities sprung up in areas where plantation and ranching agriculture was once the primary path to regional influence. Like most of the South, Corpus Christi in 1900 was surrounded by a mostly rural landscape, but a growing class of optimistic urban social elites believed that a different future lay ahead for the small seaside city. Middle class by national economic standards, this group included the town's leading lawyers, storeowners, doctors, and bankers. As a group, they wielded much influence, but it was the women among them, including their wives, who made some of the greatest strides in the early Progressive-era reforms in Corpus Christi.[2]

Very few families in the area, except ranch tycoons like the Driscolls, Klebergs, and Kings, had achieved upper-class status by 1900. These few families comprised the area's landed rural elite, who did not stand to gain if Corpus Christi became an urban epicenter. Their financial position hinged on increased agricultural production and land holdings. Conversely, those who stood to gain the most from the area's increased urbanization needed population growth to feed their service-oriented businesses, civic innovations, and political aspirations. Thus, in Corpus Christi, traditional middle-class professionals became entrepreneurial elites, separate from the rural elite. They invested time, money, and effort in city development. If it did not succeed, they would gain nothing, but if the city flourished, the possibilities were limitless. As historian Don Doyle argues, "It was largely by the process of city building that local business leaders became a class, a social entity bound by a similar view of the world, by common interests, and by associations and instruments of power that could advance those interests." It was as part of this group that the urban, educated, white, and economically secure membership of the Woman's Monday Club (WMC) developed.[3]

A closer look at the members and activities of the WMC during its developmental years and first decade of existence provides a better understanding of how urban entrepreneurial elite groups in southern cities created an identity separate from the predominantly agrarian southern powerbase and established themselves at the top of their local social hierarchy. The WMC derived its opportunities for local and regional leadership from two distinct sources. First, its members and their families occupied social, economic, and politically central positions in Corpus Christi. Second, the women's status also depended upon their civic booster activities, especially between 1900 and 1910. Their boosterism bridged the old agricultural ideals of privatized civic development with recent trends for the increased expectation of government-sanctioned civic services through efforts to clean, plan, and advertise the city in modern terms.

Shaping this urban entrepreneurial elite went through a number of stages before the WMC engaged in organized civic activism. Early on, these urban elites started strengthening local class distinctions with the formation of The Myrtle Club in 1883, claiming to be Corpus Christi's first social organization. The *Corpus Christi Caller* reported before the club's first anniversary that, "its membership comprises many of the leading men of the city and county who take evident pride in its success." This male-only association was organized for the purpose of studying literature, but it soon opened clubrooms in the Doddridge and Davis bank building. The group started with great enthusiasm; its members met often, a local storeowner sold Myrtle Club Cigars, and plans were laid for a private club library. Through the life of the club, members included influential early citizens, current and future mayors, and city aldermen.[4]

Early in 1884, the Myrtle Club established "Ladies Day" and opened their clubroom to socially elite women for four days each month. By late that year, the men's organization only congregated semi-annually. Within the next few months, though, Myrtle Club members and their wives reorganized as The Oliver Wendell Holmes Club. This association, established in early 1885 as a literary society, flourished through 1887. This group of men and women met weekly and discussed contemporary literature, literary classics, poetry, and music. In turn, the members of the Holmes Club created a new literary organization called the Fortnightly Circle, which held its first meeting on December 14, 1893. The last recorded meeting of the Fortnightly Circle was a mere six months after the first, May 25, 1894, with no explanation of its disbanding, and the town's literary activity appears to have waned for a couple of years. The next phase in Corpus Christi's literary history began in 1897 with selective personal invitations sent out to former members of the Holmes Club from Ella Dickinson Scott. This gathering was the inaugural meeting of the WMC.[5]

Including the host, all eight WMC charter members present on the first night were members of the city's social elite. Even though certain areas of the South, like Corpus Christi, embraced limited change like urbanization, the public domain was still racially segregated. The WMC was not unique in this nature; its members appear to have been willing participants in the exclusionary practices of the Jim Crow South. For decades to follow, all members recorded from the club's first meeting in 1897 were white. Furthermore, most members and their husbands were born in the United States. Among the club's twenty members who appear on the 1900 United States Census, only two were not native-born, Olivia Hirsch (France) and Margaret Coleman (England). Furthermore, of these members' seventeen husbands, only two were born outside the United States, David Hirsch (Germany) and Thomas Hickey (Ireland). Of the remaining eighteen members, only four were born in non-South states, as were four of the husbands. In 1910 none of the twenty-four club members was foreign-born, but three of the twenty husbands were not native-born: Perry Garrett (Canada), William Gerhardt (Germany), and H. S. Springwell (England). Moreover, only three club members came from non-South states, as did five of their husbands. Thus, of the WMC members and their husbands who appear on the 1900 and/or the 1910 United States census, the vast majority were born in the southern United States. Other historians have found similar trends when investigating the background of urban progressives in the New South. Historian Don Doyle, for example, also found that entrepreneurial elites in other southern cities had moved westward from different areas in the South in search of familiar places to establish new powerbases outside the control of older, more entrenched, exclusionary power structures. The majority of WMC members and their husbands fit this description.[6]

To further illustrate that the WMC consisted of individuals trying to establish a status separate from the predominantly agrarian southern powerbase, the majority of WMC members' financial resources came from non-agricultural positions. By 1910, the county population had more than doubled, from 10,439 in the 1900 census to 21,955. While more than 50 percent of the population growth in Nueces County during this decade moved to rural areas, of the seventeen WMC members' husbands who appear on the 1900 census, only three individuals made their living from agriculture. This number dropped to just two out of twenty-three of the members and husbands holding jobs in 1910, with Livingston Collins the only one in both years to be counted as an agriculturalist. Therefore, at each survey year, a significant majority of the WMC members and their husbands derived their economic well being from non-agricultural enterprises.[7]

The political power that WMC members possessed came from the fact that, like most federation clubwomen, they were well connected at the local, state, and national levels. A survey of the club's membership in 1900 showed that only three were not married: Fannie Southgate was widowed and Henrietta Mallory and Mary Thompson were unmarried. Of the remaining seventeen members, two were married to local officials. Edna Hopkins's husband, W. B., was the county judge, and Hattie Luter's husband, Henry, was the county clerk. Also, Carrie Chandler's husband, Samuel, was the Presbyterian minister. By 1910, the number of members not married increased to five: Bessie Bellinger was widowed, and Louise Brunet, Mildred Seaton, Olive Schropshire, and Mary Thompson were all unmarried. Of the twenty-one members and their husbands who were employed, eight persons held positions with possible community influence. This subgroup included a newspaper publisher, newspaper editor, district judge, county judge, county clerk, secretary of the Corpus Christi Civic Club, president of the Corpus Christi National Bank, two public school teachers, and a minister. Furthermore, of the twenty-four members, five of the women were wage earners. Maude Gerhardt, for example, worked as an editor for the *Corpus Christi Caller* and assumed the position of publisher of the *Texas Sun* for a few years after the death of her first husband, John S. Hardwicke.[8]

The connections with local government officials presented the members of the WMC with opportunities to influence city decision making. Even though state and national women's federations frowned upon overt political lobbying as late as 1902, leaders of such organizations nevertheless understood that opportunities existed for members to use their familial and social links. That year, the state's federation leaders concluded the following:

> It was decided that the [Texas] Federation as an organization wished to eschew even the appearance of meddling in matters political, hence no legislative committee had been provided.

> Following out this policy no lobbying would be permitted, but when one considered that the husbands, fathers, brothers and sweethearts of clubwomen, were men of influence in affairs of state, it was conclusive that the clubwomen were not without ways and means of influencing legislation. Hence the custom was adopted, that the [Texas Federation] president should issue circular letters to each club asking that in the home and social circles the influence of each member should be used with voters who could directly influence legislation. Thus was created a great, silent force for the enactment and enforcement of good laws.

The Texas Federation thus made a crucial developmental transition. Although they publicly stood against direct lobbying efforts, the organization henceforth encouraged women's influence and connections with men of power in politics.[9]

The impact of this shift was clear. For example, parties at the home of Gus (G. R.) and Ella Scott were legendary, none more so than the gathering they hosted for William Jennings Bryan when he came to Corpus Christi in 1908 and 1909 to recuperate from his presidential defeat by William Howard Taft. Years later, Ella Scott told an interviewer for the *Corpus Christi Caller*: "I invited a number of people and a crowd of 30 or 40 showed up." The writer added that the Scott home on South Broadway was "surrounded by what was described as the finest display of horses and buggies seen here in years."[10]

Ella Scott also serves as an example of the status achieved by some WMC members. She served from 1891–1893 as one of the vice presidents at large for the Women's World's Fair Exhibit Association of Texas during the lifetime of that organization. This association connected socially elite women from all over the state to regional and national networking and training in organizational activities. Its achieved purpose was to plan, build, and manage the Texas Building at the 1893 World's Fair in Chicago, Illinois. The building served as the Lone Star State's only representative structure at the event. Many historians consider it to have marked the gateway to the twentieth century, because of its "watershed" effect on American culture and society through its focus on American progress and innovation.[11]

At different points during her lifetime, Scott also served as director of the Corpus Christi National Bank, vice president and later life member of the Texas Women Banker's Association, president of the Texas Federation's Fifth District, and chair of the Parks and School Grounds

Committee for the Texas Federation. She also held the office of president for the City Federation of Corpus Christi. Texas's first General Federation president, Anna J. Hardwicke Pennybacker, nicknamed Scott, "Admiral of the Valley." In addition to her many honors, the Texas Federation named her as a founder of its headquarters in Austin and a life member of its board of directors. In addition to Scott's talents in financing and leadership, she was also an effective fundraiser. Her obituary in the *Corpus Christi Caller* included reminiscences from a friend that "she had a little gray horse and a buggy, and whenever a merchant would see the rig approaching he'd reach for his check book because he knew Mrs. Scott was collecting donations for some worthy cause."[12]

Scott's family connections were not just through her and her husband, who served as county attorney. Her son-in-law, Walter Pope, was District Attorney for Texas's Twelfth Judicial District, held the office of Corpus Christi City Attorney, and at one time owned the *Corpus Christi Times.* He was also a member of the Texas House of Representatives for twenty-two years. During his service in the Texas House, he was involved in the formation of Texas A&I University in Kingsville and sponsored the 1919 bill to create the Port of Corpus Christi. Scott's only child, Lucille Pope, was also a WMC member in later years, further extending the family connections between the organization and local leaders.[13]

The Scotts were not the only well-connected members of the WMC. Prominent member Maude Gerhardt almost single handedly started Corpus Christi's welfare program and served as an advocate for children for more than forty years until 1949, only the last seven of which she was a paid employee of the county. Gerhardt also served as managing editor for the *Corpus Christi Times* for one year, in 1910, and much later conducted a woman's hour on Corpus Christi's radio station KGFI. WMC member Ida Durand Redmond held the office of president of the Texas Federation from 1923 to 1924. During her term, she chaired the State Committee on Education and often influenced national federation work.[14]

The WMC fit already defined criteria as local social elites, but both the clubwomen and their husbands occupied the position of economic elites in Corpus Christi as well for two reasons. First, many of them owned businesses. In 1900, three of the members' husbands were agriculturalists, as discussed, but there were also an exports agent, a real estate merchant, and a banker. By 1910, those whose businesses obviously depended on Corpus Christi's growth and increased urbanization included a newspaper publisher, a banker, the owner of a boarding house, the president of the local bank, a building contractor, and a lumber yard owner. Second, these businesses were doing well. A survey of the Nueces County tax rolls for 1900 and 1910 reveal that the members of the WMC and their husbands held moderate to upper-middle wealth among the taxpayers listed by the collector. The highest for either year was Henrietta M. King, with \$3,555,665 in holdings in 1910. This far outweighed the assets of anyone in the WMC. More important, change was afoot. In 1900, Perry Doddridge had around \$38,880, the greatest assets of anyone associated with the WMC; in 1910, Gus Scott had the most among the WMC group, listing his total assets at around \$49,485. This increase reflects the improvement in finances among the members of the WMC as a whole. Their individual average worth in 1910 was approximately 165 percent of what it was in 1900, and the mean worth for the group was almost four times what it had been a decade earlier. This financial increase among WMC members indicates that their community investment had already begun to pay off, further defining their position as economic elites.[15]

The clubwomen's livelihood, along with that of their family, hinged on increased growth of the local population, but potentially so did their social position in the changing cityscape. Club work, which incorporated civic booster activities, offered these women the chance to define Corpus Christi's public space on their own terms. The WMC often led activities in the city with the understanding that a clean and safe environment offered opportunities for increased tourism and residual growth. This had the potential of adding more individuals and families to patronize the WMC's family businesses. The types and leaders of the boosterism also increased the likelihood that the growing population consisted of those willing to invest in the established entrepreneurial elites' vision of what Corpus Christi should be. Therefore, as economic and social elites, WMC members often participated in and led civic booster activities.

This group of clubwomen understood what a city needed to compete with other emerging urban areas. Corpus Christi needed amenities that included clean beaches, public parks, and safe recreational areas. Furthermore, the city's leaders wanted to let potential residents know about what their area had to offer—in short, they needed to "sell" the city through booster activities. The WMC's first large community building project became the Ladies Pavilion. The club's members in 1903 began the planning and construction of the building, located on a Bay Shore dock in downtown Corpus Christi, where the T-Head is currently situated. Years later, Ella Scott looked back on the Ladies Pavilion as her "pet project" and fondly remembered helping to pay for the building by serving tamales, coffee, and salads. Club members also bought and sold stock, held stockholder's meetings, and helped with construction and maintenance. The purpose of the site was to hold functions like dances, lyceum performances, social programs, and Fourth of July celebrations. Events like these increased community involvement in activities and encouraged tradition building. These structures were vital in community building, because they provided new places for the public to come together that were not associated with traditional powers, such as a church or the workplace.[16]

Before the pavilion was built, Corpus Christi residents celebrated the Fourth of July by holding a water carnival. Among the entertainments was the "landing of Columbus [played by postmaster] Julius Henry, staged … at the foot of Starr Street," as well as a parade. Yet local officials ended the yearly festivities after they were rained out several years in a row. The problem with the lack of consistent traditions was that individuals were less likely to congregate. The result was fewer activities and less community. The Ladies Pavilion provided a reliable location for residents to interact, and it placed the WMC at center stage. The building was an indoor arena with a stage designed for performances such as "A Dream of Beautiful Women." Long after its loss due to flooding during the 1916 hurricane, locals fondly remembered the concerts, parties, and Fourth of July celebrations held on its festive grounds. Furthermore, decades later, locals also recalled "the elaborate refreshments prepared for these affairs."[17]

Soon after the Ladies Pavilion's construction, the *Waco Times-Herald* reported that the WMC "influence in the community is already recognized," adding that "when the Monday Club inaugurates a move, the citizens respond almost as a unit." In September 1903, the WMC had begun studying William Shakespeare's *Julius Caesar*. Kate Friend, who was a Shakespearean scholar and Texas Federation clubwoman, as well as the society, literature, and drama editor for the *Waco Times-Herald*, designed the course. The WMC entertained Friend at their October 12 meeting. That night, she gave a lecture at the Ladies Pavilion for Corpus Christians entitled, "Shakespeare's Stratford and His Literary London." The proceeds of the evening went to the civic endeavors of the WMC, and Friend was reportedly so impressed with the members and the town that she wrote the laudatory article in the *Waco Times-Herald,* which also said, in part:

> In the evening, the pavilion was opened, a Mexican band engaged, and the clubwomen with more than the usual number of willing husbands, and friends formed a representative audience

> for Miss Friend's illustrated talk on Twentieth Century Stratford. Corsicana, which claims to be the cleanest town in the state, must look well to her laurels, when Corpus Christi comes into competition. In this regard, it is the modest city. While the club women did not superintend the cleaning, they take just pride in the fact that it has been done.[18]

By the end of October 1903, the WMC had organized a petition drive that marked the beginning of a decade-long struggle for civic sanitation, cleaning, and beautification. In their petition, the clubwomen urged the removal of the fish houses and saloons from local beaches by the city council. The WMC initiated the petition because of the health hazards that both types of establishments reportedly posed. According to them, these businesses ignored hygienic food preparation guidelines and left rotting fish entrails and oysters "to cause sickness in our midst." They were "also unsanitary because all such places such as those above mentioned have [outhouses] connected with them and in use, thereby causing offensive excrements to be deposited along our bay front all the while." Lastly, the WMC argued that the poorly constructed buildings on the beaches marred "one of the most attractive and inviting features of our city."[19]

The petition drive suggests that the clubwomen understood that unclean areas of the city hurt potential growth and development; furthermore, they knew the link this had to economic prosperity. The women tried appealing to the business-focused councilmen and mayor by pointing out that the changes would pose "little or no expense" and that if the bay front was "improved, [then, it could] be attractive and furnish a pleasant resort for ourselves and our visitors every evening year round." Furthermore, the clubwomen stated that "disreputable" individuals lurked in this area, and for that matter, vagrants in Corpus Christi increasingly accosted women in the streets. They concluded the petition with a call to arms, asking "the men of our town [to] join us in this, feeling that by such a united effort, all this can and will soon be accomplished." The club's recruitment of men for civic improvement marks their entry into local politics on behalf of the entrepreneurial elite. In their past efforts, the club usually focused on fundraising for their projects; with the petition, the women undertook a more active role, reaching across gender lines in an attempt to organize locals for the improvement of Corpus Christi's sanitary conditions.[20]

Hygiene concerns, like those expressed by the WMC, grew nationally and internationally and often became synonymous with civic activism aimed at creating a better quality of life. The professionalization of medicine changed how progressives viewed pure food and sanitation. In 1876, when Louis Pasteur and Robert Koch "proved that a specific microorganism caused a specific disease," a new world opened for medical study. The causal discoveries of disease from viral and parasitic predators soon followed. Furthermore, by the 1890s, Ellen Swallow Richard started teaching classes in "sanitary chemistry" and analyzed drinking water at the Massachusetts Institute of Technology. Moreover, Marion Talbot taught "sanitary science" at the University of Chicago, and when the Columbian Exposition opened, Bertha Palmer's opening speech at the Woman's Building emphasized "enlightened homemaking."[21]

In Texas at about the same time, the Dallas Federation of Women's Clubs began pushing its city for a water filtration plant, and in Galveston the Women's Health Protective Association funded a city sanitation survey. Clubwomen gained more information about health and sanitation on a daily basis. The WMC not only knew about these developments but also joined in the effort. After the Corpus Christi club presented its petition, the city council formed a committee to check into the matter. Despite the women's lobbying efforts, the city council committee returned with a declaration in February 1904, regarding the sanitation part of the petition, that "nothing could be done except to enforce the ordinance now in existence, which was being done." The clubwomen were ahead of local government officials in determining the steps needed for the city's further growth and success. Not until the end of the decade did local governmental officials revisit the issue, again at the WMC's insistence, and increase sanitation measures with regard to beachfront business practices.[22]

The lack of governmental action did not stop the WMC from trying to make Corpus Christi competitive in seeking the resources and recognition that were necessary for success. Potential residents and businesses looking to relocate often sought well-planned cities for efficiency, healthy living conditions, and aesthetics. One of the keys to a well-planned city was the conservation of nature within the increasingly urban environment. While the club members went back and forth with city officials over the sanitation petition, in November 1903 the WMC hosted a "reception to the citizens of Corpus Christi" at the Ladies Pavilion to celebrate Scott's appointment to the Texas Federation civics committee. At the reception, Corpus Christi women led discussions on the role of local citizens in civic work and tried to increase local interest in the matter. The newspaper reported the social aspects of the event without emphasizing its political purposes. The reception did not have an immediate effect on the decisions of city leaders regarding the petition, but the council did not forget the issues that arose concerning public safety.[23]

Examination of city council records during this era shows that its decisions regarding issues were usually reactions to suggestions made by citizens. Since the pattern was reaction, not action, it is likely that the council, when they discussed vagrancy in 1905, was reconsidering an issue raised by the WMC petition two years earlier. There is no other indication in council records of a source other than the clubwomen's request to act against vagrancy and disorderly conduct prior to council members passing an ordinance that outlawed disorderly conduct in September 1905. The ordinance's thirty-eight sections forbade making noise, swearing, and breaking the peace at public businesses, as well as using "obscene language," yelling or shrieking, and the indecent exposure or the display of "any pistol or other deadly weapon in a manner calculated to disturb the inhabitants of such place or private house." Sections six and eleven responded to the parts of the petition presented by the WMC to the council requesting that local officials intervene and stop the vagrants who accosted women in the streets of Corpus Christi. Although it had taken some time, the city council did respond to the concerns of the clubwomen.[24]

During this period, local physician and Corpus Christi mayor Hiram H. Segrest read a letter into council minutes on April 11, 1904. Among Segrest's suggestions was that "the sanitary committee [see] that all persons that breed mosquitoes or that are liable to breed disease are aborted." The mayor wanted the councilmen to approve an ordinance that required residents to reduce areas on their property prone to infestation by mosquito larvae. The following month, city attorney Delmas Givens reported to the council that "for the prevention of yellow fever and other infectious contagious diseases," the proposal appeared legal. He had checked both the charter of Corpus Christi and Texas statutes, and nothing in either contradicted the council's proposed rule. The five-part ordinance required the owners of all wells, lakes, ponds, and other receptacles of stagnant water within the town limits to screen their water reserves or coat them with oil. It provided for legal enforcement by the city marshal and the fining of citizens found in violation of this law. The council passed the ordinance, followed soon thereafter by the county commissioners, who congratulated Corpus Christi on acting to further good health.[25]

Although it appeared Mayor Segrest initiated the civic sanitation direction, the source was most likely the WMC. Segrest had been mayor since 1902, but the council had not discussed specific sanitation efforts before the clubwomen's 1904 petition for sanitation laws. The mayor's request and the council's actions mirror a directive outlined in a letter written that year by Ella Scott and the Texas Federation's civic committee. The Texas Federation's annual handbook for 1904–1905, presented to Texas clubwomen in November 1904, included the text of the letter. In part, it requested that Texas Federation affiliates pay "especial attention" to the "water supply [and] the covering and proper care of cisterns." Furthermore, Segrest moved in the same social circles with WMC members and their husbands, and he attended the First Presbyterian Church with many clubwomen, including Scott. In 1909, correspondence regarding a clash between the city council and the WMC over control of Corpus Christi's Artesian Park revealed previously unrecorded political lobbying between Segrest and Scott. In efforts aimed at pointing out the council's errors, the clubwomen referenced a verbal agreement reached in 1904 between Mayor Segrest and Scott as president of the WMC that gave control of the park to the latter group.[26]

Mosquitoes that bred yellow fever continued to plague Corpus Christi. The *Corpus Christi Caller* often ran articles that addressed the push for more eradication measures regarding the dreaded parasite, and many of the pieces gave specific information on how to do so. The issue was not just local. New Orleans suffered a yellow-fever epidemic in 1905, and the fear of death by plague swept over the nation the same year. *The Ladies' Home Journal* walked readers through the processes of eliminating breeding areas. In July 1905, nearly a year and a half after the council turned down the women's petition requesting sanitation and public decency changes, the aldermen of Corpus Christi passed an ordinance "providing for a health inspector," and it was modified the following November. In March 1906, a detailed discussion concerning the town's mosquito problem dominated a WMC meeting. As a result, the members passed a resolution to "interest [themselves] actively in the warfare against the [insects]." By the end of the year, the club petitioned the council to take up the fight against mosquitoes. A year later, the WMC continued the effort. Resolving "to take immediate steps in the extermination of the mosquito," the members in April 1907 offered to help the city council in eradicating the dangerous insect.[27]

Simultaneous with the mosquito eradication efforts, in June 1904 the WMC dedicated an entire meeting to a new potential project for the club: civic improvements to Artesian Square. Something similar had been discussed a year before, but nothing happened at that time. This plan was actually a hybrid of progressive campaigns, one dedicated to the preservation of historical sites and the other to the creation of municipal parks. Similar initiatives had focused on national historic sites such as George Washington's Mount Vernon, and in February 1904 the Daughters of the Republic of Texas (DRT) had begun work for the purchase of the Alamo in San Antonio. At the Texas Federation's meeting the following November, leaders asked members to support the DRT in saving the Alamo from destruction. For Corpus Christi, the WMC put its own spin on the campaign by combining it with the trend of conserving city space for municipal parks.[28]

America's increasingly urban areas required that progressives take measures to ensure that parts of the nation remained somewhat undeveloped. Municipal park movements worked to bring healthy environments into cities that lacked them and were part of the first urban planning movements. The idea of setting an area aside for something other than private buildings was relatively new. Conceptualizing public use of the outdoor space revolutionized how urban leaders viewed their municipalities. Municipal planning for parks eventually spread to roads, streetlights, and other public amenities. The General Federation of Women's Clubs' civic committee and its local affiliates, including the WMC, advocated many of these progressive projects.[29]

In Corpus Christi, the WMC focused on converting Artesian Square into Artesian Park. The square was originally the campsite and an artesian well dug by General Zachary Taylor's troops when they were sent to Texas when war with Mexico loomed after annexation in 1845. In 1854, the city's founder, Henry Lawrence Kinney, deeded the site to Corpus Christi. By 1900, the town had installed a bandstand, water fountain, and walkway, but it was a small area with few attractions for visitors. The square was the closest thing Corpus Christi had in ties to Texas's great battles, like the one at the Alamo, and local clubwomen decided it needed preservation. WMC members used their fundraising skills to promote concerts, receptions, and rummage sales and raised enough money for additional walkways in the square. In September 1904, the women decided to petition the city council for help. It turned the matter over to Mayor Segrest and authorized him to negotiate with the women. It was unclear what the club members had requested, but since they continued fundraising efforts for improving the square, it was possible that they needed the council's permission to renovate the town's property. The club continued discussing Artesian Square and fundraising for the site through the years of 1904 and 1905, but the council often did not respond to their communications.[30]

In May 1907, the WMC asked the council for funds to purchase lots adjacent to Artesian Square. It appropriated $1,500, but the clubwomen determined that the cost was actually $2,300. Therefore, it was up to them to raise the remaining $800. The husband of a member of the WMC Artesian Committee agreed to buy and hold the lots until the club could raise additional funds. In January 1908, the Artesian Committee presented its plans for the creation of Artesian Park. They included leveling the two new lots and adding cement walks. This added another $700 to the cost and brought the deficit to $1,500. After a vote, each member pledged fifty cents per month toward the sum. The WMC also held concerts, plays, and other fundraisers at the park, and planned to superintend the area for as long as necessary.[31]

Although the clubwomen expected to direct park planning measures, in keeping with their position at the top of the city's hierarchy, elected officials had different ideas. The key issue of ownership and control over the municipal park soon led to two fights between the city council and the WMC. To begin, the additional lots were deeded directly from the original owner, Dudley Ward, to the City of Corpus Christi. This undercut the WMC's claims of control. The conflict escalated when, for an unknown reason, city attorney Delmas Givens held onto the deeds for an extended time. Then, perhaps fearful of the council's reaction to his delay regarding Artesian Park, Givens refused the WMC's request to submit the extra paperwork necessary to first transfer the lots to them and then to the city. Through much conflict over the subject and correspondence with Givens, the club eventually dropped this part of the fight in July 1908, with the understanding that the WMC would receive credit in council records for their efforts.[32]

Although the credit to the WMC exists in the rarely read and barely accessible council minutes, this was still an important message. Lack of professional and timely record-keeping by city officials threatened the women's place in city affairs. Furthermore, the municipal council minutes read, "a committee of three ladies (Mrs. Timon, Tabor, and Coleman) appeared before the council asking that the city contribute $1000." The brief reference regarding the clubwomen only named the WMC's members by their married surnames and not in connection with an organized club. This suggested that the council did not recognize the clubwomen's position in civic matters. The fact was that the women did not hold a place in the formal political structure within which the council operated. The women could not vote, and therefore the council did not owe them anything. Much of the success the clubwomen had to this point was in the private sector or behind closed doors, relying on "silent" agreements with city leaders.

The lack of public consideration by the local officials painfully reminded the clubwomen about the existing separation between their private efforts and the council's public power. They conceded and continued work with the council and on the park, but in February 1909 the problems with the council and Artesian Park turned from bad to worse.[33]

That month the second clash over the park occurred, but this time the WMC fought back when the council turned down its petition requesting continued control of Artesian Park. A new women's club in Corpus Christi, the Altrurian Club, asked the WMC for permission to place a fountain in the park. The WMC quickly agreed. This transaction ruffled the city council, and its members soon decided that, "[the petition] not be granted and that the city reserve the right of granting permission for improvements [and that] nothing [was] to be taken from or added to without a permit from the city council." This enraged WMC members. While they apologetically communicated the news to the Altrurian Club, they also wrote to the council, stating that a verbal agreement existed between the former mayor, Segrest, and Ella Scott. And since the remaining financial responsibilities regarding Artesian Park lay with the WMC, so did control of the park.[34]

The WMC members then went a step further. The clubwomen told the council that they wanted nothing more to do with Artesian Park, and they published all financial transactions thus far in the *Corpus Christi Caller* as a political statement to local citizens. The women wanted everyone to know that credit for the creations of Artesian Park should go, not to the council, but to the WMC. The clubwomen believed they had earned the respect of locals, including the council. Years of work for the city and self-improvement through education superseded Texas Federation policies against overt political actions. The Corpus Christi women refused to allow others to reduce their role in community leadership without a fight. Rather than covert negotiations to pursue their political ends, the Woman's Monday Club then made a significant step. They openly asserted a community leadership role and hoped that respect and influence would come with that new function. When it did not, the clubwomen not only broke their silence, they let out a very public scream in print for the entire city to read. This was a complete shift from the Texas Federation leadership's frowning on such aggressive behavior.[35]

These newly raised voices also began using pressure politics as part of a pure food campaign sweeping the nation. Publicized by journalistic endeavors like Upton Sinclair's novel *The Jungle*, problems in the food industry attracted wide public attention. When the General Federation surveyed all of the states in 1906, Texas was one without any pure food legislation. This lack of state attention to public health explained the Corpus Christi women's earlier difficulty in fighting the saloons and fish houses. Laws did not provide local governments with the tools to regulate food preparation or local sanitation. Texas did not provide inspectors, legislation, or financial support, and the only incentives regarding food preparation came from unconditionally producing it quicker and cheaper. Addressing the situation, Pauline Periwinkle, a columnist for the *Dallas Morning News* and advocate for the Texas Federation, wrote, "men have shut up one eye and squinted so hard at commercial interests with the other, that they see little else. . . . The wonder is that doctors and undertakers and tombstone manufacturers don't join with the grocers in defeating measures bound to injure their trade." Women's notice of business-minded politicians acting in favor of profit was obviously not just a Corpus Christi problem.[36]

The Texas Federation and Woman's Christian Temperance Union lobbied state officials in 1906 and 1907. The WMC participated as well, corresponding with Senator Charles A. Culberson and Representative John N. Garner, both from Texas, in support of Harvey W. Wiley, the head of the Pure Food and Drug Administration. While Texas clubwomen knew their health, and more important that of their children, was in danger with every unregulated bite, control over the regulatory process was equally vital. When they asked for a state pure food commission, they requested that Texas lawmakers place the agency's headquarters at the College of Industrial Arts (now Texas Woman's University in Denton), not the uncooperative state health department or the all-male Agricultural and Mechanical College, both of which seemed to work more against women than for them.[37]

The women secured pure food legislation in 1907, but lost their request that the College of Industrial Arts house the state's agency. Yet they also recruited J. S. Abbott, a Dallas chemistry teacher sympathetic to the cause, as the new dairy and food commissioner. Another problem arose when state legislators only gave Abbott $5,000 and a stenographer for the entire state. In response, the Texas Federation enlisted a force of female inspectors from their membership, which provided Abbott with a trained if unpaid staff. Each community's local affiliate managed the activities of these inspectors through their home economics committees, including the WMC.[38]

Inspectors from the WMC visited dairies, meat-packing plants, and bakeries in and around Corpus Christi. Each time, the clubwomen made new demands and, during subsequent visits to the sites, they looked for compliance to their previous requests. Among the changes the women requested were the addition of screens to windows. Corpus Christi was very windy, so the request for screens was vital to pure food. In addition, the city continued to battle insects, such as flies, which also contaminated food preparation. Screens helped with this long-standing campaign of the WMC. The Corpus Christi club also organized educational activities for the local community. They offered cooking classes; members gave papers on food contamination, and held discussions about the local markets, dairies, bakeries and fish houses at club meetings. Local doctors gave lectures on behalf of the club, and the *Corpus Christi Caller* ran articles that chronicled the fight. The clubwomen worked hard to incorporate safe practices into Corpus Christi's culinary behaviors. As members of the entrepreneurial elite, they focused on elevating social and business standards to improve their urban environment. Their involvement in local issues lent them a certain amount of status that influenced the larger public's beliefs and activities.[39]

As part of Texas Federation network efforts, women's clubs in Dallas and Galveston sponsored pure food activities similar to those of the WMC. In 1907, after clubwomen spent three years fighting for local laws, the City of Dallas requested that a team of women help "insure [*sic*] compliance and enforcement" of its recently passed pure food and drug ordinance. Like Corpus Christi's non-existent food legislation before the progressive reforms, Galveston did not originally have ordinances that pushed for adequately hygienic food. Therefore, their Women's Health Protective Association "secured advice from sanitation experts, drew support from men's civic groups, newspapers, and the consuming public, and gained inspections and eventually appointments for themselves from state bureaucrats . . . from 1912 until its successful resolution in 1917."[40] The WMC thus found itself part of a larger progressive movement that was sweeping the state and nation.

In April 1908, Corpus Christi citizens again presented a petition to their city council for the removal of fish houses and saloons from the community's beaches. The council referred it to a committee to research the legality of the issue. Legislators were concerned that the city might not have the authority to limit private business. City officials discovered that they could legislate against unsafe practices, and in November, they held a special meeting and passed an ordinance "forbidding fish and oyster houses on Corpus Christi beaches or within city limits." In December 1908, when a group of area citizens signed a petition requesting the nullification of the above-mentioned ordinance, the council refused and upheld the long-delayed abolition of the establishments. This was a big victory for the WMC. Their agenda for the city's urban atmosphere had triumphed over a more privatized view of unrestricted business practices.[41]

In participating in the early phases of the city planning movement, the WMC members were "selling" Corpus Christi and Texas as unique regions involved in modern development. These types of activities marked cities as part of the changing New South instead of the closed system revolving around planter families. This type of civic marketing attracted more population and economic growth by individuals with similar goals. As the New South became increasingly urban after the turn of the twentieth century, often groups within cities began actively working to help their communities grow. These groups often used booster activities to advertise their city as the best way to attract both people and resources. The growth of their community in population often fed these boosters' economic investments by providing more people to buy their goods or services, while city growth also promised the possibility of increased social and political status within the region. Often the position of leader in these cities, as entrepreneurial elites, came with requirements for social, political, and economic status within the local community. It was not enough that the community looked at individuals as leaders; these people also had to provide a great amount of effort and innovation in community growth. The WMC of Corpus Christi was one of these early groups. After 1910, the members stayed active in the community and often occupied civic leadership roles, but other civic and women's clubs formed. Furthermore, by that time local government officials also took increasingly active roles in planning and boosterism, and soon the WMC no longer had to be a major source of civic direction or innovation.[42]

Notes

1. Portions of this chapter appear in Jessica Sutton Brannon-Wranosky, "The Civic Development in Corpus Christi, Texas, by the Woman's Monday Club from 1897–1913" (M. A. thesis, Texas A&M University-Corpus Christi, 2004); Jessica Brannon-Wranosky, "Corpus Christi History before La Retama [2004]" La Retama Club: Corpus Christi Public Libraries 100 Years of Service, 1909–2009, http://www.cclibraries.com/local_history/laretama/lrhistory.htm (accessed 8 Oct. 2005). The author wants to thank those who invested time and effort in earlier versions of this work, my M. A. chair and committee, Anthony Quiroz, David Blanke, and Sarah Heath, and in later years, Randolph B. Campbell, to whom this anthology is dedicated.

2. For further discussion of urbanization in the South and in Texas, see Char Miller and David R. Johnson, eds., *Urban Texas: Politics and Development* (College Station: Texas A&M University Press, 1990); Bradley R. Rice, *Progressive Cities: The Commission Government Movement in America, 1901–1920* (Austin: University of Texas Press, 1977); Patricia Evridge Hill, *Dallas: The Making of a Modern City* (Austin: University of Texas Press, 1996); Don H. Doyle, *New Men, New Cities, New South: Atlanta, Nashville, Charleston, Mobile, 1860–1910* (Chapel Hill: University of North Carolina Press, 1990).

3. *Handbook of Texas Online* [hereafter cited as *HTO*], s. v. "Henrietta Chamberlain King," http://www.tsha.utexas.edu/handbook/online/articles/view/KK/fki16.html (accessed 10 Oct. 2005); *HTO*, s. v. "Richard King," http://www.tsha.utexas.edu/handbook/online/articles/view/KK/fki19.html (accessed 2 Feb. 2004); *HTO*, s. v. "Robert Justus Kleberg II," http://www.tsha.utexas.edu/handbook/online/articles/view/KK/fkl4.html (accessed 2 Feb. 2004); *HTO*, s. v. "Laurels Ranch," http://www.tsha.utexas.edu/handbook/online/articles/view/LL/apl4.html (accessed 2 Feb. 2004); Doyle, *New Men, New Cities, New South,* 19; Clubs and Organizations Collection: Woman's Monday Club Papers, Local History and Genealogy Room Archives, Corpus Christi Public Library (hereafter referred to as WMC Papers); Records of the Comptroller of Public Accounts, Ad Valorem Tax Division, County Real and Personal Property Tax Rolls, Nueces County, 1900 and 1910, Archives Division, Texas State Library and Archives, Austin, (hereafter referred to as Nueces County Tax Rolls). "Federated clubwoman" refers to members of clubs networked as part of the General Federation of Women's Clubs and its state and local affiliates. The Texas Federation of Women's Clubs was the organization for federated Texas clubwomen. By 1903, the Women's Monday Club was member organization of both. For further discussion of federated clubwomen, see Elizabeth Hayes Turner, *Women, Culture, and Community: Religion and Reform in Galveston, 1880–1920* (New York: Oxford University Press, 1997); Judith N. McArthur, *Creating the New Woman: The Rise of Southern Women's Progressive Culture in Texas, 1893–1918* (Urbana: University of Illinois Press, 1998); Meagan Seaholm, "Earnest Women: The White Woman's Club Movement in Progressive Era Texas, 1880–1920" (Ph. D. Diss., Rice University, 1988); Karen J. Blair, *The Clubwoman as Feminist: True Womanhood Refined, 1868–1914* (New York: Holmes & Meier, 1980); Betty T. Chapman, "From the Parlor to the Public: New Roles for Women in Houston, 1885–1918," *The Houston Review: History and Culture of the Gulf Coast* 15 (1993): 31–44; Maureen Flanagan, "Gender and Urban Political Reform:

The City Club and the Woman's City Club of Chicago in the Progressive Era," *The American Historical Review* 95 (Oct. 1990): 1,032–50; Paula Baker, "The Domestication of Politics: Women and American Political Society, 1780–1920," *The American Historical Review* 89 (June 1984): 620–47; Anne Firor Scott, *The Southern Lady: From Pedestal to Politics 1830–1930* (Chicago: University of Chicago Press, 1970). It is widely accepted that Blair's book is one of the best histories of the General Federation's beginnings.

4. Corpus Christi City Council Minutes, Vol. D and Vol. E, City of Corpus Christi, City Secretary's Office, City Hall, Corpus Christi, Tex.; *Corpus Christi Caller,* 30 Sept., 14 Oct., 4 Nov. 1883, 17 Feb., 18 May, 30 May, 19 Oct., 23 Nov. 1884, 15 Nov. 1885, 16 Feb. 1887; Brannon-Wranosky, "Corpus Christi History before La Retama." For further information on leisure time, see Kathy Peiss, *Cheap Amusements: Leisure in the Turn of the Century New York* (Philadelphia: Temple University Press, 1986), 116, 123, 129–32, 142, 164–68, 183–84.

5. *Corpus Christi Caller*, 17 Feb., 18 May, 30 May, 19 Oct., 23 Nov. 1884, 15 Nov. 1885, 16 Feb. 1887. The last real mention of The Myrtle Club was in a memoriam article in the *Corpus Christi Caller* in January 1887 on the death of member John S. Givens, signed by a committee comprised of P. Doddridge, G. R. Scott, G. W. Westervelt, D. McNeill Turner, and Thomas Hickey. Most issues of the *Corpus Christi Caller* from 1886–1887 carry meeting notices for the Fortnightly Circle. See also Minutes, WMC Papers, Item 1.01, pp. 1, 24. Unfortunately, it may be impossible to ever gain a complete list of WMC members. Because the Fortnightly Circle minutes book was used to record the first minutes of the WMC, newspaper articles about both organizations were glued over half of the WMC members list.

6. Twelfth Census of the United States, 1900, Texas, Nueces County, Schedule 1: Population, National Archives and Records Administration, Washington D. C.; Thirteenth Census of the United States, 1910, Texas, Nueces County, Schedule 1: Population, NA. For a discussion of the nature of segregation in the Post-Reconstruction South, see Edward L. Ayers, *The Promise of the New South: Life After Reconstruction* (New York: Oxford University Press, 1992), 136–46; Glenda E. Gilmore, *Gender and Jim Crow: Women and the Politics of White Supremacy in North Carolina, 1896–1920* (Chapel Hill: University of North Carolina Press, 1996). Doyle, *New Men, New Cities, New South.* There was a three-year gap in the minutes book from the last meeting of the Fortnightly Circle in 1894 to the first meeting of the WMC in 1897. Locals and clubwomen called the

WMC "the first woman's club in CC." Minutes, WMC Papers, Item 1.01, p. 24; Scrapbook #1 (1897–1949), WMC Papers, 37.

7. Twelfth Census, 1900, Nueces County, Schedule 1; Thirteenth Census, 1910, Nueces County, Schedule 1; Thirteenth Census, 1910, Nueces County, Schedule 5: Agriculture.

8. Twelfth Census, 1900, Nueces County, Schedule 1; Thirteenth Census, 1910, Nueces County, Schedule 1; Thirteenth Census, 1910, Nueces County, Schedule 5; *Corpus Christi Caller*, 15 Nov. 1965; *Corpus Christi Times*, 15 Nov. 1965; *Corpus Crony*, 26 Dec. 1908.

9. Stella L. Christian, ed., *The History of the Texas Federation of Women's Clubs* (Houston: Dealy Adey Elgin Company, 1919), 44–45; Scott, *Southern Lady*, 167; Judith N. McArthur and Harold L. Smith, *Minnie Fisher Cunningham: A Suffragist's Life in Politics* (Oxford: Oxford University Press, 2003), 31–32, 34–35; McArthur, *Creating the New Woman,* 103, 108. For more about influential members of federated clubs, see Blair, *Clubwoman as Feminist*. In it, she discusses members like Phoebe Hearst, "an active clubwoman and wife of a United States Senator and mining magnate, she was [also] the mother of William Randolph Hearst, founder of the Hearst chain of newspapers." Blair, *Clubwoman as Feminist*, 95.

10. Scrapbook, WMC Papers, Item 23.01, p. 6; *Corpus Christi Times*, 3 Mar. 1944, 9 Apr. 1949.

11. Jeffrey A. Zemler, "The Texas Building and the Women's World's Fair Exhibit Association of Texas," *Southwestern Historical Quarterly* (July 2011): 19–23; Daphne Spain, *How Women Saved the City* (Minneapolis: University of Minnesota Press, 2001), 16–17; Judith A. Adams, "The American Dream Actualized: The Glistening 'White City' and the Lurking Shadows of the World's Columbian Exposition," in David J. Bertuca, Donald K. Hartman, Susan M. Neumeister, eds., *The World's Columbian Exposition: A Centennial Bibliographic Guide* (Westport, Connecticut: Greenwood Press, 1996), xix–xx.

12. Scrapbook, WMC Papers, Item 23.01, p. 6; *Corpus Christi Times,* 3 Mar. 1944, 9 Apr. 1949.

13. W. E. Pope Papers, Special Collection and Archives, Texas A&M University-Corpus Christi, Tex.

14. Scrapbook, WMC Papers, Item 23.01, p. 20.

15. Nueces County Tax Rolls 1900 and 1910.

16. *Corpus Christi Caller*, 18 Feb. 1898, 1 Sept. 1939, 3 Mar. 1944; WMC Papers, Item 1.01, p. 56; Doyle, *New Men, New Cities, New South;* Blaine A. Brownell, "The Commercial-Civic Elite and Urban Planning

in Atlanta, Memphis, and New Orleans in the 1920's," *The Journal of Southern History* 41 (Aug. 1975): 339–68; Jon C. Teaford, "New Life for an Old Subject: Investigating the Structure of Urban Rule," *American Quarterly* 37 (1985): 326–56; Robert Wiebe, *The Search for Order, 1877–1920* (New York: Hill and Wang, 1967), 167–70.

17. Scrapbook, WMC Papers, Item 23.01, 6; *Corpus Christi Caller*, 1 Sept. 1939.

18. *HTO*, "Kate Harrison Friend," http://www.tsha.utexas.edu/handbook/online/articles/ view/FF/ffr22.html (accessed 1 Apr. 2004); WMC Papers, Item 1.01, p. 86. The article from the *Waco Times-Herald* entitled "Woman's Sphere," by Kate Friend, was reprinted as part of a local article in *Corpus Christi Caller*, 23 Oct. 1903.

19. A copy of the petition, excluding signatures, can be found in *Corpus Christi Caller*, 23 Oct. 1903; City of Corpus Christi Minutes, Vol. E (5 Oct. 1903): 135.

20. *Corpus Christi Caller*, 23 Oct. 1903; City of Corpus Christi Minutes, Vol. E (5 Oct. 1903): 135.

21. Wiebe, *Search for Order,* 114; McArthur, *Creating the New Woman*, 31.

22. Ibid., 34; City of Corpus Christi Minutes, Vol. E (5 Oct. 1903): 135; *Corpus Christi Caller*, 9 Oct., 6 Nov., 11 Dec. 1903, 8 Jan., 5 Feb. 1904, 1 Sept. 1939.

23. Christian, *History of the Texas Federation of Women's* Clubs, 124; Scrapbook, WMC Papers, Item 23.01, 6; City of Corpus Christi Minutes, Vol. D and Vol. E.

24. City of Corpus Christi Minutes, Vol. E (9 Sept. 1905): 259–67.

25. City of Corpus Christi Minutes, Vol. E (11 Apr. 1904): 163, (7 May 1904): 170; *Corpus Christi Caller*, 23 Sept. 1904, 25 Aug. 1905.

26. Texas Federation of Women's Clubs Program, 1904–1905, Woman's Collection, Texas Woman's University, Denton, Texas; WMC Papers, Item 1.02, pp. 145–52; Dermot H. Hardy and Ingham S. Roberts, eds., *Historical Review of South-East Texas and The Founders, Leaders and Representative Men of Its Commerce, Industry and Civic Affairs* (Chicago: Lewis Publishing Co., 1910), 628–29; *Corpus Christi Caller*, 9 Apr. 1949; "Mayors and Council Members" in Miscellaneous Information Notebook, Local History and Genealogy Room Archives, Corpus Christi Public Library.

27. *Corpus Christi Caller*, 23 Sept. 1904, 28 July, 25 Aug., 13 Oct. 1905; "To Get Rid of Mosquitoes," *Ladies Home Journal,* reprinted in *Corpus Christi Caller*, 4 Aug. 1905; Minutes, WMC Papers, Item 1.02, pp. 16, 39, 49; City of Corpus Christi Minutes, Vol. E (6 Apr. 1907): 377.

28. Christian, *History of the Texas Federation of Women's Clubs,* 120, 124–25.

29. Blair, *Clubwoman as Feminist*, 103; Mary Ritter Beard, *Woman's Work in Municipalities* (1915; repr., New York: Arno Press, 1972), 293–96. For further information regarding the environmental conservation movement, see Samuel P. Hays, *Conservation and the Gospel of Efficiency: The Progressive Conservation Movement, 1890–1920* (1959; repr., New York: Atheneum, 1979).

30. Texas Historical Commission Marker: Artesian Park Site (Corpus Christi, Texas, 1976); *HTO*, "Corpus Christi, Texas," http://www.tshaonline.org/handbook/online/articles/hdc03 (accessed 2 Feb. 2004); WMC Papers, Item 1.01 B, pp. 88–90, Item 1.01, p. 100; City of Corpus Christi Minutes, Vol. E (15 Sept. 1904): 201.

31. Minutes, WMC Papers, Item 1.02, pp. 56–58, 80–82, 99–104, 118.

32. Ibid.; Delmas Givens to Woman's Monday Club, n.d., WMC Papers.

33. City of Corpus Christi Minutes, Vol. E (7 May 1907): 379.

34. City of Corpus Christi Minutes, Vol. E (2 Feb. 1909): 609; WMC Papers, Item 1.02, p. 145.

35. Ibid., pp. 145–52.

36. Upton Sinclair, *The Jungle* (New York: Barnes & Noble, 1906); "Baby Protection," in *The Sherman Democrat*, reprinted in *Corpus Christi Caller*, 7 Dec. 1906; *Dallas Morning News*, 11 Feb. 1907.

37. WMC Papers, Item 1.04, p. 8; Scrapbook, WMC Papers, Item 23.01; McArthur, *Creating the New Woman*, 43.

38. Ibid., 43–45.

39. Ibid., *Creating the New Woman*, 44–45; Minutes, WMC Papers, Item 1.05, pp. 51–52, 78–79; Minutes, WMC Papers, Item 1.04, p. 67; Minutes, WMC Papers, Item 1.03, pp. 71–76; copies of *Corpus Christi Caller* articles concerning local pure food activities can be found pasted in Minutes, WMC Papers, Items 1.03–1.04.

40. Elizabeth York Enstam, *Women and the Creation of Urban Life: Dallas, Texas, 1843–1920* (College Station: Texas A&M University Press, 1998), 143; Turner, *Women, Culture, and Community,* 217.

41. City of Corpus Christi Minutes, Vol. E (13 Apr. 1908): 529–30, (24 Nov. 1908): 564–69, (4 Dec. 1908): 579.

42. WMC Papers; *Corpus Christi Caller* from 1908 to 1913.

Tank rolling through courthouse square in Denton during World War I. Courtesy of Denton Public Library

Denton County, Texas, and the Draft During the First World War

Gregory W. Ball

The Denton County courthouse was quiet on July 20, 1917. The local newspaper noted that "nothing was filed in county court, no filings were reported in the district court, no birth or death certificates and no marriage licenses were applied for." The reason for the lack of official business was obvious to county residents: the first draft since the Civil War was taking place in Washington, D.C. As blindfolded administration officials pulled numbers from a glass bowl, they were passed by telegraph to a waiting nation. In Denton, the *Record-Chronicle* reported that many of the county officials were "in the selective draft age," and "seemed rather indisposed toward work" as they waited to see if their number was called. Thus, the one area filled with activity in an otherwise quiet courthouse was the county courtroom, where interest in the draft was "at fever heat," and the "telephones were kept busy all day answering queries from anxious ones who wanted to know whether or not a certain number was drawn." It was a "quiet, earnest crowd intent on knowing how each man came out in the drawing."[1]

An important aspect of the United States' involvement in World War I was the implementation of a selective draft. While drafts occurred during the Civil War, the draft as implemented during World War I enrolled more men and succeeded in meeting its primary goal: fielding the largest army the nation had ever seen while maintaining a strong economy as millions of men left the workforce and donned the "khaki." The draft was based on the concept of a universal liability to serve in time of war, and the United States called nearly 3,000,000 men to service, or 20 percent of the male population between the age of eighteen and forty-five. This was done in less than two years, between the summer of 1917 and the fall of 1918.[2]

In order to prevent damage to the nation's agricultural and industrial bases, the Army had to determine who would fight and who would not. The Army developed, through trial and error, a complex system of determining who would be drafted. But, in order to ascertain the influence of the draft on local communities, it is more useful to look at the men who were drafted rather than to analyze technical aspects of the draft. Furthermore, it is possible to compare men who were drafted with those who were granted exemptions or with men who volunteered for military service. Denton County, Texas, provided an excellent opportunity to study those three groups, as the county was a fairly representative agricultural county in 1918, yet also was close enough to the urban centers of Dallas and Fort Worth to represent a transition between the urban and farming areas of North Texas. Additionally, the county also raised a volunteer company of National Guardsmen for service in the war. It is possible, then, to determine the socio-economic backgrounds of men in each group and learn whether they shared any similarities or displayed significant differences. Were exempted men more likely to be married and have families than the men who were drafted or those who volunteered? Did race play a factor? What influence did the local draft board have on these men and on the community? Answering such questions points out the importance of studying national issues at the local level in order to understand better how those issues influenced individuals and communities and helps complete the story of the Great War not only in Denton, but in Texas as well.[3]

Although the background of the United States' intervention in World War I is best explored elsewhere, the United States government shifted from a policy of neutrality in 1914 to one of open belligerency by April 6, 1917. A fundamental part of that policy shift was centered on the issue of preparedness, especially after the sinking of the *Lusitania* in the spring of 1915. The question became to what extent should the United States actively prepare for war? While this debate raged, the war in Europe continued to worsen, causing both President Woodrow Wilson and Congress to address the issue of expanding the armed forces should the country be drawn into the war. In November of 1915, the president proposed a "reorganization and expansion" of the military, although he was very careful to avoid the implication that the United States might intervene in the war. In 1916, the issue of preparedness began to hinge on the value of using volunteers to strengthen the army or the implementation of a draft.[4]

That issue remained important into 1917. As late as two months after the United States had broken diplomatic relations with Germany in February of that year, the government still expected to rely solely on voluntary enlistments to increase the army's size. By March 1917, however, the situation had changed, and Secretary of War Newton D. Baker admitted that a draft might be required at some future date but only after the volunteer system could no longer provide the required number of soldiers.[5]

President Wilson had long remained a proponent of raising a wartime army through the volunteer system. By the end of March, however, Wilson concluded that a wartime draft was the only way to raise an army of the size required should the United States enter the war. As it turned out, less than two weeks before the United States declared war on Germany, the United States Army found itself with a president who had decided that a draft was more appropriate, and who expected to field an army of at least 500,000 soldiers but had yet to offer any legislation for implementing a draft or creating the administrative apparatus to carry one out.[6]

After a fierce struggle in Congress, the Selective Service Act authorizing a draft passed both houses on April 28, 1917. The president signed it three weeks later. The men to be drafted would enter the new "National Army." Along with the Regular Army and a federalized National Guard, they would represent the preponderance of United States manpower on the Western Front. Once the act was signed, the administration of the draft had to proceed rapidly, in part because the president called for a nationwide registration of all men between the ages of twenty-one to thirty to take place on June 5, 1917. Once it was became law, the focus shifted from the national to the local level, where the process of registering, selecting, examining, and sending men off to training camps took place and where the nature of the draft and those who were involved with it could be studied with profit.[7]

Through the operation of more than 4,500 local exemption boards and with the help of county officials, the selective service system registered just less than 24,000,000 men for the draft. In Texas, 990,522 men (4 percent of all registrants) were registered, which ranked fifth among the states. Only Illinois, New York, Ohio, and Pennsylvania registered more men. Of the men who registered in Texas, 712,629 (72 percent) were actually classified by local boards, and 251,242 were "held for service" (35 percent). The national average of men held for military service was 36 percent. Of Texas men held for service, local boards actually inducted 127,797 men (13 percent), which amounted to 4 percent of the total draftees in the United States. In Texas, dependency deferments were granted in 323,677 cases (45 percent), which was slightly above the national average of 39 percent.[8]

Regarding industrial and agricultural exemptions and deferments, Texas boards granted 3,361 (.5 percent) of industrial and 8,051 (1 percent) of agricultural claims, both of which were slightly below the national averages. Texas boards also registered a little more than 54,000 alien residents while granting slightly more than 12,000 exemptions for other reasons. As for those who resisted and evaded the draft, out of 24,000,000 registrants, the Provost Marshal General reported a nationwide total of 489,003 desertions (2 percent of all registrants). Of that total, more than 150,000 thousand were eventually accounted for, leaving 337,649 cases of desertion in the United States (1.41 percent of all registrants). In Texas, out of the 990,000 registrants, 25,178 were initially classified as deserters (2.54 percent). Fourteen thousand of these were accounted for, leaving Texas with 10,113 desertion cases (1.11 percent of Texas registrants). Taken as a whole, Texas was neither far above nor far below the national average in any of the major statistical categories of the World War I draft.[9]

If Texas fits the national average of the draft, how did Denton County compare with Texas? Denton County registered 7,579 men (.8 percent of total Texas registrants) during the three registration periods spanning June 1917 to September 1918. Of those registered, the Denton County exemption board inducted 921 men into military service (12 percent). As for exemptions and deferments, the Denton County board granted 1,670 exemptions for dependents (22 percent). Of the 280 local boards in Texas, Denton County ranked eighteenth in the number of dependency claims granted. However, Denton accounted for just twenty-seven agricultural exemptions and only one industrial deferment. Denton County generally paralleled Texas as a whole, particularly in inducting men for service, where the percentages were almost identical.[10]

At the state level, the selective service system relied heavily on county level government for support and was specifically designed to be decentralized and quickly implemented. The Army's Provost Marshal General, Maj. Gen. Enoch Crowder, served as the Army's senior official in charge of the selective service system. Below the national level, state governors were charged with authority for the draft within their states. Below the governors were district boards, of which Texas had four. The Northern District was in Fort Worth, the Southern District in Houston, the Eastern District in Tyler and the Western District headquartered in Austin. The district boards had two primary functions. First, they were to review decisions made by the county exemption boards "upon appeal," and second, they were to make all decisions regarding exemptions for the draft based on agricultural or industrial claims. The district boards, according to General Crowder, were to provide "a check on irregularities by local boards . . . and assured to every registrant the opportunity of a rehearing before a court removed from local prejudice and influence." The four district boards in Texas contained twenty-eight members, with eight additional members serving at one time or another.[11]

The central component of the World War I draft system was the county exemption board. In the United States, there were 4,648 local boards with slightly more than 14,000 members. In Texas, this amounted to 280 boards, one for every county and city with a population of 30,000 or greater. During the war, approximately 841 individuals served on Texas exemption boards, each of which was comprised of three men from the county or city. These boards were, in essence, the "front line" between the citizens and the government. As General Crowder wrote in a report to the Secretary of War: "Long after the selective service machinery will have been dismantled, and the processes of the draft will have faded from memory, the term 'local board' will hold its place in our speech as the typical mark of the system that lifted America from the most peaceful of Nations to a place of first magnitude among military powers." A central feature of these local boards was that the board members were not military officers, nor were they specially trained civilians. Rather, they were members of the local community who were expected to know the particular situation of their county, understand the local nuances and character of the residents, and thus be in a position to *impartially* select men to be drafted. According to the Provost Marshal General, board members were chosen for "their unquestioned patriotism, fair-mindedness, and integrity, and [they were] impelled solely by the motive of patriotic self-sacrifice." Of course, this did not necessarily reflect the reality of each board's operations.[12]

Local exemption boards played an essential role as the "buffer" between the federal government and the citizen and "attracted and diverted, like local grounding wires in an electric coil, such resentment or discontent as might have proved a serious obstacle to war measures, had it been focused on the central authorities." In one way, these local boards were the face of the government, acting as friendly local citizens who would bear the brunt of criticism of the draft. In an effort to appoint men who would remain above the influence of petty criticism, the men named to the local boards were chosen by the president, upon the recommendation of state governors. Such a system, of course, brought about some complaints of political interference. Although there was doubtless some political maneuvering for these positions, of the 14,000 local board members across the nation, more than 4,200 listed their occupations as "medicine," while slightly more than 2,800 listed "public office" as their occupation. This was followed by law and agriculture as the top four occupations of board members.[13]

The local boards were not created until after the initial draft registration of June 5, 1917. From that point on, however, they were responsible for the administration of the draft until the end of the war on November 11, 1918. In short, the local exemption board was charged with every aspect of the draft, including registration, determination of order numbers, classification of registrants, and calling those to be inducted as well as shipping them to training bases. Indeed, local board members had to be familiar with 433 pages of selective service regulations as well as master "for daily and instant use" more than 100 different forms. Assisting the local boards were medical and legal advisory boards as well as instructors to teach registrants rudimentary military skills before they were inducted and sent to training camps.[14]

By all accounts, Denton County residents were patriotic and supported America's intervention in the war against Germany and its allies. Patriotic celebrations and parades were commonplace, and thousands of American flags were sold across the county. This patriotism however, had a darker side as fears of German sympathizers were also common. Suspicious men traveling through the county, rumors of German flags being raised while American flags were burned, and investigations into illicit telegraph stations sending messages to German spies in Mexico were common not only in the county but throughout North Texas. In one instance, several boys playing in a barn came across dynamite. The find was brought to the courthouse square where, the local newspaper noted, it was examined by a "large number of persons, who hatched several very vivid imaginary stories of 'German spies' 'anarchists' and the like." After closer investigation, it was discovered the dynamite was for destroying tree stumps.[15]

County Sheriff Pat Gallagher was charged with implementing the draft registration. All male citizens within the specified age group of twenty-one to thirty-one years old were required to fill out a registration card that included the registrant's age, present address, place of birth, citizenship status, occupation, place of occupation, dependent relatives, prior military service, marital status, race, and whether the registrant planned to claim exemption from the draft. If the registrant was an African American, the bottom left corner of the registration card was cut off, making those cards easier to identify. General Crowder reflected the reality of the time when he wrote that "color and race were, of course, not material under the law and the regulations for the purpose of the classification. But the organization of the Army placed colored soldiers in separate units."[16]

Sheriff Gallagher prepared for registration day by bringing in volunteers to help with the enormous task before the draft bill had even been signed, although only three men at first volunteered their assistance. Because of his position, Gallagher became a focal point for curiosity about the registration, although the government initially told him very little about how the draft would work. Gallagher commented at one point that he "had received no further instructions on the manner of registering and selecting the army under the draft bill." He did, however, receive blank registration forms.[17]

Gallagher worked closely with the County Clerk's office, which also received numerous inquiries about the draft, particularly after the sheriff and Earl Ross, a local notary, spent two days and one night traveling through the county appointing registration officials in each voting precinct. The two men did not sleep while they were gone, nor did they have qualms about waking people in the middle of the night to swear them in to their new positions. The *Denton Record-Chronicle* reported that Gallagher and Ross were no "respecters of persons or sleep" in their desire to finish their task. In this period, Gallagher and Ross appointed sixty-nine officials in thirty-one county precincts to help conduct the registration. These men were told that they could "draw fees" for the work but were encouraged to assist in the registration without pay.[18]

Soon, all of the men selected to assist in the registration were brought to Denton for a "school" held at the county courthouse, so they would "have a definite idea of what is required of them and thus make fewer mistakes in registering the men." But, as registration day neared, questions about the draft increased. For example, what would happen if a registrant was not going to be in his home county on registration day? There were also plenty of questions on exactly how to fill out the registration cards. The County Clerk's office, busy registering non-residents of the county for the draft, learned much from that experience. In one day, County Clerk Roy Mays reported the registration of fifty-one non-residents and sent a special courier to the town of Justin, in the southwest part of the county, to register an expected two hundred transient workers who were building a pipeline. Based on his experience with the first group of those non-residents, Mays told Denton County residents that they should "read more about how to answer the questions asked by the registrar before submitting themselves for registration." Apparently, the non-local registrants had failed to show "a practical knowledge of the questions to be asked and therefore are incapable of answering them as rapidly as it is desired." According to Mays, it had taken some men twenty minutes to answer the twelve questions, when in his opinion "it should take but a few moments."[19]

When Mays reported that 98 percent of the non-residents and county residents who would be out of town on registration day had claimed exemption from the draft, questions about those exemptions became a prominent discussion topic. To clarify things, the *Denton Record-Chronicle* published specific instructions issued by General Crowder concerning exemptions. The instructions warned that men who claimed exemptions because of dependents "must be certain that the person they have in mind is 'solely' dependent on them. Otherwise, they must not hide behind petticoats or children." But, they also noted that "if it is true that there is another mouth than your own which you alone have a duty to feed, do not let your military ardor interfere with the wish of the nation to reduce the war's misery to a minimum."[20]

For the initial draft registration, there were several ways to claim exemption. From the national standpoint, far and away the largest group of men exempted from the draft claimed dependents, nearly seven million out of seventeen million men who were classified by local draft boards (40 percent). Agricultural and industrial claims could also earn an individual exemption from the draft, although exemptions for those reasons were not nearly as common as those for dependents. For example, agricultural and industrial deferments combined totaled 824,000, far less than the seven million dependent claims granted nationwide. Other ways men could claim exemption from the draft included being a member of a religious group that opposed war, being an "executive, legislative, or judicial" official at the state or national level, being currently enrolled in the military, or being a felon or otherwise "morally deficient."[21]

While Denton County generally supported the draft, there were several instances of protest in the region as registration day approached. In one cryptic reference to an unnamed section of the county, the *Record-Chronicle* reported "some evidence of disaffection and opposition to the selective draft registration." Although the paper was not specific, it did note that opposition was not organized, "but rather sporadic and only one or two localities are affected." The county authorities, it stated, were keeping a close watch on the situation "with a view to taking prompt and effective steps if necessary." In nearby Dallas, anti-draft registration circulars were found that proclaimed "Down with conscription—refuse to register." Apparently, the circulars were not from the local area, although they succeeded in arousing the "vigilance of government agents." And in Fort Worth, after the draft began, hundreds of falsified registration cards were discovered. In addition, registrants were advised to carry a copy of their registration card with them at all times, especially if they left the local area as "peace officers everywhere will be on the lookout for slackers and if one has not the certificate of registration, they will probably cause some embarrassment."[22]

Regardless of disaffection in the county, Sheriff Gallagher and his assistants continued with their preparations, registering prisoners in the county jail and those in the county "convict camps." In an effort to ensure support, Denton Mayor Paul J. Beyette proclaimed that registration day would be a city holiday. Beyette wrote that "everyone should realize fully the importance of this action [draft registration]. I believe that every true and loyal American is anxious to 'do his bit.'" Three days after this announcement, however, O. M. Curtis of the Denton Chamber of Commerce announced that no celebrations would be held. Curtis wrote that "offering oneself for the defense of one's country, while it is a privilege, it is a very serious matter and should be gone about and done in a very serious way," and therefore should not be accompanied by music and parades. Curtis's speech also drew connections between patriotism and service to the country and illustrated the view some Texans held about wartime service: "Giving one's self for the defense of one's country is of course a very serious thing for it means loss of life, not all the lives that are offered but some of them sure. Giving one's self for this purpose looked at from one angle is a glorious privilege for I do not believe death could come in a nobler or more glorious way than in fighting for one's country." Statements such as this certainly put pressure on young men to register or even volunteer.[23]

Denton County's draft registration day began at seven in the morning. By noon, the *Record-Chronicle* reported that an estimated 65 percent of the eligible population had registered. Officials believed there were nearly 4,000 men within the age group in the county who were expected to register, and by the end of the day, Denton County officials estimated that 3,070 men registered for the draft. Instead of a band and parades to mark June 5, 1917, Denton County residents pinned a red, white, blue, and khaki "badge of honor" on registrants. The names of these men were inscribed on an "honor roll," published in the *Record-Chronicle* and posted on the door of the County Clerk's office. The paper also reported that there had been no trouble at any registration center and that no one within the eligible ages had refused to register, although early on draft day the *Record-Chronicle* reported that few African Americans had registered, noting it was "not known whether they did not intend registering or expected to come to the offices after work hours."[24]

Of course, not everyone did register that day. Most, however, failed to register because of extenuating circumstances rather than opposition. In Denton County, the case of John Riley Allbert is illuminating. Allbert "presented himself for registration at the County Clerks' office" nearly two weeks after registration day. He was accompanied by his father, who spoke on John Riley's behalf because his son was a mute. Neither he nor his father had left their farm for more than a month and neither claimed to know about the registration until John Riley and his father had come into Denton on business. There, John Riley found out about the draft after signing with another mute. The County Clerk wasted no time in registering John Riley, although it is doubtful if he was ever called. Another man from the county mailed his registration card in from Dallas but it was delayed in the mail and eventually returned to the individual. Rather than risk being labeled a "slacker," the man hand delivered it to the County Clerk's office in Denton.[25]

Once registration day was over and the preliminary work of sorting and numbering the registration cards had been completed, the citizens of the county had to wait for the local board to meet before further steps could be taken. The composition of the Denton County exemption board was not announced, however, until June 27, 1917, three weeks after registration day. The initial members of the board were Frank A. Wright, a banker from Pilot Point, A. Wayne Robertson, a retired farmer from Little Elm, and Dr. J. C. Copenhaver of Aubrey. According to the *Record-Chronicle*, while there was "general satisfaction" with the composition of the board, there was criticism that no member was from Denton, the county seat and largest town in the county. Shortly thereafter, the men met at the courthouse and chose Frank Wright as chairman and took care of "preliminary work" while awaiting instructions. Future meetings of the board would take place in the county courtroom of the Denton County courthouse.[26]

The local exemption board did not begin the process of classifying and exempting men whose numbers had been called in the July 20, 1917, draft lottery until the end of the month. The process initially consisted of compiling lists based on the selected draft numbers and then calling groups of registrants in for physical examination. Those who passed the physical examinations would then either be certified for military service, or, if they had requested an exemption, the board would consider their request. Based on the population of the county and the number of men who had registered, Denton County's initial draft quota was 245 individuals. To ensure that the county examined enough men to fill the quota, 200 percent, or 490 men, were initially called to the local exemption board because of the expectation that a certain number of men would not pass their physical exams.[27]

Exemptions were the central function of the board, and the fundamental question it had to answer was: who should be exempt from the universal liability to military service? Further complicating matters was that when the draft registration cards were examined, county officials found that of the original 3,042 registrations, 1,877 recorded a reason for exemption (62 percent). According to a report in the *Record-Chronicle*, out of a total of 2,794 white registrants, 1,710 requested exemptions (61 percent). The county initially registered 276 African Americans, 143 of whom requested exemptions (52 percent). For both groups, dependent relatives were the main reason for exemption requests. But, as the Provost Marshal General had made clear, a registrant would not be exempted solely for marital or dependent status. Rather, each registrant would be assessed individually with the determining factor expected to be whether the man's spouse could work or there were relatives who could support the wife and children.[28]

Even though a registrant claimed exemption on his registration card, further action on his part was required. The federal regulations stated: "The statement on the registration card of any such person that exemption or discharge is claimed shall not be construed or considered as the presentation of a claim for discharge." If a man wished to claim exemption from the draft, he was required to present his claim, in the form of an affidavit, to the exemption board, with no verbal argument, "not less than five days" after receiving his notice to appear before the board. The exemption board would then consider the case and make a decision. All dependency claims were eligible for appeal to the district board. Finally, men who were exempted by the board faced the prospect of being recalled, reexamined, and called to service. Indeed, in order to ease complaints about men exempted from the draft, the Denton board required exempted registrants to explain in what ways they had been "helping the country in this hour of need." Those who failed to answer to the satisfaction of the board were liable to be "called in and asked to show cause why they should not be placed in Class 1," or the group of draft-eligible men. Later in 1918, the local board was asked to revisit their lists of deferred and exempted men to see if the status of any man changed. The exemption board chairman stated that "the board will greatly appreciate suggestions from any person who knows of any registrant whose condition has changed." Furthermore, he noted, "it was a patriotic duty that every man owed to his country to assist in this work and let the burden fall on every man alike."[29]

The work of the local exemption board was a continuous process of classifying registrants, managing the physical exams of hundreds of men, deciding exemption claims, processing paperwork, and ensuring men inducted into the military were sent off to training camps on schedule. Local residents also expected board members to provide news about the draft and men in the army. The work was long and difficult, and it caused the membership of the county board to change several times. The first change occurred shortly after the board sent its first quota of men to Camp Travis in San Antonio. Frank A. Wright resigned on September 19, 1917, after less than three months on the job, citing the lack of time to devote to his business. He was replaced, according to a telegram sent by Texas Governor William P. Hobby, by John W. Bailey. Bailey, who lived in Denton and had two sons in the military, remained the chairman of the exemption board until it completed its work in late 1918.[30]

Because the activities of the local exemption board were often administrative and complex, perhaps the best way to assess the influence of the board is to study the men that it either did or did not draft. By examining a random sample of 100 of those individuals, it can readily be ascertained who was drafted, what their ages and occupations were, and then compare that sample with a random sampling of 100 men who received exemptions. Such an analysis could then be compared with a similar group of volunteers. As noted, a unit existed in Denton County that permits such a comparison. Company M, 7th Texas Infantry, Texas National Guard, formed in Denton County at the same time as the first registration and draft occurred. Company M was then sent to Camp Bowie in Fort Worth, where it joined the 142nd Infantry Regiment, 36th Division and saw combat in France in the fall of 1918. By examining this group, the importance of the local exemption board in the lives of the citizens of Denton County becomes clear.[31]

Soldiering is a job for young men. Although the draft initially brought in men between the ages of twenty-one and thirty, an analysis of age characteristics is still useful. In September of 1918, the draft eligible ages were expanded, when those required to register included all men between the ages of eighteen and forty-five. As might be expected, the youngest were the volunteers of Company M, whose average age was twenty-two, the youngest being eighteen and the oldest, the company commander, thirty-eight. On one hand, as volunteers, these men might have been more eager to serve, and at their age they likewise had fewer obligations and responsibilities than other groups. On the other hand, conscription carried negative connotations in the early stages of American involvement in World War I because of memories of the Civil War draft. This caused some men to volunteer rather than wait to be drafted.[32]

Drafted men were slightly older than the volunteers, with an average age of twenty-four. Not surprisingly, the sample of men who were exempted from the draft was the oldest. The average age for that group was twenty-six years. Such a breakdown of the ages indicates that the men who were exempted likely had more time to get married, start families, and make their way in business, while the volunteers and draftees generally had fewer life experiences, and, in most cases, had less time to develop their careers or start families. The point is evident upon closer examination. The majority of draftees were below the age of twenty-five, with fifty-eight men (58 percent) falling within this category, while the remaining forty-two (42 percent) were between twenty-five and thirty years old. Of the draftees, only eight men out of the sample of 100 (8 percent) were twenty-nine or thirty years old.[33]

On the other hand, exemptees displayed the opposite characteristics. Forty-one men (41 percent) of the sample of 100 exempted from the draft were below the age of twenty-five while the majority, or fifty-nine men (59 percent), were twenty-five to thirty. Also, twenty of the men granted exemptions (20 percent) were twenty-nine or thirty years old, more than twice the number of draftees who fell into this category. Thus, were men drafted or exempted based solely on their ages? In examining the average ages of twenty-four and twenty-six, it appears not to have been the case. Again, individual circumstances rather than age may well have been given greater consideration by the board.[34]

To what extent were occupations of interest to the board considering that men could claim exemption on agricultural or industrial grounds? One of the main points of the draft was the desire of the federal government to build an army quickly without disrupting the nation's economy, and exemptions on occupational grounds played a role in determining which men would be drafted. One would expect that Denton County, being a rural county, would have a large number of men engaged in agriculture. But what was the occupational breakdown among volunteers, draftees, and exemptees, and what were the occupations of those more likely to be drafted in Denton County?[35]

For all three groups, farming was the majority occupation. Of the volunteers of Company M, thirty-four were farmers, while fourteen men were classified as unskilled laborers. The volunteers also included a range of individuals engaged in skilled jobs such as auto mechanic, well driller, tailor, printer, and machinist. Of the men who were drafted, however, sixty-six men claimed farming as their primary occupation (66 percent). Thirteen men were categorized as unskilled workers (13 percent), six as skilled workers (6 percent), eight as clerical workers (8 percent), five had unknown occupations (5 percent) and three were unemployed. Did the local exemption board tend to draft farmers or was the occupational breakdown similar for those who were exempt?[36]

Sixty-five of the men who received draft exemptions also claimed farming as their occupation (65 percent). Eleven men were unskilled workers (11 percent), seven were skilled (7 percent), thirteen were clerical workers (13 percent), one was an officer of the government (1 percent), and three had unknown occupations (3 percent). Obviously, due to the similar breakdown in occupations among the drafted and exempted registrants, the local board certainly did not single out any particular occupation as liable for the draft.[37]

If the Denton County exemption board was just as likely to draft or exempt a man because of his occupation, how did they respond to men who claimed dependents or were married? First of all, the vast majority of the volunteer unit from Denton was comprised of unmarried men. Ninety-seven percent of Company M was not married. Only three men on the initial roster of the company were married, including the commanding officer. This further supports the claim that the volunteer soldiers were younger and perhaps had not yet established themselves, or were eager and swayed by patriotism. As for dependents, fifteen of the soldiers (10 percent) in the volunteer company claimed dependent relatives.[38]

Along similar lines, the men who were drafted were also less likely to be married. Of the sample of drafted men, only sixteen (16 percent) were married. Although most of the draftees were not married, forty (40 percent) did list dependents, but only seven of the forty (18 percent) listed their dependents as a wife and at least one child. Thus, if a draftee claimed dependents, it was more often than not a dependent mother or father, rather than a wife or child. Almost the exact opposite was true among men who were exempted from the draft. Eighty-eight men of that sample group were married (88 percent). Even more striking, only four of the men who were exempted from the draft did not claim any dependents. An overwhelming number (96 percent) of exemptees did have dependents. Furthermore, of the 96 percent who had dependents, the majority (71 percent) listed a wife *and* at least one child as their dependents, a far greater percentage than the draftees. Those statistics show that the Denton County exemption board focused not only on a man's marital status but the *type* of dependents he supported.[39]

For the purposes of the draft, dependency was defined as having a family that was solely dependent on the male for support. Did the Denton County exemption board follow this guidance? Without question, it appears the most significant element in determining a man's liability for the draft was his marital status and not only dependents, but what kind of dependents. The board, however, tried to explain that a man would not be exempt from the draft solely because of marriage or children. In fact, in a report submitted to the Provost Marshal General's office in December 1917, the board claimed they were "careful to instruct registrants of their rights to claim exemptions and the meaning of the law as applied to dependents." In response to a query by the Provost Marshal General's Office asking if marriage or children should be the sole grounds for exempting a man for dependency, the Denton board responded with a single word: "No." The Denton board also claimed they did not exempt "virtually all married men." The local newspaper, however, reported that although the board had not explicitly stated so, "it is fairly evident after a scrutiny of the exemption claims rejected and accepted that the board has adopted a rule that men with dependent wives and children generally speaking shall be exempt." Men with only wives dependent on them, the paper reported, were more likely to be drafted. Although the board believed this was a misinterpretation and attempted to correct that impression in a newspaper article, the sample of drafted men and exempted men certainly lends merit to the newspaper's claim.[40]

The Denton board finally explained its interpretation of granting exemptions based on dependency: "Where mode of family living, if not extravagant, would be seriously disturbed by absence of husband, discharges were granted. In cases where there was enough independent income for support of family in practically former condition discharges were refused. Also refused where husband had in the past failed to furnish proper support and wife had been compelled to work." The board was also leery of granting discharges to men who had married after May 18, 1917, in what many considered "slacker marriages," assuming that such marriages were entered into simply to keep the husband from being drafted. Also, the board reported that the "most severe criticisms" of the regulations (but not the board itself) "are in cases where men have been exempted when it is a well known fact that every want of the wife would be provided for by relatives." Why the board would level such criticism of the "regulations" is unclear since the board itself was the authority on dependency claims in the county. This statement also suggests that the board did not follow the national guidelines in every case if residents criticized them for this. Nevertheless, dependency remained a sensitive issue and was often difficult to decide objectively even in the most straightforward cases, and there was often a subjective element in deciding claims.[41]

It is also instructive to examine how many men claimed exemptions from the draft and yet were drafted. Of the draftees, 40 percent believed that they had grounds for exemption and stated so at the time they registered. Of those forty men, twenty-four requested exemptions because of dependents (60 percent). Interestingly, fifteen men had dependents but did not initially request an exemption and were drafted, as did twenty-five men who were eventually granted exemptions. Eleven of the men who were drafted initially claimed exemption on occupational grounds. As mentioned, the Denton County exemption board was required to pass occupational claims on to the district board. Those eleven men had their occupational claims denied by the district boards. As historian Jeannette Keith has argued, the selective service system was created in such a way as to make "small farmers expendable," and this appeared to be the case in Denton County as only a handful of men received occupational exemptions.[42]

Two draftees initially also reported they should be exempt for medical reasons. Elmer Swofford, an unmarried farmer from Justin, Texas, claimed to have an "enlarged liver," while Earl Collins, a Denton grocery clerk, simply wrote "physical disqualification" on his registration card. Most claims for medical exemptions were proven false when the men were examined by doctors. Perhaps these two men, among others, were what spurred the Denton board to report that the biggest problem encountered with physical examinations was the "complaint of diseases which did not exist," even though they also pointed out that "very little" falsification during physical examinations was attempted. The work of examining the registrants was tedious. For example, on one draft call four doctors each examined forty men in one day, and legitimate failures of physical examinations were more common than many officials expected. In the initial group of registrants, for example, the Denton board reported that of 146 men examined in one day, 50 failed the physical examination (34 percent), while three days later 40 out of 80 men were rejected physically. The large numbers of men initially rejected on physical grounds also caused some grumbling from local residents. In one instance, the local paper printed a letter written by a woman opposed to the discharge of some "strong young men" because of medical reasons, although they had been legitimately rejected by the physical examining board. On the other hand, Gentle Price, an African American, was examined by the physicians and approved for military service although he had just lost several fingers in a shotgun accident.[43]

One draftee, George E. Tyson, listed his occupation as farmer but claimed exemption as a "minister." Religion could factor into the draft in several ways, examples of which occurred in Denton County. First, a man was eligible for exemption if he was a "student of divinity." Problems arose, however, when boards were confronted with determining not if the man was actually a student, but whether the school *qualified* as a divinity school. In fact, the board believed that the rules regarding "students of divinity schools should be more defined." The Denton board also reported that there were "some attempts to evade [the] draft on this ground in this county which were aided by certificate from schools which we are sure could not be classed as 'recognized divinity schools.'" Second, some claimed exemption as conscientious objectors due to their religious beliefs. Joel R. Chambers was a married farmer from Argyle, Texas. He claimed exemption on the grounds that he was a member of the Church of Christ. The Denton County exemption board was very clear on how they interpreted the draft rules for these types of claims: "We have very little patience with such of these as have made claims and believe in most cases . . . these claims have been solely for the purpose of evasion." Chambers was drafted, and it appeared the same would happen to David F. Koiner of Krum, also a member of the Church of Christ. Koiner, however, eventually secured an exemption on occupational grounds.[44]

In general, Denton County had few problems with men who refused to register or who deserted or evaded the draft, although the county was not completely immune. In total, the Denton exemption board reported 92 men as "delinquents and deserters." However, after the cases were investigated, only nine were determined to be "willful" or "deliberate" deserters. One example of draft resistance in Denton occurred in September 1918 when the board prepared to send a group of men to San Antonio's Camp Travis. One man, Marion Swindell, failed to answer the roll call. After being questioned as to why he failed to show up, Swindell allegedly responded that "he did not care anything about the nation and that he was not coming." When Swindell was brought to the courthouse for further questioning, he refused to walk from the car and had to be carried into the courthouse. Eventually, he was put on the train with the other men and sent to Camp Travis as a "prisoner who refused to respond when called." The *Denton Record-Chronicle* followed up Swindell's story the next day by interviewing his mother, who claimed that her son was not an anarchist but a conscientious objector. His mother stated that Swindell "has never had even a toy gun in his possession and knows nothing more about shooting than a little child. He does believe in a Supreme Being—one who rules over all nations alike and for this reason does not believe wars between nations right." Swindell himself claimed that he would not go to war voluntarily "but that the government would have to come after him." Only then would his conscience be clear.[45]

Finally, what about race? Were African Americans in Denton Country drafted more frequently than others? Were their exemption claims taken seriously? Of the 7,579 registrants in Denton County, there is no complete analysis of the white and African-American registrants. Twenty draftees in the sample were African-American (20 percent). Of those twenty men, eight (40 percent) requested exemptions but were denied as opposed to thirty-two whites in the same situation (40 percent). These eight men were married with dependents. Also, of the twenty men, all were engaged in farming, except one who was a dishwasher. Overall, there appeared to be little distinction between white and African-American draftees, at least in Denton County. Of the sample of men exempted from the draft, however, there were fewer African Americans. In fact, out of the sample of one hundred men exempted from the draft, only five (5 percent) were African-American and one was Hispanic. Of these five men, three claimed exemption because of dependents, and one had dependents but did not claim exemption at the time of registration, perhaps unaware that he could. It is difficult to draw specific conclusions based on the sample size, because in November 1917, the *Record-Chronicle* reported that 148 African Americans had been granted exemptions. While the sample suggests that the board may not have given serious attention to all the claims of local African Americans, it is impossible to know to what extent racism played a part in drafting or exempting them. Anecdotal evidence, however, points to the attitude toward African Americans common at the time, as Chairman Bailey commented that "the drafted negroes are pretty patriotic as a rule. They are just about as anxious to fight for their country as the enlisted men, once they are called." Furthermore, when African-American registrants failed to appear when called by the board,

Chairman Bailey announced that unless these men communicated with the board "immediately," they would be "posted as deserters."[46]

The Denton County exemption board took a set of rules created by the national government and attempted to apply them at the local level in an effort to find men they thought could best serve the nation during wartime while not disrupting the economic base of the country or leaving families unable to take care of themselves. In Denton County and Texas, industrial and agricultural claims lagged far behind claims for dependency. Dependency, not marriage, was the key factor in the county in determining whether or not a man would be called upon to serve. Although dependency is difficult to define, it appeared that in Denton County the board exempted far more men because of wives *and* children than for other reasons. Regardless, determining whether the board made the right choice in selecting a man for service or exemption was no easy task. What is possible to determine, however, is that the board interacted on an individual level with the community and attempted impartiality, although such was impossible when the people who were responsible for bringing men into the Army lived in the same area, were familiar with local circumstances, and knew many of the same people.

But the most important thing is not determining whether the board succeeded in its task. Instead, the more important factor was the men themselves, who, for whatever reasons, volunteered, were drafted, or were exempted. The Denton County exemption board influenced the lives of these three groups. Some volunteered to escape the draft, some were forced through the concept of universal liability to serve, and some were released from military duty. All, however, as individuals interacted with the national government through the medium of the local exemption board. And while the local board sent some men home to grow old with their families, it in turn doubtless sent some men to their deaths. By that fact alone, the Denton County exemption board played an integral part in the lives of Denton County residents during the First World War.

Notes

1. All quotes from *Denton Record-Chronicle*, July 20, 1917.

2. John W. Chambers, *To Raise an Army: The Draft Comes to Modern America* (New York: Free Press, 1987), 98, 200–1; David M. Kennedy, *Over Here: The First World War and American Society* (1980; repr., New York: Oxford University Press, 2004), 154.

3. Lonnie J. White, *Panthers to Arrowheads: The 36th (Texas-Oklahoma) Division in World War I* (Austin: Presidial Press, 1984); Lonnie J. White, *The 90th Division in World War I: The Texas-Oklahoma Draft Division in the Great War* (Manhattan, KS: Sunflower University Press, 1996).

4. Chambers, *To Raise an Army*, 79, 103, 105, 128.

5. Ibid., 130, 133.

6. Ibid., 136, 138.

7. Ibid., 166, 170.

8. Enoch H. Crowder, *Final Report of the Provost Marshal General to the Secretary of War on the Operations of the Selective Service System to July 15, 1919* (Washington, D.C.: Government Printing Office, 1920), 19–24, 54–55. It should be remembered that these numbers only reflect draftees and do not represent *all* soldiers who fought in World War I or who served from Texas.

9. Ibid., 20–24, 52–53.

10. Enoch H. Crowder, *Second Report of the Provost Marshal General to the Secretary of War on the Operations of the Selective Service System to December 20, 1918* (Washington, D.C.: Government Printing Office, 1919), 586–87.

11. Ibid., 268, 364–65 (first quote), 479.

12. Ibid., 276, 479.

13. Ibid., 277 (first quote); Kennedy, *Over Here*, 155.

14. A legal advisory board was not appointed for Denton County until late November 1917 and consisted of three local lawyers, H. R. Wilson, F. F. Hill, and Joe S. Gambill. They were to "assist registrants in filling out the questionnaire." *Denton Record-Chronicle*, Nov. 27, 1917; Crowder, *Second Report*, 279–80, ix–x.

15. Denton routinely had parades and celebrations throughout the war, see *Denton Record-Chronicle,* Aug. 28, 1917, Mar. 26, Apr. 6, 1918, for examples; for the dynamite story, see *Denton Record-Chronicle*, Feb. 18, 1918; for flag sales, see *Denton Record-Chronicle*, Apr. 4, 7, 1917; for German sympathizers, see *Denton Record-Chronicle*, Apr. 4, 9, 13, 14, 1917.

16. Crowder, *Second Report*, 191.

17. Meirion and Susie Harries point out that to decrease the time between legislation and implementation of the draft, Secretary of War Newton Baker and Gen. Enoch H. Crowder "illegally" had draft registration cards printed "covertly," and distributed them around the country swearing people to secrecy. See Meirion and Susie Harries, *The Last Days of*

Innocence: America at War, 1917–1918 (New York: Vintage, 1997), 94. Sheriff Pat Gallagher apparently had no qualms about announcing that he had received draft registration cards; see *Denton Record-Chronicle*, May 9, 20 (quote), 1917.

18. This was an issue that recurred throughout the draft period as the members of the exemption board complained about being paid on time, see Denton Board Report; *Denton Record-Chronicle*, May 22, 24 (quote), 1917. It was not until September 1918 that a "new schedule of pay" was approved, which paid board members between $50 and $200 per month based on the number of registrants in the county. Based on the number of registrants, the *Denton Record-Chronicle* speculated that the board members would receive the maximum allowable stipend; see *Denton Record-Chronicle*, Sept. 24, 1918.

19. County Clerk Roy Mays also expressed surprise at the number of transients in the county who had registered at his office, estimating that nearly 400 non-county residents had been registered, including the two hundred men working in Justin on the pipeline, *Denton Record-Chronicle,* May 30, 1917. Mays also feared that a number of non-county residents were working in the "harvest fields" might have disregarded the order to register, *Denton Record-Chronicle,* June 4, 1917. See also *Denton Record-Chronicle*, May 24 (first quote), 29 (second and third quotes), 1917.

20. Ibid., May 24 (quote), 30, 1917.

21. Instead of granting clear-cut exemptions, by December 1917 the War Department had shifted to a system of classification, in which men eligible for service were put in Class 1, while men who were previously exempted were now placed in deferred classes II–V. In total, there were twenty-five subgroups that a man could be classified under. See *Denton Record-Chronicle*, May 24, 1917, Nov. 26, 1918; Crowder, *Final Report*, 20–21.

22. While no "slacker" roundups were held in Denton, one did occur in nearby Fort Worth, in which more than 1,200 men were "herded into the city hall for investigation as to whether or not they were slackers." See *Denton Record-Chronicle*, June 1 (first three quotes), 4 (fourth quote), 2 (last quote), Sept. 5, 1917, Aug. 16, 1918.

23. Christopher C. Springer might have acted under such pressure. Springer, who lived in Pittsburgh, Pennsylvania, was "certified into service" by the Denton County board for "failure to appear when called." Upon receiving this notice he wrote to the board that he was "ready and willing to serve" and that he would come back to Denton if transportation

could be provided. When he did not hear from them, he spent his own money and traveled home to Denton to report in person, whence he was sent to Camp Travis. See *Denton Record-Chronicle*, June 1 (first quote), 4 (second quote), Sept. 13, 18, 1917, Apr. 30, 1918 (third quote).

24. Prior to the draft, the African-American community issued a statement that "we, the colored citizens of Denton, declare our allegiance to the American people and our loyalty and patriotism to the Stars and Stripes." See *Denton Record-Chronicle*, Apr. 12, June 5 (quote), 6, 11, 1917; Crowder, *Second Report*, 587. The *Record-Chronicle* published the list of those who registered for the draft on June 16, 1917, revealing the county had few ethnic groups and aliens. In November 1917, the *Record-Chronicle* reported registration of the following ethnic groups: Twelve Mexicans, one Bulgarian, one Austria-Hungarian, one naturalized German, four Russians, three Germans, one Austrian, two Greeks, and one Italian. See *Denton Record-Chronicle*, Nov. 21, 1917.

25. *Denton Record-Chronicle*, June 16, 25, 1917.

26. Ibid., June 27, July 2, 24, 1917.

27. This was not the only draft call, merely the first. As the war continued, Texas and Denton County constantly received numerous draft calls. Thus, the work of the board continued on a routine basis throughout 1917 and 1918. See *Denton Record-Chronicle*, July 25, 1917.

28. Board Chairman John W. Bailey later stressed to the citizens of the community that they should not sign off on affidavits in support of exemptions unless they were sure of the information they contained because "some men are prone to sign affidavits on the very slightest provocation. They never stop to think that if they swear to facts that are questionable and let a man loose from his service … they are by that act sending another man in his place." *Denton Record-Chronicle*, June 7, July 2, Oct. 18 (quote), 1917.

29. Registrants could claim exemption on more than one ground. In Denton County, Emmett H. Whitehead claimed exemption on industrial grounds and was denied. He then requested an exemption because of a dependent wife, had that claim rejected by the local board, and then appealed to the district board rather than be drafted. See *Denton Record-Chronicle*, Oct. 24, 1917. Another man requested exemptions for a dependent father, then on agricultural grounds, and finally as a divinity student. All claims were denied. Registrants of this sort were called "persevering exemptionists" by Bailey. *Denton Record-Chronicle*, July 13 (first and second quote), 28, Nov. 5, 1917, Apr. 26 (third quote), May 10, 1918 (fourth quote).

30. J. M. Gary eventually replaced A. W. Robertson on the board, which cited his "home and interests" as being in the eastern part of the county and that he had "already sacrificed nearly a year's time to this arduous work." However, B. F. Paschall succeeded Gary in September 1918 because of illness; see *Denton Record-Chronicle*, June 4, Sept. 24, 1918. Joe R. Bailey served with the 344th Field Artillery (*Denton Record-Chronicle*, Oct. 11, 1917, July 28, 1918), and John W. Bailey Jr. was the "second Denton boy" to become a pilot in the Air Service (*Denton Record-Chronicle*, Oct. 5, Nov. 6, 1917).

31. American Battle Monument Commission, *American Armies and Battlefields in Europe: A History, Guide, and Reference Book* (Washington, D.C.: Government Printing Office, 1938), 516. The three groups of registrants were based on initial company rosters for Company M from Ed F. Bates, *History and Reminiscences of Denton County* (1918; repr., Denton: Terrell-Wheeler, 1976). Reports of draftees shipped to training camps by the Denton Board are available in the Records of the Selective Service System (World War I), Texas, Denton County, Record Group 163, National Archives, Washington, D.C. See also newspaper lists of exempted men published in the *Denton Record-Chronicle*. The draftees and exemptees were randomly selected to generate a sample of one hundred for each group. For each group, data was taken from the Selective Service Registration Cards for World War I (Texas) available at the National Archives and Records Administration, Southwest Region, Fort Worth (Microfilm M1509, Reels 43–45).

32. Indeed, during the debates on the draft, Speaker of the House James B. Clark stated that "there is precious little difference between a conscript and a convict." See Chambers, *To Raise an Army*, 165; Gregory W. Ball, "Over the Top: Denton County Soldiers of the Great War, 1917–1918," *Southwestern Historical Quarterly* 114 (Oct. 2010), 137.

33. Selective Service Registration Cards for World War I (M1509, Reels 43–45).

34. Ibid.

35. While the district board generally considered agricultural and industrial claims, they did handle appeals as well. In one case, the County Judge of Denton County, Fred M. Bottorff, was originally denied his exemption claim of a dependent wife and daughter as well as holding a county office by the local board, but was granted his exemption by the district board; see *Denton Record-Chronicle* Sept. 1, 21, 1917. According to instructions received by the Provost Marshal General's office, in 1918 the Denton board began to classify men based on occupation. In order

to forestall complaints, Chairman Bailey stated that "the occupational classification ... is simply to show the War Department where a man can best be used after he is called to service," and would not affect the time of year he might be called or any deferments based on agricultural or dependent grounds. See *Denton Record-Chronicle*, Jan. 24, 1918.

36. Information on fifty-five men of Company M could not be found; see Ball, "Over the Top," 137.

37. Selective Service Registration Cards for World War I (M1509, Reels 43–45). In support of this point, it did not appear that drafting a large number of farmers had a major impact on agriculture, at least cotton production. The *Denton Record-Chronicle* noted in October 1918 that at least 90 percent of the year's cotton crop had been picked, although experts predicted that the 1918 yield would be "less than half of an average crop." See *Denton Record-Chronicle*, Oct. 10, 1918; one draftee, Jerry Scott Fowler, worked for the *Denton Record-Chronicle* and wrote a number of pieces to the paper about his experiences. For example, see *Denton Record-Chronicle*, Oct. 18, 1917.

38. Ball, "Over the Top," 137.

39. Selective Service Registration Cards for World War I (M1509, Reels 43–45).

40. Records of the Selective Service System (World War I), Provost Marshal General's Office, Local Board Experience Files, Texas, Denton County, Topic III: Exemption and Discharge in General and Topic VI: Discharge for Dependency, RG 163, NA; *Denton Record-Chronicle*, Aug. 16, 17, 1917.

41. If there is any doubt that marriage and children were a key consideration, the *Denton Record-Chronicle* published an overview of the draft in the county up to that point in November 1917. For men who were "called and accepted for service," 61 were married, while 300 were single. On the other hand, of those who were "called but not accepted," 719 were married, while 321 were single. See *Denton Record-Chronicle*, Aug. 1, Nov. 21, 1917; Local Board Experience Files, Texas, Denton County, Topic VI: Discharge for Dependency.

42. The *Denton Record-Chronicle* reported on two men who had been drafted because their claims of dependency were denied by the local board. However, both had their claims reversed by the district board, along with nineteen other men. These two, R. C. Leuty and Emory Beck, were already at Camp Travis in training and were expected to be sent home. See *Denton Record-Chronicle*, Sept. 24, 1917; Selective Service Registration Cards for World War I (M1509, Reels 43–45); Jeannette

Keith, *Rich Man's War, Poor Man's Fight: Race, Class, and Power in the Rural South during the First World War* (Chapel Hill: University of North Carolina Press, 2004), 82.

43. Injuries did keep some men from being drafted. Jerry Giles, a farmer in Sanger, Texas, claimed exemption for a "bad left eye" although he was married with one child. Charlie King, a married farmer in Pilot Point, Texas, claimed a "crooked left arm." Both were exempted from the draft. In order to solve the issue of too many physical disqualifications, the government began to ease the rules for physical exams. See *Denton Record-Chronicle*, Aug. 3, 7, 10, 28, Sept. 12, 1917; Selective Service Registration Cards for World War I (M1509, Reels 43–45); Local Board Experience Files, Texas, Denton County, Topic II: Physical Examinations.

44. Another man, William Henry Veale, claimed exemption as a divinity student but also requested to go into the hospital corps of the Army; see *Denton Record-Chronicle* Aug. 25, Sept. 12, Oct. 25, 1917; Local Board Experience Files, Texas, Denton County, Topic III: Sundry Exemptions and Topic VIII: Religious Objectors, Morally Unfit.

45. Records of the Selective Service System (World War I), Final List of Delinquent Registrants and Deserters, 1919, Texas, Denton County, RG163, Southwest Branch, Fort Worth, Texas; *Denton Record-Chronicle*, Sept. 5 (first two quotes), 6 (last two quotes), 1918.

46. An indicator of the attitude of Denton County residents was that when white soldiers left for training camp, they were often given a celebratory send off. In one example, the "Young Men's Business League entertained the men at a picture show Saturday afternoon and arranged for a short program after escorting them to the station. The citizens of the city were asked to be present at the station to bid the men Godspeed." See *Denton Record-Chronicle*, Mar. 30, Apr. 27, 1918. On the other hand, when African-American soldiers were sent off, the newspaper did report it, but there was usually little evidence of any celebration, although in one instance the local paper reported that "a large crowd was at the station Wednesday afternoon to see the men leave"; see *Denton Record-Chronicle*, Apr. 1, July 18, 1918; Selective Service Registration Cards for World War I (M1509, Reels 43–45; *Denton Record-Chronicle*, Oct. 23, Nov. 5 (Bailey quote), 21, 1917.

Edmundo E. and Jovita González Mireles. Portrait by Estevan Medrano

"Gente Decente": Tejanos Jovita González and Edmundo E. Mireles

Harriett Denise Joseph, Alix Riviere, and Jordan Penner

When Jovita González married Edmundo E. Mireles in 1935, she had already accomplished more than most Mexican Americans of her generation, male or female. By the time she was thirty, the Tejana was an acclaimed folklorist, historian, speaker, author, and teacher. González's marriage, however, would dramatically change the course of her life and career. Her interests became secondary to those of her husband, the Mexican-born Mireles, who was destined to become a renowned pioneer in bilingual education. At a critical time in American history, González worked with him to promote the teaching of Spanish language and culture in public schools. As Mireles gained prominence on the local, state, and national scenes, his wife's earlier accomplishments faded into the background. Her identity became that of Mrs. Edmundo E. Mireles. Not until the late twentieth century, after Jovita and Edmundo were dead, did the efforts of a few dedicated scholars renew appreciation of González's historical importance. Today she is recognized as a ground-breaking Mexican-American woman, even more celebrated than her husband. To understand how and why she became more famous in death than in life, one must examine the lives of this remarkable couple: Jovita González and Edmundo E. Mireles.

Jovita González came from a family with proud roots but few financial resources. Her mother, Severina Guerra Barrera, was a housewife whose Spanish ancestors held an impressive land grant in the Rio Grande region during the colonial period. Her father, Jacobo González Rodríguez, was a teacher in Tamaulipas, México. Born around 1904 on her grandparents' San Román Ranch in the border region near Roma, Texas, Jovita's early years on the ranch significantly shaped her life. She and her sister would go horseback riding with their grandfather, take long walks with their father, and visit with the *vaqueros*. The girls were fascinated by the cowboys' tales of "ranch lore" and border ballads. Also entertaining were stories about ghosts and witches. These experiences helped the sisters gain pride in their Hispanic heritage. From their grandmother they also learned that family roots had been planted in Texas long before the Anglos arrived, and she impressed upon them that "Texas is our home. Always remember these words: Texas is ours."[1]

Regarding the Spanish language as an integral part of the family's identity, Jovita's father initially did not allow English spoken in his home. But his pride in being a Mexican American did not blind him to obstacles facing Tejanos in the early twentieth century. With the coming of the railroad and increased Anglo migration from the American Midwest, the border region was changing to the disadvantage of Mexican Texans, regarded as inferior by the rapidly growing Anglo population. These concerns and the realization that his children were receiving an inferior education at the small one-teacher, ranch-supported school convinced Jacobo of the need to relocate. The senior González decided to move his family to San Antonio in 1910, but the children's adjustment to that Anglo-dominated city proved difficult. Fortunately, Jovita was a talented student who earned the equivalent of a high school diploma while still in her teens.[2]

Jovita's high school education was an unusual accomplishment for a Mexican-American woman in that era, but she longed for additional learning. Her goal was to attend The University of Texas at Austin, an institution then admitting only a small number of Mexican Americans. Although the young Tejana had academic ability, financial necessity forced her to delay her dream, and she enrolled in a much less expensive normal school. There she earned a teaching certificate in two years. Then, with the assistance of her uncle, Jovita landed a teaching position in Rio Grande City. She lived there with him and his family to save money and attain her goal of attending The University of Texas at Austin.[3]

In the early 1920s, González's efforts enabled her to enroll at The University of Texas at Austin. Jovita studied Spanish under Professor Lilia Casis, who became a role model for the younger woman. Unfortunately, she was forced to return to San Antonio within a year when her funds ran out. There she directed a small school until she received a scholarship in 1924 to cover her major expenses at Our Lady of the Lake College. With this assistance, she earned a Bachelor of Arts degree in Spanish in 1927. Determined to study under Casis, even while enrolled at Our Lady of the Lake, Jovita managed to take summer courses in Austin with her role model. This also afforded the young Tejana a chance to interact with other noted members of The University of Texas faculty, such as folklorist J. Frank Dobie, who was to play a critical role in her life, and historian Carlos E. Castañeda, who was a friend of Jovita's family.[4]

Dobie, "the man who had put Texas folklore studies on the map," became Jovita's mentor for about twenty years. Early in their relationship, the two were formal in their interactions with each other. Later, however, Jovita came to address him as "my godfather" and "*muy amigo mío*" (my very good friend). The famed folklorist had a profound influence on the Tejana. Although she had always been fascinated by folk tales of the border region, Dobie helped her to understand their importance to other people; and he encouraged her to record those stories in written form. At his urging, González began collecting and writing border history. Her specialty became transforming oral traditions into short stories or sketches that appealed to "readers who preferred a refined quality of literature."[5]

Dobie helped open doors for the Tejana that would otherwise have been closed to a minority woman. González's talents, however, allowed her to take advantage of opportunities that presented themselves. Her mentor was a prominent figure in the Texas Folklore Society (TFS), and because of him, Jovita gained acceptance into that prestigious group. Assisted by Dobie, González first appeared on the annual TFS program in 1927. Despite her own impressive ancestry, Jovita chose not to talk about "the landed proprietor who, in my part of the state, forms the better class." Instead, she focused on "the socially alienated *vaquero*." Jovita's formal presentation was accompanied by Mexican cowboys who sang ballads. Not only was the speech well received by the audience, but it also led to her first publication, an article in *Texas Southwestern Lore*, the official journal of the TFS.[6] This possibly was the first time a Mexican American in Texas had published an essay in English, and the Tejana was just getting started. Soon thereafter, she became a regular speaker at the TFS's annual program.

At the 1928 TFS conference, Jovita presented a story entitled "The Woman Who Lost Her Soul," which was also later published. The tale involves Don Francisco, who changes as a result of meeting a young woman named Carmen. "Spoiled and selfish," Carmen has an affair with her best friend's fiancé. The devastated friend, as she lies dying, warns Carmen that "my spirit will torture yours from Hell." Carmen's mother then dies of shame, and people treat the young woman as an outcast. "A living corpse," she believes that her soul is with her "victim in Hell." With the intervention of a priest, Don Francisco learns a valuable lesson about forgiveness of his own daughter, as he and his wife try to help Carmen "become her old self again."[7]

Through tales such as "The Woman Who Lost Her Soul," the Tejana sought to create "tolerance and mutual understanding" between Anglos and Hispanics. That her efforts were effective is evident by the recognition she received early in her career. By the end of the 1920s, González's speeches and publications made her one of the "stars" of the TFS. After serving two terms as secretary, the Tejana was elected vice-president of the organization in 1929.[8]

Despite her literary accomplishments, Jovita was determined to continue her formal education. But, again, money was a problem. By 1927, she had taken a position as a Spanish teacher at Saint Mary's Hall in San Antonio. With the help of Saint Mary's director and Professor Dobie, within two years Jovita received the Lapham Scholarship. This finally allowed her to pursue graduate studies at The University of Texas. Being a Tejana at The University of Texas brought mixed blessings. As a graduate student under the direction of historian Eugene C. Barker, Jovita had access to a quality education, available to few of her gender or ethnicity. Indeed, she was one of perhaps thirty Mexican Americans from the Rio Grande Valley and one of about 250 from the entire state who attended the university at the time. Outside the classroom, González had time to embrace her Hispanic heritage by joining the Latin American Club, the Newman Club for Catholic students, and the *Junta del Club de Bellas Artes* (Fine Arts Club).[9] Celebrating that same heritage in the classroom, however, proved much more difficult.

Jovita learned hard lessons as a Hispanic woman at a university then controlled by Anglo males. White professors praised the role of Anglo Americans in Texas's past but ignored the injustices done to Mexico and its people. Minorities were presented as "inferior . . . and wholly unequal to the [other] Texans." Upset by what was being taught in some of her courses, the Tejana nevertheless understood that to challenge openly her professors would threaten her status as a graduate student and future teacher. Although she kept her tongue in the classroom, González found other means by which to express her views. Based on her love and understanding of border people, she proposed to do her master's thesis on social life in three heavily Hispanic South Texas counties, but her major professor declared the topic unsuitable, and it was certainly nontraditional. Acting on González's behalf, Castañeda argued that her work would prove useful "in the years to come as source material." Persuaded, Barker let the Tejana proceed with one of the few theses being written at the time that did not present "Mexicans as a social problem."[10]

In planning her research trips into Cameron, Starr, and Zapata counties, the Tejana knew that women of her day did not normally engage in activities like her undertaking. People in South Texas might well be reluctant to share their histories with her, so she needed them to understand that she was a "proper woman," even though she was pursuing a career path usually reserved for men. To increase her chances of success, Jovita got letters of introduction from Catholic and Episcopal officials and clergy on the border that referred to her as "Maestro Jacobo's daughter . . . and Don Francisco Guerra's granddaughter," as well as "*una persona decente*" (a decent or refined person). To be seen as one of the "*gente decente*" was very important to Jovita González, because the words meant that one had good breeding, as opposed to the less refined and poorly educated "*gente corriente*" (common people). Even though her family was "lower middle class" during her lifetime, she never forgot that her ancestors once had been among the elite. That she worked to preserve the culture and customs of lower-class Hispanics, a group from which birth set her apart, was only one of several ironies that marked her life.[11]

Another irony was that González's thesis on "Social Life in Cameron, Starr, and Zapata Counties" presented Texas history differently from that taught by her major professor, Barker. He and other historians of the time wrote books that, for the most part, justified "Anglo imperialism." Whereas Barker considered the Texas Revolution of 1836 to be "at the veritable center of Texas history," González pointed out that Spaniards and Mexicans had been in the state long before Texas was Texas. Jovita's thesis contained chapters on topics such as "Present Mexican Population in the Counties Considered," "Border Politics," and "What the Coming of the Americans Has Meant to the Border People." She believed the early twentieth century was bringing a "Renaissance to the border counties [and] an awakening in every sense of the word." A new generation of Tejanos, with "a clearer understanding of the good and bad qualities of both races," was becoming Americanized. Presciently, she wrote that they had "a store of traditions" behind them and "a struggle for equality and justice before the law" in front of them. González concluded her thesis with the hope that this new generation would "bring to an end the racial feuds that have existed in the border for nearly a century."[12]

Despite its controversial nature, "Social Life in Cameron, Starr, and Zapata Counties" helped González meet the requirements for her master's degree. She graduated from The University of Texas in August 1930. After finishing her graduate studies, she continued to teach at Saint Mary's Hall, to be active in the TFS, and to be a publishing scholar. More than that, by 1930 Jovita's star was shining so brightly that she became the first ever Mexican-American woman to be elected president of the TFS, an office to which she was reelected the next year. Since the TFS had few female or Hispanic members, her two terms in its highest office were especially noteworthy. In that same year, she felt secure enough to vent some of her frustrations, and not just remain silent. In an article entitled "America Invades the Border Towns," she criticized Anglos and Hispanics for their roles in the "racial struggle" that gripped South Texas from 1848 to 1930. She described Anglos as "an aggressive, conquering, and materialistic people" but also labeled people of her ethnicity as "a volatile but passive and easily satisfied race." With this published article, her completed thesis, and Dobie's support, the Tejana received a prestigious Rockefeller Grant in 1934. This enabled her to take a year's leave from teaching "to research and write a book on South Texas history and culture." The materials gathered for her book were used later on for program presentations at professional meetings and for additional published articles.[13]

Although the professional side of Jovita's life was going remarkably well, she was still single at age thirty. Reasons for her delaying marriage perhaps seem obvious, because educational and professional goals had consumed the Tejana's time and energy for years. And even into her early thirties, she still held hopes of pursuing a doctorate degree. The severe economic depression in the United States also complicated Jovita's life. As a working woman and graduate student, Jovita not only had to support herself, but she also was forced to help her family as the economy worsened in the 1930s.[14] But not all obstacles to marriage were financial considerations for the Tejana. As a proud Hispanic woman, González probably wanted to marry within her ethnic group, but if she desired an educated and ambitious Latino as her husband, he might well be wary of marrying an independent, intelligent, and non-traditional woman. Another complication was that Jovita lived in an era when men were dominant over women in American society. This dominance was even more pronounced in Hispanic culture. Having already learned some hard lessons about silence and submission, González undoubtedly had serious reservations about surrendering her independence.

Regardless of the factors that had kept her single, the Tejana put aside these concerns and married Edmundo E. Mireles in 1935.[15] The two had met while students at The University of Texas. Later, during their long years together, Jovita González de Mireles would learn that marriage to a strong Hispanic male was not that different from being a graduate student at The University of Texas. She had to make difficult compromises, put her career second to Edmundo's, and learn once again when it was prudent to stay silent.

Who was this man for whom González was willing to make such sacrifices? Mireles, in many respects, was a worthy partner for this accomplished Mexican-American woman. His father, Sostenes, was a merchant in Mexico, where Edmundo was born in late 1905. The circumstances of his upbringing are unclear, but it is certain that Edmundo grew up in San Antonio, where he was schooled and learned English. Young Edmundo graduated from Main Avenue High in 1926, took classes at San Antonio College, and then transferred to The University of Texas to study classical languages. Active in extra-curricular activities and a promising student of Greek and Latin, Edmundo became president of the Classical Language Club. He also served as editor of the university's first Latino newspaper. After receiving his college degree in 1931, Edmundo returned to San Antonio to teach at the same high school from which he had graduated and married Jovita González four years later.[16]

The two Hispanics had much in common, even though Edmundo was born in Mexico and Jovita in Texas. Both were literate in English, as well as Spanish. Both were alumni of The University of Texas, and given their levels of education and career opportunities, they differed significantly from the vast majority of Hispanics in Texas. Nevertheless, the two of them took pride in their heritage, as evidenced by extra-curricular involvement in college. Mireles was no doubt impressed with his wife's accomplishments, and perhaps even a bit intimidated by them. That González was his equal was apparent. The question of whether such an unusually accomplished Latina would make a satisfactory wife was another matter altogether. Nonetheless, despite any misgivings they probably shared, their marriage lasted for almost fifty years until "death did them part." With the help of Professor Castañeda at The University of Texas, the newlyweds were hired by the San Felipe School District in Del Rio, Texas. Edmundo became a high school principal, while Jovita taught English and served as department head. Together they played a significant role in public education for the community of San Felipe.[17]

After her marriage, the Tejana remained active for a time as a folklorist, and she published articles appearing in the mid-1930s. Among her better known works from this period is "Bullet Swallower." This title was Jovita's contribution to *Puro Mexicano* (*Pure Mexican*), a compilation of Mexican folklore edited by Dobie and published in 1935. "Bullet Swallower" is narrated by Antonio, "a landowner by inheritance, a trail driver by necessity, and a smuggler and gambler by choice." As they cross the Rio Grande, Antonio and his companions are confronted by Texas Rangers. The men resist, because "it was not ethical among smugglers to lose the property of Mexicans to Americans." Death would be better than dishonor. During the confrontation, one of the Rangers shoots Antonio, but he survives. Later he boasts that "the bullet knocked all of my front teeth out, grazed my tongue and went right through the back of my neck. Didn't kill me, though." After this episode, the Hispanic folk hero is called Antonio Bullet-Swallower. As he brags: "It takes a lot to kill a man . . . who can swallow bullets."[18] Jovita González de Mireles made another presentation in the mid-1930s at the twenty-second annual meeting of the TFS in Austin. She was one of only two Hispanics on the program that year.

While his wife was busy as a teacher and folklorist, Edmundo endeavored to improve conditions for fellow Hispanics. He helped found a political group called *Club Político Latino* (Latino Political Club), and he also played an active role in the League of United Latin-American Citizens (LULAC), an organization composed of United States citizens of "Latin or Mexican descent." Mireles thought LULAC worthwhile, because it worked "to improve the citizenship of the community" and "to make [the United States] a better nation."[19]

In the late 1930s, the Mireleses moved to Corpus Christi, because LULAC members from that coastal city had recruited them. In their new home, Edmundo became a fifth grade teacher at Southgate School, while Jovita taught at a high school. In Corpus Christi, Jovita continued to work on a project dear to her heart: a historical novel, based in part on research funded by her Rockefeller grant. She wanted to record the culture of South Texas as it had existed before the Anglos arrived in the 1840s and imposed their way of life on those living along the border. Before moving to the Gulf Coast, González had asked Margaret Eimer of Del Rio to serve as co-author of the proposed novel. Perhaps the Tejana believed that a story about "the Mexican side of the war of 1848" would have a better chance of publication with an Anglo's name also appearing on the title page. No doubt the difficulty of completing the novel without assistance, given other demands on her time, likewise influenced the Tejana's decision. In any event, Eimer accepted the invitation but, given the controversial nature of the project, chose to write under the pseudonym Eve Raleigh. For years the two women "worked so hard to finish and get the manuscript on the market" that they were "sick of the thing" when it was finally completed. They nonetheless submitted the novel to three publishers, one of which "admitted that the background is interesting, the plot stirring, [and] the characters alive."[20] But in the end, all three firms sent rejection notices. Discouraged, the co-authors then abandoned the project.

Their unpublished novel focuses on the elite Mendoza y Soría clan during the period when the United States militarily occupied South Texas from 1845 to 1848, with flashbacks to earlier periods. The family head, don Santiago, is proud and domineering. He and other aristocrats are determined "to resist Anglo intruders to the death." Their daughters and sisters, however, react differently, and some of them form unions with the Anglos, relationships that "become the glue for a new society." Significantly, Edmundo Mireles was not unhappy that his wife's co-authored manuscript had been rejected for publication. She had wanted to deliver a message about the past, while his focus was on the present. He shared his wife's desire to be regarded as among the "*gente decente*," but in his view, her novel put them at risk. He and Jovita were especially vulnerable in their positions as public school teachers in Corpus Christi, where "the walls of racial prejudice" were high. Edmundo also feared that the themes of injustice by Anglo Americans, as presented in his wife's manuscript, would anger Anglo bigots and Latino nationalists. Since Jovita had decided to put aside plans to publish the novel, Edmundo insisted on destroying the manuscript, despite her objections. Once again, circumstances had forced concessions on the Tejana. She did not openly defy Edmundo but instead secretly saved a copy of her manuscript. She did, however, give up all hope of publishing it in her lifetime.[21]

Probably in reaction to her failed publication, as well as her husband's objection to it, Jovita "limited her folklore writing and focused . . . [instead] on teaching Spanish and on being a wife." As time passed, people in Corpus Christi knew her only as Mrs. Edmundo E. Mireles and were unaware of her earlier accomplishments. Edmundo took center stage, and as his star began to shine more brightly, hers dimmed. The couple increasingly devoted their energies to his passion, bilingual education.

In Corpus Christi, Mireles proved to be the right man in the right place at the right time. He and Jovita helped to change the face of public education in that city and beyond. As an educator committed to the teaching of Spanish to English-speaking students, Edmundo Mireles faced many obstacles. Not the least of these was a law enacted by the Texas legislature in 1918, more than twenty years before the Mireleses moved to Corpus. This legislation required all public school classes, except foreign language courses, to be taught in English. Foreign languages could not be taught in all lower grades.[22]

Patriotism was used to justify the "English Only" policy, adopted during World War I, when the United States was at war with Germany. The Lone Star State, of course, had a large German population, dating back to the mid-1800s. The original immigrants and their descendants had maintained their native language and culture, which made them objects of suspicion in wartime. This enabled supporters of the 1918 law to insist "that they were defending the culture of those who died at the Alamo" against undesirable foreign influences. However, long after the war ended, the English-Only rule persisted in Texas, with the new target being Mexican-born Texans. Fleeing from the chaos of the 1910 Mexican Revolution, increasing numbers of Mexico's citizens had been drawn to the United States by its geographic closeness, its economic opportunity, and its political stability. Texas's leaders were concerned about immigrants who came to the United States but did not understand English. These concerns bled over to Mexican Americans as well. They, too, were suspect as "men and women, born and reared in the Lone Star State, who speak a foreign tongue and cherish the habits and ways of another country."[23]

Forcing Mexican Americans to become "Americanized" became a major goal in the Lone Star State. For example, in 1930 the State Department of Education created a special English-Only curriculum for Spanish-speaking children in first and second grades, and the policy "was applied ruthlessly." In extreme cases, Hispanic children could be suspended from school if they spoke a single word in their birth tongue. Besides being made to feel ashamed of their language, Spanish-speaking children had trouble comprehending what was being taught in the classroom. Labeled slow learners, these youngsters were separated from other students.[24] Poor scores on intelligence tests seemed to justify the low opinion of their abilities, and many educators chose to overlook the possibility that English-language tests did not fairly measure the intelligence of minority children.

That Hispanics were darker-skinned than whites was another strike against them. Regarding people of color as inferior, whites kept apart from minorities as much as possible. African-American students, of course, were prevented by law from attending the same schools as whites, but Mexican-American students with their Spanish and Indian parentage were considered white. They were not subject to legal segregation based on race, but the English-Only policy led to the same practical results—de facto "segregated schools for Tejanos." Mexican-American students were further handicapped since many of them lived in poverty with poorly educated parents clustered in low-income neighborhoods with substandard schools. Not surprisingly, then, Mexican-American youths had a "shocking failure or dropout rate," which further reinforced notions of their inferiority.[25]

Long overdue changes were on the horizon by the time the Mireleses moved to Corpus Christi near the end of the 1930s. Once again international events and a world war fostered changes in the educational system. This time, however, the reforms would work to the benefit of Hispanic students. With Germany and Japan engaged in aggressive actions abroad, the United States faced possible involvement in another world war. Concerned American officials knew that poor relations between the United States and Spanish-speaking nations in the Western Hemisphere could be exploited by an enemy in time of war. So the United States government moved to adopt a “Good Neighbor Policy,” aimed at improving relationships in Latin America.[26]

Acutely aware that any successful Good Neighbor effort had to begin at home, in 1940 President Franklin D. Roosevelt named Nelson Rockefeller as Coordinator of Inter-American Affairs. Rockefeller’s duties included introducing “Good Neighborism” into the nation’s public schools. And somewhat surprisingly, Texas became “the most involved and cooperative state” in those efforts. The state’s leaders pledged “to bring about a greater interest in our neighbor republics,” as well as promote “more tolerance, acceptance, and understanding of Mexican Americans.” To help achieve these goals, a state law, passed in 1941, called for the teaching of Spanish beyond the second grade in public schools. Legislators in Austin recognized the change as vital to the interests of their state and the United States.[27]

After more than two decades, English-Only was dead. The State Department of Education was instructed by the Texas legislature to create a “course of study for the teaching of Spanish to all Texas schoolchildren from the third to the eighth grade.” And, of course, the state had a pioneer educator who had already created such a curriculum in Corpus Christi—Edmundo E. Mireles. He had long concluded that the future of the United States depended largely on “our ability to understand and influence other nations and to cooperate with them.” His belief that “we shall never really know a people until we understand their language” explained why he had learned—and spoke—eight languages. Significantly, to Mireles language was about “biculturalism” as much as about “bilingualism.” Joining Mireles in his crusade was Corpus Christi’s school district superintendent, R. B. Fisher. For the 1940–1941 academic year, the two men proposed a Spanish language program to help “the child to speak, read, and write the Spanish language,” while also giving “the children the proper knowledge of Latin-American customs, history, and traditions.” Students in grades three through eight would participate.

However, because the proposed bilingual program was illegal under Texas law at that time, the district had to request special permission from the state. With that accomplished, Spanish instruction began in all Corpus Christi elementary schools in September 1940.[28]

Edmundo E. Mireles served as Coordinator of Spanish for the city's public schools. Initially, he oversaw more than seventy teachers and their more than five thousand students. Faced with a lack of qualified Spanish-language teachers, Mireles exhibited a practical side. He insisted that it was "unnecessary to know much Spanish to teach a little." And, the Tejano did everything he could to ensure that teachers knew more than just "a little." He offered popular weekly training seminars and night courses, as well as reviewing lesson plans submitted by the head Spanish teacher in each school.[29]

The educator also worked with his wife and Superintendent Fisher on a textbook entitled *Mi Libro Español: Libro Uno (My Spanish Book: Book One)*. That Jovita became involved in writing this book and in other aspects of her husband's bilingual program was not surprising. After all, she was a native Spanish speaker, an experienced language teacher, and a published author. Apparently, her husband had no objection to her writings when they suited his purposes. In *Libro Uno*, the authors explained that a simple and logical method was being used in the Spanish program to avoid traditional, boring exercises in grammar. As a result, the 6,500 students who had participated were reportedly "eager to continue." Also, the first year of the pilot program "proved that a modern language properly presented is relatively easy for young children." The authors listed the three major objectives of the Spanish language program. They were "to give the child the ability to speak and read a language he hears daily," to help him or her become familiar with "Latin American history and culture, conditions and customs," and "to create a sympathetic attitude toward other peoples and their ways." The thirty lessons in the textbook were designed to accomplish those objectives. Also recommended were that at least twenty minutes a day be spent in the classroom on Spanish instruction and that each school create a Pan American Club to meet about an hour each week. In all, three volumes of *Mi Libro Español* were published for use in Spanish language instruction. The Mireleses in the 1940s also produced a six-part textbook series for the bilingual program called *El Español Elemental* (*Basic Spanish*).[30]

Edmundo E. Mireles was dedicated to the success of the Spanish language program, which he directed for a quarter of a century. And, succeed it did. Praise came from many quarters. A university professor complimented him for "pioneering in a movement which is of vital interest to Americans today and especially to Texans." As evidence of this, requests for copies of Corpus Christi's "Spanish course of study" came from as far away as New Jersey. Powerful national figures also recognized the value of the Corpus Christi model. In 1940 Congressman Richard Kleberg of Kingsville, Texas, noted that a "neighborly and friendly relationship between North and South America" was very important. Because the elementary grades were the "time to master a foreign language," he declared his support for Mireles's "fine program." Even more impressive, Good Neighbor Coordinator Nelson Rockefeller wrote Mireles that he "was most interested to hear of your work in teaching Spanish in Corpus Christi." He added, "It is most important for North Americans to know Spanish and for South and Central Americans to know English in order that a deeper understanding and friendship may be achieved." And First Lady Eleanor Roosevelt wrote, "I hope that every school in this country will teach the children to consider Spanish as their second most important language. I am studying Spanish every day I can."[31]

Time magazine in February 1944 featured an article on the Corpus Christi model and the "passionate" Mireles. The educator himself was described as a "Mild-mannered Teacher" who was a mixture of Latin and American. The author noted that Mireles kept "two books on his desk: Shakespeare and Cervantes," which represented the best of literature in English and Spanish. Mireles was quoted as hopeful that bilingual children would lead "adults a long way toward inter-American understanding." Indeed, the article reported that "in Corpus Christi more than 600 adults have enrolled in night Spanish classes in order to keep up with their children."[32]

Despite national attention, probably the greatest impact of the Spanish program was within Texas. In 1942 Thurmond Krueger of the Texas Junior Chamber of Commerce declared that Mireles's language program had "put Corpus Christi and Texas on the map." The intense focus on the Spanish language model was caused in part by the entry of the United States into World War II in 1941. As millions of Americans entered the armed forces, serious labor shortages resulted. One solution was a formal arrangement for Mexico to send workers to its northern neighbor. The historically poor treatment of Hispanics in the Southwest complicated the process, however, because the Mexican government wanted guarantees of protections for its citizens involved in the *bracero* program, which allowed the legal importation of workers from Mexico. Although the program formally began in 1942, Texas's record of discrimination caused the Mexican government to refuse to allow that state to participate until 1947. Better treatment of Latinos became necessary for the sake of the war effort, however, and attempts were made to increase public awareness about the "discrimination being practiced . . . against Mexican nationals." In a powerful newspaper piece, Undersecretary of State Sumner Welles insisted that workers came north to seek good-paying jobs "to better themselves and the members of their family." They helped the "national war effort by relieving labor shortages." He believed many Americans were unaware of discrimination against Mexicans. This mistreatment must end, he declared, or "the term 'good-neighbor policy' will lose much of its real meaning."[33]

The Mireleses worked inside and outside of the classroom to promote Pan Americanism. As one aspect of this work, they helped create the non-profit Pan American Council of Texas. Chartered in 1943 to do business in Corpus Christi, the organization was open to anyone over the age of eighteen with an interest "in the study of the Spanish language and the Latin American Republics." Jovita, under the name Mrs. E. E. Mireles, was a charter member, while Edmundo was not only president of the Council but also held a position on the Board of Directors. A formal goal of the Council was to have April 14 observed annually as Pan American day, beginning in 1943.[34]

Corpus Christi benefited because of the efforts of Edmundo E. Mireles, who found many ways to channel his talents and energy. He helped the community at large by serving as Director of the Nueces County Tuberculosis Association, as well as being a member of the Corpus Christi War Housing Board and Family Service Board. At one point, Mireles decided that he could better serve the people of the coastal region as a public official. He set his sights on a legislative seat in the 71st District, which included Nueces, Jim Wells, and Duval counties. Although Edmundo advertised himself in the Democratic primary as a highly qualified candidate who "brought national recognition to Corpus Christi," he was unsuccessful in his bid for public office. Rebounding from his failure to achieve a seat in the Texas legislature, Mireles used the radio to campaign effectively for other Mexican-American candidates running for public office. Urging Latinos to vote "in favor of our own," he insisted that they must be active in the civic and political arenas. For some twenty-five years, Mireles presented radio talks on a number of topics, many of which related not only to politics but also to education. His broadcasts informed Spanish-speaking parents on how to enroll their children in the public schools and explained the process by which low income students could receive free meals at school.[35]

Mireles also used the written word to good effect. In a Spanish-language article written for *Texas Outlook* in 1951, he provided an update on the language program in Corpus Christi. He restated his belief "that the greatest means of promoting friendship between Anglo Americans and Mexican Americans is for each to learn the language of the other." He reported that the Corpus Christi Spanish Program in its tenth year had 180 teachers and almost 10,000 students, which constituted "a contribution" to the efforts of the government to achieve "international peace." Similar information was presented two years later in an English-language piece by Mireles in *The American School Board Journal.* In that article the program was reported to have 229 teachers and more than 10,500 students, notable growth for such a short period of time. That a man as involved as Mireles in multiple undertakings found time to pursue his own higher education is truly remarkable, but he not only took graduate courses in Austin but also earned a master's degree in Spanish in the early 1950s from a college in Monterrey, Mexico.[36]

While Edmundo was involved in bilingual education, politics, public service, speaking, writing, and studying, Jovita worked as a classroom teacher and by the mid-1950s was the Head Teacher in the Spanish program for Ray High School. The Tejana also directed "*pastorelas*, pageants, and Christmastime *posadas* with local Mexican children as . . . pilgrims for the entertainment of a mostly Anglo Audience." As always, however, what Jovita did was overshadowed by her renowned husband. In her personal life, she became distant from "the Mexican American local community." To the Anglos she was "upper crust." To her own people "she was either not known" or seemed "aloof, mixing only with the highly educated people of Anglo and Spanish/Mexican society." Her friends, whether Anglo or Hispanic, were "people of prestige."[37] This is not surprising, especially when one considers her level of education, as well as her desire to be considered a cultured person. Her husband probably approved of Jovita's limiting her social circle to the "upper crust," because he valued respectability, and it benefited his career.

Edmundo E. Mireles continued to play a key role in educational reforms in Corpus Christi for decades. In the 1950s, city leaders realized that "lack of the English language" placed Latino children at a disadvantage. They often had to repeat the same grade "again and again . . . through no fault of their own." A new summer program was begun in 1956 to prepare "six-year-old Non-English speaking children to enter the first grade." The LULAC-supported pre-school training program taught a vocabulary of 500 English words and some 50 common expressions. Of the 152 students who participated in the first year, only 3 "failed to pass" to the next grade. By 1959, 680 children were enrolled in the rapidly growing program. And, of course, the coordinator of the Corpus Christi pre-school program was none other than Mireles. The Corpus Christi experiment attracted the attention of the Texas Education Agency, as well as state politicians. Mireles later claimed that this led to passage of House Bill 51 in the 56th legislature. That law established optional "Head Start" pre-school training for non-English speaking students in all Texas school districts. Again, Corpus Christi led the way with Mireles playing a key role.[38]

Thoughtful people at all levels of government recognized that educational needs were not limited to children. The Economic Opportunity Act, passed by the United States Congress in 1964, aimed "to mobilize the human and financial resources of the nation to combat poverty in the United States." Consequently, Corpus Christi began an Adult Basic Education Program (ABE) for people eighteen or older who were unable to make a decent living because of illiteracy in English. Beginning in 1965 with 560 registered adults, the free program had 721 students by its third year of existence. It went far beyond the teaching of English by offering a variety of other subjects as well.[39] By the early 1970s, the aging Edmundo Mireles was Coordinator of the ABE Program for Corpus Christi, yet another in his long line of administrative positions.

As it turned out, Edmundo remained active in the workforce longer than Jovita, who retired in 1967, in part because she suffered from diabetes and had become reclusive. Attempts to write her autobiography proved unsuccessful. If she were to be remembered after her death, it would have to be because others recognized the value of her early accomplishments. Fortunately, the "dynamic duo" of Jovita González and Edmundo E. Mireles came to the attention of historian Marta Cotera, who interviewed the couple during the 1970s. Having heard about the unpublished novel that Gonzáles had written with Eimer, the interviewer asked about it. Edmundo responded that he had destroyed the manuscript, but Jovita made a little gesture that only Cotera could see. The interviewer believed that Jovita was trying to let her know that a copy of the novel still existed. For reasons that will become apparent, that gesture proved significant after the couple were deceased, following nearly fifty years of marriage.[40] Jovita died in 1983, followed by Edmundo four years later.

Many in Corpus Christi wanted to honor the Mireleses for their tireless service to their community, and naming a school after them seemed a fitting tribute. However, the first two attempts to achieve this goal failed. In the late 1990s, renewed effort came from a committee determined to pursue "Project Mireles." It finally achieved success, and the press announced that a new elementary school was to be named "for the famous educator and his wife." As before, Edmundo was referred to as a "famous educator," while Jovita was simply "his wife." While the issue of naming a school for the Mireleses was under consideration in Corpus Christi, events occurred elsewhere that would make Jovita more than just Edmundo's wife. During their lifetimes, the couple had acquired printed materials, correspondence, handwritten notes, books, photographs, artifacts, and sound recordings.[41] With no children as heirs, the Mireleses left their estate to an employee, María Isabel Cruz. Although she donated the bulk of their library and papers to Texas A&M University at Corpus Christi, some materials found their way to The University of Texas at Austin and Texas State University in San Marcos. These collections were treasure-troves that led to Jovita again becoming a person of well-deserved renown.

The Tejana's resurrection was due in part to the efforts of Teresa Palomo Acosta and Cynthia E. Orozco. At a 1990 conference on "Mexican Americans in Texas History," these two scholars helped call attention to what an exceptional woman González had been.[42] Others interested in the life and works of Jovita González included María Eugenia Cotera, whose mother interviewed the Mireleses in the 1970s, and José E. Limón, who had graduated from Ray High School in Corpus Christi. By the early 1990s, Cotera was a graduate student at The University of Texas at Austin, where Limón was a professor. Working together, the two searched the Mireles and González papers and found Jovita's historical novel. Subsequently, María Cotera and José E. Limón edited the long-lost work, finally published under the title of *Caballero* in 1996.

Limón's search in the following year resulted in the publication of another book-length work by González. "A collection of folklore loosely woven together into a semi-autobiographical novel," *Dew on the Thorn* deals with "elite ranching families." This second novel takes place in the early twentieth century at a time of dramatic changes in South Texas. The region has been enjoying "peace and stability," in part because of the "pattern of intermarriage" of Mexicans and Anglos—a theme first introduced in *Caballero*. And Spanish is celebrated in *Dew* as having "again become the language of society" along the border. The major conflict in the second novel results from the arrival in South Texas of a new wave of Anglos, "brought by the railroad." The newcomers display prejudice against Hispanics, and Fernando Olivares, a major character in the novel, is a member of "one of the mixed families." The discrimination that he experiences in Corpus Christi shocks him. "Had he received a slap on the face he could not have felt worse. That his family had been in the country for five generations meant nothing to these Americans." To them, "he was just a Mexican, and a Mexican was something to be treated as an inferior being." Fernando, however, does not submit to discrimination without protest. He fights back through political involvement. Exhorting his fellow Hispanics "to exercise their rights as American citizens," Olivares also advises them "to learn English . . . to send our children to American schools. Not because we are ashamed of our Mexican traditions, but because this will make us know how to protect ourselves against them [the Anglos]."[43]

Dew on the Thorn mirrors the lives of Jovita González and Edmundo E. Mireles. Both were born into a minority group that was treated as inferior, yet neither meekly accepted that situation. While valuing Mexican traditions, both of them learned English, became Americanized, and were active citizens. Like Fernando Olivares in her novel, Jovita came from a family that had been in Texas for generations. Nevertheless, she was considered inferior by those who arrived much later than her ancestors. She, however, was determined to make her mark in a world that placed many obstacles in the path of a Mexican-American woman, and she did. Although life forced compromises on the Tejana, she persisted as a student, a professional, and a wife. Rather than being ashamed of her people's heritage, she brought their story to Anglos who would not otherwise have been exposed to the rich traditions and history of South Texas. In so doing, she also preserved that heritage for the generations of Mexican Americans to follow. And, in the end, although posthumously, she found ways to be heard, despite the best efforts of her husband to silence her.

Edmundo E. Mireles, on the other hand, bore a strong resemblance to fictional Fernando Olivares in urging Hispanics to be politically active and in trying to gain political office for himself. A brilliant man with tremendous energy, he dedicated his life to bettering the condition of fellow Latinos. Ultimately, however, he chose to work from within the system and take a less militant approach than some of his countrymen. Aware that knowledge is power, Mireles focused on education as the best avenue for his efforts. And as a pioneer in teaching Spanish language, culture, and history to young Anglos, he helped reduce ignorance and prejudice in their parents as well. By encouraging native Spanish-speakers of all ages to learn English and helping them to become better educated in general, he improved the quality of their lives.

As individuals and as a team, Jovita González and Edmundo E. Mireles stood head and shoulders above the crowd. Before they married, she was the better known of the two because of her achievements as folklorist, historian, writer, and speaker. After they wed, she became literally and figuratively Mrs. E. E. Mireles. As a couple they worked together, but their efforts were directed primarily at fulfilling Edmundo's goals. This was not a total sacrifice on Jovita's part, because she and her husband shared much in common: the love of their native language, appreciation of their Spanish heritage, the desire to improve Anglo-Hispanic relations, the will to help their people, the calling to teach, the ability to write, and a love of learning. Their shared passions have left a joint legacy that continues to inform and inspire people of all ethnic groups.

Notes

*This term is borrowed from Leticia Magda Garza-Falcón's book, *Gente Decente: A Borderlands Response to the Rhetoric of Dominance* (Austin: University of Texas Press, 1998), and translates as "people of good breeding."

1. Sergio Reyna, "Introduction," *The Woman Who Lost Her Soul and Other Stories*, by Jovita González (Houston, TX: Arte Público Press, 2000), xi; Andrea R. Purdy, "Jovita González de Mireles (1904–1983)," in Laurie Champion, ed., *American Women Writers, 1900–1945: A Bio-Bibliographical Critical Sourcebook* (Westport CT: Greenwood Press, 2000), 143; Garza-Falcón, *Gente Decente,* 258; Rosemary A. King, *Border Confluences: Borderland Narratives from the Mexican War to the Present* (Tucson, AZ: The University of Arizona Press, 2004), 28.

2. The Handbook of Texas Online, "González de Mireles, Jovita," http://www.tsha.utexas.edu/handbook/online/articles/view/GG/fgo34.html (accessed July 16, 2001); Garza-Falcón, *Gente Decente*, 258; María Eugenia Cotera, "Introduction: A Woman of the Borderlands," in *Life along the Border: A Landmark Tejana Thesis*, by Jovita González (College Station: Texas A&M University Press, 2006), 10.

3. José E. Limón, *Dancing with the Devil: Society and Cultural Poetics in Mexican-American South Texas* (Madison: The University of Wisconsin Press, 1994): 61–62; Garza-Falcón, *Gente Decente*, 258.

4. Ibid., 258; Teresa Palomo Acosta and Ruthe Winegarten, eds., *Las Tejanas: 300 Years of History* (Austin: University of Texas Press, 2003), 94; Cortera, "Introduction," 11.

5. Limón, *Dancing with the Devil,* 61; Garza-Falcón, *Gente Decente*, 258; Laurie Champion, "Introduction," in *American Women Writers*, xv.

6. Sylvia R. Longoria, "González's Works Inspire Local Scholars: Library Yields Unpublished Writings by Famed Historian," *Corpus Christi Caller Times,* Aug. 1, 1999; Purdy, "Jovita González de Mireles," in *American Women Writers*, 143; Garza-Falcón, *Gente Decente,*, 259.

7. Jovita González, *Woman Who Lost Her Soul*, 143–145,151.

8. Reyna, "Introduction," xix; Garza-Falcón, *Gente Decente*, 259.

9. Biographical note in "A Guide to the Edmundo E. and Jovita González Mireles Papers, 1921–1993," Southwest Writers Collection, Albert B. Alkek Library, Southwest Texas State University, San Marcos, http://www.lib.utexas.edu/taro/tsusm/00051/00051-P.html (accessed Apr. 18, 2012); Garza-Falcón, *Gente Decente,* 259; Handbook of Texas Online, "González de Mireles, Jovita."

10. Garza-Falcón, *Gente Decente*, 1, 260; Limón, *Dancing With the Devil,* 68–69; Acosta and Winegarten, *Las Tejanas,* 94; Benjamin Johnson, "Engendering Nation and Race in the Borderlands," *Latin American Research Review* 37 (2002): 269; Handbook of Texas Online, "González de Mireles, Jovita."

11. Garza-Falcón, *Gente Decente,* 88–89, 259; Handbook of Texas Online, "González de Mireles, Jovita;" Reyna, "Introduction," xix.

12. Cotera, "Introduction," 4, 16–17; González, *Life along the Border*, 41, 109, 116.

13. Acosta and Winegarten, Las Tejanas*,* 94; Garza-Falcón, *Gente Decente,* 260; Jovita Gonález, "The Devil on the Border," in *Hecho en Tejas: An Anthology of Texas-Mexican Literature*, ed. Dagoberto Gilb (Albuquerque: University of New Mexico Press, 2006), 102–5; Limón, *Dancing with the Devil,* 65–67; Handbook of Texas Online, "González de Mireles, Jovita;" Purdy, "Jovita González de Mireles," 142; José E. Limón, "Introduction," *Caballero: A Historical Novel, by Jovita González and Eve Raleigh* (College Station: Texas A&M University Press, 1996), xvii; Reyna, "Introduction*,*" xi–xiii, xx–xxi.

14. Ibid., xix.

15. Ibid., xiii; Limón, "Introduction," xvii; Handbook of Texas Online, "Mireles, Edmundo Eduardo, 1905–1987," http://www.tsha.utexas.edu/handbook/online/articles/
view/MM/fmi90.html (accessed July 16, 2001).

16. Handbook of Texas Online, "Mireles, Edmundo Eduardo;" Garza-Falcón, *Gente Decente,* 78; "Vote for E. E. Mireles for State

Representative” (Leaflet, Edmundo E. Mireles papers, 1940–1971, Benson Latin American Collection, General Libraries, The University of Texas at Austin [hereinafter cited as EEM Papers]).

17. Garza-Falcón, *Gente Decente*, 77–78; Handbook of Texas Online, “Jovita González de Mireles.”

18. Garza-Falcón, *Gente Decente*, 82; González, *Woman Who Lost Her Soul*, 47–49.

19. League of United Latin-American Citizens, “LULACS,” EEM Papers.

20. Garza-Falcón, *Gente Decente,* 114, 261; Limón, “Introduction,” xvi–xvii, xix.

21. Johnson, “Engendering Nation,” 269; González and Raleigh, *Caballero*, 5, 194–95; Garza-Falcón, *Gente Decente,* 95, 112–13, 198; Limón, “Introduction,” xxi–xxii.

22. Reyna, “Introduction,” xiii, xxi; Carlos Kevin Blanton, *The Strange Career of Bilingual Education in Texas, 1836–1981* (College Station: Texas A&M University Press), 65.

23. Ibid., 67–68, 76–77.

24. Ibid., 70–71, 76, 82.

25. Ibid., 85, 88.

26. Ibid., 96.

27. Ibid., 97–98; Senate Bill No. 67, March 4, 1941, EEM Papers.

28. Blanton, *Bilingual Education in Texas,* 100–103; Edmundo E. Mireles, “Philosophy,” and Edmundo E. Mireles, “Corpus Christi Spanish Program, 1950–51,” EEM Papers.

29. Handbook of Texas Online, “Mireles, Edmundo Eduardo;” “¿Habla Vd. Inglés?,” *Time* (Feb. 14, 1944), 72; Blanton, *Bilingual Education in Texas,* 102–3.

30. Edmundo E. Mireles, R. B. Fisher, and Jovita González Mireles, “Introduction,” *Mi Libro Español: Libro Uno* (Austin, TX: Benson & Company, 1941), vii–viii. Volumes one and three of *Mi Libro Español* and volumes two and six of *El Español Elemental* can be found in Jovita González Mireles, Manuscripts and Works, ca. 1925–1980, Benson Latin American Collection, General Libraries, The University of Texas at Austin.

31. Earle Hamilton, Feb. 11, 1941, William H. Wilson, Sept. 10, 1941, Nelson Rockefeller, Aug. 11, 1940, and Eleanor Roosevelt, n.d., as quoted in “Comments from Educators on Corpus Christi Spanish Program, 1939–1941,” EEM Papers.

32. “¿Habla Vd. Inglés?,” 72.

33. Thurmund Krueger, "Letter to School Superintendent of Spanish Program from Junior Chamber of Commerce," Feb. 24, 1942, and Sumner Welles, "Good Neighbor Policy and Discrimination in Southwest," in *Pan American Day Brochure: A United Front* (1944), EEM Papers.

34. Pan American Council of Texas, *Organization, Constitution, By-Laws, Committees, Motion to Incorporate, Charter*, (n.p., n.d.), 3, 19–20; Edmundo E. Mireles, "History of the Council," in *Saludos Amigos* (Pan-American Day Dinner Dance Program, 1946), EEM Papers.

35. "Vote for E. E. Mireles for State Representative" (Leaflet, n. d.), Edmundo E. Mireles, "Radio Talks on Behalf of Mexican American Candidates [on KWBU]" (July 24, 1948), Edmundo E. Mireles, "Radio spots for the beginning of classes in public schools" (1946), Edmundo E. Mireles, "Pláticas de Educación" (n.d.), EEM Papers; Handbook of Texas Online, "Mireles, Edmundo Eduardo."

36. Edmundo E. Mireles, "Los Niños de Corpus Christi Son Bilingues," *Texas Outlook* (May 1951); Edmundo E. Mireles, "The Teaching of Spanish in Our Public Schools," *The American School Board Journal* (Nov. 1953): 33–34, 92; Biographical Note in "A Guide to the Edmundo E. and Jovita González Mireles Papers."

37. Corpus Christi Public Schools Division of Curricular Services, "Report of Spanish Department 1955–56," EEM Papers; Garza-Falcón, *Gente Decente*, 97–98.

38. Edmundo E. Mireles, "Report to Corpus Christi Public Schools: Summer English Program for Pre-School Non-English Speaking Children" (1962), EEM Papers.

39. "Status and Progress Report of Adult Basic Education Program" (Nov. 21, 1967), "Adult Basic Education, 1969–1970" (n.d.), EEM Papers.

40. Garza-Falcón, *Gente Decente,* 131, 261; Limón, "Introduction," xxi–xxii.

41. Jonathan Osborne, "School May Bear Name of Mireles," *Corpus Christi Caller Times,* July 25, 1999; Content Note in "A Guide to Edmundo E. and Jovita González Mireles Papers."

42. Garza-Falcón, *Gente Decente,* 74.

43. Johnson, "Engendering Nation," 270; Jovita González, *Dew on the Thorn*, ed. José Limón (Houston: Arte Público Press, 1997), 151–52 (quoted in Johnson, "Engendering Nation," 270).

Sunnyside residents in Houston protest "instant slums" in November 1966. Courtesy of Houston Metropolitan Research Center

National Ideal Meets Local Reality: The Grassroots War on Poverty in Houston

Wesley G. Phelps

President Lyndon B. Johnson's War on Poverty, launched in August 1964 with the passage of the Economic Opportunity Act as part of his larger Great Society project, proved to be a bold and ambitious series of initiatives fueled by the spirit of 1960s American liberalism. The act created the Job Corps to provide unemployed and underemployed young men with marketable skills, Volunteers in Service to America (VISTA) to tap the great resource of idealistic youth eager to take an active role in fighting poverty, and the Community Action Program (CAP) to mobilize local resources for a comprehensive attack on poverty. The massive federal antipoverty program would be administered by the newly created Office of Economic Opportunity (OEO).[1]

Despite the importance of Johnson's War on Poverty to American history in the twentieth century, and particularly to the history of the volatile 1960s, the best-known accounts tend to focus on a broad, national narrative and are mostly concerned with policy analysis. While these works are vitally necessary for understanding the ideas and politics that shaped national policy, they tend to obscure the multitude of ways that poverty warriors actually implemented these policies in local communities. As historian Allen J. Matusow argued nearly twenty-five years ago, the real story of community action in the War on Poverty rests with organizations "in one thousand communities across the country" working to implement their vision of effective antipoverty programs. Since most historians know little about how War on Poverty programs operated at the local level, continued Matusow, no final judgment of them is possible "until an army of local historians recovers the program's lost fragments."[2]

This essay will investigate one of these "lost fragments" of the War on Poverty by exploring the fate of the Community Action Program in Houston during its most radical and confrontational phase between the fall of 1966 and the spring of 1967. Focusing the lens on a single location reveals that the War on Poverty created a significant conflict over the meaning of American democracy and the rights of citizenship.

Grassroots activists in Houston—if only for a short period of time—were able to use the War on Poverty to advance an agenda of social change that included empowering the city's poor and helping them engage in confrontations with local elites. In so doing, they contested mainstream definitions of democracy. These often fierce political battles spawned by the War on Poverty revealed a fundamental disagreement over what democracy meant, how far it should extend, and who should benefit from it. Reflecting the renewed focus on citizen participation that was prevalent during the 1960s, local implementers of the War on Poverty in Houston took seriously the federal mandate to empower the poor as they pushed for a more participatory form of democracy that would include more citizens in the political, cultural, and economic life of the city. Seen in this new light, the War on Poverty appears as an integral part of the democratic experiment in America, and its implementation in Houston reveals both the possibilities and the limits of American democracy.

Local Houston antipoverty activists were able to use the War on Poverty to expand democracy in the city primarily because the concept of community action, which guided the Community Action Program, was ill-defined and open to a multitude of interpretations. At its core, community action presented a new way of thinking about both the causes of and solutions for poverty. According to Matusow, the CAP called for local communities to create agencies that would be capable of "mobilizing local resources for a comprehensive attack on poverty." The goals of this direct attack on poverty would be threefold: 1) to create and provide new social services for the poor; 2) to provide centralized coordination of all social services available to the poor; and 3) to bring about institutional change that would benefit those living in poverty. This final CAP objective of reforming local institutions proved to be political dynamite in many communities because it implied a direct challenge to the balance of power, especially in the larger cities. A good portion of the architects of the federal War on Poverty had learned "to despise local schools, police, welfare departments, and private charity institutions," Matusow argued, "for dispensing demeaning, fragmented services to the poor." While more and better services were certainly needed, many federal planners believed that social and institutional change were required in order to attack poverty in any meaningful way.[3]

As Matusow pointed out, the reformers among the War on Poverty planners recognized that local institutions would be openly defiant of efforts to change them. The reformers' solution to this problem was to declare that all community action agencies must be administered with the "maximum feasible participation" of a community's poor residents. "Community action," concluded Matusow, "would seek to reform institutions by empowering the poor." The edict of maximum feasible participation could operate in three ways: 1) poor residents could serve on the governing boards of the local community action agencies; 2) the poor could be hired to work in the various programs; or 3) local community action agencies could employ community organizers to help empower the poor to make demands on local institutions and elected officials. This final application of maximum feasible participation, which called for nothing short of the politicization and empowerment of the poor to demand a greater share of a community's resources, offered local Houston activists the opportunity to use the federal program to advance a broader critique of how democracy operated in the city.[4]

Grassroots antipoverty activists in Houston interpreted the goals of the CAP and the strategies for the "maximum feasible participation" of the poor in a much more confrontational fashion than most national planners. For a brief moment between the fall of 1966 and the spring of 1967, grassroots antipoverty activists in Houston were able to shape national War on Poverty policies by implementing their own radical interpretation of the community action concept and locating a few sympathetic allies in Washington. These activists, working within the city's community action agency, implemented a radical CAP that called for the organization and empowerment of Houston's poor communities in order to initiate confrontations with local elected officials and institutions, and this approach ultimately propelled activists to challenge mainstream definitions of democracy. Armed with a radical ideology that placed human rights above property rights and called for the empowerment of the poor, these activists not only challenged the local power structure's resistance to change, but they also exposed the fallacies and naivety of the liberal dream of a War on Poverty that would neither challenge entrenched middle-class interests nor confront city governments or other pillars of local power. By exposing the structural and institutional limitations placed upon the poor, grassroots antipoverty activists in Houston, through their implementation of a radical interpretation of the community action concept, showed that confrontational tactics could be effective in addressing the needs of the poor and changing the meaning of democracy on the ground in Houston.

The radical vision for the CAP was strongly encouraged by William V. Ballew Jr., a local attorney who took over as head of the Houston agency in January 1966. Ballew had been involved in antipoverty efforts in Houston since the early 1960s and was an early advocate for the implementation of the new federal War on Poverty in the city. Ballew's election as the new head of the city's CAP certainly meant a dramatic shift in the focus and direction of the War on Poverty in Houston. While most of the early organizers of the program in Houston had a conservative interpretation of community action and were cautious about the maximum feasible participation of the poor, Ballew firmly believed that broad community organization, mobilization, and empowerment of the poor to challenge the city's elected officials and institutions were the most important parts of the War on Poverty.[5]

As soon as Ballew took over as chairman it became apparent that not only did he have a radically different interpretation of community action, but he was also a believer in what was known as the Saul Alinsky Method. Saul Alinsky was the radical community organizer who in 1939 helped create the Back of the Yards Neighborhood Council in Chicago and had received national attention by traveling the country training organizers in his methods. Alinsky argued that individuals, especially those trapped in poverty, had little hope of successfully dealing with any city's government agencies or welfare organizations because of the overwhelming amount of power an urban bureaucracy possessed over its poor citizens. According to Alinsky, it was only through organization, as labor had accomplished through the creation of industrial unions, that the poor could attempt to match the power of a city's government and bring about needed change in their communities. Alinsky's method of organizing and mobilizing poor communities was attractive to some antipoverty workers across the country because Alinsky seemed to understand that the problems of poverty boiled down to one core issue—power relations. Alinsky's followers believed that only through upsetting the traditional balance of power between a city's political and economic elites and its poor residents could the demons of poverty be exorcised from society.[6]

To remove any doubt about his antipoverty philosophy and commitment to community organizing, Ballew required that every member of the Houston agency carefully read Alinsky's *Reveille for Radicals*, a book published in 1946 that laid out Alinsky's blueprint for the organization of poor communities to challenge urban power structures. And in February 1966, one month into Ballew's tenure as head of the city's CAP, Alinsky brought his radical message directly to Houston's poverty workers when he spoke on the campus of the University of Houston about his experiences organizing several poor communities and how these organizational tactics could be used in the federal War on Poverty.

The main shortcoming of the national antipoverty effort, according to Alinsky, was that it "looks at deprivation only in terms of money and not of power . . . To expect to funnel federal funds through local administrations is like giving an employer money to funnel into the organization of labor unions that someday might strike against him." Alinsky argued that the only way to make the War on Poverty successful in eradicating poverty in Houston was to organize poor people into powerful blocs that could confront the city's public officials and force them to address the needs of impoverished neighborhoods. Apparently this suggestion that poor people should organize to claim power and control over their own lives was too much for some audience members to withstand. After just a few minutes of Alinsky's speech, one woman in the front row jumped out of her seat and shouted, "Well, that's enough for me!" and walked out of the auditorium. About twenty-five others followed her, including about a dozen Ku Klux Klan members in full regalia. When asked about Alinsky's visit a few days later, Houston Mayor Louie Welch stated, "I don't think extreme philosophies of either side are needed in this community. Any philosophy which sets class against class is, in my opinion, un-American." Ballew undoubtedly faced an uphill battle in following the Alinsky model of community organizing in Houston.[7]

In the spring and summer of 1966, Ballew launched a public relations campaign in Houston to explain how the Alinsky method would be applied to the implementation of the War on Poverty in the city. During a speech delivered to a group of Houston businessmen during the summer of 1966, Ballew echoed Alinsky's sentiments and argued that the "basic concept [of community action] is radical, yes, even revolutionary; but so was the beginning and the development of our American democracy and economy . . . Recall the labor movement in America. Most manufacturers did not improve wages and working conditions until workers in America organized and became a political and economic force in our country." Ballew argued that just like the labor movement, poor people in the United States must be organized to put pressure on and if necessary to force confrontations with the city's power structure to make sure their needs are addressed. For this reason, argued Ballew, "the war on poverty cannot be a mere extension of existing social and welfare programs. Existing agencies, for all their decent efforts and good intentions, are not getting through to the poor." Instead, Ballew pledged that Houston's CAP would encourage poor people themselves to plan, develop, and implement antipoverty programs in their own communities, even though this plan was "not necessarily welcomed by existing power structures."

This goal would be reached through community organization, a tactic to which Ballew referred as "our single most important program. This is more than an extension of social and welfare services; it is a new departure—it is grass roots involvement of the poor in their own programs and decisions in connection with meeting their needs in the community . . . When these people meet in their civic organizations and clubs, get to know each other and articulate their needs, requests are bound to be made upon the county courthouse, the city hall for services, etc. As labor organizers in the '20s and '30s were labeled agitators, or worse, community organizers today in the war on poverty may be likewise reviled. If we are wise, we will exercise extreme patience and understanding while these people go about their work."[8]

As Ballew laid out his plans for the course of the War on Poverty in Houston, he remained steadfast in his commitment to Alinsky-style community organization and maximum feasible participation of the poor despite some opposition. Although some conflict did arise with other board members, Ballew was able to lead the CAP in a more confrontational direction primarily because he located an important ally in the regional OEO office. William Crook, regional director of the southwest division of OEO and who would later become national director of the VISTA program in 1967, strongly supported the use of community organizing and favored more activist community action agencies like the one Ballew was trying to build in Houston.

Ballew arranged for Crook to speak to Houston's antipoverty workers in 1966, and Crook used the occasion to stress that the CAP should be used to expand democracy. Crook argued that community action "contains whatever hope we have for a successful conclusion to the war on poverty." In response to those who opposed the idea of community organization, Crook pointed out that it was the only part of the federal antipoverty effort that attempted to restore the initiative to local citizens and for this reason should be welcomed rather than feared. According to Crook, the ideas fueling the CAP, including the prospect of organizing and empowering the poor, "is as valid a form of democratic decision [making] as the Constitution of the United States. It is as much a part of the tradition of this land as the old New England town meetings . . . It is the philosophy of a free people applied practically to a local situation." Rather than bowing to the irrational fears of local politicians, Crook implored Ballew's staff to expand the CAP and use it to bring about lasting democratic change.[9]

Although Ballew and other antipoverty activists in the community action agency worked to expand some social service programs in the city such as Legal Services and Head Start, they focused most of their energy on community organizing in an effort to empower poor Houston citizens to confront local governing elites. In early November 1966, Ballew issued a memorandum in which he stated, "Since money . . . is not only in short supply but is also restricted in many cases, our effective area of operation is in community organization, development and action. Our primary effort, I repeat, is in the neighborhoods and our primary responsibility is placing good people there as community organizers and neighborhood developers. This is essential." Ballew argued that community organizers should live in Houston's poor neighborhoods with the residents they were attempting to empower through community organization. Community organizers, therefore, should be chosen based on whether or not they could commit to this new focus. "This requires a special commitment," Ballew continued, "not normally found in some social worker types who want a good paying job and spend too much time protecting that job. In the war on poverty, we are all expendable." Ballew also advised giving individual community organizers as much freedom as possible to carry out their efforts. "Once we have good people working in the neighborhoods," Ballew stated, "we should give them as much independence and responsibility as possible." The ultimate goal, according to Ballew, was to get community organizing activities initiated quickly in order to begin empowering the poor to make demands on the public officials and local institutions that affected their daily lives.[10]

To give the organizing effort clear direction, Ballew appointed Reverend Earl E. Allen as director of community organization. Allen was a native Houstonian, a local Methodist minister, and director of the Wesley Foundation at Houston's all-black Texas Southern University. Allen certainly had plenty of experience with community organizing. He had been a regional representative of the Congress of Racial Equality (CORE) in Dallas while he attended seminary at Southern Methodist University, and in that position Allen had organized a month-long civil rights protest in 1964 to desegregate downtown restaurants and cafeterias. Like Ballew, Allen had read Alinsky's work on community organizing and was committed to the idea of fully empowering the poor in Houston to confront the city's public officials and institutions. "I wanted to change the status quo," Allen said in a recent interview, "so I was abrasive and not afraid of confrontation." In hiring Allen to focus solely on community organizing, Ballew sent a clear message that neighborhood organization, community empowerment, and even protest activity would be a major thrust of his effort to implement the War on Poverty in the city of Houston.[11]

Allen immediately recognized that Ballew's staff would need to be retrained in Alinsky-style community organizing. He issued a memorandum in early December 1966 in which he stated that his goal was to find "both a relevant and a realistic approach to achieving the maximum feasible participation of the poor in the total decision-making process in Houston-Harris County." Allen had a broad interpretation of the meaning of community action and maximum feasible participation of the poor. He certainly agreed with both Ballew and federal War on Poverty planners that poor residents should be involved in the planning and implementation of antipoverty policies and programs in their own communities, but he carried this edict even further by arguing that poor Houston residents should also enjoy full participation in the social, political, and economic life of the city. In short, Allen advocated the New Left philosophy of participatory democracy and believed that the CAP called for the use of effective organizing in order to restore to Houston's poor population a degree of power over their own lives.[12]

The traditional view of poverty posited that poor people themselves were the cause of their own poverty because they had failed to adapt to an advanced industrial economy with an increasing number of highly skilled jobs. In order to remedy this, welfare agencies and social workers sought to change the individual behavior of poor people. An emerging group of antipoverty activists in the 1960s, however, including Allen and a few national War on Poverty planners, believed there were structural limitations that severely reduced the power poor people had over their own lives. Institutional racism, discrimination, complex and aloof municipal bureaucracies, cumbersome local welfare agencies, and a lack of educational and employment opportunities were structural forces that oppressed poor people and were more responsible for persistent poverty than individual behavior. The solution to poverty, therefore, which was included as a small but significant component of the CAP, was community organizing with the ultimate goal of empowering the poor. According to Allen and many other community organization proponents, Alinsky had been correct; the only effective solution to the problem of poverty was to restore power to poor communities through organization.[13]

In his plan for community organization in Houston, Allen instructed his staff first to enter a poor neighborhood and develop a profile of the community that would present a "realistic picture" of the particular area and uncover specific problems that needed to be resolved. Once the community organizer had identified the major problems of a particular neighborhood, Allen instructed them to draw the attention of neighborhood residents to a "gut issue," which was a specific situation that served to dramatize a particular problem. For example, specific gut issues stemming from the problem of inadequate housing in poor neighborhoods could be rat infestation, high rents, unresponsive landlords, a lack of trash cans, or a wide array of other issues that would serve to dramatize the larger problem of inadequate housing. Allen told his community organizers to rally residents around this gut issue and bring those citizens who were concerned about this particular issue together in order to work on possible solutions and initiate any necessary action. Allen stated, "Your job is to dissect a poor community and find out what's buggin' it. You have to build a concern for participation—find a gut issue, but find one which can be solved quickly. We need victories. Victories build confidence." By bringing residents together to work on common problems in the community, according to Allen, organizers would be able to identify leaders within the community and could begin developing this leadership to tackle future problems and issues. This process could be repeated for a series of gut issues until the neighborhoods were organized into action groups capable of successfully confronting the city's public officials and dedicated to solving the problems of the community. Allen stated that these various action groups should eventually be brought together to form neighborhood councils that would try to deal with problems affecting the entire neighborhood. In turn, neighborhood councils would eventually be brought together to form area councils that would be sufficiently large and diverse to address problems affecting an entire area of Houston. Allen argued that once these area councils had been formed, community organizers should work to strengthen each organizational group so they would be able to carry on without the leadership provided by the professional organizer.[14]

Ballew and Allen, along with a staff of approximately 140 community organizers, decided to focus their initial efforts in a large African-American neighborhood northeast of downtown Houston known as Settegast. At one time the neighborhood had been a haven for lower-middle-class African Americans who wanted to own their own homes, but by the mid-1960s Settegast had deteriorated, primarily because it failed to keep pace with standard city improvements through the years such as modern sewage systems and paved roads. By 1960 the median income in Settegast was a little more than half of the average income for Harris County, and despite the fact that homeownership rates remained high, housing conditions there were among the worst in the city. Settegast residents suffered from a number of problems, not the least of which stemmed from municipal officials' indifference to their problems and business and real estate developers' exploitation of the relatively powerless and uneducated community. Allen and Ballew believed that what was needed in the area was community organization to bring about lasting social change capable of producing permanent improvements in the lives of Settegast residents. Only by organizing the residents of Settegast could they be mobilized and empowered, which would enable them to make demands on the city government, local businesses, and other institutions to remedy the problems associated with poverty in the neighborhood.[15]

The community organization tactics developed by Ballew and Allen produced almost immediate results, and by the end of 1966 the two activists could reasonably claim that their strategy of mobilizing poor communities in the city was producing small yet important victories, particularly in Settegast. When Allen's community organization staff began working in Settegast in November, it was clear that the grotesquely unsanitary water supply in the area would serve as an effective issue to dramatize the problem of inadequate city services. Organizers discovered that the majority of homes in Settegast were served by backyard water wells, which frequently became contaminated with bacteria and parasites because disease-carrying sewage was seeping into the wells from septic tanks and outhouses. Although community organizers did not carry out a scientific study, it seemed likely that the extraordinarily high rate of kidney disease in the neighborhood was a direct result of residents drinking contaminated water on a daily basis. Armed with this information, community organizers and a large group of Settegast residents walked into a city council meeting in mid-November and demanded that Mayor Louie Welch extend city water services to their neighborhoods. Faced with this delicate political issue and clearly not wanting to appear to deny Houston residents sanitary drinking water, Welch immediately ordered city workers to place emergency water spigots on the city's fire hydrants in Settegast to provide clean water to the residents. Welch also quickly drew up a plan to extend city water services to the area and instructed one of Houston's city attorneys to investigate the possibility of filing a lawsuit against the company that knowingly sold water from contaminated wells to unsuspecting families in Settegast. Ballew immediately claimed victory for this exercise in Alinsky-style community organization and pointed out that at the urging of community organizers, residents "went to City Hall and demanded a city water supply to replace their contaminated one—and they got it." The event produced such a surprising victory that a *Houston Post* reporter covering the story declared that the "dawn of a quiet revolution may have broken over Houston" when the

Settegast group arrived at City Hall to begin receiving a redress of grievances that were a long time coming. "In a modern city such as Houston," a *Houston Post* editorial asserted a few days later, "no person should be threatened by contaminated water, or be dependent upon a fire hydrant for pure water. Our consciences should not permit it."[16]

Ballew and Allen even encouraged the community organizers to help plan and participate in organized protest activities to bring attention to the plight of their communities. While Settegast residents were putting pressure on Mayor Welch and the Houston City Council to address their water problems, residents from some of the same neighborhoods began staging demonstrations at their local schools protesting the lack of sanitary conditions there. Not only was there contaminated water coming into many of the schools, but there simply was not enough water pressure for the use of drinking fountains or even to flush toilets. Many students and teachers had to bring thermoses to school filled with enough water for the entire day. After protesting for several weeks with no response from the all-white Northeast Houston School District Board, several Settegast neighborhood councils, which had been formed with assistance from Allen's staff, launched a write-in campaign to get two African-American residents elected to the board who promised to address these problems. These two candidates lost by a very narrow margin, but nevertheless these neighborhood councils were successful in encouraging more residents to assume an active role in the administration of their local schools. A *Houston Post* reporter commented, "With almost 1,000 Settegast votes to reckon with, it is doubtful that the school board out there will ever be quite the same again." The protests also had an effect on Welch—he ordered his staff to obtain water samples from Settegast schools to check for contamination.[17]

After achieving some success getting city officials to address the problem of contaminated water in Settegast, Allen's community organizers focused on the absence of medical treatment facilities. Community organizers were shocked to discover that there were absolutely no healthcare facilities in Settegast or in any of the surrounding communities. There was not a single doctor or dentist who practiced in the area, and if residents needed medical attention, they were forced to travel twenty miles to Ben Taub Hospital in the Texas Medical Center, which was the nearest public health facility to the Settegast community. Many residents lacked the means of transporting themselves or family members to the hospital, and since ambulance services were only available to those who could pay for them, most Settegast residents simply received no medical attention when they were sick or injured. Rather than establishing a temporary health clinic or hospital in the area funded by the federal government or local charities, members of Allen's staff began organizing neighborhood residents to put pressure on the Harris County Hospital District to build and maintain a permanent branch of the public hospital system in Settegast. One of Allen's community organizers argued that the proposed Settegast healthcare facility would set an example for the rest of the city and become the first of several clinics established in poverty neighborhoods. "These clinics would help decentralize charity medicine in Harris County," the organizer stated, "and make services available to the poor in outlying areas." As Allen's staff began organizing residents into pressure groups, Harris County Hospital District officials responded slowly but generally favorably to the idea of creating a branch of the city's public hospital in Settegast. By early January the hospital district board had placed the issue on the agenda for their meeting that month.[18]

In order to make sure that Harris County Hospital District members would address the absence of healthcare facilities in Settegast, community organizers and neighborhood residents marched to city hall in downtown Houston where the meeting was taking place to demand the creation of a branch of the public hospital in their neighborhood. The strategy worked—the hospital district voted to establish a branch in Settegast immediately. Located inside a building donated by the Houston City Council, the new Settegast Clinic opened during the last week in January and served 175 poor residents in its first week of operation. The opening of the clinic was a "breakthrough event," Ballew remarked, and clear evidence that the "War on Poverty in Houston is beginning to go." Most importantly, the creation of the Settegast Clinic was a major victory for Ballew, Allen, and their community organization staff because it showed what the community organizing strategy could accomplish in Houston.[19]

After some early successes, Ballew encouraged the spirit of organized protest to carry beyond the neighborhood of Settegast. For example, community organizers and a group of residents from a mostly African-American neighborhood on the west side of town called Blossom Heights organized a twenty-mile protest march to call attention to the fact that their children were bused that far to attend school when an all-white school was just two miles from their homes. In the Sunnyside neighborhood, a poor area south of downtown, community organizers found that residents had recently formed the Sunnyside Housing Committee through which they were attempting to put pressure on the Houston City

Council to prevent slumlords from building inadequate and unsafe housing in that part of the city. Members began showing up at Houston City Council meetings in October to demand a change in the city's building code and an end to land zoning practices that allowed unscrupulous residential builders to erect high-density, low-quality housing that had a tendency of turning older neighborhoods into "instant slums." With the help of Allen's staff, Sunnyside Housing Committee members launched a protest campaign against the real estate developers who were beginning to build slum housing in the area. In November 1966 approximately fifty people marched in front of the proposed building sites carrying signs that read "Don't Move In" and "I Wouldn't Let My Dog Live in These Shacks." Clarence White, leader of the protest, told members of the press to spread their message all across the city of Houston. "This is pathetic," White exclaimed. "What kind of kids could you raise in those shacks? This is what breeds crime. People say, 'Why so much crime among the Negroes?' Then they come out here and help build crime." Addressing the other marchers, White pointed out that the slums were being built by two real estate developers—one white and one black, although the race of the guilty parties was of no real importance. White continued, "It doesn't matter what color your skin is. If you're moving shacks into Sunnyside, we're your enemy." Other marchers told the reporters that this protest was only the beginning of their effort to take control of their own neighborhood.[20]

The involvement of employees of Houston's CAP in protest activities provoked many questions from city officials and Houston residents about the proper role of poverty workers and community organizers around the city. In response to these questions, Ballew defended both the organizers' actions and the use of protest demonstrations. "It seems to me our organizers are going to have to be with the people and work with them," argued Ballew to a *Houston Post* reporter. "As long as the protests are peaceful, I see nothing wrong with our people taking part in them." A federal inspection team from the OEO in Washington concurred with Ballew's assessment of the role of Allen's community organization staff. During an official inspection of the War on Poverty in Houston conducted in February 1967, inspectors concluded in their report that one of the ways Ballew had improved the antipoverty effort in Houston when he became chairman of the city's community action agency was the hiring of Allen and their increased focus on community organizing. One OEO inspector noted that the success of the community organizing effort was apparent all over the city and that Allen's community organization staff was "reaching someone in Houston since they are creating a great deal of foment." Another inspector commented that Allen was "bright, imaginative, and knowledgeable about the process of community organization" and possessed the necessary competence to iron out any problems that naturally arise from trying to organize the poor.[21]

It was clear by the spring of 1967 that Allen's community organizing efforts, particularly in the Settegast area, were paying dividends to poor residents and were beginning to change the very meaning of democracy. Ballew could finally boast that Houston's Community Action Program was waging a concerted attack on the structural and institutional causes of poverty in the city and was enjoying a series of small but important victories. The Alinsky method seemed to be working quite satisfactorily during Ballew's first year as chairman, primarily because he enjoyed a tremendous amount of support from his staff and OEO officials in Washington. By the spring of 1967, however, their actions had provoked a powerful backlash from local public officials and conservative defenders of the status quo. Members of the city's power structure, particularly Mayor Louie Welch and Police Chief Herman Short, launched an all-out assault on Ballew, Allen, and the CAP, especially after it came to light that several poverty workers were involved in protests on the campus of Texas Southern University preceding the "riot" that occurred there in May 1967.[22] At the same time a conservative mood overtook War on Poverty officials in Washington that resulted in a diminished amount of support for confrontational community action agencies like Ballew's. Members of Houston's CAP quickly retreated from the radical interpretation of the community action concept, forced Ballew out of office, reined in the activities of Allen so drastically that he resigned, and committed themselves to a more conservative program of social service delivery. Ballew's experiment in the Alinsky method in Houston thus ended just as it was beginning to achieve some small victories.

Yet the relatively short amount of time Ballew and Allen had to implement their confrontational vision for the CAP in Houston offers valuable insights into how these ideas operated on the ground. Ballew, Allen, and their community organizing staff members showed that community organization and mobilization could be effective in empowering poor Houston residents to confront the city's power structure and bring about needed changes in their neighborhoods. The small victories they achieved illustrated that the Alinsky method could be successful not only in bringing about a degree of social change necessary to begin addressing the problems of poverty but also in expanding the meaning of democracy. For a brief moment, grassroots activists in Houston successfully transformed an inadequate liberal program for eradicating poverty into a radical effort to bring about real and lasting social change in the city. Their experiences show that if historians want to understand how the War on Poverty and the CAP really worked, they must investigate it at the grassroots level where activists implemented their own vision of community action.

It is only at the grassroots level that one can see that the federal antipoverty program opened up a space to challenge mainstream definitions of democracy. Together with civil rights legislation, for a few years the federal government placed its power and authority behind the idea of broadening democracy, and a significant number of grassroots activists capitalized on the opportunities created to change the status quo. Grassroots activists in Houston, armed with a mandate from the federal government, challenged mainstream definitions of democracy and, at least for a short period of time, broadened the scope of democracy in the city and empowered poor residents to take an active role in civic life. By demanding a voice in the decisions that affected their lives, local activists and poor Houston residents demanded a voice in local politics. At least for a brief moment, poor Houstonians and their activist allies achieved some important victories and managed to expand the meaning of democracy. The fluid interaction between federal policies and grassroots activists made it possible to use the War on Poverty to bring about social change in Houston and to make the concept of democracy meaningful in the lives of poor residents.

Notes

1. "Economic Opportunity Act of 1964," S2642, *United States Serial Set*, 88th Cong., 2nd sess. (Ser. 12616-3).

2. Allen J. Matusow, *The Unraveling of America: A History of Liberalism in the 1960s* (New York: Harper & Row, 1984), 254–55.

3. Ibid., 244–45.

4. Ibid., 245. See Office of Economic Opportunity, Community Action Program, *Community Action Program Guide* (Washington, D.C., Feb. 1965) and Office of Economic Opportunity, Community Action Program, *Community Action Program Workbook* (Washington, D.C., Mar. 1965).

5. Minutes of Houston-Harris County Economic Opportunity Organization Board of Directors, 10 Jan. 1966, Box 266, Folder H-HCEOO

Board of Directors Minutes, Leon Jaworski Papers, Texas Collection, Baylor University Library, Waco, Texas (hereafter cited as Jaworski Papers); George Bush to Bill Ballew, 15 Jan. 1966, Box 265, Folder Houston-Harris County Economic Opportunity Organization—Correspondence, Jaworski Papers; Leon Abramson, "Summary Report on the Investigative Task Force of the Ad Hoc Subcommittee on the War on Poverty Program," Box 6, Folder Report/Investigative Task Force, Mar. 1966, Ad-Hoc Subcommittee of War on Poverty, Records of the General Counsel, President's Task Force in the War Against Poverty, Record Group 381, National Archives and Records Administration, College Park, Maryland (hereafter cited as NARA); Noe Perez, "Jaworski Quits Local Antipoverty Group," *Houston Chronicle*, Jan. 11, 1966.

6. William V. Ballew Jr., "The Way We Were," Address to Twentieth Anniversary Symposium, Gulf Coast Community Services Association, 19 Nov. 1986, Box 1, W. V. Ballew Collection, Houston Metropolitan Research Center, Houston Public Library, Houston, Texas (hereafter cited as Ballew Collection). For the life of Saul Alinsky, see Sanford D. Horwitt, *Let Them Call Me Rebel: Saul Alinsky—His Life and Legacy* (New York: Knopf, 1989).

7. Ballew, "The Way We Were," Ballew Collection; Saul Alinsky, *Reveille for Radicals* (Chicago: University of Chicago Press, 1946); Austin Scott, "Saul Alinsky, Professional Radical, Aids 'Have-Nots,'" *Houston Chronicle*, Feb. 20, 1966; Noe Perez, "Slum-Dweller Organizer Hits Poverty War," *Houston Chronicle*, Feb. 25, 1966 (quotations).

8. William V. Ballew Jr., "The Anti-Poverty Program in Houston," Address to Young Presidents' Club of Houston, Texas, 17 Aug. 1966, in author's possession.

9. Minutes of Houston-Harris County Economic Opportunity Organization Board of Directors, 7 June 1966, Box 265, Folder H-HCEOO Information, Jaworski Papers.

10. William V. Ballew Jr. to Charles Kelly, memorandum, 2 Nov. 1966, Box 1, Folder 3, William V. Ballew Jr. Papers, 1965–1968, MS 254, Woodson Research Center, Fondren Library, Rice University, Houston, Texas (hereafter cited as Ballew Papers).

11. Charles Kelly to Don Hess, 26 July 1966, Box 13, Folder Administrative, Texas, 1966, OEO CAP Records of the Director, State Files, 1965–1968, RG 381, NARA; "E. E. Allen Named to EOO Post," Houston Post, Nov. 20, 1966; H-HCEOO, "Resume of Proposals," 23 Mar. 1966, Minutes of H-HCEOO Board of Directors, 10 Apr. 1966, Box 1, Folder Minutes 1966, Ballew Papers; Ballew to Lucile Johnson, 8 Apr.

1966, Box 1, Folder Correspondence January-June 1966, Ballew Papers; Earl E. Allen, interview by Wesley G. Phelps, 11 Dec. 2008, Houston, Texas (quotation).

12. Earl E. Allen to All Community Organization Staff, memorandum, 9 Dec. 1966, Box 59, Folder Houston Texas CAA 1968, OEO CAP Records of the Director, Subject Files, 1965–1969, RG 381, NARA (quotation); Office of Economic Opportunity, Office of Inspection, "Houston-Harris County Economic Opportunity Organization," Feb. 1967, Box 10, Folder Contracts, Office of Economic Opportunity, Southwest Region, Community Action Programs, District Supervisors, Records Relating to City Economic Opportunity Boards, 1965–1968, RG 381, National Archives and Records Administration, Southwest Region, Fort Worth, Texas (hereafter cited as NARASW); E. R. Brown to Marlene Futterman, memorandum, 13 Feb. 1967, Box 73, Folder CAP, Houston, Harris County, Texas, Jan.– Mar. 1967, OEO Inspection Division, Inspection Reports, 1964–67, RG 381, NARA; Allen, interview.

13. Allen to All H-HCEOO Personnel, memorandum, 21 Dec. 1966, Box 59, Folder Houston Texas CAA 1968, OEO CAP Records of the Director, Subject Files, 1965–1969, RG 381, NARA; Marlene Futterman, "Inspection Report for H-HCEOO and HAY," Feb. 1967, Box 73, Folder CAP, Houston, Harris County, Texas, Jan–Mar 1967, OEO Inspection Division, Inspection Reports, 1964–67, RG 381, NARA.

14. Allen to All H-HCEOO Personnel, memorandum, 21 Dec. 1966, Box 59, Folder Houston Texas CAA 1968, OEO CAP Records of the Director, Subject Files, 1965–1969, RG 381, NARA (quotations); Saralee Tiede, "Outlook Called Hopeful in War on Poverty Here," *Houston Chronicle*, Jan. 1, 1967.

15. Houston-Harris County Economic Opportunity Organization, "The Settegast Report: A Program for Community Development," 31 Aug. 1966, Box 59, Folder Houston Texas CAA 1968, OEO CAP Records of the Director, Subject Files, 1965–1969, RG 381, NARA.

16. Blair Justice to Louie Welch, memorandum, 6 Sept. 1966, Box 33, Louie Welch Papers, Houston Metropolitan Research Center, Houston Public Library, Houston, Texas (hereafter cited as Welch Papers); Tiede, "Outlook Called Hopeful" (first quotation); Harold Scarlett, "Poverty's Captives: Planners Finally Get Some Action," *Houston Post*, Nov. 10, 1966 (second quotation); "Water Emergency," *Houston Post*, Sept. 9, 1966 (third quotation).

17. Justice to Welch, memorandum, 6 Sept. 1966, Justice to Welch, memorandum, 19 Sept. 1966, Darrell Williams to Gene Gatling, 21 Sept.

1966, Welch to Williams, 28 Sept. 1966, Welch to D. H. Germany, 28 Sept. 1966, Justice to Louie Welch, memorandum, 30 Sept. 1966, Box 33, Welch Papers; Joe Smith, "Schools Without Water: Children Are Sent Home," *Houston Post*, n.d., newspaper clipping, Box 33, Welch Papers; Tiede, "Outlook Called Hopeful;" Scarlett, "Poverty's Captives" (quotation).

18. Minutes of Houston-Harris County Economic Opportunity Organization Executive Committee, 19 Dec. 1966, Box 73, Folder CAP, Houston, Harris County, Texas, July–Sept 1967, OEO Inspection Division, Inspection Reports, 1964–67, RG 381, NARA; Saralee Tiede, "EOO to Ask Hospital District To Set Up Settegast Clinic," *Houston Chronicle*, Dec. 15, 1966 (quotation); H-HCEOO, "Narrative Statements on Needs and Functions, Decentralized Medical Facility, Settegast Community," Dec. 1966, Box 1, Folder Minutes 1966, Ballew Papers.

19. Office of Economic Opportunity, Office of Inspection, "Houston CAP," Feb. 1967, Box 10, Folder Contracts, Office of Economic Opportunity, Southwest Region, Community Action Programs, District Supervisors, Records Relating to City Economic Opportunity Boards, 1965–1968, RG 381, NARASW; Minutes of Houston-Harris County Economic Opportunity Organization Executive Committee, 23 Feb. 1967, Box 73, Folder CAP, Houston, Harris County, Texas, July-Sept 1967, OEO Inspection Division, Inspection Reports, 1964–1967, RG 381, NARA; Ballew to Ralph Yarborough, 2 Feb. 1967, Box 1, Folder Correspondence January-February 1967, Ballew Papers (quotation).

20. Tiede, "Outlook Called Hopeful"; Scarlett, "Poverty's Captives"; "Residents March in Protest: Sunnyside Fights 'Instant Slums,'" *Houston Post*, Nov. 8, 1966 (quotations).

21. Scarlett, "Poverty's Captives" (first quotation); E. R. Brown to Marlene Futterman, memorandum, 13 Feb. 1967 (second quotation), Futterman, "Inspection Report for H-HCEOO and HAY," Feb. 1967, Box 73, Folder CAP, Houston, Harris County, Texas, Jan.– Mar. 1967, OEO Inspection Division, Inspection Reports, 1964–1967, RG 381, NARA (third quotation).

22. For the effect of the Texas Southern University Riot on the War on Poverty in Houston, see William S. Clayson, "The War on Poverty and the Fear of Urban Violence in Houston, 1965–1968," *Gulf South Historical Review* 18 (2003): 38–59.

Contributors' Biographies

Gregory W. Ball has been a civilian historian with the United States Air Force since 2009 and is currently the historian for 24th Air Force in San Antonio, Texas. He earned his Ph.D. under the direction of Randolph B. Campbell, and his book on the 7th Texas Infantry in World War I is a forthcoming publication of the University of North Texas Press.

Alwyn Barr is a Professor Emeritus of History at Texas Tech University and a former chair of the History Department. Many of his five authored books, including *Black Texans: A History of African Americans in Texas, 1528–1995* (2nd ed. 1996) and *African Texans* (2004), address questions and themes central to Campbell's work. He is a Fellow and former president of the Texas State Historical Association.

Walter L. Buenger is a professor of History and former History Department chair at Texas A&M University. He is an award-winning author or co-author of four books and the co-editor of two others. His most recent book, *Beyond Texas Through Time* (2011), co-edited with Arnoldo De León, describes how Texas history has changed since 1991. A longtime friend of Campbell's, he is a Fellow and former president of the Texas State Historical Association.

Gregg Cantrell holds the Erma and Ralph Lowe Chair in Texas History at Texas Christian University (following several years as Campbell's colleague at UNT). He is the author or editor of numerous award-winning books and articles, including *Stephen F. Austin, Empresario of Texas* (1999) and *Lone Star Pasts: Memory and History in Texas* (2006). He is a Fellow of the Texas State Historical Association and will serve as its president in 2013–2014.

Donald E. Chipman is an Emeritus Professor of History at the University of North Texas. He is the author or co-author of seven books. His *Spanish Texas, 1519–1821* (Rev. ed. 2010) is a multiple prize-winner, as is *Notable Men and Women of Spanish Texas* (1999), which he co-authored with Harriett Denise Joseph. Chipman is a member of the Texas Institute of Letters and Fellow of the Texas State Historical Association. In 2003 King Juan Carlos I of Spain appointed him to the Order of Isabel la Católica, the highest honor available to a non-Spaniard. Chipman arrived at UNT two years before Campbell, and they have been close friends since.

Bradley R. Clampitt is an assistant professor of History at East Central University and the author of *The Confederate Heartland: Military and Civilian Morale in the Western Confederacy* (2011). At the University of North Texas, he worked with Campbell as a graduate student and teaching assistant.

Light T. Cummins is the Guy M. Bryan Professor of American History at Austin College and the author of eight books. A longtime friend of Campbell's, he has been a Fulbright Scholar, a member of the Board of Directors of the Louisiana Historical Association and of the Texas Council for the Humanities, a chair of the Grayson County Historical Commission, and, most recently, State Historian for Texas. A Fellow of the Texas State Historical Association, he received the Premio de España y America in 1994 from King Juan Carlos I of Spain.

Harriett Denise Joseph is a professor of History at the University of Texas at Brownsville. An award-winning author or editor of four books and many articles, she earned her Ph.D. at the University of North Texas, where Campbell became one of her mentors while she worked closely with Donald E. Chipman. Students Alix Riviere and Jordan Penner assisted Joseph with the compilation of her contribution.

Andrew F. Lang, a doctoral candidate in History at Rice University, is currently writing his dissertation, "Challenging the Citizen-Soldier Ideal: Culture, Race, and the Problem of Military Occupation during the American Civil War Era." Campbell served as one of his undergraduate and graduate mentors at the University of North Texas.

Carol Lipscomb received her Ph.D. in American History from the University of North Texas, where she studied under Campbell. She contributed numerous entries to *The New Handbook of Texas* (1996) and was the translator for Robert S. Weddles's *After the Massacre: The Violent Legacy of the San Saba Mission* (2007). She continues to research and write from her home in Fort Worth.

Richard B. McCaslin is the chair of the Department of History at the University of North Texas. He is an author or editor for sixteen books, five of which have won awards, and has contributed many chapters and articles to other publications. He is a Fellow of the Texas State Historical Association and serves on its Board of Directors. As a graduate student, he took a course from Campbell, who continues to serve as his mentor as well as a colleague and friend.

Laura Lyons McLemore is the William B. Wiener Jr. Professor of Archives and Special Preservation at Louisiana State University-Shreveport, where she serves as Head Archivist for Archives and Special Collections. She has many publications, including a dissertation written under the direction of Campbell that was published as *Inventing Texas: Early Historians of the Lone Star State* (2004). She is a past president of the Society of Southwest Archivists and a member of the Board of Directors for the Louisiana Historical Association.

Carl H. Moneyhon is a professor of History at the University of Arkansas at Little Rock. He is a multiple award-winning author of four books and many articles on Texas and Arkansas in the Civil War and Reconstruction era, as well as in the New South. A longtime friend of Campbell's, he is also a Fellow of the Texas State Historical Association.

Wesley G. Phelps is an assistant professor of History at Sam Houston State University. His forthcoming book, *A People's War on Poverty: Urban Politics, Grassroots Activists, and the Struggle for Democracy in Houston, 1964–1976*, will be published by the University of Georgia Press. He completed his master's degree at the University of North Texas under the direction of Campbell before earning his doctoral degree at Rice University.

Mark Stanley holds a Ph.D. in History from the University of North Texas. His research focuses on Texas and southern politics, and his dissertation was a biography of Governor Pat M. Neff of Texas, who was instrumental in the passage of the poll tax and Terrell Election Laws. Campbell directed his master's thesis and served on his doctoral committee.

Andrew J. Torget is an assistant professor of History at the University of North Texas. He is the editor of several books on the Civil War and has won several awards for his pioneering work in the field of digital humanities scholarship. Campbell's *An Empire for Slavery* was part of the inspiration for his current book project, *Cotton Empire*, which he is completing as Campbell's colleague at the University of North Texas.

Jessica Brannon-Wranosky is an assistant professor of History at Texas A&M University in Commerce. Active in many organizations, she completed her Ph.D. at the University of North Texas, where Campbell served on her doctoral committee. She is revising her dissertation for publication and has several forthcoming chapters and articles.

Index

A

Abbott, J. S., 326
Abert, James W., 96
Acosta, Teresa Palomo, 377
Adams, John, 69
Adams, John Quincy, 72, 75
Adams-Onis Treaty, 62, 76
Adult Basic Education Program (ABE), 376
African Americans, xii, 5–9, 11, 15, 16, 18, 19, 114, 121, 149, 151, 187, 204–206, 208, 213–215, 223–232, 239, 296, 384 (*see also Texas: lynching, disfranchisement, slavery*)
  churches, 235, 269, 283
  education, 268, 269, 283, 396
  health care, 277–284, 395, 396
  housing, 265–277, 284, 393–397
  segregation, 8, 9, 18, 265–283, 297, 313, 341, 370
  and Democrats, 235–237, 240–244
  and Populists, 229–238, 240, 241, 243, 244, 249, 293
  and Republicans, 231, 234–237, 240
  in World War I, 340, 344, 345, 351, 352
Alabama, 107, 109–112, 1114, 118, 121, 191, 196
Alamán, Lucas, 121
Alamo, 5, 7, 10, 11, 44, 45, 48, 50, 323, 370
Alinsky, Saul, 388–392, 394, 398
Allbert, John Riley, 344
Allen, Eliza, 90
Allen, Earl E., 391–398
Allred, James V., 47, 48
Alpine (Texas), 44
American Revolution, 4, 64, 71, 85, 212
Atlantic World, 17, 24, 108, 109
Antoine, C. C., 282
Arciniega, José Miguel de, 117
Argyle (Texas), 351
Arizona, 162
Arkansas, 48, 66, 84, 85, 87–90, 92, 98, 112, 161, 162, 209
Arkansas Gazette, 93, 94, 277
Arnold, Ben, 233
Arredondo, Joaquín de, 74
Aubrey (Texas), 344
Austin (Texas), 9, 21, 51, 205, 245, 314, 316, 338
Austin *State Journal*, 205, 211
Austin, Dorothy, 51
Austin, James "Brown," 110, 113, 116, 120
Austin, Stephen F., 42, 51, 54, 106–123, 132, 134
Autry, Gene, 44, 45
Ayers, Atlee B., 45
Azcárate, Juan Francisco, 115

B

Baenziger, Anne P., 215
Bailey, Ellis, 215
Bailey, John W., 346, 352, 353
Bainbridge, John, 19
Baker, Newton D., 336, 337, 339

Ballew, William V., Jr., 387–398
Banks, Nathaniel P., 167
Barbé– Marbois, Francois, 66
Barber, Isaac Newton, 234
Barker, Eugene C., 20, 42, 107, 364, 365
Barrera, Severina Guerra, 361
Beauchamp, Evan, 206, 207
Bee, Hamilton P., 167
Beeson, Benjamin, 112
Bell County (Texas), 208
Bell, C. K., 248
Bell, Thomas, 112
Bellinger, Bessie, 314
Bexar County (Texas), 282
Beyette, Paul J., 343
Bickett, John H., 236, 237
Big Show, The, 45
Binkley, Christopher C., 192
Black, James, 161, 165
Blair, James K., 190, 191
Boles, John, 47
Bonaparte. Joseph, 68
Bonaparte, Napoleon, 65, 67, 68
Bonaparte, Napoleon III, 212
Bonham (Texas), 50, 51
Bonham News, 298, 299
Bonham, James Butler, 50, 51
Booth, Charles L., 207
Booth, Richard R. Jr., 205, 207, 211
Bosque County (Texas), 204, 205, 213, 214
Bourland, James G., 198
Bowman, James, 139
Bowman, Thomas, 134, 139
Bracero program, 373
Brackenridge, Mary Eleanor, 12, 17, 19
Bradley, L. D., 170
Brasher, Seymour C., 145
Brazoria County (Texas), 164
Brazos County (Texas), 131–152, 212, 240, 246
Brazos Santiago (Texas), 167
Brearley, David, 91
Brewer, S. S., 235
Brice, Donaly E., 215
Brightman, John Claver, 168
Brooks, George, 149
Brown, Milton, 44
Brownsville (Texas), 157, 162, 167
Brundage, W. Fitzhugh, 38, 41
Brunet, Louise, 314
Bryan (Texas), 148
Bryan, William Jennings, 238, 241, 293, 300–302, 315
Buenger, Walter L., 40
Burnet, David G., 98
Bush, George W., 40
Bush, John E., 273
Bustamante, Anastacio, 120
Bywaters, Jerry, 44

C

Cabeza de Vaca, Alvar Núñ ez, 71
Calhoun, John C., 75, 86–90
California, 9, 18, 41, 45, 47, 65, 99
Cameron (Texas), 230–237, 239–241, 243, 248, 364
Cameron County (Texas), 364, 365
Cameron Herald, 239, 241
Camp Bowie (Texas), 346
Camp Travis (Texas), 346, 351, 352

Campbell, Randolph B., ix–xiii, xv, xvi, 20, 37–40, 72, 108, 148, 187, 203, 229, 230, 249, 306
Campbell, Thomas M., 248, 249
Cantrell, Gregg, 38, 40, 107, 108
Carnegie, Andrew, 22
Carter, Amon G., 46
Carter, Richard, 134, 140
Caruth, Walter, 193
Caruth, William, 193
Casis, Lilia, 362
Cass, Lewis, 95, 96
Castañeda, Carlos E., 363, 364, 367
Centennial News, The, 47–49
Central America, 18, 19
Chambers, Joel R., 351
Chandler, Carrie, 314
Chandler, Samuel, 314
Charles III (Spain), 62
Charles IV (Spain), 61, 66–68
Chicago, 15, 51, 271, 315, 320, 388
Chief Bowl, 97
Childress, R. C., 270
Chouteau, August Pierre, 90, 92
Civil War, 6, 7, 9, 13, 19, 21, 131, 144–148, 152, 157–172, 185, 187, 193, 207, 212, 230, 265, 272, 276, 281, 282, 294, 335, 347 *(see also Confederate States of America, United States Army)*
Civil Rights movement, 16, 18, 19
Claiborne, William C. C., 73
Clark, Edward, 146
Clark, George, 234
Clark, William, 67
Clarksville (Texas), 11, 12
Clayton, Charles, 139
Cleburne (Texas), 208
Clements, A. Q, 166
Clemons, Leigh, 40, 41
Cleveland, Grover, 294
Clifton (Texas), 204
Coahuila-Texas, 65, 110, 116, 118, 119
Coleman, Margaret, 313, 324
Coleman, Wiatt, 135
Collin County (Texas), 187, 194
Collins, Earl, 350
Collins, Livingston, 314
Collins, Mary, 136
Colorado, 17
Colored Knights of Pythias, 280
Colquitt, Oscar B., 248
Community Action Program (CAP), 385–399
Confederate States of America, 6, 7, 9, 10, 14, 19, 22, 131, 158, 186–198
- military, 158–173, 186, 188, 193, 196, 197, 205, 209 (*see also Texas units*)
- morale, 171, 157–174
- nationalism, 6, 158–161, 170–174
- reunions, 6, 10, 232
- symbols, 10, 14, 21
- Trans-Mississippi, 168, 196, 212

Congress of Racial Equality (CORE), 391
Connally, Tom, 48
Connecticut, 188, 197
Cooke County (Texas), 187, 190, 198, 295–307

Copenhauer, J. C., 344
Copland, Aaron, 44
Coppini, Pompeo, 2, 21, 22, 44, 51
Coreth, Rudolf, 167
Coronado, Francisco Vazquez de, 70, 71, 76
Corpus Christi (Texas), 162, 167, 311–328, 368, 369, 371–378
  Artesian Park, 322–325
clubs, 312–314, 325
  KGFI (radio station), 316
  Ladies Pavilion, 310, 317, 318, 320
  Woman's Monday Club, 312–328
Corpus Christi Caller, 312, 314–316, 322, 325–327
Corpus Christi Times, 316
Corsicana (Texas), 45
Cotera, María Eugenia, 377
Cotera, Marta, 376, 377
Covington (Texas), 207, 215, 216
Cox, George H., 206
Cox, William O., 206
Cress, Thomas, 135
Crisp, James E., 44
Crockett, Davy, 20
Croix, Teodoro de, 64, 71
Crook, William, 390
Crouch, Barry A., 215
Crowder, Enoch, 338, 339, 340, 342, 345, 349
Crowell, John, 91
Crutchfield, Thomas F., 194
Cruz, María Isabel, 377
Culberson, Charles A., 238, 300, 301, 326
Curtis, O. M., 343
Custis, Peter, 67

D

Dahl, George, 51
Dallas (Texas), 8, 10, 43–49, 51, 52, 297, 320, 326, 327, 336, 342, 344, 391
Fair Park, 44, 51
Dallas County (Texas), 189, 193, 194
Dallas *Herald*, 211
Dallas Morning News, 296–298, 300, 326
Daniels, G. W., 145
D'Anville, Jean Baptiste Bourguignon, 71
Darden, Stephen H., 214
Daughters of the Republic of Texas, 12, 323
Davidson, James, 203, 205, 206–212, 214, 215
Davidson, R. V., 248
Davis, Edmund J., 203, 205–216
Davis, J. D., 283
Davis, James H. "Cyclone," 233
Davis, Jefferson, 22, 164
Decatur News, 298
DeGress, Jacob C., 216
Del Rio (Texas), 367, 368
Democratic Party, 10, 23, 195, 203, 211–216, 230–249, 282, 293–295, 297, 299–303, 305–307
DeMumber, James T., 208, 209, 215, 216
DeMumber, Mary Jane Gathings, 209
Denton (Texas), 334, 335, 341, 343–346, 348–351
Denton County (Texas), 187, 335–353

Denton *Record-Chronicle,* 335, 341–345, 352
Dewey, John, 42
Dobie, J. Frank, 20, 43, 49, 362–364, 366, 367
Doddridge, Perry, 317
Dodge, Augustus C., 99
Douglas, Charles, 114
Douglass, Astyanax M., 209–216
Douglass, Charlotte Ann Gathings Wier, 209
Douglass, James Gathings, 215
Doyle, Don, 311, 313
Dozier, Otis, 44
Driscoll Family, 311
Dumas, James P., 193
Duncan, William B., 161
Durant, George W., 162
DuVal, Edward W., 90–92
Duval County (Texas), 374

E

Eaton, John, 91–93
Edwin, L., 151
Eilers, Adele A., 13
Eimer, Margaret *(AKA Eve Raleigh),* 368, 376
El Paso (Texas), 11, 14, 67
Ellis, David, 50
Ellis County (Texas), 187, 190, 194
Ely, Glen Sample, 37
Estes, Aaron, 174
Europe, 4, 17, 18, 23
Evans, William E., 206
Evia, José Antonio de, 71

F

Fannin, James, 51
Fannin County (Texas), 187, 190, 193–196, 298
Farmer, T. F., 300
Farmers' Alliance, 230–232, 239
Faulkner, William, xii, xiii
Fayette County (Texas), 23
Ferdinand VII (Spain), 76
Ferguson, Miriam A., 19, 23
Ferguson, William M., 241–243
Fisher, R. B., 371, 372
Fisher, S. Rhoads, 121, 122
Florida, 64, 70, 75, 76, 84, 88, 271
Foik, Paul, 49
Ford, Lynn, 51
Ford, O'Neil, 45, 46
Fort Brown (Texas), 167
Fort Cobb (Indian Territory), 191
Fort Esperanza (Texas), 166
Fort Gibson (Indian Territory), 92, 93, 95, 96
Fort Hebert (Texas), 161
Fort Smith (Arkansas), 91, 191
Fort Worth (Texas), 46, 48, 49, 336, 338, 343, 346
France, 62, 66, 69–72, 121
Frazier, John R., 273
Frear, Yvonne Davis, 39
Freeman, Abraham, 193,194
Freeman, Thomas, 67
Friend, Kate, 318
Fulshear, Churchill, 113

G

Gaceta de México, 69
Gaines, Edmund P., 88
Gainesville (Texas), 198, 300, 302
Gainesville *Daily Hesperian*, 296
Galbraith, James, 190

Galbraith, Samuel, 190
Gallagher, Pat, 340, 341, 343
Galveston (Texas), 132, 146, 148, 156, 158–172, 174, 320, 327
Women's Health Protective Association, 320, 327
Galveston & Red River Railroad, 137, 141
Galveston Daily News, 233–235, 237
Galveston News, 148
Galveston *Tri Weekly News,* 212, 213
Gálvez, José de, 62, 63
Gardiner, Charles W., 212
Gardoqui, Diego de, 64
Garibay, Pedro de, 68
Garner, John N., 326
Garrett, Perry, 313
Gassiot, Juan, 64
Gathings, Benjamin C., 208, 209, 211
Gathings, David A., 209, 211
Gathings, George W., 208, 209, 211
Gathings, James J. Jr., 203–207, 209–211, 215
Gathings, James J. Sr., 202–215
Gathings, Laura A. Sedberry, 215
Gathings, Martha, 207, 208
Gathings, Philip, 207, 209, 215
Gathings, Philip W., 207
Gathings, William C., 207–209, 211
Gathings Male and Female College, 207
General Federation of Women's Clubs, 316, 323, 325
Georgia, 8, 21, 84, 86, 89, 109, 112, 172, 196
Gerhardt, Maude, 314, 316
Gerhardt, William, 313
Gibbs, J. M., 208, 209
Gillette, L. E., 212
Givens, Delmas, 321, 324
Godoy, Manuel, 66
González, John Morán, 40
González County (Texas), 21
Good Neighbor Policy, 371, 373, 374
Grace, John P., 207, 209, 211
Grange, 230
Grasty, G. J., 297
Grayson County (Texas), 187, 188, 190–193, 299
Great Britain, 64, 109, 110, 114, 115, 118, 119
Great Depression, 40, 41
Great Hanging, 198
Green, Thomas, 144
Grimes County (Texas), 208
Groce, Jared, 112, 113, 117
Guerrero, Vicente, 119, 120
Guion, David, 44
Gulf of Mexico, 69, 109
Gutiérrez de Lara, José Bernardo, 72–75

H

Hackett, Charles Wilson, 61, 72
Haiti, 121
Hamilton, Andrew J., 189, 196, 211
Hamilton, Samuel S., 94
Hamtramck, John, 90, 92
Hardeman, Michael, 147
Hardy, Henderson, 151
Hardwicke, John S., 314

Harn, Carroll P. D., 212
Harn, Isaac, 280
Harper, William, 282
Harris County (Texas), 281, 392, 393, 396
Harris, Ethel Wilson, 51
Harris, Thomas, 283
Harrisburg (Texas), 4
Harrison County (Texas), x
Hawkins, Joseph, 111
Hays County (Texas), 21
Head Start, 376, 390
Hefley Family, 239
Hempstead (Texas), 141
Henderson, Thomas S., 233
Henry, H. R., 144
Henry, Julius, 318
Herrera, Simon de, 67, 74
Hickey, Thomas, 313
Hidalgo, Miguel de, 72–74
Higgs, George, 144
Hill County (Texas), 65, 203–216
Hillsboro (Texas), 205, 208, 209, 214
Hirsch, David, 313
Hirsch, Olivia, 313
Hobby, William P., 346
Hogg, James Stephen, 22, 234, 239, 248, 249
Hogg, Will C., 45
Hogue, Alexandre, 44
Holleday, Samuel, 139
Holt, Harrison, 208
Honey Grove (Texas), 194
Hord, W. H., 189
Hooper, William, 206
Hoover, J. Edgar, 49
Hopkins, Edna, 314
Hopkins, W. B., 314
Houston (Texas), 8, 39, 47, 49, 51, 132, 137, 141, 146, 148, 163, 167, 168, 266–283, 338, 384–399
Houston & Texas Central Railroad, 141, 146, 148
Houston *Tri Weekly Telegraph*, 276
Houston Post, 238, 267, 394, 395, 397
Houston Telegraph, 164
Houston *Telegraph and Texas Register*, 98
Houston *Union,* 211, 212
Houston, Sam, 51, 82–90, 93–98,101,164, 207
Howard, William, 106
Hubbard, David, 191
Hubbell, Jay, 42
Hudson, V. B., 242, 248
Hughes, Jeremiah E., 190
Humphrey, William, 11
Hunt County (Texas), 187, 193–197
Huntsville (Texas), 210

I

Ibarbo, Antonio Gil, 63
Immigration, 16, 273–276, 296
Illinois, 195, 197, 237
Indianola (Texas), 167
Indians, 7, 8, 15–18, 43, 69, 70, 83–85, 89, 92–101, 113, 115, 166, 187, 189, 191, 192, 197
  Cherokees, 83–97, 100
  Choctaws, 84, 91
  Comanches, 16, 17, 95, 96, 116, 191
  Creeks, 75, 84, 88, 91, 109

Delawares, 191
Hiwasee Agency (Tennessee), 85, 86, 88, 89, 91
Osages, 87, 90–92
Pawnees, 87, 95
Plains, 95, 97
Removal, 84, 85, 89, 92
Shawnees, 191
Seminoles, 75, 84, 88
Wichita Agency (Indian Territory), 191, 192
Indian Territory, 90, 93, 97, 98, 187, 191, 192
International & Great Northern Railroad, 233
Iturrigaray, José de, 68
Ivins, Molly, 17

J

Jackson, Alexander, 112
Jackson, Andrew, 75, 76, 84, 86, 89–94
Jay, John, 64
Jefferson *Jimplecute*, 9
Jefferson, Thomas, 61, 66–69, 75, 84
Jim Wells County (Texas), 374
Johnson, Andrew, 185–188, 192–193, 196–198
Johnson, Barney L., 195
Johnson, Lyndon B., 14, 385
War on Poverty, 385–399
Johnson County (Texas), 187, 208
Johnson's Island (Ohio), 188
Johnston, Albert Sidney, 22
Johnston, J. D., 298
Jolly, John *(AKA Oo-loo-teka)*, 86, 87, 89, 90
Jones, Martha, 134
Jones, Randall, 114
Juneteenth, 7
Justin (Texas), 341, 344, 350

K

Kansas, 21
Kaufman County (Texas), 187
Kearby, Jerome C., 238, 300, 301
Keith, Jeannette, 350
Kentucky, 11, 66, 111, 195, 268, 271
Kemble, Josiah W., 213, 214
Kemp, Jeff D., 248
Kemp, Louis Wiltz, 49, 50
Key, V. O., 306
King, Henrietta M., 317
King Family, 311
Kingsville (Texas), 373
Kinney, Henry Lawrence, 323
Kirby, Jack Temple, 229
Kleberg, Richard, 373
Kleberg Family, 311
Koch, Robert, 320
Koiner, David F., 351
Kousser, J. Morgan, 294, 305
Krueger, Thurmond, 373
Krum (Texas), 351
Ku Klux Klan, 7, 8, 14, 18, 23, 149, 208, 211, 389
Kuykendall, William, 162

L

La Bahía (Texas), 74, 116
La Salle, René Robert Cavelier, Sieur de, 70
Lack, Paul D., 20
Lamar, Mirabeau B., 83, 97, 98
Lángara, Juan de, 60, 71
Langley, Bill, 51

Lanham, S.W.T., 248
Las Casas, Juan Bautista de, 72, 73
Law of April 6, 1830, 120
Lawrence, Alexander M., 205, 211
Lea, Tom, 44, 51
League, Thomas Jefferson, 161
League of United Latin-American Citizens (LULAC), 368, 375
Lee, Robert E., 22, 163
Lee, Roswell W., 188
Leeper, Matthew, 191, 192
León, Alonso de, 70
León, Juan Ponce de, 70
Level, Gus, 280
Lewis, Meriwether, 67
Lewis, William J., 144
Limón, José E., 377
Lincecum, Gideon, 162,163
Lincoln, Abraham, 144, 297
Lindsay (Texas), 296, 303
Little Elm (Texas), 344
Little Rock (Arkansas), 264, 266–283
  Arkansas Baptist College, 269
  Howard School, 268
  Philander Smith College, 269
Littlefield, George W., 9, 21, 22
Livingston, Robert R., 66
Los Adaes, 63, 67
Lost Cause, 6, 13, 19, 22, 40, 232
Louis XIV (France), 70
Louis XV (France), 62
Louisiana, 62, 63, 66–70, 72, 73, 109, 111, 112, 282
Louisiana Purchase, 61, 71, 75, 84
Lowe, Richard G., x, 306
Luter, Hattie, 314
Luter, Henry, 314

M

Macune, Charles W., 230, 237, 238, 241, 244, 248
Madison, James, 72, 73, 75
Magee, Augustus William, 73, 74
Magruder, John Bankhead, 163–170, 172
Mallory, Henrietta, 314
Marchbanks, George F., 190
Marfa (Texas), 47
Martinez, Antonio, 75
Massachusetts Institute of Technology, 51, 320
Massanet, Damián, 70
Matagorda Bay (Texas), 168
Matagorda Committee of Safety, 4
Matagorda Island (Texas), 167
Mattox, J. W., 145
Matusow, Allen J., 385–387
Maxey, Samuel Bell, 211
Mays, Roy, 341, 342, 344
Maysfield (Texas), 235
McAnally, Oscar F., 239, 241, 244, 245, 248
McClellan, William, 91
McGahey, Alex, 136
McIntosh, William, 144
McKenney, Thomas L., 94
McKeon, A. C., 162
McKinley, William, 238, 300–302
McLennan County (Texas), 65, 206
McLeod, Hugh, 97
McMahan, A., 139
McMichael, Kelly, 49

McMinn, Joseph, 86–88
McMurray, Fred, 43
McMurtry, Larry, 20
Medford, H. C., 169
Medina River, Battle of, 74
Meigs, Return J., 85–88, 91
Mexican War, 98, 172, 323
Mexico, 4, 5, 14, 18, 23, 45, 47, 61–69, 73, 74, 95, 107, 108, 110–120, 146, 340, 361, 367, 374, 375
  Constitution of 1824, 4, 115, 116
  Inquisition, 68, 70
  Revolution of 1910, 16–18, 370
Mexico City, 61, 63, 68, 70, 115, 120, 121, 172
Meyers, Robert, 152
Mézières, Athanse de, 71
Michigan, 16
Milam County (Texas), 230–231, 234–241, 243–249
Milam News, 241, 248
Milano (Texas), 232
Miller, Dale, 47, 48
Miller, G. S., 245, 246
Miller, John, 162
Millican (Texas), 141, 143, 144, 146–149
Millican, Elliott, 134, 135, 139, 140, 152
Millican, F. M., 152
Millican, J. E., 152
Millican, J. H., 139
Millican, John, 131, 134–136, 139–141, 143, 152
Millican, John E., 152
Millican, Robert Hemphill, 134, 135, 152
Mireles, Edmundo E., 360, 361, 366–370, 379
Mireles, Jovita González de, 360–379
Mireles, Sostenes, 367
Mission San Francisco de los Tejas, 70
Mississippi, xii, 8, 9, 16, 17, 21, 70, 109–111, 114, 118, 207, 209, 215
Missouri, 66, 111, 162, 167
Mitchell, Harvey, 147, 150
Mitchell, Jack, 213
Mitchell, Jeff P., 147
Moneyhon, Carl H., 215
Monroe, James, 66, 72, 73, 75, 84, 87–89
Montague County (Texas), 187
Montero, Bernardino, 73
Moore, Monta J., 239–242, 244
Morgan, Gideon, 88
Morgan, Jeff, 167
Muenster (Texas), 296
Mud Island (Texas), 170
Mumford, Lewis, 42
Músquiz, Ramón, 120

N

Nabours, W.A., 236, 238, 241, 245, 248
Nacogdoches (Texas), 63, 67, 73, 75, 100, 112
Nagle, Pierce, 206
Napier, Edward H., 208, 209
Nast, Thomas, 184
Natchitoches (Louisiana), 73
Nava, Pedro de, 65
Navarro, José Antonio, 117
Navasota County (Texas), 132

Neblett, William H., 165, 167, 168, 171
Neches, Battle of the, 97
Nelson, Donald, 51
Neutral Ground Agreement, 68, 71–73
Neve, Felipe de, 64
New Mexico, 9, 21, 66, 70
New Orleans, 62, 64, 65, 73, 110, 111, 112, 268, 271, 280, 281, 322
New Spain, 18, 61–64, 68, 70, 114
    Commandancy General of the Interior Provinces, 63–65, 67, 74
New York, 48, 92–94, 110, 337
New York Times, 48
Ney, Elisabet, 50
Nicholson, Soltolla, 204, 205, 209, 215
Nolan, Philip, 65, 75
North Carolina, 144
Nueces County (Texas), 313, 317, 374
Nugent, Thomas L., 236, 246
Nunn, William C., 215

O

Oakie, Jack, 43
Odom, Howard, 42
Office of Economic Opportunity (OEO), 385, 390, 397
Ogden, Fredric D., 293, 294, 297
Ohio, 48, 139, 193, 271, 337
Omaha *Breeze*, 9
Onís, Luis de, 72, 76
Oregon, 99
Orozco, Cynthia E., 377
Our Lady of the Lake College, 362
Owens, William A., 20

P

Pack, Leonard, 48
Palmer, Bertha, 320
Park, Milton, 298
Parker, Alton B., 303
Parker, David, 88
Parker County (Texas), 187
Pasteur, Louis, 320
Payne, Stanley G., 76
Pearre, Charles B., 213, 214
Peñalosa, Diego de, 70
Pennsylvania, 48, 121, 337
Pennybacker, Anna J. Hardwicke, 316
Periwinkle, Pauline, 326
Perry, Emily Austin, 113
Peru, 68
Pettit, John, 100
Petty, Elijah, 160
Phelps, James, 114
Phillips, Michael, 39
Pichardo, Jose Antonio, 61, 62, 66–76
Piguese, George, 194
Pike, Albert, 96
Pike, Zebulon, 67
Pilot Point (Texas), 344
Pinney, Elbert, 197
Pinney, Henry, 194
Plainview (Texas), 11, 12
Polley, Joseph B., 163
Pope, Lucille Scott, 316
Pope, Walter, 316
Populists *(AKA People's Party)*, 216, 229–249, 293–306

Port Lavaca (Texas), 165, 167
Price, Gentle, 351
Pritchett, W. T., 204–215
Progressives, 40, 229–250, 311, 317–328
Prohibition, 16, 18, 19
Pye, Edward, 168

Q

Quayle, William, 195, 196

R

Rabb, William, 112
Ragsdale, Kenneth, 46
Ramsdell, Charles W., 42
Rand, Sally, 45
Ratcliff, James T., 214
Raymond, James H., 214
Rayner, John B., 233, 234
Reagan, John H., 22, 299
Reagan, Ronald, 17
Reaugh, Frank, 43
Reconstruction, xi, 6, 7, 17, 18, 131,149–152, 185, 189–192, 197, 203–216, 229, 231, 282
Redmond, Ida Durand, 316
Reed, Wilson, 139, 150
Republican Party, 17, 230–245, 151, 189, 197, 203, 205, 206, 212, 214–216, 267, 282, 298–304, 306
Richard, Ellen Swallow, 320
Richmond (Virginia), 162, 268, 271
Riego, Rafael del, 76
Rio Grande City (Texas), 362
Roark, James, 131
Robertson, A. Wayne, 344
Robertson, Felix D., 23
Robertson, John W., 211, 212
Robertson County (Texas), 233
Rockdale (Texas), 231–235, 239
Rockdale Messenger, 241
Rockdale Reporter, 228, 247
Rockefeller, Nelson, 371, 373
Rodríguez, Jacobo González, 361
Rogers, Ginger, 47
Roma (Texas), 361
Roosevelt, Eleanor, 373
Roosevelt, Franklin D., 40, 48, 371
Roosevelt, Theodore, 303
Rose, Billy, 46
Rose, H.R.S., 190
Rose Bowl, 47
Ross, Earl, 341
Ross, James, 112
Rubí, Marqués de, 62, 63
Runnels County (Texas), 215
Rushing, Joseph C., 194, 195
Russell, J. H., 164

S

Sabine Pass, 157, 162, 164, 166, 167
Sabine River, 67, 68, 73
Salado Creek, Battle of, 74
Salcedo, Manuel, 73, 74
Salcedo y Salcedo, Nemesio, 65, 67
Saltillo (Mexico), 116–119, 122
Saluria (Texas), 167
San Angelo (Texas), 44
San Antonio (Texas), 10, 12, 45, 47, 61, 63, 67, 72–75, 95, 115–119, 266–282, 346, 351, 362, 367

San Antonio *Express,* 211
San Antonio *Herald,* 211, 214
San Augustine (Texas), 97
Santa Anna, Antonio López de, 4, 74
Santa Fe (New Mexico), 67, 70
Santa Fe Trail, 96
Sarmiento, Domingo Faustino, 65
Schropshire, Olive, 314
Schulenberg (Texas), 12, 13
Schulenberg Sticker, 23
Scott, Ella Dickinson, 313, 315–317, 320, 325
Scott, Gus (G. R.), 315–317
Scott, Paul R., 145Seale, C.C., 147
Seaton, Mildred, 314
Sedberry, Alexander Rush, 208, 215
Sedberry, Merritte A., 208
Segrest, Hiram H., 321–323, 325
Seguin, Erasmo, 115
Shannon, George R., 210
Shelby, Clair Charmion, 61, 72
Shelton, J. D., 239, 242, 245
Sherman (Texas), 191
Sherman Register, 299
Short, Herman, 398
Shreveport (Louisiana), 267–269, 273, 274, 276–284
Sinclair, Upton, 325
Singletary, Otis, 214
Sigüenza y Góngora, don Carlos, 70
Smith, Charles, 150
Smith, Edmund Kirby, 168
Smith, J. H., 283
Smith, M. W., 4
Smith, William, 85, 86
Socialist Party, 249, 299
Sorelle, W. J., 194
Soto, Hernando de, 71
South Carolina, 109, 112, 271
Southern Methodist University, 42, 47, 391
Southgate, Fannie, 314
Southwest Review, 42
Spain, 43, 61–76, 114
Sparks, S. A., 136
Spencer, Harriett, 147
Splawn, Mary Ruth, 61, 72
Springwell, H. S., 313
Spruce, Everette, 44
Stanbery, William, 95
Stapp, Sinclair, 194
Starr County (Texas), 364, 365
Staub, John, 45
Steinbeck, John, 19
Still, William Grant, 273
Strabo, 71
Streetman, Sam, 236
Strong, Donald S., 295, 296
Strong, Henry, 209, 215
Stuart, J.E.B., 212
Sul Ross University, 44
Swindell, Marion, 351
Swofford, Elmer, 350

T

Tabor, Mrs. I. C., 324
Taft, William Howard, 315
Tahlontuskee, 87
Talamantes, Melchor de, 68
Talbot, Marion, 320
Tarrant County (Texas), 187
Tauch, Waldine, 44
Taylor, Zachary, 323

Tejanos, 4, 7, 12, 15, 16, 18, 19, 115–117, 240, 273, 279, 280, 282, 352, 361–379
Tennant, Allie Victoria, 44, 50, 51
Tennessee, 10, 48, 83, 84, 86–90, 93, 111, 139, 161, 172, 195
Temple, Shirley, 49
Terrell, Alexander W., 294, 295, 299, 306
Texaco, 49
Texas,
- annexation, 5, 99
- architecture, 43, 45, 51
- art, 43, 44, 51
- cattle, 2, 7–10, 39, 47, 135, 139, 140, 142, 150, 152, 207
- Centennial (1936), 41–43, 45–52
  - Board of Control, 46, 47, 49
  - Board of Historians, 43, 49, 50
  - Rangerettes, 49, 51, 52
- Confederate forces, 145, 146, 158–173, 186, 188, 193, 198, 205
  - Battalions,
    - 1st Cavalry, 197
    - Spaight's Cavalry, 161
  - Regiments
    - 1st Cavalry, 162
    - 1st Heavy Artillery, 161, 165
    - 3rd Infantry, 165, 166
    - 4th Infantry, 163
    - 7th Cavalry, 164
    - 8th Cavalry *(AKA Terry's Texas Rangers)*, 21
    - 8th Infantry, 165
    - 8th [12th] Infantry, 209
    - 10th Infantry, 145, 160, 161
    - 12th Cavalry, 204, 207
    - 17th Infantry, 160
    - 20th Infantry, 165, 171, 174
    - 21st Cavalry, 145
    - 25th Cavalry, 145
    - 32nd Cavalry, 167
    - Mann's Cavalry, 156
    - Terrell's Cavalry, 166
- cotton, 7, 12, 17, 20, 108–112, 116–119, 122, 130, 132, 135, 142–144, 146, 148–150, 230
- cultural identity, ix–xii, 3–23, 36–52
- Declaration of Independence, 7, 134
- disfranchisement, 21, 229, 243–249, 293–307
- European immigrants, 7, 14–16, 18, 19, 45, 273, 274, 276, 296, 313, 369
- land grants, 111, 112, 134
- legislature, 7, 19, 203–205, 210–214, 216, 239, 240, 244, 245, 249, 294, 295, 306, 316, 369, 371, 376
- lynching, 8–10, 21, 28, 29, 30, 149, 234
- Mexican colony, 107–120
- militia, 206–208, 216
- music, 43–45
- National Guard, 336, 337, 346–348
- Republic, xv, 4, 5, 10, 18, 83, 96–98, 101, 132, 159

Revolution, 4, 5, 10, 18, 48, 50, 95, 212, 365
secession, 5, 6, 18, 144, 187–189, 192, 194–197, 205, 207
slavery, x, xi, 4–6, 13, 18, 20, 21, 107, 108, 110–123, 131, 132, 136, 140, 142–144, 148, 187, 192, 194, 207, 306
Spanish colony, 61–68, 71–75
State Fair, 13, 18, 36, 40
State Guards, 208–210, 212, 213, 216
State Police, 203–209, 213–216
State Troops (13th Brigade), 189
Unionists, 189, 190, 192, 193, 196, 198
Texas A&I University, 316
Texas A&M University, 326
Texas A&M University (Corpus Christi), 377
Texas Federation of Women's Clubs, 12, 314–316, 318, 320, 322, 323, 325–327
Texas Folklore Society, 363–366, 368
Texas Institute of Letters, xi
Texas Philosophical Society, xi
Texas Rangers, 47, 48, 51, 98, 214, 367, 368
Texas Southern University, 391, 398
Texas State Federation of Labor, 298
Texas State Historical Association, x–xii, 12, 38, 50
Texas State University, 377
Texas Sun, 314
Texas Western University, 11
Texas Woman Suffrage Association, 12
Texas Woman's University, 12, 326
Thompson, Mary, 314
Thornton, R. L, 48, 51
Throckmorton, James W., 192, 193
Timon, Bessie Baker, 324
Toledo, José Álvarez de, 74
Toler, Thomas V., 195, 196
Towner, William L., 209, 215
Tracy, Harry, 235
Treaty of Paris (1763), 62
Treaty of Paris (1783), 64, 75
Treaty of San Ildefonso, 66, 69
Treaty of Tordesillas, 61
Turner, Elizabeth Hayes, 38
Turner, Frederick Jackson, 11
Tyler (Texas), 338
Tyson, George E., 351

U

United Confederate Veterans, 10, 215
United States, xvi, 17, 18, 64
Army, 8, 73, 88, 100, 149, 167, 186–188, 190, 192, 208, 277,
in Civil War, 157, 158, 159, 166–168, 172–174, 191, 281
in World War I, 335, 337
Bureau of Indian Affairs, 86, 94, 98, 100
Bureau of the Census, 132, 313

Bureau of Refugees, Freedmen and Abandoned Lands, 149, 277, 278, 281, 284
Congress, 48, 64, 88, 90, 92, 94, 95, 98–101, 118, 186, 190, 197, 213, 336, 337, 376
Constitution, 19, 192, 213, 297, 390
Indian Agency, 87–94
Military Academy (West Point), 73, 187, 188
Naval Academy (Annapolis), 187
Selective Service, 335–355
War Department, 87–89, 95, 96
University of Chicago, 320
University of Houston, 388
University of Kentucky, 11
University of North Texas, ix, xi, xii, xv
University of Texas, 2, 9, 11, 22, 42, 43, 48, 49, 362, 364–367, 375, 377
University of Virginia, ix, xii, 188

V

Val, Edward W. du, 90, 91, 92
Van Fossen, John, 92, 94
Vandiver, Frank, 37
Velasco (Texas), 161, 167
Vicksburg, 165, 166
Vinovskis, Maris A., 157
Virginia Point (Texas), 162
Virginia, ix, xv, 5, 112, 134, 162, 163, 172, 195
Volunteers in Service to America (VISTA), 385, 390

W

Waco, 9, 10, 204, 206, 213
Waco *Examiner,* 211
Waco Times Herald, 318, 319
Walker County (Texas), 209, 211
War of 1812, 84, 109
Ward, Dudley, 324
Warfield, Charles A., 194
Washburne, Elihu, 197
Washington County (Texas), 132, 135, 152, 162
Washington, D.C., 48, 73, 85, 87, 88, 92, 95, 162, 197, 398
Washington Monument, 21
Washington, Jesse, 9
Washington, George, 4, 21, 22
Watson, Tom, 238
Waxahachie (Texas), 50
Wayne, John, 8, 20
Webb, Walter Prescott, 11, 20, 42, 43, 214
Weber, David J., 65, 75
Weddle, Robert S., 69
Welch, Louie, 389, 394, 395, 398
Welles, Sumner, 374
West, Perry Kincheon “Kinch,” 206, 207
Westhall, Thomas, 113
Wharton, William H., 95
White, Clarence, 397
Whitis, Charles H., 214
Wier, Frank T., 209, 215
Wier, Joseph P., 207, 209
Wiley, Bell I., 157
Wiley, Harvey W., 326
Wilkinson, James, 67

Williams, B. F., 245, 246
Williams, David R., 45, 46
Williams, Henry, 209, 215
Williams, Jackson D., 136
Williams, Thomas H., 206
Williams, Thomas R., 193
Williamson County (Texas), 208
Willingham, Elizabeth, 204, 207, 213, 214, 216
Willingham, Joe, 204, 207, 213, 24, 216
Willingham, Lewis, 204
Wills, Bob, 44
Wilson, Harvey, 147
Wilson, John S., 140, 141
Wilson, L. J., 145
Wilson, Thomas C., 140, 141, 143, 147
Wilson, William C., 139
Wilson, Woodrow, 22, 336, 337
Wise County (Texas), 187, 298
Womble, John E., 146
Womble, K., 144, 147
Woman's Christian Temperance Union, 326
Women's suffrage, 10, 12, 13, 17, 19, 23
Wood, J. P., 211
Wood, James M., 156
Woods, Randall B., 22
Woods, P. C., 160
Woodward, C. Vann, 229, 298
Wooters, James C., 208
World War I, 12, 16, 22, 41, 42, 45, 335–353, 369, 370
World War II, 371, 373
Wright, Frank A., 344, 346
Wright, M. H., 193
Wright, William B., 196

Y

Yellow Bayou, Battle of, 207
Young, William Hugh, 188, 189
Yrujo, Carlos Martinez de, 69

Z

Zapata County (Texas), 364, 365
Zespedes, Vicente Manuel de, 64